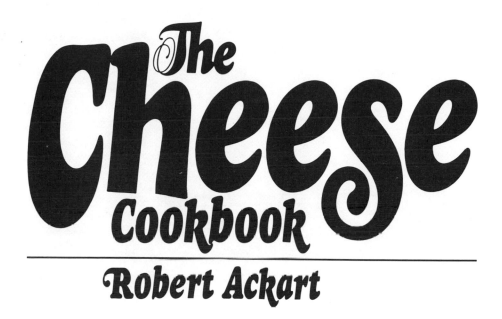

The Cheese Cookbook

Robert Ackart

Drawings by Marjorie Zaum

Publishers · GROSSET & DUNLAP · New York
A FILMWAYS COMPANY

For
Roberta, Carolyn, and Lynne

CONTENTS

Introduction

Cheese—what a fascinating food it is! It can be purchased in almost any weight—from a few ounces to over 200 pounds. It is found in every shape—round, triangular, oblong, cylindrical. It comes in many colors—from pure white to deep orange, from the shade of freshly made butter to blue-green. And it has countless tastes—from sweet to salty, from mild to pungent or aromatic.

The varied and exciting adventure of cheese may take two directions. First, there is the experience of meeting new and heretofore untasted cheeses offered as a course or as an accompaniment to salad (if desired) or fruit (preferably). And there is the intriguing experience of cheese in cooking—the subject of this book.

During these days of high food prices, one hears that "cheese is a good meat substitute." Good? No, it is better than that. Five quarts of milk are needed to make 1 pound of Cheddar, a fact illustrating how concentrated a food cheese is. The protein content of cheese is eight times that of an equal weight of milk, and it is a better source of protein than meat. In addition, cheese provides calcium, phosphorus, and various essential vitamins. Thus, cooking with cheese may be not only a new culinary adventure for you, but also a very wholesome source of nourishment.

This book is divided into three sections. Section I deals with what cheese is and how it is made. Section II lists alphabetically the individual cheeses used in cooking; more than eighty cheeses are briefly described.

The main part of the book, Section III, is a selection of recipes for cooking with cheese. Included are approximately 330 classic and unusual recipes, arranged according to the customary menu categories (appetizers and first course dishes, soups, meats, poultry, fish, egg dishes, vegetables, farinaceous foods, salads, breads, desserts, and sauces and dressings). They are designed to serve six persons unless otherwise indicated. Directions for doubling the recipe, as well as for refrigerating and freezing it, are given. The length of time required to prepare the dish and the length of time required to cook it also are given. A point at which one "may stop and continue later" is indicated, so that the dish may be made either in one session or, if desired, in two. If the recipe is ovencooked, the temperature setting is given at the beginning of the directions, so that the oven will be ready when needed. Ingredients are listed in order of their use, and for cooks who, like myself, arrange their spice shelves alphabetically, seasonings are listed in that manner.

I feel that cooking is a personal and creative experience. This is especially true of cheese cookery, for these dishes are often capable of variation. The recipes, invented, begged, borrowed, stolen from family or friends, and researched for this book, all have been adapted to a format which, I feel, is easily read and easily used. Sometimes, if a recipe is of personal interest, I share an anecdote about it or comment on it. For the interest of the cook, the country of origin is given when the dish has a particular national flavor.

Although related only indirectly to the use of cheese in cooking, I feel it may be helpful to set down a few suggestions for "cheese-tastings" (an increasingly popular social entertainment), and for serving cheese as part of a meal. These ideas are found in the brief Appendix.

Robert Ackart

Katonah, N.Y.

Acknowledgments

To Mr. Edward Edelman, owner-proprietor of the Ideal Cheese Shop, 1205 Second Avenue, New York City, who has graciously shared his knowledge of cheese by reading and making suggestions for the sections on "The Miracle of Cheese," "A Cheese-Tasting Party and a Few Hints on Serving Cheese," as well as the cheese glossary. For his offer of time and expertise, I am warmly appreciative.

To M. Pierre Androuët, leading authority on the cheeses of France, for valuable material and for various visits to his celebrated cheese restaurant in Paris, always informative and memorable gastronomic adventures.

To Mr. H. John Bessunger of the Haram-Christensen Corporation for use of his valuable brochure "Cheese Panorama."

To Mrs. Stella Blitchfeldt, director of public relations of Landbrugsraadet, Copenhagen, and to Mr. Peder Holm, assistant export manager of Brel Foods, Ltd., Copenhagen, for their share in making possible observation of Danish cheese manufacture.

13

To Mr. Frank O. Fredericks, president of the Roquefort Association, Inc., New York City, for arranging a sojourn in Roquefort-sur-Soulzon. While there, I was the guest of M. Jean Rouquet, products manager of Roqueforts-Société, who guided me through the Cambalou Mountain and through each step of the *affinage* of the celebrated cheese, and who presented me to M. Edouard Gaffier, secretary general of the Roquefort Confederation; my thanks to both gentlemen for the information they offered. To the Roqueforts-Société I am indebted for various culinary ideas using Roquefort: dips or fillings, butters, sauces, Roquefort Puff, and—a special favorite—Roquefort Soufflé.

To Mr. Heinz Hofer, president of the Switzerland Cheese Association, Inc., New York City, for his introduction to Mr. Willy Buehlmann, director of public relations, Swiss Cheese Union, Inc., Berne, with whom I visited the Emmenthaler creamery at Krauchthal, a trip which was singularly rewarding in the writing of this book. I am grateful to the Swiss Cheese Union, Inc., for permission to adapt several of their recipes: Flour Soup, Swiss Onion Soup, Swiss Cheese Soup, Ham Loaf, *Poulet à la Reine, Ramequin Vaudois,* Eggs *en Cocottes,* various ideas for fondues, Cheese Mousse I, Easter Monday Tart, Sbrinz *Quiche,* Vegetable *Quiche,* Baked Rice, Swiss Toast, Dill Salad Dressing, Sapsago Salad Dressing, and various cheese butters.

To Mr. Helge W. Leeuwenburgh, of the Holland Cheese Exporters Association, New York City, for his introduction to Mr. Eit Hendricks, export manager of the Zuivelverkoopcentrale in Meppel, Holland, who showed me through several Edam-producing installations; and to Miss Lucia Hilbers, director of public relations of the Netherlands Zuivelbureau, Rijswick, who, together with Mrs. Debbie DeBie, dietician and cooking instructor, contributed the recipes or ideas for the following: Cold Cucumber Soup, Corn Chowder, Fish Chowder with Gouda, Moussaka with Gouda, Baked Fish, Paella with Gouda, Fondue with Gouda and Peppers, and *Ratatouille* with Gouda. These recipes were translated from the Dutch into English by Mr. Jan Willem Aschenbrenner of Rotterdam.

To Professor Luigi Volpicelli of the Instituto della Cucina Italiana, Rome and Milan, for helpful articles and suggested sources for materials on Italian cheeses.

To the Ronson Corporation, Richard A. Vaill, vice president, for generously supplying a "Table Chef" butane burner, the safest I know for at-table cooking, with which I tested various fondue recipes.

To the Dairy Produce Advisory Service of the Milk Marketing Board of England and Wales. With Robin Wynne-Jones, export manager of the Creameries Division, I visited the J. M. Nuttall and Company Stilton creamery at Hartington, Derbyshire, where the plant manager, Mr. Ian Millward, was very helpful. Mr. Wynne-Jones also arranged a visit to Aspatria, the Cheddar creamery in Cumberland, where I was the guest of Mr. Charles Hares, manager of that ultramodern, handsomely designed operation. Miss Mandy Hill of the Publicity Department of the Milk Marketing Board offered various photographs and Miss Carole Clarke, food consultant, supplied the following recipes and cooking ideas which I have adapted to American kitchens: Onion Soup with Cheddar, Cream of Tomato Soup, Baked Pork Chops, Ham and Banana Rolls, Sausage in Cheese Sauce, Cheese Charlotte, Cheese Ramekins, Arbolettys, Cucumber Mousse, Stuffed Peppers, Scones, Cheddar Cheesecake, Apricot Pudding, Basic Cheese Sauces, Cheese and Peanut Stuffing for Poultry, Stuffing for Fish Filets, Stilton Salad Dressing, and Cheese Mayonnaise.

To Miss Mary Lyons, director of public relations, Food and Wines from France, Inc., New York City, for writing to the Société pour l'Expansion et la Vente de Produits Agricoles et Alimentaires (SOPEXA), Paris. Mme. Jacqueline Pery, the warm-hearted and gracious director of public relations of SOPEXA, who has become an esteemed friend, arranged introductions to and visits with authorities on French cheeses and a tour of several days' duration through the Pays d'Auge, the Camembert-producing region of Normandy. On this excursion, I was privileged to make the acquaintance of M. Paul Buquet, president of the Laiteries Buquet, Chambois, a genial, cultivated, and vital gentleman who was particularly helpful in illuminating the methods of Camembert manufacture; I also met the hospitable M. Daniel Courtonne, whose Camembert *fermier* operation is described on page 46. Mme. Simone Cointat, dietician and food editor of SOPEXA, and M. Jean-Louis L'homme of the executive staff were also helpful in supplying culinary ideas for cheese, of which Beef Patties with Gouda and Roquefort Ramekins are but two examples.

Finally, to my neighbor, Helga Fast, for typing the manuscript and for many valuable suggestions as we worked together.

No book on food and cookery is the work of one author; many persons and many traditions also add their special and invaluable contributions. My grateful thanks go to those persons mentioned above; this book is their book as well as mine.

I
THE MIRACLE OF CHEESE

[1]

Cheese-Making

It is only natural that cheese is called the wine of food. As wine comes solely from the grape, so cheese comes solely from milk. And, just as wine is characterized by countless subtle variations in flavor and *bouquet*, cheese, too, is capable of myriad tastes and textures. As a true appreciation of wine comes only with long acquaintance with it, so familiarity with cheese breeds admiration for its many forms and flavors. Similarly, just as the savoring of wine demands refinement and development of the palate, so, too, does the enjoyment of cheese.

Cheese is one of our most ancient foods—indeed, it is very probably our oldest "man-made" nourishment. There is a legend that prehistoric nomads in what we now call the Middle East carried milk in sacks made from the stomachs of young cattle. The heat of the day and the rennin inherent in the lining of the stomach pouch caused the milk to coagulate and separate the solids from the watery liquid, or whey. When this phenomenon first occurred, the man deprived of his milk was probably very angry; but he soon discovered that, once coagulated and removed from the whey, the milk solids kept rather well—much longer, in any case, than milk in liquid form—and they tasted good, too. Thus, in its crudest form, cheese was "invented." Only experimentation and ingenuity were needed to develop this food in various ways in terms of color, form, taste, and texture.

Testifying to the antiquity of cheese, the Old Testament refers to "cheese of the herd" being given to King David (II Samuel 17:27–29). Various cheeses adorned the banquet tables of the ancient Greeks and Romans, and the Romans in their conquest of northern Europe experienced cheeses unknown to them in the south. Shakespeare makes several allusions to cheese in his plays—proof, I feel, of its popularity with the common people, for the dramatist almost invariably chose his imagery from areas readily comprehensible to the general public.

Our increasing enthusiasm for cheese in the United States is caused in some measure by Americans' increasing travel abroad. This fact is interesting—at least to me—because cheese was originally the poor man's substitute for meat, whereas now it is sometimes a symbol of affluence. In Tudor England, "white meats"—cheese and eggs—were more often than not the principal source of the peasant's protein. Some cheeses, indeed, were first produced to meet a specific economic need; the Welsh Caerphilly, for example, was developed to provide Welsh coal miners with a highly nourishing and inexpensive food that could be readily packed in a boxed lunch.

Modern words for cheese have interesting derivations. The Greeks drained off the whey of their cheese in a wicker basket called a *formos*. With the advent of Roman domination, *formos* became, in Latin, *forma*, from which we derive the modern Italian and French words for cheese, *formaggio* and *fromage*. On the other hand, the native Latin word for cheese was *caseus*, a root still to be found in the German *Käse*, the Dutch *Kaes*, and even the Spanish *queso*. Our present-day English word *cheese* also comes from this Latin root, by way of the Old English *cese*, which once was said with a hard "c" but later was pronounced as "ch." The relatively new word *turophile*, "lover of cheese" or "cheese-fancier," comes from the Greek *tyros*, "cheese," and *phile*, "loving."

There are literally hundreds—perhaps thousands—of varieties of cheese, all based upon the following eighteen prototypes. Brick, Camembert, Cheddar, Cottage, Cream, Edam, Gouda, Hand, Limburger, Neufchâtel, Parmigiano (Parmesan), Provolone, Romano, Roquefort, Sapsago, Swiss, Trappist, and, finally, the whey cheeses

(Ricotta). Of these hundreds of varieties, at least fifty to sixty kinds are available in our better supermarkets. Between supermarkets and specialty shops, America has full access to the world's cheeses. The U.S. Department of Agriculture estimates that the average American eats 14 pounds of cheese a year. The world's oldest "convenience food" (the first cheese dates back some 10,000 years), still manufactured basically as it was then, is today grouped into what are known as *natural* and *process* cheeses.

Natural cheese—the cheese with which this book is concerned—is made directly from curds and, sometimes, whey; it is varied in color, texture, and flavor by the kind of milk used and by the method of ripening and seasoning the coagulated curd. Process cheese is made from one or more natural cheeses which have been ground, heated, and mixed with emulsifiers and water to assure a uniform consistency. Unlike natural cheese, which continues to age or ripen as a living food, process cheese is a case of "arrested development." It is a good "keeper" in the refrigerator. It is easily melted for smooth if uninspired sauces. But I personally feel its only honest calling is in a Sunday night supper's toasted cheese sandwich—and even then I prefer a natural cheese, which has greater character and taste of its own. Rindless cheeses, sometimes mistaken for process cheeses because they are similarly packaged, are natural cheeses wrapped in film to prevent drying; this film, in turn, acts as the crust or rind. Denmark produces various rindless cheeses; the label on the package will confirm that it is a natural product. (Denmark, by the way, annually exports over 70,000 tons of cheese of over fifty different types made from pasteurized cow's milk under government inspection.)

Cheese is made from the milk of cows, ewes, goats, asses, water buffalo, mares, yaks, llamas, reindeer, and camels. As long as there is milk and some agent to coagulate it, cheese is a certainty. The milk itself may be varied by adjusting its fat content, by combining yields from different milkings (night and morning milkings, for example), and by combining the milk of different animals (that is, of different herds of cows or goats—less often by combining the milk of different species of animals).

Cheese-making as we would recognize it began as a home enterprise; some of the world's finest cheese continues to be produced only in domestic surroundings and thus in small quantity. Even today Gruyère is made locally from the combination of a few milkings collected from only a few farms. An increased ability to control milk quality, a growing awareness of cheese-making techniques and possibilities, and—perhaps most important—improved transportation and storage facilities have spurred the cheese-making art to the point that it is now largely a factory industry. This fact has obvious advantages: It standardizes quality and it assures purity. But it also precludes some of the individuality which cheese had when made at home in small quantities; it also limits somewhat the number of varieties. Nevertheless, factory-made cheese is available to every consumer attracted by this increasingly popular food, and one is grateful for that.

Cheese-making requires approximately ten volumes of milk for each volume of cheese. In this highly concentrated form, such a cheese as Cheddar, for example, contains about 36 percent moisture, 34 percent fat, 24 percent protein, 1.7 percent salt, and 4.3 percent miscellaneous milk solids. One ounce of Cheddar is composed of the following: protein, 7.2 g.; fat, 9.8 g.; calcium, 230 mg.; iron, 6.20 mg. It has no carbohydrates (these have been lost in the whey). But it does contain vitamins A, C, and D, as well as thiamine and riboflavin. Three and one-half ounces of Emmenthaler (better known as "Swiss" cheese) is made up of 30 percent protein (supplying 40 percent of the estimated minimum daily adult requirement), 31 percent milk fat (equaling one-third of the daily adult energy requirement), six-tenths percent phosphorus (or 50 percent of the usual daily adult requirement), and 1.1 percent calcium (equaling the normal daily adult requirement). Three and one-half ounces of Gruyère supply more than one-third of the daily adult requirement of vitamins A and D; the B-complex vitamins, vitamins E and K, and the provitamin carotene are also properties of this cheese. One and one-quarter ounces of cheese contain the same amount of calories as about 2 ounces of meat, one glass of milk, or 2½ pounds of oranges. Seven ounces of cheese more than replaces the protein value of 10 ounces of meat. And what of the caloric count of cheese? In such cooked, pressed cheeses as Cheddar and Emmenthaler, for example, there are about 370 calories per 3½ ounces, while the same amount of some soft-ripened and fresh cheeses contains approximately 280 and 100 calories, respectively.

Because all cheese is derived from a single source—milk—and because all milk—whether from a cow, sheep, goat, water buffalo, or some more exotic beast—contains virtually the same nutrients, the food values of Cheddar, Emmenthaler, and Gruyère may be assumed to represent approximately those of other cheeses. True, some cheeses are richer and have a higher caloric count than others—the soft-ripened double and triple *crèmes*, for example, to which extra cream has been added. The higher percentage of butter fat in a given cheese does not change its food value; it only means that because of its richness one eats less of it than of a "leaner" cheese.

Cheese is costly, some will say. True, cheese is not an inexpensive food; yet if it is sometimes priced higher than meat, it has no waste (frequently the toughest rind can be grated and incorporated in some dish or other).

There are six basic steps in cheese-making:

1) The coagulation or curdling of the milk by the addition of rennet (rennin) and/or cultures of lactic acid. (The enzyme rennin is derived from the fourth stomach of milk-fed calves. Kept in a salt-brine solution, it is called rennet and, chemically, is exactly the same as the rennet tablets from which our childhood junket was made; the curd of coagulated milk contains all of the nutrients of fresh milk.)

2) The cutting of the curd to allow the whey (the water content of milk) to run off.

3) The shaping of the curd in molds of various sizes and shapes, through which more whey is drained.

4) The salting of the yet unmolded but slowly hardening curd, either by brushing with or immersion in saline solution, or by "hand tossing" with dry salt.

5) The continued draining and drying of the cheese.

6) The ripening or aging of the cheese under conditions favorable to the development of its particular qualities.

The miracle of cheese (or perhaps one should say the miracle of milk) is that it is capable of seemingly endless variations. If there are only eighteen basic cheeses—just as, we are told, there are only three plots in literature and five melodies in music—there are hundreds of different possible tastes and textures. These differences can be accounted for by the following considerations:

1) What kind of milk is used to make the cheese—milk from a cow, goat, ewe, water buffalo, or—more unusually—reindeer, camel, or llama? (The milk of each animal has its own distinctive flavor which, in turn, affects the taste of the cheese.)

2) What kind of food is eaten by the animal? Is it, for example, mild pasturage or is it aromatic wild grasses? (The diet of the animal will affect the flavor of the milk and, therefore, the taste of the cheese.)

3) Is raw milk used to make the cheese, or (as is often the case today, especially in commercial production for export) is pasteurized milk used? (Raw-milk cheeses are, by law, ripened over a longer period than are those made of pasteurized milk; for this reason, raw-milk cheeses, such as those of the Cheddar family, have substantial flavors. Cheeses made of pasteurized milk are marketable in a short time and therefore their taste tends to be mild.)

4) To what temperature is the milk heated before the addition of rennet and/or cultures of lactic acid? (The temperature affects the speed with which the milk coagulates and the consistency of the curd.)

5) What is the proportion of rennet to lactic acid culture? (Hard cheeses are produced by adding more rennet and less lactic acid; soft cheeses result from the addition of more lactic acid and less rennet. Thus, hard cheeses may contain about 35 percent water; soft cheeses, about 50 percent; and fresh cheeses, as high as 80 percent. It should be added that when milk coagulates, practically all the carbohydrate content goes into the whey; the carbohydrate content of cheese is dependent upon how much whey, or water, is retained by the finished product.)

6) What other cultures or agents are added to the milk at the time of renneting or to the freshly coagulated curd? (In the case of Roquefort, for example, *Penicillium roqueforti* is added.)

7) Is the curd "cooked" by being heated to and held at a certain temperature for a given length of time? (This procedure, which gives the curd greater solidity and increases the expulsion of the whey, is part of the production of Cheddar, Emmenthaler, and the Italian *grana* cheeses.)

8) Is the freshly molded curd pressed to force out the whey—as in the case of such a cooked cheese as Cheddar—or is it left to drain without pressure—as it is in Camembert? (Pressing the curd yields hard cheese; cheese from self-draining curd is soft.)

9) What is the method of salting the cheese? (Dry salt is added to the cooked curd of Cheddar before it is milled to uniform size for molding and pressing; Pont l'Évêque is brushed with saline solution to form a crust; Parmigiano, Emmenthaler, Camembert, and Brie are submerged in salted water for as long as twenty days for Parmigiano, up to forty-eight hours for Emmenthaler, about one hour for Brie, and often as little as forty minutes for Camembert. Each of these different techniques and timings affects the fermentation or flavor or texture of a particular cheese. In the case of Emmenthaler, the rounds are also turned and washed with salt solution at regular intervals, a procedure contributing to the flavor, size of the "eyes," or holes typical of Swiss cheese, and the formation of the rind. In the case of Camembert, the salting contributes to the fermenting process and somewhat to the flavor, but it does not affect the salt content of the cheese—a fact making Camembert an excellent cheese for people on low-salt diets.)

10) At what temperature and at what degree of humidity does the cheese continue to drain and dry? At this time is any further agent added to the crust? (Both temperature and dampness factors differ in the manufacture of French and Swiss Gruyère; the colder, drier conditions of French Gruyère ripening produce a moister, softer-textured cheese than is made in Switzerland. In many commercial dairies, a culture of mold and bacteria, *Penicillium candidum*, is sprayed on such soft-ripening cheeses as Camembert and Brie to grow into the velvety crust of the finished product.)

11) Finally—for the purposes of this expressly simplified outline—at what temperature and at what degree of humidity does the cheese complete its aging and ripening, or *affinage?* (A singular example of the importance of these conditions is Roquefort, ripened in the caves of the Cambalou Mountain near the village bearing the name of this renowned cheese. The temperature, humidity, and molds unique to these caves make Roquefort what it is; other warehouse-ripened blue cheeses are just as good in their own right, but they are separated by subtle differences of flavor and texture from the unique cheese bearing the name Roquefort.)

Using as a touchstone the six basic steps in cheese-making, together with the eleven most conspicuous areas of variation, we may explore the production of a few representative cheeses. The cheeses I have chosen were selected on the basis of my own familiarity with their use in the kitchen and with their method of manufacture rather than because of any desire to make this chapter "scientific." (One may read the entry on "Cheese" in any encyclopedia for that information.) I propose, instead, to write informally of some experiences I have enjoyed in observing the making of cheese in the countries of their origin. The cheeses discussed here will also be found in the Glossary of Cheeses, pages 57 to 76.

[2]
Swiss Cheese

To produce a medium-sized 180-pound "Swiss" cheese, or Emmenthaler—the most famous and most imitated of the cheeses from Switzerland—approximately 220 gallons of milk are required. (In the case of Emmenthaler, the larger the cheese, the better it is; the flavor is fuller and the eye formation more uniform. Thus, a 210-pound Emmenthaler is to be preferred to a medium-sized one.) One-half of the necessary milk is the evening milking allowed to rest overnight, and one-half is morning milk freshly delivered to the cheese-maker. Partly skimmed and combined in large vats, the slowly stirred milk is heated to a uniform 89° to 95° Fahrenheit. Rennet and lactic acid bacteria, used to promote fermentation and curing, are added, and at once the milk begins to coagulate. The curdled milk is cut several times, by means of a copper-strung "harp," into small equal-sized particles called "cheese grains." The whey separates from the curd and, as it does so, the cheese grains become firmer. While being gently stirred, the mixture is heated to

The verdant, well-kept, peaceful Swiss countryside provides the special forage for the rich, sweet milk needed for making Emmenthaler.

Milk collected from neighboring farms has been transported to the local creamery in this manner for generations.

Milk, weighed and tested, is poured into vats. Rennet will be added to the milk to produce the coagulation necessary to form the curd.

about 127° Fahrenheit for thirty minutes, or until the grains have reached proper size and consistency.

To remove the curd from the whey, a cheesecloth is stretched over a semicircular form having the same shape as the bottom of the vat. Drawn along the wall of the vat and passed beneath the curd, it collects the cheese grains in a large mass. The curd is transported by pulley to the pressing table, where it is put, still cradled in its cheesecloth, into a wooden hoop about 5½ inches high and of adjustable diameter. The cheesecloth is smoothed so that no imprint of its folds will mark the surface of the cheese. A mechanical or hydraulic press exerting up to 3,300 pounds is used to remove the whey, which is collected and used as cattle fodder.

The cheese, turned several times and rewrapped during the day, is virtually dry by night. The following morning it is stamped with its date of production and maker's code and taken to the salting cellar, where salt (spread over its surface and thus releasing further moisture) begins to harden the protective rind and, through absorption, flavors the body, or *pâte* (dough), of the cheese. Twenty-four hours later, the cheese is immersed for two days in brine (a 20- to 23-percent solution of common salt); during this period the loaves lose water and absorb salt.

An important characteristic of Emmenthaler is the lactic acid fermentation, beginning in the original milk vat and continuing through the brine bath. Following the brine bath, the cheese is placed in a 73° Fahrenheit damp cellar and continues to ferment, which produces carbonic acid. A resulting gas, collecting at various spots in the cheese and unable to escape, forms the holes, or "eyes," typical of Emmenthaler. The eyes require eight to twelve weeks to develop to their ideal size (about the size of a cherry). To achieve uniformity of eye size, the cheeses are turned twice weekly and washed with brine.

Finally, the cheese is moved to a warehouse curing-cellar, where the constancy of temperature and dampness produce the necessary ripening. Four months are required to age a mild Emmenthaler; more highly flavored ones require up to ten months' maturation. During this period, those cheeses manufactured for export are stamped radially with the word "Switzerland," the trademark of the Swiss Cheese Union, Inc.

Gruyère, Emmenthaler's closest but stronger-tasting relation, is made in virtually the same way. The Gruyère wheel is smaller (about 77 pounds), with eyes the size of peas and sometimes small fissures in the "dough." Gruyère comes generally from western Switzerland, the French-speaking area, where it was first made in the town of La

Coagulated milk is cut through with a "harp" of copper wire strung tightly on a frame. Cutting the coagulated milk allows the whey to run off.

The curd is stirred with wooden paddles, further releasing the whey. Note the "harp" on the right.

Curd, cradled in cheesecloth, is hoisted into molds which will determine the shape and size of the finished cheese.

The cheesecloth is carefully smoothed to prevent any imperfections appearing on the surface of the finished cheese. Note the size of this "medium" cheese.

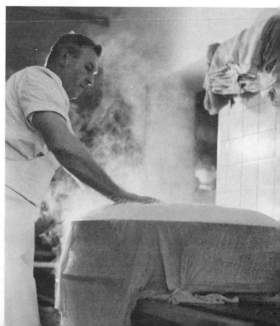

Gruyère, whereas Emmenthaler is indigenous to the German-speaking area of Switzerland. The chief difference in manufacture is that the temperature in the Gruyère fermenting cellar is lower than that of the Emmenthaler cellar; less carbonic acid is formed and, therefore, the eyes are fewer and smaller. Gruyère, unlike Emmenthaler, is not washed during fermentation and curing; it is kept constantly moist with brine, a fact accounting for the rind and odor typical of Gruyère. Gruyère is mature at five months.

I had the opportunity of visiting an Emmenthaler creamery in the village of Krauchthal, nestled in the hills of Bern Canton, where the fall foliage looked like vast oriental carpets thrown carelessly over the mountain sides. Accompanied by my genial host, Willy Buehlmann, Director of Public Relations of the Swiss Cheese Union, I was fortunate to have an intimate glimpse of this traditional art. I learned, for example, that virtually every important village in German-speaking Switzerland has its family-owned Emmenthaler factory—some 2,000 of them—using local milk to produce two wheels per day per factory. To become

Cheeses, removed from their molds, are floated in brine and salted, a process which flavors the cheese and encourages further release of the whey.

Machines are used to turn the heavy cheeses so that they will be of uniform texture and flavor. When they are turned, they are also wiped with brine.

The cheeses are aged under conditions of controlled temperature and humidity.

The cheese is tested for flavor, texture, and size of "eye."

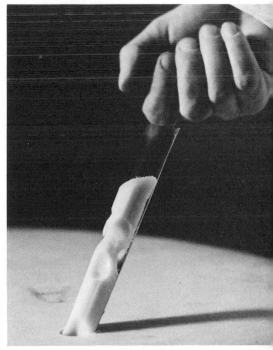

To assure the authenticity of the product, the word "Switzerland" is radially stamped on all Emmenthaler cheeses manufactured under the stringent surveillance of the government-affiliated Swiss Cheese Union.

a master cheese-maker, still largely a father-to-son profession, one must be at least twenty-five years old and have served an apprenticeship of three years in a creamery; one year's formal training in dairy school, with diploma, is required, as are four additional years of work in a cheese factory (this latter period includes the obligatory Swiss military service).

The creamery at Krauchthal, typical of those throughout the cooperative system in Bern Canton, also serves as domicile for its owner, Andreas Zaugg, and his family. There are only three workers in addition to Herr Zaugg, who takes an active part in certain steps of the cheese-making and vigilantly oversees the entire process. He also keeps the books and tests the milk. His wife makes their home on the second floor of the building and runs the small ground-level shop, a part of every village cheese factory, where dairy products and such staples as coffee and chocolate are sold.

[3]
Cheddar

What a contrast to this simple and traditional mode of cheese-making is Aspatria, the glistening new $10 million Cheddar factory opened in August 1974 by the Milk Marketing Board of England and Wales. The M.M.B., as it is familiarly called, is a large cooperative supported by the 65,000 milk-producers of England and Wales (Ireland and Scotland have their own bureaus) to promote consumption of dairy products and to create marketing outlets for them. Aspatria, in Cumberland, less than 10 miles from the Scottish border, is the first creamery to come fully under the operating aegis of the Board. From my host, Charles Hares, manager of the creamery, I learned that 90 percent of English cheese manufacture is devoted to Cheddar or Cheddar-related cheeses. The fact that Aspatria alone daily produces two thousand 40-pound blocks of Cheddar gives credence to this figure. The creamery has transformed Aspatria, once a dying mining town, into an agricultural center of some 4,000 inhabitants, many of whom are connected with cheese-making. The 300 milk-producers in the immediate area account for much of the population; they supply the factory with 50,000 gallons a day.

Satiny stainless steel equipment and computerized technology further separate Aspatria from Krauchthal. But the cheese is produced, save for the special differences which give Cheddar its own quality, very much like Emmenthaler. The finished cheese appears in about twelve hours after rennet has been added to milk freshly pasteurized and cooled to 86° Fahrenheit in double-lined 1,000-gallon vats. The process consists of the following steps:

1) The starter of lactic acid culture is added to the milk to achieve the desired acidity (at this time, too, *annatto,* a vegetable coloring derived from a tropical American plant, may be added; *annatto* is used in the manufacture of various cheeses—Edam is another example).

2) Rennet is added and coagulation commences.

3) The curd is cut to the size of a corn kernel (with Emmenthaler, it is cut to the size of a grain of wheat).

4) The curd is cooked by steam forced into the pocket of the double-walled vats.

5) The whey is drained (and dried into whey powder for human and animal consumption).

6) The curd is "Cheddared" for one and a half hours (Cheddaring refers to the period following the removal of whey and before the addition of salt—in other words, the curd rests).

7) The curd is milled and salted (with Emmenthaler, salt is added from the "outside in," by means of rubbing and immersion in brine).

8) The curd, pressed into plastic forms, hardens for eight hours.

9) The shaped cheese is cut into 40-pound blocks (no longer the traditional rounds, because of the space-saving and ease of packaging made possible with a rectangular shape).

This firm cheese, originally from the Somersetshire village of Cheddar (although it is no longer made there) is aged, with regular turning, from two months to two years, depending upon the degree of sharpness and crumbliness desired; young Cheddar is mellow, creamy, and easily sliced.

In the United States, law imposes a quota on the import of English Cheddar, because Cheddar and its near relatives (Monterey Jack, Coon, "store" cheese) are among the most widely produced American cheeses. American production started in the early nineteenth century in New York State, then the center of our cheese industry; in 1851, the first factory system for making Cheddar was developed near Rome, New York, on the Erie Canal. Today, Cheddar is produced in several parts of the country—New York, Vermont, Ohio, Illinois, Nebraska, Iowa, Minnesota, California, with perhaps the largest production centering in Wisconsin.

A first-cousin of English Cheddar is Cheshire (originally called Chester), the origins of which date from the first century A.D. Caesar's Twentieth Legion enjoyed it as a sheep's-milk cheese, but it has been made from cow's milk since the dissolution of the monasteries under Henry VIII. Until the nineteenth century it was used by English farmers to pay rent. Originally deriving its character from the salt meadows where the cattle grazed and from the high cream content of the milk, Cheshire has been a favorite cheese of such literary luminaries as Jonson, Herrick, Johnson, Boswell, and Shaw. Other Cheddar relatives from the British Empire include Caerphilly, Derby, Dunlap, Gloucester, Lancashire, Leicester, and White Wensleydale.

[4]
Blue-veined Cheeses

There are over fifty varieties of blue-veined, or blue-mold, cheeses. They are produced the world over—in the United States, Ireland, Holland, Argentina, Switzerland, Israel, Denmark, South Africa, Germany, Canada, Austria, and Australia—as well as, of course, in France, Italy, and England, the respective producers of Roquefort, Gorgonzola, and Stilton. Of these three, Roquefort, produced in southern France, in the region northwest of Marseilles, is the only sheep's-milk blue cheese imported to this country (there are other blue-veined sheep's-milk cheeses—Bleu de Corse, for example—but they are not exported). Roquefort, the oldest and most celebrated of all the blue-veined cheeses, must, by law, be aged in the limestone caves of Cambalou Mountain near Roquefort. Gorgonzola, made since the ninth century in the Po Valley on the plains of Lombardy, is named for a village near Milan. Stilton, popular since the early eighteenth century, has been called King of English Cheeses. Each is a great blue-veined cheese and each has its particular qualities differing it from the others; comparisons among them are useless.

The United States is a large producer of blue-veined cheese, most often and most honestly called simply "blue cheese." Our domestic "Gorgonzola," for example, is only just satisfactory, lacking the creamy smoothness of the Italian original. But blue cheese, making no pretense at being a special variety, is very good both at the table and in cooking. Denmark, too, since 1914, has been a large producer of superior blue cheese (called "Danablu"), the least expensive of imported blue-veined cheeses.

To produce blue-veined cheeses, a mold, either *Penicillium glaucum* or *Penicillium roqueforti,* is introduced in one of three ways: It may be added directly to the milk before coagulation takes place (the technique used in making Roquefort, Gorgonzola, and Danish blue-mold cheeses); it may be added to the curd before pressing (the method largely used in the production of Stilton); or it may be injected into the finished cheese as smears on piercing needles (the oldest method and still sometimes used in traditional farm-produced blues). Regardless of how the mold gets into the cheese, the dormant spores will not develop until the cheese is pierced to allow oxygen to reach them; it is this contact with oxygen which activates the mold and stimulates its growth.

Served by Rabelais, extolled by Pliny and Casanova, imported from France by some sixty-five countries, Roquefort is reputed to be one of the world's most expensive cheeses, the most glamorous of the blue-veined family. Charlemagne, returning from battling the Saracens in Spain, was introduced to Roquefort at the very place where it is aged today; he relished it and commanded that two *caisses* of it be brought annually to his castle at Aix-la-Chapelle. So popular and distinctive was the cheese that in the early fifteenth century, by royal decree, King Charles IV restricted use of the name "Roquefort" to the blue-veined ewe's-milk cheese made in the area of Roquefort-sur-Soulzon in Aveyron. In 1666, the Parliament of Toulouse confirmed the word "Roquefort" to apply only to that cheese aged in the Cambalou caves at Roquefort; a fine was imposed for fraudulent use of the name. Today, Roquefort is readily recognizable by the figure of an encircled sheep in red on the foil wrapping; it is illegal to use the patented name for any other blue cheese.

For the most part, the Roquefort area is arid, a land of jagged, rock-ledged mountains and sere plains, cut through by narrow, fast-moving rivers. Here a geological upheaval took place millions of years ago; an earth shift under the crest of Mont Cambalou brought into being a network of some twenty-five limestone caves, comprising over 125 acres, one leading into another, anthill fashion. At the same time, small fissures, called *fleurines,* appeared in the walls of the caves, forming 4 miles of corridors extending from the high plateau to the River Tarn, far below. By an accident of nature, perpetual cross currents of cool, moist air were created in the caves—a gigantic air-conditioning system which remains throughout the year at a uniform temperature of about 45° Fahrenheit and a steady humidity of 95 percent. To the best of our knowledge, this phenomenon at Roquefort is unique, and, since the cheeses are aged in the caves of Cambalou, the phenomenon also helps explain why Roquefort itself is unique among cheeses.

Fourteen individual cheese-makers belong to the Roquefort Confederation, an organization working for Roquefort cheese in much the same way as the English Milk Marketing Board works for British dairy products—promoting production, maintaining standards, protecting and creating markets for the product. Over 25 million pounds of Roquefort (or well over 5 million individual loaves) are produced annually, of which the United States, the largest importer, consumes some 2 million pounds.

As the villagers of Roquefort-sur-Soulzon (population under 2,000) busy themselves with testing, aging, packing, and shipping cheese, sheep-raisers on 14,000 farms supplying the cheese-makers concern themselves with their 700,000 Lacaune sheep. These gentle beasts lactate only four months of the year, producing 1 quart daily (or about 30 gallons annually); for this reason, Roquefort-making is today regulated by refrigeration to be a partially year-round enterprise, but by far the greatest quantity of cheese is made in the spring and early summer. Cheese-makers throughout the area, as well as in the Pyrenees receive each morning their quota of ewe's milk—today collected by milking machines—which is thoroughly filtered and heated to about 80° Fahrenheit before the addition of rennet and *Penicillium roqueforti.* (*Penicillium roqueforti,* botanically a member of the mushroom family, is specially grown on stale rye bread mixed with vinegar and active leaven and then ground to a fine powder.) Coagulation takes place within two hours, when the cut curd is put into cylindrical molds and allowed to drain for four or five days before being brought to Roquefort's Mont Cambalou. There it is rubbed with salt and pierced with stainless steel needles. In the caves, the cheese is then stood on wooden shelves (on edge, to expose to the air its largest possible area) and so begins its ripening. After about thirty-five days the cheese begins to acquire its typical appearance and flavor and it continues to do so during the required time of ripening—from three months (for cheese exported to the United States) to six months, depending upon the strength of taste desired. At the end of several weeks and after many turnings, the finished cheese is wrapped in foil and placed in a cold room to retard the aging process, which, unless checked, continues until the cheese becomes almost inedibly strong tasting.

Roquefort cheese is such an integral part of life to Roquefort's people that *le fromage* refers specifically to Roquefort. A housewife will tell her neighbor that she is going to market for ". . . *Gruyère pour faire une sauce, mais aussi il me faut du fromage.*"

Often a small amount of Roquefort is blended with milk in a baby's bottle; it is believed that enzymes in the cheese aid digestion and contribute significantly to the child's nourishment.

Just as the Romans knew Roquefort, they also knew—not surprisingly—Gorgonzola, a cow's-milk blue-veined cheese. Cattle, which had grazed in the Lomellina Valley south of Milan (an area today devoted to rice growing), returned north at the end of summer and, en route, were rested and milked at Gorgonzola, a little town on the Bergamo road northeast of Milan. Whatever milk was not immediately consumed was made into cheese, which, in turn, was aged in the mountain caves of the Valtellina, where the dampness and constant temperature prompted growth of the natural mold. Except for the fact that Gorgonzola is turned frequently and pierced with copper wire to ensure even spreading of mold, it is aged today very much as it was in earlier times. Gorgonzola is now produced in Milan, Novara, Lodi, Como, Cremona, Pavia, and Brescia.

Like Roquefort, Gorgonzola travels well; to assure its best possible quality for exportation, it is aged for three months or more. This measure, however, would not appeal to an Italian cheese-fancier, for at home the celebrated Italian blue is eaten when only two months old, very soft and creamy, without a strong graining of mold and with the wrinkled, grayish crust showing only a blush of red. Gorgonzola is, I feel, best enjoyed this way; it is, nevertheless, a superb cheese, a delectable companion at the table and, in certain dishes, a fine cohort in the kitchen.

While the guest of Robin Wynne-Jones, Export Manager of the Creameries Division of the Milk Marketing Board of England and Wales, I visited the Nuttall dairy in Derbyshire, the largest-producing of nine Stilton factories. Other Stilton producers are located in Leicestershire and Nottinghamshire; all belong to the cooperative Stilton Cheese Makers' Association, an organization, like the Roquefort Confederation, promoting and protecting the cheese and its name. To support the work of the Association, each creamery is levied a certain sum for every 1,000 gallons of milk used.

The Dove Dairy of J. M. Nuttall and Company, nestled in the countryside outside the picture-book village of Hartington, is surrounded by stone farmhouses, high dry-walls, narrow serpentine roads, and vegetation—both trees and grass—almost incredibly verdant. As Ian Millward, the dairy's manager, showed us about, he explained that "Nuttall's," as the creamery is familiarly called, makes both white and blue Stilton and Wensleydale. The white cheeses have not been allowed to develop mold; their taste and texture, therefore, are quite different from the blue-veined varieties.

At "Nuttall's," only local milk coming from within a 6-mile radius or so of the dairy is used. Daily, about 7,500 gallons of the richest milk, with added cream, are processed to yield 250 cheeses (17 gallons of milk make one 14-pound cheese); the rounds are aged for four months. The making of Stilton, with its golden-red wrinkled crust and creamy white body patterned with blue veins, is confined to the rural Midlands.

Though no longer farm-produced, it cannot be made by large-scale factory methods. No one attempts to explain why this is so, but accepts the fact without question, just as a vintner knows instinctively that certain wines must be made in limited amounts to assure their quality.

Large curds are stirred with a "pitchfork" to assure the release of the whey in the manufacture of Wensleydale.

[5]
The Hard, Grating Cheeses

Cheeses suitable for grating are merely those which, firm-textured by nature, have been allowed to age longer and to harden more than would be the case in their customary use. Emmenthaler, Gruyère, and Cheddar, for example, fine table and cooking cheeses, become harder and drier with age and ultimately grate well for use as a condiment. Selecting cheeses suitable for grating as a cooking ingredient or condiment depends, in large measure, on what flavor and texture you want a particular dish to have. Obviously, one does not grate Camembert or Gorgonzola, but any hard or semi-soft cheese may be grated (or shredded). A list of cheeses suitable for grating is found on page 80.

The most famous of the grating cheeses are the Italian *granas,* so named because of their grainy texture, which is caused by minute crystals in the body of the cheese. The most celebrated of Italy's various *granas* is Parmigiano-Reggiano, popularly exported to the United States with its name stenciled on the rim. (Other Parmesan-type cheeses, made in other countries, are also imported by the United States.)

Parmigiano, the *grana tipico,* is named for the city of Parma in the area where the cheese was first made; today, it is produced in many cities of the Reggio-Emilia region—Modena, Bologna, Mantua, Ferrara, and Piacenza—and is made from local milk in the same way that it was made in the thirteenth century. During its aging, it is frequently turned, scrubbed, and tapped with hammers for the sound of ripeness. A two-year-old wheel is said to be *vecchio* (old), and, while not hard, is ready to be cut as a table cheese—one of the most delectable I know. A three- or four-year-old wheel is *stravecchio* (very old), and is solid enough to grate well (including the rind) into a powder which melts in cooking but which does not form strings, as does Gruyère, for example. Of course, *stravecchio* Parmigiano may be as old as twenty years; its antiquity will only improve and mellow its yellow-beige body shot through with a network of nearly invisible holes and with myriads of tiny lactic crystals, the *grane,* yielding the typical minutely beaded texture.

The traditional producing season is from the first of April until mid-November. Evening and morning milk are skimmed, then combined in open copper kettles; to them is added fermenting whey of *lactobacilli* and *streptococci,* from the previous day's cheese-making. The milk is then heated and diluted rennet is added. The curd, once broken, is gently "cooked" and drained (most of the whey is fed to pigs, thereby producing the famous Parma hams). The cheese is then molded and pressed, in a process very similar to that used for Emmenthaler save that the salt immersion lasts for three weeks rather than two days. Approximately 1,500,000 cheeses, each stenciled "Parmigiano Reggiano," are made annually by some 1,700 dairies. All Parmigiano-Reggiano is made under carefully controlled conditions set by the Consorzio del Formaggio Parmigiano-Reggiano; the product, like Switzerland Swiss cheese and Roquefort, is safeguarded by trademark, albeit other countries use similar names, spelled differently, for the same type of *grana* cheese.

[6]
Two Semi-soft Cheeses: Edam and Gouda

Among the celebrated and popular semi-soft cheeses made in much the same way as their Swiss and English relatives, Emmenthaler and Cheddar, are the Dutch Edam and Gouda. I have visited an Edam factory at Zuidwolde, near Meppel, Holland as guest of the Zuivelbureau of the Nationale Cooperatieve Zuivelverkoopcentrale, or the Dutch Dairy Bureau, an organization which, like the British M.M.B., is run by the dairy industry itself to promote production and consumption of its products both at home and abroad. With branch offices in Aachen, Brussels, London, and Paris, it offers lectures, classes in cooking with dairy products, and brochures on various aspects of dairy foods. The vigor of this program may in part explain the position of Holland as the world's largest cheese exporter. The Dairy Board has under its aegis some thirty-five creameries manufacturing such traditional Dutch cheeses as Edam, Frisian Clove, Leyden, and Gouda, the latter the most important Dutch cheese, accounting for 60 percent of the total national cheese production. At Zuidwolde, 50,000 gallons of milk are transformed each day by forty workers into plump round-sided Edams. They are trucked to nearby Meppel, where, in a large curing-house, they are aged and packed before shipment. At Meppel, I was shown about by Eit Hendricks, the North American Export Manager. The Meppel installation directed by Mr. Hendricks handles about 25 percent of the annual Dutch export to our continent. (Ninety percent of the total export market, he explained, is in Germany as mild young cheeses, the preferred taste there.) Mr. Hendricks also stated that the total cheese export from Holland in 1973 was about 203,000 tons, of which the installation at Meppel supplied 60,000 tons, or just under 30 percent of the total. Always fascinated by statistics, I was especially impressed by these figures.

Edam is made in the north of Holland, Gouda in the south; each has a history of production going back over eight hundred years. Traditionally, they are "thumped" or tapped, to determine whether or not they are adequately aged. A dull thump of the knuckles on the cheese means good quality; a sharp thump indicates that more aging is necessary. Both Edam and Gouda are whole-milk products. In the case of both, size affects the taste, the larger being preferred by Dutch turophiles.

[7]
Two Peerless Soft-ripened Cheeses: Camembert and Brie

Camembert and Brie, perhaps the most glamorous of the soft-ripened cheeses, are made following the six basic steps outlined at the beginning of this chapter on page 23. Certain, seemingly slight variations give each cheese its particular personality. In the case of Camembert, lactic acid is added when the milk is at 85° Fahrenheit. Usually, the curd is not cut before it is put into 4½-inch draining hoops; the curd, broken as little as possible, then must settle in a carefully controlled 70° Fahrenheit temperature. At the end of two days, when the cheese is about 1½ inches thick, it is salted either with fine dry salt or by immersion in brine for about one hour or less; it also may be treated with a mold-bacteria culture (*Penicillium candidum*), which is sprayed on the cheese in solution. Curing, the most difficult aspect of the process, requires three weeks. During curing, the cheeses are on open wood frames at a temperature of 55° Fahrenheit and a relative humidity of 85 to 90 percent; the cheeses are turned often.

Brie, Camembert's near relative, comes in three sizes, rounds of 16, 12, and 5½ inches respectively. Like Camembert, Brie is ripened by yeasts and molds growing on the surface of the cheese. Unlike Camembert, it is often started with the addition of slightly ripened skim milk. Heated to nearly 90° Fahrenheit, and with rennet added, the milk coagulates in about two hours, and large horizontal slices of the curd are transferred to metal draining hoops set on straw or rush mats in a temperature of 65° Fahrenheit. With the hoops removed, the cheese is further drained and frequently turned on clean straw mats. Fine dry salt is rubbed on the surface of the cheese daily for two or three days. The cheese is then placed in a well-ventilated room, with the temperature at 55 to 60° Fahrenheit, for eight days, at which time a velvety mold begins to grow on the surface. Then at a temperature of 52° Fahrenheit, a relative humidity of 85 percent, and with little ventilation, the cheeses are cured for about three weeks. Brie, like Camembert, may be inoculated with micro-organisms.

The details of difference in making these soft-running cheeses are given to illustrate not only the importance of each step in cheese production, but also the remarkable differences which these details make in the finished product. Truly, the art of the cheese-maker is a celebration of the miracle of milk!

In the heart of well-ordered Normandy, with its apple orchards and soft green meadows bordered by flower-covered hedges, is found the cradle of Camembert country—the "Pays d'Auge." Camembert has been made in the carefully tended Auge region since the eighteenth century. There are two stories about the origins of Camembert in Normandy. One is that Marie Harel, wife of a prosperous farmer, discovered the secret of making Camembert. The other, more generally accepted story is that a priest, fleeing the dangers of the French Revolution, took refuge in the Harel farmstead and, in thanks for his safety, revealed to his benefactress the mystery of making Camembert, a secret which he had brought with him from his abbey. In any case, today statues and plaques in the village of Camembert and at nearby Champsoult, where she is buried, commemorate the good Mme. Harel—as well they should—for her priceless gift to turophiles the world over.

Camembert, like Roquefort, is peculiarly a product of one region, being made from the milk of Normandy cows pastured among the sweet grasses of the Auge countryside. Unfortunately, unlike Roquefort, Camembert has no patent, no "appellation d'origine," to protect its name from indiscriminate use. The Normandy Dairy, Ltd. (Normandie-Lait) works valiantly to identify and protect genuine Normandy Camembert and to promote it properly, but despite these efforts "Camembert" is now produced not only throughout France itself, but also in Denmark and the United States.

These "imitative" Camemberts are not the same cheese as the Normandy original; there is no point in pretending they are. Nor is a Normandy Camembert fermier—that is, one made of unpasteurized milk by a small cheese-maker—the same as Camembert laitier—one made of pasteurized milk by a commercial dairy. The supreme Camembert—Camembert fermier—is, alas, unavailable in the United States, where pure-food laws require pasteurization of imported milk products. But dairy-made Normandy Camembert is available, if one searches it out. And the search is well worth any effort.

(I should add here that anyone will be fortunate to visit well-tended Normandy—a land of handsome châteaux, owned by prosperous farmers, surrounded by lovely countryside, at once radiant and brooding, verdant and luxuriant. On any visit, inquire about a *fromagerie fermière*—and buy a Camembert on the spot. I did, from genial M. Daniel Courtonne, a third-generation Camembert-maker, who daily produces about 300 cheeses in the rambling basement of his home. The memory of the taste of the one I enjoyed will long remain with me, a prized souvenir—as will the flavor and smoothness of the *calvados* (Norman apple brandy) which M. Courtonne's father made fifty years ago and which I was offered with justifiable family pride.)

Upon another occasion, I had the privilege of visiting the Fromagerie Buquet at Chambois, another third-generation family enterprise, which, according to M. Paul Buquet, its energetic and affable president and owner, "just grew, a little at a time." Located in the center of the *patrie* Marie Harel—of whom M. Buquet is a descendant—the dairy, operated by some eighty-five workers and administered by a staff of twenty, produces daily some 50,000 individual Camemberts, 85 percent of which are exported (chiefly to America). The milk, collected in the immediate vicinity from an area of about twenty-five square kilometers, includes that of M. Buquet's own herd. The dairy at Chambois pasteurizes the milk for export trade—pasteurization standardizes quality and helps to conserve the cheese. But at another Buquet dairy nearby, which produces Camembert for the domestic market, raw milk is used in deference to French taste.

[8]
Cream Cheese

The term "cream cheese" applies not only to the smooth, foil-wrapped household staple with which we have been familiar since carrying sandwich lunches to school, but also to any cheese made with the addition of cream to the milk. The ensuing richness of the cheese, dependent upon the amount of cream used, is well defined by the French practice of labeling them as *crème, double crème,* and *triple crème,* the third category being that richest in butter fat—*matière grasse.* Except in this technical sense, however, there is no similarity between our homely cream cheese and the remarkably subtle and sophisticated *crèmes* which are most often—and should be—served with pride as part of a cheese course at a well-appointed dinner.

Save for the supplemental cream used in their production, cream cheeses are made by the same basic procedure as we have observed with Cheddar, Emmenthaler, Gruyère, Roquefort, and the like. Popular in both Europe and America, the creams, like all soft cheeses, tend to deteriorate quickly; they must be well refrigerated and protected with plastic wrap. If old or carelessly kept, they have a strong taste.

The rectangular shape which makes American cream cheese immediately recognizable was the idea of William E. Lawrence and Son, cheese-makers of Chester, New York, who produced in the early part of this century both Neufchâtel—similar to cream cheese, but containing less butter fat—and the richer cream cheese. Shortly thereafter, a village west of the Catskills began to make a cream cheese so smooth that it was dubbed "Philadelphia Cream Cheese"—a promotional name deriving from the prestige of the City of Brotherly Love, which in those days was considered a center of gastronomy. Within fifty years "Philly," as it is now popularly called, had become the world's largest-selling packaged cheese. Today, we produce annually some 130 million pounds of it, and over 5 million pounds of Neufchâtel.

The crustless cream cheeses, such as "Philadelphia" or Neufchâtel or Gervais, have the same consistency as butter. Most frequently used as table cheeses, they are also excellent cooking cheeses, particularly in sauces and desserts, the most celebrated of which is cream cheesecake.

Cheesecake, known in some form throughout virtually every Western country for hundreds of years, was eaten by Elizabeth I of England, was admired by Pepys, and continues, in the form we know today, to be one of our most popular sweet dishes.

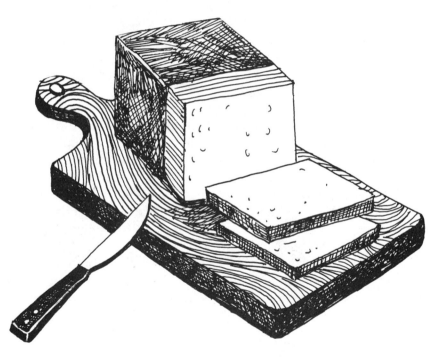

[9]
Fresh Cheeses

There are myriads of fresh, or soft unripened, cheeses. Of the estimated 480-odd cheeses in France, the great majority are fresh. There are many of them, too, in Italy. For the most part, they are unavailable to us; indeed, we frequently do not even know their names because they are often eaten the day they are made (or very shortly thereafter) and do not travel far from their place of production. What a pity for the American cheese-lover! There are European fresh cheeses so fine, so unusual and delicious, that travelers to Europe seek them out in local restaurants or food shops in order to enjoy them, just as they do celebrated paintings in Europe's museums or the continent's beautiful and varied scenery.

Because all fresh cheeses are perishable and do not travel well, it is natural to give attention to those readily available to us. Of these, of course, the best known to most Americans is cottage cheese. Made of skimmed milk or reconstituted skimmed milk with added dried milk solids, cottage cheese may be enhanced by the addition of cream stirred into the curd. To be labeled "creamed cottage cheese" or "cream-style cottage cheese," the product must contain 4 percent or more added cream. By far the largest-selling and most used cheese in the United States—we consume over 1 billion pounds annually—cottage cheese is a pleasant companion at the table, and, together with Ricotta, is a fine ingredient in many recipes.

You can make your own cottage cheese, or a cheese food somewhat similar to it, at some saving over the market price and with considerable personal pleasure. For "diet" cottage cheese, in a soup kettle or large saucepan, combine three 1-quart envelopes of dried milk and 2 quarts of cold water, stirring to dissolve the crystals; salt the liquid to taste. In a little cold water, dissolve a rennet, or "junket," tablet. Heat the milk until it is lukewarm; remove it from the heat, stir in the dissolved rennet, and allow the milk to sit, undisturbed, for ½ hour, or until it has coagulated. Using a spatula, cut the coagulated milk north-to-south, east-to-west, and diagonally—this will release the whey. Return the coagulated milk to a gentle heat; and, stirring slowly but constantly, heat it until it feels just barely warm. At once remove it from the heat. With a piece of cheesecloth, line a colander, then put the colander in a large bowl (to collect the whey, which is a very healthy drink). Pour the curd into the cheesecloth and draw the corners of the cloth together to form a bag (similar to a jelly bag); tie the corners securely and hang the bag over the whey pan to drain for one hour. Place the cheese in a clean container with a tight-fitting lid and refrigerate it; bottle and refrigerate the whey, if desired.

Perhaps our second best-known fresh cheese—and surely it is number one in its native Italy—is Mozzarella. In America, however, Mozzarella is not always "fresh" cheese; this plastic curd cheese, commercially made on a large scale, with added preservatives and vacuum-packed, has a much longer life than the fresh Mozzarella. We know it, alas, chiefly as an essential ingredient of pizza and, to a less extent, of such Italian dishes as eggplant Parmigiana. But in Italy Mozzarella has a much nobler status: It is a superb table cheese. At its best, Italian Mozzarella is made of the milk of water buffalo; otherwise, cow's milk is used. It is usually ball-shaped and is considered at its best when still oozing its whey. In southern Italy, where it originated and where it is still produced on a large scale, it is eaten the day it is made. It is also available, in Italy, with a lump of clear yellow *manteca*—sweet butter made of whey—at the center. Originally produced in this exotic manner to keep butter from spoiling in the heat of southern Italy, this cheese, accompanied by a substantial Italian country bread, is a delicacy which I continually recall from various trips to Italy and which I always seek out whenever I return.

It is sad to have to admit—but one must do so—that Mozzarella produced in the United States has suffered a considerable change. The light, buttery quality of its Old World ancestor is missing; so, too, is the nutlike flavor with its pleasant ever-so-light edge of acidity. As a cheese to eat at the table, commercially produced Mozzarella tends to be rubbery and bland. It is quite acceptable for use in recipes calling for it. Of course, all domestic Mozzarella is a cow's-milk product; no water buffalo has come near it. But in cities with large Italian communities specialty-food shops still make their own Mozzarella or are supplied it by some small producer. For your own pleasure, seek out such a source—doing so is well worth the effort.

[10]
Goat and Sheep Cheeses

The cheese of goats and sheep are probably the parent cheeses of myriad varieties which have been developed since the beginning of time. In the story of Polyphemus, Homer speaks of goat- and sheep-milk cheeses. Throughout Homer's world of Asia Minor, even today most cheese is produced from goat's and ewe's milk because these animals, hardier than cows, are best able to forage nourishment from a land of dry, arid vegetation.

Surely the most famous of all sheep's-milk cheeses is Roquefort (see pages 35 to 39 and the Glossary on page 57), the history of which is as old as that of any cheese eaten today. Other non-cow's-milk cheeses, however, also have their solid place in the affection of turophiles. Most such cheeses are made in France, and often one must seek them out in their native regions in order to enjoy them. But many travel well and are readily available in this country. Many hard, grating sheep's-milk cheeses of Italy are also for sale in America; some of them, still bearing their Italian names, or variants of them, are produced in the United States from cow's milk.

Greek Feta, exported to the United States as well as made here, may be a goat's- or ewe's-milk product, or a combination of the two; preserved in brine, its curd is firm and its taste rather acid and salty. Feta may be eaten as a table cheese or used, to pleasant effect, in cooking, especially in Greek and Middle Eastern dishes.

Of the sheep's-milk cheeses, Pecorino Romano—next to Roquefort, of course—is best known in America. A hard, grating cheese, it is stronger flavored than Parmesan; a mixture of the two is often suggested in Italian recipes, and with good reason, for they are an excellent combination. Although Sardinia produces Pecorino Sardo, "the flower of Sardegna," one-half of Italian ewe's-milk cheese comes from the province of Latium, near Rome. From Greece we import Kasseri, a sheep's-milk cheese considerably harder than Feta and with a more stalwart flavor. Kasseri is used as both a table and cooking cheese, and in Greece is often served thick-sliced, grilled under a hot broiler, and dressed with olive oil and lemon juice.

Goat and sheep cheeses, tending toward pronounced flavor and sometimes saltiness, are complementary companions to fruits, tomatoes, honey, and, sometimes, sugar; and some of them, fine in cooking, make excellent fillings for meat "pies" and such pasta as *ravioli*.

[11]
Buying and Storing Cheese

Buying Cheese

Buying cheese, like buying produce, demands a certain know-how which is easily and quickly developed with practice. If you deal with a cheese shop, your problems are minimized because the proprietor will probably offer you a tasting of your selection. Whenever possible, sample cheese before buying it. Patronize a store with a large turnover: doing so is insurance against purchasing over-ripe cheese. If you buy cheese, as most of us do, at a supermarket, there are a few rules to follow (these also apply to buying at a specialty shop):

1) The cheese should look good—that is, fresh, clear, and appetizing.
2) Cheeses bought in bulk should not have cracks on the surface, which indicate a growing dryness.
3) Veined cheeses should look moist.
4) Soft-ripening cheeses should look plump.
5) Some cheeses, such as Liederkranz, are dated for your protection; Switzerland Swiss cheese is stamped "Switzerland." For grated cheese, you will do well to buy a piece and grate it at home; pre-grated cheese quickly loses its flavor, in the same way as does a bottle of wine too long uncorked.

Keeping and Storing Cheese

Cheese does not require refrigeration if eaten reasonably soon after purchase. To keep it for any length of time, however, it should be refrigerated. If your refrigerator has a "cheese drawer," use it. If not, use a middle shelf where the temperature is at a mean between the top or bottom of the unit.

Wrap cheese well with plastic wrap; be sure that the wrap tightly covers the cheese, thus sealing out as much air as possible. Serve only as much as you anticipate will be eaten, for taking cheese in and out of the refrigerator, wrapping and unwrapping it, will reduce its freshness and taste. If mold appears on the cheese, scrape it off and serve the cheese with assurance; the mold is quite harmless. This suggestion does not, of course, apply to blue-veined cheeses, in which the mold is part of the cheese. Soft cheeses, of course, should be used within a few days of purchase.

Freezing cheese is not suggested. Soft-ripening cheeses will *not* freeze; blue-mold cheeses tend to become dry and very crumbly. Certain cheeses will tolerate freezing (but doing so will not improve them). If small amounts are tightly wrapped in plastic, Edam, Gouda, Port Salut, Pont l'Évêque, Emmenthaler, Gruyère, Provolone, Mozzarella, Münster, Cheddar, and cheeses of similar consistency may be frozen for brief periods. It is not recommended, however.

II
A GLOSSARY OF CHEESES
USED IN COOKING

The following glossary of cheeses is purposely restricted to (1) those cheeses mentioned in the reading matter of the text, (2) those cheeses suggested for use in Section III, "Cheese in Cooking—A Selection of Classic and Unusual Recipes," and (3) those cheeses which may be used in cooking at the discretion of the reader.

If desired, all cheeses listed here may be served as table cheese; this list, however, expressly omits many other table and cooking cheeses either because of their rarity in this country or because they do not fall within the scope of this book. The cheeses included are available from specialty shops, department stores, supermarkets, and grocery stores.

Arranged alphabetically by the name of the individual cheese, each entry indicates its country of origin and/or production, gives some facts of its history, and suggests certain characteristics. Strongly subjective reactions—to taste, texture, and aroma, for example—are expressly omitted; to describe these qualities of cheese is as impossible as it is to define the *bouquet* of different wines.

The Cheeses Listed by their Country of Origin and/or production:

Alsace: Münster

America: Baronet, Blue cheeses, Brick, Cheddar, Colby, Coon, Cottage, Cream, Farmer, Liederkranz, Monterey, Neufchâtel, Ricotta, Sage, "Store" cheese

Argentina: Sardo

Austria-Hungary and *Romania:* Kashkaval

Belgium: Limburger

Denmark: Danablu, Havarti

Great Britain: Caerphilly, Cheddar, Cheshire, Dunlop, Lancashire, Leicester, Stilton, Wensleydale

France: Bonbel, Brie, Camembert, Cantal, Comte, Gervais, Livarot, Münster, Neufchâtel, Pont l'Évêque, Port Salut, Reblochon, Roquefort, Saint-Paulin

Germany: Limburger, Tilsiter

Greece: Feta, Kasseri, Kefalotyri

Italy: Asiago, Bel Paese, Cacciocavallo, Emiliano, Fontina, Gorgonzola, *Grana*, Mozzarella, Parmigiano, Pecorino, Provolone, Reggiano, Ricotta, Romano, Taleggio

Netherlands: Edam, Gouda, Mimolette

Norway: Jarlsberg

Switzerland: Appenzeller, Bagnes, Emmenthaler, Glarus, Gruyère, Raclette, Sapsago, Sbrinz, Schabziger, Spalen, "Swiss," Vacherin Fribourgeois

Yugoslavia: Trappist

Appenzeller

(Switzerland) From the Canton of Appenzell, this pressed, cooked cheese, somewhat similar in taste to Emmenthaler and Gruyère, has been made since the eleventh century. Usually a skim-milk cheese, it is also produced in Bavaria and the Austrian Alps. Its delicate, fruitlike flavor derives from daily brushing with salt and wine or cider. A fine table offering and excellent for fondues.

Asiago

(Italy) Cured for one year or more, this very hard grating cheese, originating in the Province of Vicenza, is now produced throughout the north of Italy. Made of partly skimmed sweet cow's milk, Asiago is an uncooked, pressed *grana* with a pungent aroma and taste, similar to that of French Cantal. In America, where it is produced in Michigan and

Wisconsin, it is available either soft (fresh) or well-aged. It is used both as a grating and as a table cheese.

Bagnes

(Switzerland) Fromage à Raclette (French "scraper," as it is also known), comes from the Bagnes Valley in the Canton of Valais. Usually farm-produced, it is a hard, cow's-milk cheese with an aromatic flavor. Used in preparing "raclette" (page 214), the dish for which it is named, it is also served as table cheese.

Baronet

(America) This mild, smooth-textured cheese, evocative of both Fontina and Port Salut, is a good cooking and table cheese.

Bel Paese

(Italy) This popular cheese not only is imported, but also is made in Wisconsin. Of creamy texture, it has a pleasant hint of tartness in its fruity flavor. An excellent all-purpose cheese of standardized manufacture, the Italian import is packaged in foil showing its trademark, a map of Italy; the domestic product is similarly packed with a map of the United States. A small round is available under the name "Baby Bel."

Blue

(America, Denmark, Canada) Blue, blue-mold, or blue-veined are all generic names for this type of cheese made in the United States, Canada, and Scandinavia. *Penicillium roqueforti* or *Penicillium glaucum* is the mold usually added. Cow's milk is used, and the conditions of aging differ from producer to producer in the various countries which make blue-veined cheeses. Danablu is the well-known Danish blue. There are various American makes. All blue cheese becomes stronger as it ages; for this reason, it should be used shortly after purchase.

Bonbel

(France) Brand name of a commercially produced Port Salut. (See Port Salut.)

Brick

(America) A smooth, light-yellow to orange cheese made from whole cow's milk, Brick, first made in 1877, is one of two cheeses of American

origin (the other is Liederkranz). Produced in Wisconsin, it tastes similar to both Cheddar and Limburger, but is less pungent. Its body is less firm than Cheddar but stronger than Limburger. Characterized by numerous round and irregular eyes, Brick probably derives its name from its shape or from the bricks once used to press it.

Brie

(France) Still produced as it was centuries ago, in the Department of Seine-et-Marne, Brie is made from cow's milk and is available in rounds varying from 5½ to 16 inches in diameter. Brie is similar to Camembert in that both cheeses are ripened by molds and bacteria growing on their surface, but the characteristic flavor and aroma of each differs. Brie is made by a complicated and exacting method of production, which requires mixing evening with morning milkings, a prolonged period of salting, and curing in high humidity, with little ventilation. Brie may be shipped before it is ripe, but the ripening continues until the moment the round is cut—one reason why finding a "perfect" Brie is difficult. The thin, white, brownish-dusted crust, as well as the creamy yellow interior, is edible. Called the "Queen of Cheeses," it is a superb table offering, but also is occasionally used in cooking (including the rind). Denmark and the United States also produce Brie. (See also page 44.)

Cacciocavallo

(Italy) First produced in southern Italy, this cow's-milk cheese is now also made during the summer in the north, primarily for export. The smooth, firm-bodied cheese is gourd-shaped, and, when aging, two cheeses are tied together and hung over a pole, rather like saddle bags across a horse; hence, possibly, the name "cheese on horseback," *"caccio a cavallo."* The young cheese is suitable for table use; that cured for six months to a year or longer is used for grating. Its flavor is delicate and mildly smoky—albeit it is not a smoked cheese, as its near-cousin Provolone often is; the light-tan crust is not edible.

Caerphilly

(England) A crumbly, very white cooked cheese related to Cheddar and made in 9-pound rounds, Caerphilly tastes somewhat like buttermilk (real buttermilk, that is, not cultured) with a slightly salty and acid tang. Originally made in Wales of skimmed milk, an easily digested, inexpensive staple for miners' lunches, today's whole-milk product is its

best at three weeks of aging. It is a very good table cheese and, I find, a reliable cooking cheese for mild-flavored dishes.

Camembert
(France) The secret of its making, allegedly first revealed in 1791 by a farmer's wife in a Norman village in the Pays d 'Auge, this celebrated cheese is now commercially made from pasteurized milk throughout France. Named for the village of Camembert this cheese has a pleasing creaminess and a flavor somewhat similar to Brie, but milder and smoother. Made year-round in creameries and—more rarely—on individual farms, Camembert should have a white rind, firm texture, and a pleasantly aromatic flavor. Denmark and the United States also produce Camembert. (see also page 44.)

Cantal
(France) This close-textured cow's-milk cheese with piquant flavor has been produced for centuries in the mountains of the Department of Cantal. The method of manufacture remains primitive even today; uncooked, pressed, brushed with salted water, and cured in the shape of tall cylinders, Cantal has a pronounced lactic acid smell when cut. However, its nutlike taste makes it welcome as a table or cooking cheese and as a condiment when grated.

Cheddar
(England, America, Canada, Denmark) Named for the village of Cheddar in Somerset, England, where it was first made, Cheddar has

Forty-pound blocks of Cheddar are transported by conveyor belt to be wrapped and boxed at the modern creamery of Aspatria.

Curd which will shortly become Double Gloucester, a Cheddar-related cheese, is cut by hand in a small English creamery.

been produced since the latter sixteenth century. Knowledge of making it was brought to America by the colonists. The first American commercial cheese enterprise, in New York State, produced Cheddar in 1851. Today over 1 billion pounds of Cheddar are produced annually in the United States. Sometimes called American, or "store," cheese, Cheddar at its best is made from pasteurized sweet whole cow's milk. Its color may vary from nearly white to orange, depending upon the amount of *annatto* added; its shape depends upon the manufacturer and weight of the cheese. It may have an artificial wax "rind" or be rindless. Its flavor ranges from mild to sharp depending upon its period of aging. Farm-produced English Cheddar is not exported; the commercially-made product is very similar to the best New York State, Vermont, Wisconsin, or Canadian Cheddars. A first-rate table cheese, it is perhaps also the most versatile of cooking cheeses. (See also page 33.)

Cheshire
(England) This superb English cheese, also known as Chester, has a distinctive and pleasantly salty flavor. Of moist and crumbly consistency,

it was first produced, as we know it today, in the village of Chester on the river Dee in the twelfth century. Elizabeth I is said to have been fond of it. Alice's "Cheshire Cat" in the Lewis Carroll masterpiece was not a pet but a traditional measure of the cheese as served in taverns. Cylindrical in shape, Cheshire may be white, but is more often a deep yellow, caused by the addition of *annatto*. Of the early-, medium-, and late-ripening Cheshires, the latter is most often available in America. A fine table cheese, it is also used in cooking, being especially suited to Welsh rabbit. (See also page 34.)

Colby
(America) Similar to Cheddar, save that it has a less dense texture and contains more moisture, Colby is made from either raw or pasteurized whole milk. It does not keep as well as its cousin. Available in light-yellow to orange cylinders, it is mild-tasting, suitable for table use or cooking. Denmark also produces a Colby.

Comté
(France) A Gruyère-related cheese from eastern France, Comté is a cow's-milk cheese, pressed and cooked, with a natural rind. Available in cylindrical wheels of about 80 pounds, it has little odor but has a salty, strong taste. A table and cooking cheese.

Coon
(America) A Cheddar cured by a special patented method, requiring a fine quality of "raw" cheese, in which both temperature and humidity are kept high, allowing unwanted mold to form easily. The cheese is crumbly and very sharp. For use as a table cheese and, if you enjoy a strong taste in dishes, as a cooking cheese.

Cottage
(America) Also called pot cheese, Dutch cheese, or Schmierkäse, this pasteurized, large-grained fresh cheese is highly nutritious; it is also made from skim milk with added skim milk concentrate or reconstituted nonfat dry milk. Because of its high moisture content, it is perishable, must be refrigerated, and should be used within a reasonably short time after purchase. The origin of this universal cheese—virtually every country has a version of it—is uncertain. Its mild flavor is complementary to many recipes. A half cup of it added to four beaten eggs before scrambling results in a delicious, light, and tasty dish. (See also page 49.)

Cream
(America) Mild, rich, smooth, buttery, and nutritious, cream cheese is made of cream or a mixture of cream and milk. Similar to unripened Neufchâtel (See page 47) but with a higher fat content, it is one of our most popular soft cheeses, being used at the table and in cooking. Bought individually packaged or in bulk, it should always be very white. I find it an excellent cheese in dishes requiring a smooth, rich sauce. (See also page 47.)

Danablu
(Denmark) One of the best known of the Scandinavian blue-veined cheeses. (See Blue.)

Dunlop
(Scotland) Formerly the Scottish national cheese and the only cheese native to that country, Dunlop is now superseded to a large extent by Cheddar, which is very like it. The flavor and uses of both are similar, the taste of Dunlop closely resembling that of a young English Cheddar. It is an excellent melting cheese.

Edam
(Netherlands) A cheese of light and buttery flavor, Edam is, historically, one of the oldest of all cheeses—Holland exported it during the Middle Ages. A sweet-curd, factory-made cheese of high-quality cow's milk to which color may be added, it was first produced near Edam in the Province of North Holland. There is also a domestic American Edam. Usually shaped like a flattened ball, Edams weigh from ¾ to 14 pounds. Imported Edam is packaged in transparent wrapping; in the United States it is paraffin-dipped. Other producers of Edam are Denmark, France, and Norway. (See also page 42.)

Emiliano
(Italy) A *grana*, or Parmesan-type cheese, available in cylinders which weigh from 45 to 65 pounds, it is very similar to Reggiano (see page 40); indeed, some say that there is no difference between them. Varying in flavor from mild to sharp and with its particular granular texture, this cheese, cured for at least one year, is very useful in cooking. (See also Parmigiano.)

Emmenthaler

(Switzerland) Named for its place of origin, the Emme Valley in Bern Canton, Emmenthaler, together with Gruyère, is the most celebrated Swiss cheese. It is mentioned as *"caseus armentatis"* by a second-century Latin writer. From early times, it was made during the summer's heavy milking season to be used as a meat substitute in winter. It was first produced in the United States in 1850 by Adam Blumer, a native of Glarus Canton, who had moved to Wisconsin. Generally called "Swiss" cheese by Americans, it has a nutty flavor and a sweetish aftertaste. In Switzerland, these qualities are attributed to the particular grazing vegetation and the glacial waters found there. "Swiss cheese" is produced in the United States, Austria, Denmark, Germany, and Ireland, among other countries. Elastic, oily of texture, and with an inedible rind, the pale-yellow cheese develops an increasingly pronounced flavor as it ages. The wheels vary in weight from 10 to 220 pounds, the quality of which, in Switzerland, is rigidly controlled by the Swiss Cheese Union, which passes on its eye (hole) formation, texture and color, flavor and aroma, exterior appearance, and storage quality. Cheeses are shipped at the age of three months, but optimum curing requires at least one year. A fine table and cooking cheese. (See also page 26.)

Farmer

(America) Also known as Pressed cheese and sometimes, incorrectly, called Cream cheese, Farmer cheese, originally firm-textured, varies in density because of the different ways of making it in different localities. Usually a whole-milk cheese, it is bland-tasting and substitutes well in recipes calling for cottage cheese.

Feta

(Greece) A cheese refrigerated and stored in a mixture of milk, salt, and water, Feta has a somewhat sharp and pungent flavor, and is an excellent accompaniment to any Middle Eastern meal. In Greece, it is produced from ewe's milk by shepherds in the mountains near Athens; in America, it is made of cow's milk. Ready to cut after one week, the white, crumbly cheese is delicious sprinkled over salads; it is also a good cooking cheese in Middle Eastern dishes. When you cook with Feta, adjust the seasoning of the recipe to allow for the saltiness of the cheese. (See also page 51.)

Fontina

(Italy) One of the superior Italian cheeses, this buttery, slightly yellow cow's-milk delight is made in large wheels of about 40 pounds. It tastes like Gruyére with a dash of Brie, and may have a few small eyes. It keeps well and is a pleasant table cheese when young; it is a fine cooking cheese when somewhat older and firmer. Produced in the Piedmont hills, Fontina has a smooth rind and body. It is reputed to have been served by the Dukes of Savoy in the eleventh century. Danish Fontina, also good, is usually wax-covered and, like young Italian Fontina, soft and sliceable. An American Fontina is also available.

Gervais

(France) Originally a brand name and today used as the generic name for a French cream cheese available in the United States in 2-ounce foil-wrapped portions. Known for over a century, this double *crème* is a mild, rich table cheese, which may also be used in cooking.

Glarus

(Switzerland) Another name for Sapsago (see page 73).

Gorgonzola

(Italy) The great Italian blue cheese, made similarly to Roquefort and Stilton (page 35), is a superior table cheese, admirable with fresh fruit, and excellent in certain recipes.

Gouda

(Netherlands) Smooth and mellow, with a flavor similar to that of Edam, Gouda is always made from whole milk (Edam may sometimes be made from partially skimmed milk), and is therefore creamier in texture. Ordinarily, only young Goudas are available in the United States; yet an aged Gouda is worth searching for, since it has a considerably fuller flavor. Shaped like a flattened ball, it was first made during the Renaissance near Gouda, a small river port in southern Holland. Produced year-round by commercial creameries, the pale-yellow Gouda has a smooth shiny rind (edible when the cheese comes sealed in red paraffin, as it usually does in this country) and a nutlike, buttery taste. Best known for table use, it is a fine cooking cheese, giving a mild and pleasant flavor to dishes in which it is used. (See also page 42.)

Grana

(Italy) "*Grana*" is the Italian generic name for any of several long-aged, very hard cheeses, usually grated for use as a condiment or in cooking, but also *excellent* table cheeses once one has grown accustomed to their resistant texture and the crunchy "crystals" characteristic of them. The *grana* flavor is sharp, intense, exquisite. Made in the Po Valley since about A.D. 1200, there continue to be three principal varieties of *grana*: Parmigiano (Parmesan), Reggiano, and Emiliano (which see). Parmesan is that variety most often exported to the United States, with Reggiano following in second place. Both are made in the United States and, with a similar but different name, in South America. (See also page 40.)

Gruyère

(Switzerland) As Swiss as the Alps or yodeling, Gruyère resembles Emmenthaler in appearance but is more flavorful, probably the preferred of the two when a Swiss diner makes his choice. Our domestic Gruyère, often individually foil-wrapped in triangular shapes, has little in common with the nutty, fruitlike quality of the original cheese. Made in essentially the same way for over 600 years, Gruyère takes its name from the chateau village of the Counts of Gruyère, albeit the cheese itself was first made as tax payment to the Abbey of Rougemont. As a result, it soon also became popular in France. Today, Gruyère is made in the areas of Fribourg, Vaud, Neufchâtel, and the Bern Jura. Made from whole cow's milk and cured for not less than ninety days, it is a remarkable all-purpose cheese, equally at home on the dining table or stove. (See also page 28.)

Havarti: The Danish Tilsiter.

(Denmark) (See page 75.)

Jarlsberg

(Norway) The Norwegian "Swiss" cheese has a nutlike flavor and an exceptionally pleasing aftertaste, both of which improve with aging. A first-rate cheese for use at the table or in cooking.

Kashkaval

(Austria–Hungary, Romania) Also spelled "Kaskaval," made of partly-skimmed ewe's milk in Serbia, Bulgaria, Macedonia, as well as in

Romania, this cheese is similar to the Italian cow's-milk Cacciocavallo (whence its name). Kashkaval is salty and sharp and has an inedible rind. When young, it is suitable as a table cheese; when old, it is used for grating.

Kasseri
(Greece) Redolent of the flavor of ewe's milk, Kasseri has the same uses as Feta, its fellow-countryman, being both a table and cooking cheese. Also made in neighboring Slavic countries.

Kefalotyri
(Greece) Sometimes spelled "Kefalotyrie," this goat's- or ewe's-milk cheese is named for its resemblance to a Greek hat, the *kefalo:* it is also made in Syria. Its salty flavor makes it an excellent grating condiment for sprinkling over cooked foods.

Lancashire
(England) One of the most popular of English cheeses, Lancashire is somewhat similar to Cheddar and Cheshire, but white rather than yellow, and softer, moister, and somewhat more flavorful. Especially suitable for making Welsh rabbit, it is a thoroughly dependable table and cooking cheese.

Leicester
(England) First made in the English midlands, this mild cow's-milk cheese, reputedly one of the finest of England, is considered by many

To protect the cheese and strengthen the rind, cheesecloth is "painted" with a thin solution of flour and water onto this Leicester, a relative of Cheddar cheese.

turophiles to be equal in quality to the splendid blue-veined Stilton, although cheddar-related. Yellower than Cheddar (it is always colored with *annatto*) and moister, it has a rich flavor and a somewhat flaky texture. A high quality table and cooking cheese.

Liederkranz
(America) Its name means "Crown of Song." This American cheese was first developed at Monroe, New York, in 1882. It should be eaten fully ripened, when the cheese is soft and has the texture of thick honey. Unlike many soft-ripening cheeses, Liederkranz is dependable and far more delicate to the palate than to the nose. A highly recommended cheese.

Limburger
(Belgium, Germany) One of the strongest-smelling cheeses, Limburger has a substantial but surprisingly subtle flavor. Originally made in the Belgian town of Limburg, it is now produced commercially not only in its homeland, but also in Germany and the United States.

Livarot
(France) Named for a village in the Department of Calvados and one of the oldest of Normandy cheeses, Livarot comes in cylinders of about 1 pound, often banded with marsh grass and sometimes boxed. Strong-tasting with a spicy flavor.

Mimolette
(Netherlands) Made year-round by commercial creameries principally in the Province of North Holland, this pasteurized cow's-milk cheese has a compact texture and a pleasantly nutty taste. Eaten at breakfast in Holland, it is a dependable table and cooking cheese.

Monterey
(America) Sometimes called Jack or Monterey Jack, this Cheddar-related cheese was first made in California's Monterey County at the close of the last century. It is produced from pasteurized whole, partly skimmed, or skim milk, its degree of hardness depending upon the milk from which it is made. Thus, it may be used as either a table or a grating cheese. Available in white wheels of smooth texture, it is mild-flavored.

Mozzarella

(Italy) Originally made from water buffalo's milk in southern Italy, Mozzarella is now also produced from cow's milk both in Italy and the United States. Ricotta (see page 72) is often made from its whey. Used when fresh, with little or no ripening, it is rindless, variably shaped, and available in different weights. It is very white, elastic to the touch, and has a mild taste. Generally used in cooking, it is very good—I think—sprinkled with a little fine olive oil and salt and pepper. Served this way with sliced tomatoes and buttered toast, it provides a pleasant luncheon. (See also page 50.)

Münster

(France) First developed in Alsace during the Middle Ages, Münster (or Muenster) is made in France of pasteurized cow's milk. It is also produced in the United States, Germany,. and Denmark. Alsatian and French Münster is strong-tasting and has a penetrating odor. American and Danish Münster is blander and smoother, and tastes very little like the Alsatian. The cheese sold in bulk (flat cylinders) I find superior to the packaged variety. It is an excellent table and cooking cheese.

Neufchâtel

(America, France) Similar to cream cheese in taste, color, and texture, Neufchâtel contains less butterfat and more protein. American Neufchâtel, richer than the French version and much easier to procure, is a mild table cheese and, in cooking, is interchangeable with cream cheese. (See also page 47.)

Parmigiano

(Italy) Also called Parmesan, this superb grana has been known for centuries. Parmesan is in reality a generic name for Reggiano, Lodigiano, Lombardy, Emiliano, Veneto and Bagozzo—all grana cheeses important in Italian cuisine for over eight hundred years. They differ in size and shape, as well as in the degree to which they are made of skimmed milk, and there are slight variations in their manufacture. But they are the same type of cheese. Fully cured (one to two years or longer) Parmesan keeps indefinitely. Considerable quantities are imported by the United States, although we have a successful domestic product. The crust is inedible. The flavor is sharp, but the cheese melts in the mouth—literally and figuratively. Lauded by Boccaccio, Molière, and Pepys, I too sing its praises—as one of the best cheeses to accompany fresh fruit and a *sine qua non* in the kitchen. (The face of Santa Lucia, the Italian patron saint of cheese manufacture, adorns the pure gold medal awarded annually to the cheese-maker of Lombardy yielding the most and best Parmesan. With Gorgonzola, Parmigiano establishes Italy among the world's great cheese-producers.) (See also page 40.)

Pecorino

(Italy) Any Italian ewe's-milk cheese, the most common of which is Pecorino Romano, made on mainland Italy and also, since 1920, on Sardinia, where it is called Sardo Romano. A Sardo also is made in the United States and Argentina. Pecorino, when young, is a pleasant table cheese. Generally used as a very hard, sharp-tasting grating cheese.

Pont l'Évêque

(France) One of the most important cheeses of France—on a par with Brie, Camembert, and Roquefort—this monastery cheese dates from the thirteenth century. Named for the bishop's bridge across the River Tongues in the area of Trouville, it is described in a poem of that period. Its surface, washed as the crust is forming, is affected by a fungus, *Monila candida,* which turns the rind a reddish gold. Square in shape, Pont l'Évêque is at its best during autumn and winter. Unlike Port Salut, it cannot be imitated. Its taste is considerably milder than its scent. When at its best, plump and soft to the touch, it is a fine table cheese and an almost perfect complement to red wine.

Port Salut

(France) Also called "Port du Salut," "Port Salut" is the licensed name of a cheese made by arrangement with the Abbey of Notre Dame du Port Salut in the Mayenne; the same cheese, dairy-produced, is called Saint-Paulin. "Abbey" is merely the sobriquet for a Port Salut–type cheese. Port Salut is mild-flavored and smooth-textured. The Danish and American versions, available at half the price of the French cheese, are somewhat more dependable; but they are really different cheeses.

Provolone

(Italy) First made in southern Italy, it is now produced throughout its native land and also in the United States. Light-colored, mellow, smooth, and sliceable, it is often molded by hand, and hence comes in a

variety of shapes. According to its age, it is mild or sharp-tasting with a slightly smoky flavor. It may also be purposely smoked. The young cheese is suitable for table use; older cheeses are used for cooking and grating.

Raclette
(Switzerland) French "scraper"—a hard cow's-milk cheese, used in the dish of the same name. (See Bagnes.)

Reblochon
(France) This cow's-milk cheese from Savoy is pale cream-colored with a reddish crust. If old, it tends to turn bitter, but when à point, it has a distinctive and delicious flavor, mild and creamy. It is named for a slang word, reblocher, referring to the dripping from a cow's udder after milking. A first-rate table cheese.

Reggiano
(Italy) Closely related to Parmigiano (see page 70), Reggiano is a grana originally made in Reggiano Emilia but now produced in the United States and other countries. A grating cheese. (See also page 40.)

Ricotta
(Italy, America) Creamy and white with a bland and slightly sweet taste, Ricotta, as old as Rome itself, is the cottage cheese of Italy, but smoother and without separate curds, often made from the coagulable substance in whey derived from other cheese manufacture. In this country, Ricotta is produced from a combination of whey and whole milk. Sprinkled with sugar, it may be eaten as a dessert; sprinkled with salt and pepper, it provides a pleasant luncheon dish. An excellent cooking cheese.

Romano
(Italy) Made of ewe's or cow's milk, or sometimes a combination of both, Romano was first produced in Latium, near Rome, and is now manufactured throughout southern Italy and Sardinia. It is similar to Pecorino and Sardo (see pages 71 and 74).

Roquefort
(France) Named for its native village in Aquitaine, Roquefort is the most famous of the blue-veined cheeses. Produced under strictest con-

trol, only genuine Roquefort is franchised to carry this name. Made from ewe's milk, it is characterized by its sharp, piquant flavor and by the blue-green veining caused by the addition to the milk curd of *Penicillium roqueforti*. One of France's oldest cheeses, it is mentioned by Pliny the Elder and was Charlemagne's favorite cheese. The special quality of Roquefort is the result of aging in humid limestone caves near Roquefort-sur-Soulzon; these conditions cannot be duplicated. Hence Roquefort's uniqueness and its careful protection by its producers and the French government. (See also page 35.)

Sage
(America) Sage cheese is really a bland, white Cheddar flavored with oil of sage, imported from Arabia. However, since discovering that the best of Vermont and Wisconsin export-quality sage is made this way, with alfalfa or young corn leaves added for bits of color, I have made my own: In a mortar or the container of an electric blender, combine ½ cup chopped fresh sage leaves (dried will not work), 2 tablespoons vegetable oil, and 2 tablespoons dry white wine. Grind the leaves with a pestle and strain the mixture, or chop them fine in the blender. Combine the sage mixture with ¼ lb. finely grated mild Cheddar cheese and one 8-oz. package cream cheese. Allow the mixture to stand at room temperature several hours, creaming it often before filling small containers or shaping it into balls. Refrigerate the cheese. The English Sage Darby is a combination of 2 parts white to 1 part flavored Darby, mixed together (originally layered). In France, dried sage is added when the curd is nearly setting—so it goes to the bottom. A celebrated Christmas cheese.

Saint-Paulin
(France) A mild-flavored and smooth-textured cheese. (See Port Salut.)

Sapsago
(Switzerland) Made for at least 500 years in the Canton of Glarus, this small cheese is made from slightly sour skim milk, buttermilk; a powder prepared from clover leaves, *Melilotus coerulea*, added to the curd, gives a sharp, pungent taste and a light-green color. The rindless, foil-wrapped, cone-shaped cheese is used, grated, as a condiment. Known also as Glarus and Schabziger or Schabzieger, of which the name Sapsago is a corruption.

Sardo

(Argentina) A Romano-type cheese used for grating. (See Pecorino and Romano.)

Sbrinz

(Switzerland) Made year-round by small dairies, this cow's-milk cheese is cured for two or three years in large wheels which may weigh over 125 pounds. The inedible dark yellow rind covers a dense yellow, strong-smelling, strong-tasting interior. Oldest of the Swiss cheeses, Pliny mentions it as *caseus helveticus* ("Swiss cheese"). Reputedly the most digestible of hard-crusted cheeses, it is used chiefly for grating but is sometimes served at the table.

Schabziger

(Switzerland) Another name for Sapsago (see page 73).

Spalen

(Switzerland) Named for the wooden containers (*spalen*) in which they are shipped, this cow's-milk cheese is the same as Sbrinz.

Stilton

(England) Perhaps the crowning triumph of English cheese-making. Produced from whole milk with added cream, Stilton has been praised by Alexander Pope, Jane Austen, and Charles Lamb. It tastes like a

A mold is filled with the curd which will one day emerge as a Stilton, perhaps the glory of English cheese-making.

combination of blue-veined cheese and Cheddar; it is mellow and crumbly. It does not keep very well and should be kept wrapped in a moistened cloth. It should never be bathed with Port wine or served with a scoop; rather, it should be cut horizontally. Rich, mellow, milder than either Roquefort or Gorgonzola, it is a superb table cheese and may also be used in certain recipes. (See also page 35.)

"Store" Cheese
(America) A familiar name, used throughout the United States for (American) Cheddar. (See Cheddar.)

"Swiss" Cheese
(Switzerland) (See Emmenthaler.)

Taleggio
(Italy) Made in the high valleys of Bergamo and the Lombardy plain at the foothills of the Alps, this cow's-milk cheese is available in thick 8-inch squares. Its yellow interior is tender, its odor full, and its taste pronounced but very pleasant; recommended both for table use and cooking.

Tilsiter
(Germany) First made by Dutch immigrants near Tilsit, a port town in East Prussia where Napoleon made his tenuous truce with the Russians, Tilsiter is also produced by Denmark, Norway, Switzerland, and the United States. It is often flavored with caraway seed. A white to yellow cow's-milk cheese similar to American Brick, it may sometimes have small round eyes. Its flavor, though not its consistency, recalls a *very* mild Limburger (see page 69). The Danish Tilsiter, called Havarti, is milder. A good table and cooking cheese.

Trappist
(Yugoslavia) First made in 1885 at a Yugoslavian monastery, it is now produced in many parts of Europe and resembles France's Port Salut. This pale yellow cheese, cured like hard cheeses, is produced from cow's milk, but ewe's or goat's milk may be added. For use at the table and in cooking.

Vacherin Fribourgeois

(Switzerland) Produced by small dairies, this cow's-milk cheese is available in wheels of about 20 pounds weight. Wrapped in resinous bark, it has a thin yellow-gray rind, a scent of resin, and a somewhat sour, pinelike taste. Named for the type of milk from which it is made and for its place of origin, it is used in fondues and sometimes as a table cheese.

Wensleydale

(England) First made in Yorkshire from whole cow's milk, blue Wensleydale is similar to Stilton in size and shape, but its flavor is stronger. Its texture is flaky. A rewarding table cheese.

III
CHEESE IN COOKING—
A SELECTION OF CLASSIC
AND UNUSUAL RECIPES

Cheese should be cooked rapidly and at medium temperatures. That is a general rule; there are exceptions which you will find in individual recipes. Prolonged cooking at high temperatures tends to make cheese stringy and rubbery. Therefore, shred, dice, grate, or crumble cheese to speed its cooking. In making sauces for use at a later time, use a double-boiler, in order that the cheese does not come into direct contact with the heat. Always bring cheese to room temperature before cooking with it. Aged cheese has more flavor than young cheese; you will need smaller quantities of the former to give the same taste in cooking. In these recipes, the amounts of cheese called for are suggestions, not hard rules. Taste the cheese before adding it to the other ingredients; you may wish to use less or more than suggested—your palate supported by a little experience will soon tell you. For soufflés and other dishes in which a light consistency is important, use well-aged cheese. (See also page 202.)

A Note on These Recipes

Cooking with cheese is capable of infinite variety. As given here, the recipes call for the cheese traditionally used in the dish. If the dish is of my invention, I suggest a cheese I enjoyed; and I suggest variants in many instances in the hope that you will experiment, too. I urge you, therefore, to use the cheese *you* prefer in the recipe of your choice. Ability to interchange cheeses in recipes will increase as your acquaintance with cheese grows. If you bear in mind the varying strengths of flavor of different cheeses, I know you will find cheese in cooking a delightful and creative culinary adventure.

When recipes call for grating cheeses, the choice is great and possibly confusing. For this reason, there follows a list of cheeses especially suited to grating (albeit the list does not preclude grating or shredding other varieties for use where "grating cheeses" are called for):

Asiago, Cacciocavallo, Cantal, Cheddar, Cheshire, Colby, Coon, Dunlop, Emiliano, the *grana* cheeses (Emiliano, Parmigiano, Reggiano), Gruyère, Jarlsberg, Kashkaval, Kasseri, Kefalotyri, Monterey Jack, Münster, Parmesan (Parmigiano), Provolone, Reggiano, Romano, Sapsago (as a flavoring only), Sardo, Sbrinz, Spalen, Tilsiter

For the information of calorie-conscious cooks, the following cheeses *may* be made with skimmed or partially skimmed milk (the list is limited to cheeses discussed in this book):

Appenzeller, Asiago, Cottage, Edam, Feta, Kashkaval, Lancashire, Livarot, Monterey, Pont l'Évêque, Port Salut, Sapsago, Spalen, Tilsiter

APPETIZERS AND
FIRST-COURSE DISHES

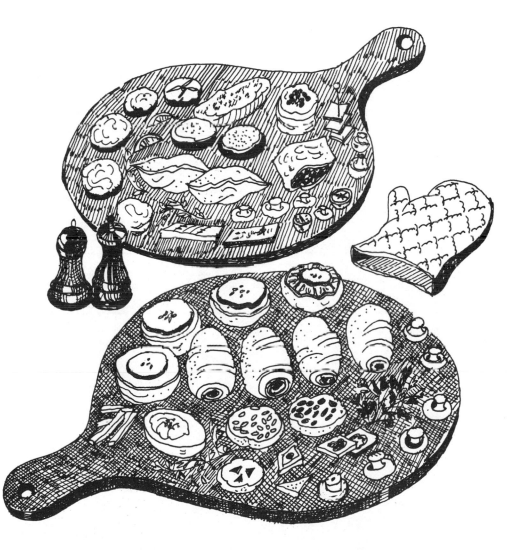

Stuffed Mushrooms: Italy

18 mushrooms · Doubles · Refrigerates
Preparation: 30 minutes · Cooking: 10 minutes in a 400° oven

Delicious with drinks or as an elegant first course.

1 cup Ricotta ¼ cup parsley, chopped ¼ cup finely chopped 　cooked ham 1 tablespoon lemon juice 1½ teaspoons salt Grinding of pepper	In a mixing bowl, combine and blend until smooth these six ingredients.
4 tablespoons butter 18 large mushroom caps	In a skillet, heat the butter and in it cook the mushroom caps for 2 minutes on each side. Drain them, smooth side down, on absorbent paper. Arrange them in a lightly oiled baking dish.
18 ¼-inch cubes Mozzarella	Mound the mushroom caps with the Ricotta mixture. Add a piece of Mozzarella to each. *At this point you may stop and continue later.* Bake the mushroom caps at 400° for 10 minutes, or until the filling bubbles.

Roquefort à la Royale

(a cocktail spread offered at Maxim's in Paris): With a fork, blend thoroughly 1 cup (4 oz.) Roquefort, crumbled, and 2 tablespoons butter, both at room temperature, a grating of pepper, and 1 tablespoon cognac. Roll the mixture into a ball and refrigerate it for at least 2 hours, so that the cognac "works." Serve the *bombe* with Melba toast.

Asparagus Rolls

Approximately 12 rolls
Preparation: 45 minutes · Cooking: 15 minutes in a 450° oven

This recipe—very good and *very* rich—is contributed by James Barnovitch, a friend in Boston.

1 egg
1 4-oz. package blue cheese, at room temperature
1 8-oz. package cream cheese, at room temperature

In a mixing bowl, beat the egg well. Add the cheeses and whip the mixture with a fork until it is smooth.

1 9-oz. package frozen asparagus spears, cooked as directed on the package and drained well on absorbent paper

1 loaf sliced good white bread

Trim the crusts from the bread slices. (Decrust only as many slices as you have asparagus spears.) Using a rolling pin, roll each slice as flat as possible.

2 sticks butter, melted

Spread each slice with some of the cheese mixture. Add 1 asparagus spear. Roll the bread slice around the asparagus and then dip the roll in the melted butter.

On a piece of foil, arrange the asparagus rolls. Place them in the freezing compartment of the refrigerator for at least 30 minutes.

When needed, remove as many asparagus rolls as desired, cut each roll into 4 or 5 segments, and bake them in a lightly oiled baking dish at 450° for 15 minutes, or until they are golden.

Stuffed Eggs with Roquefort

Hard boil, cool, peel, and halve lengthwise 6 eggs. Remove the yolks to a mixing bowl and to them add 1 cup (4 oz.) Roquefort, crumbled, 1½ tablespoons butter, both at room temperature, and salt and pepper. Using a fork, blend the mixture thoroughly and with it fill the egg whites. Arrange the stuffed eggs in a lightly buttered baking dish. Make 2 cups of Mornay Sauce, page 347, and pour it over the eggs. Bake the dish at 400° for 10 minutes, or until the sauce bubbles.

Miniature Pastry Puffs

36 puffs · Doubles · Refrigerates · Freezes
Preparation: 15 minutes · Cooking: 35 minutes, in a 400° oven

Festive for cocktail parties, these little pastries may be filled with any of the dips included here. If desired, the filled puffs may be heated at 375° for 5 minutes before serving.

½   cup water
4   tablespoons butter
¼   teaspoon salt
½   cup flour

In a saucepan, combine the water and butter. Over high heat, bring the water to the boil and, when the butter is melted, stir in the salt and then, all at one time, the flour. Off heat, stir the mixture vigorously until it draws from the sides of the pan and forms a ball.

2   eggs

Vigorously beat in each egg, one at a time.

Drop the dough by the teaspoonful onto an ungreased baking sheet. Bake the puffs at 400° for 35 minutes, or until they are risen and golden. Allow them to cool on a wire rack and freeze now if desired.

Filling of your choice (see pages 87–92)

Or remove their tops, add the filling of your choice, and freeze if desired (allow the filled puffs to come to room temperature before heating them).

If desired, ¼ cup (1 oz.) Gruyère, grated, may be blended with the flour.

Blue Cheese Dip or Filling

2 cups · Refrigerates
Preparation: 15 minutes

1½ cups (6 oz.) blue cheese, crumbled
4 tablespoons butter, softened
4 tablespoons heavy cream
1 egg yolk
¼ cup parsley, chopped
Grating of pepper

In a mixing bowl, using a fork, cream together the blue cheese and butter until the mixture is smooth. Add the remaining ingredients and beat the dip thoroughly to blend it well.

Blue Cheese and Brandy Dip or Filling

1⅔ cups · Refrigerates
Preparation: 15 minutes

1 cup (4 oz.) blue cheese, crumbled
1 8-oz. package cream cheese, at room temperature
3 tablespoons brandy
2 tablespoons heavy cream
¾ teaspoon dill weed, finely ground in a mortar

In a mixing bowl, using a fork, cream together the blue and cream cheeses until the mixture is smooth. Add the remaining ingredients and beat the dip thoroughly to blend it well.

Cheddar Dip or Filling

2 cups · Refrigerates
Preparation: 15 minutes

1 cup (4 oz.) sharp Cheddar, grated
1 cup sour cream
4 tablespoons sherry
2 drops Tabasco sauce

In a mixing bowl, combine these four ingredients and blend them until the mixture is smooth.

Cheddar-and-Beer Dip or Filling

2½ cups
Preparation: 15 minutes

This appetizer is a traditional delicacy from the southern United States.

2 cloves garlic, put through a press
½ teaspoon dry mustard
1 tablespoon Worcestershire sauce
2 drops Tabasco sauce
½ cup warm beer
2 cups (8 oz.) sharp Cheddar, grated
Salt, if needed

In a mixing bowl, combine the first six ingredients and blend the mixture until it is smooth. Adjust the seasoning.

Clam Dip or Filling

2½ cups · Doubles · Refrigerates
Preparation: 15 minutes

1 8-oz. package cream
cheese, at room
temperature
½ cup (2 oz.) blue cheese,
crumbled
1 small onion, grated
1 tablespoon chives,
chopped
2 drops Tabasco sauce
¼ teaspoon salt

In a mixing bowl, combine these six ingredients and, using a fork, beat them until they are well blended.

1 7½-oz. can minced clams,
drained (reserve the
liquid)

To the cheese mixture, add the clams. Add sufficient clam liquid for the desired consistency. Blend the dip well.

Cream Cheese Dip or Filling

1¼ cups · Refrigerates
Preparation: 15 minutes

1 8-oz. package cream
cheese, at room
temperature
Milk

In a mixing bowl, using a fork, blend the cream cheese and a little milk until the mixture is smooth; add milk, a little at a time, as needed to achieve the desired consistency.

1 small onion, grated
¼ cup parsley, minced
1½ tablespoons prepared
horseradish
½ teaspoon salt
Pinch of white pepper

Add these remaining ingredients and beat the dip thoroughly to blend it well.

Feta Dip or Filling

2½ cups · Refrigerates
Preparation: 15 minutes

2 cups (8 oz.) Feta, sieved
8 tablespoons sweet butter, softened
3 tablespoons chives, chopped
¼ cup parsley, chopped
¾ teaspoon paprika
¾ teaspoon thyme, finely ground in a mortar

In a mixing bowl, combine the ingredients and blend them until the mixture is smooth.

Gouda Dip or Filling

2½ cups · Refrigerates
Preparation: 15 minutes

1 8-oz. Gouda, shredded
¾ cup (3 oz.) blue cheese, crumbled
½ cup sour cream
4 tablespoons butter, softened
2 tablespoons lemon juice
1 onion, grated
Pinch of cayenne
Salt

In a mixing bowl, using a fork, cream together the two cheeses and sour cream until the mixture is smooth. Stir in the butter and the lemon juice; add the seasonings to taste and beat the dip thoroughly to blend it well.

Pierre Androuët's
Roquefort Dip or Filling

2½ cups · Refrigerates
Preparation: 15 minutes

M. Androuët, our leading authority on French cheese, is a warm and genial person, the owner-proprietor of Paris's most renowned cheese restaurant. I have adapted his recipe as a filling for cocktail puffs. (See Miniature Pastry Puffs, page 86.)

6 tablespoons sweet butter, softened 2 tablespoons flour	In a mixing bowl, using a fork, blend the butter and flour.
1 egg yolk 2 cups (8 oz.) Roquefort, crumbled and at room temperature Milk, as needed	Add the egg yolk and cheese and beat the mixture to yield a smooth paste. If necessary, a little milk may be added to achieve the desired consistency.

Wensleydale Dip or Filling

1½ cups · Refrigerates
Preparation: 15 minutes

1 cup (4 oz.) Wensleydale, crumbled
¼ cup heavy cream
1 onion, grated
¼ cup chopped nuts of your choice
¼ cup watercress, finely chopped
Pinch of cayenne
Salt

In a mixing bowl, using a fork, whip together the cheese and cream until the mixture is smooth. Add the grated onion, nuts, watercress, and seasonings to taste. Beat the dip thoroughly to blend it well.

Cheese Puffs Port Salut

Follow the recipe for Miniature Pastry Puffs, page 86, fill them with 1 cup *panada,* page 345, made with 2 cups (8 oz.) Port Salut, shredded. (For a main dish at luncheon or a first course at dinner, make 12 pastry puffs and fill them with this mixture. Serve the puffs hot, accompanied separately by thin Béchamel Sauce, page 347, seasoned with chopped parsley.)

Roquefort Puff

Make ½ the recipe for *Gougère,* page 306, omitting the cheese; divide the dough in 6 equal strips and bake them as directed. Split them horizontally and arrange the bottom halves in a lightly buttered baking dish. Over them spread 1 cup of Mornay Sauce, page 347, to which ½ cup (2 oz.) Roquefort, crumbled, has been added. Replace the tops of the puff pastry. Over them, spoon 1 cup Béchamel Sauce, page 347, and dot them with butter. Bake the puffs at 400° for 10 minutes, or until the sauce is bubbly and golden.

Vegetable Tarts

(a festive and elegant first course): Line individual tart shells with short pastry; prebake for 10 minutes in a 400° oven. Fill each tart shell two-thirds full with cooked and seasoned vegetables (choose from the list on page 230). Add Mornay Sauce, page 347, and a dot of butter. Heat the tarts in a 400° oven for 10 minutes, or until the sauce is bubbly.

Roman Cheese Loaf

Serves 6 to 8
Preparation: 20 minutes · Cooking: 20 minutes in a 350° oven

Spiedini alla Romana is a popular appetizer in the Italian capital. It also serves well as a supper dish.

1   1-lb. loaf Italian bread

Without cutting through the bottom crust, slice the bread in ¾-inch pieces.

8   tablespoons sweet butter, melted
1   2-oz. can anchovy filets, chopped, with their oil
½   teaspoon oregano

To the butter, add the chopped anchovy and oregano. With this mixture, brush each side of the bread slices. Reserve any remaining anchovy mixture.

1   1-lb. package Mozzarella, sliced
¼   cup (1 oz.) Parmesan, grated

Between each slice of the bread, insert a slice of the cheese. Skewer the loaf lengthwise. On a lightly buttered baking sheet, arrange the loaf. Brush it with any remaining anchovy mixture. Sprinkle it with the Parmesan.

At this point you may stop and continue later.

Bake the loaf at 350° for 20 minutes, or until the cheese is melted and the loaf is crusty. Upon removing the skewer, separate the slices with a serrated knife. Serve the loaf hot.

Scrambled Egg Toast

For each serving, allow 2 pieces of buttered toast; cover each toast slice with a slice of Gruyère and bake at 400° for 10 minutes, or until the cheese is melted. Meanwhile, using your preferred method, scramble 2 eggs per person and, when the toasts are ready, top them with the eggs; garnish the dish with chopped parsley. A delightful way to serve scrambled eggs.

Fruit Toast I

(*I discovered this simple but unusual appetizer in Holland.*): For each serving, top a slice of buttered toast with half a canned pear, well drained, the cut side down; season with a grating of pepper, and cover with a ⅛-inch slice of Edam. Bake the toast at 400° for 10 minutes, or until the cheese is melted.

Fruit Toast II

Combine 1 beaten egg with 1½ cups (6 oz.) Gruyère, grated (or any other firm-textured cheese of your choice, such as Appenzeller, Emmenthaler, or Tilsiter); if necessary, add a little cream to yield a spreadable mixture. With this, spread 6 slices of toast; top each slice with fresh apple slices (tossed with lemon juice to prevent their discoloring) or a canned fruit half (such as apricot, peach, pear, or pineapple). Bake the toasts at 400° for 10 minutes, or until the cheese mixture is melted. If desired, the toasts may be lightly sprinkled with the juice of the fruit used before being spread with the cheese mixture. Allow one toast per serving.

Mushroom Toast

In 3 tablespoons butter, sauté ½ lb. mushrooms and 1 small onion, both finely chopped; stir in the juice of ½ lemon; stir in 1 teaspoon flour and 3 tablespoons cream; season the mixture with salt to taste. Spread an equal amount of the mixture on 6 slices of toast, and cover each with a ⅛-inch slice of Gruyère; sprinkle with paprika. Bake the toasts at 400° for 10 minutes, or until the cheese is melted. Allow one toast per serving.

Roquefort Toast

Blend ¾ cup (3 oz.) Roquefort, crumbled, two 3-oz. packages cream cheese, and 4 tablespoons butter, all at room temperature; add ½ cup chopped walnuts or pecans and a pinch of cayenne. Spread the mixture on 12 lightly toasted bread slices, sprinkle with buttered bread crumbs, and bake at 400° for 10 minutes, or until they are golden brown. Allow two toasts per serving.

Savory Toast
Combine and blend 2 tablespoons mayonnaise, 2 tablespoons tomato paste, 3 cloves garlic put through a press, and ¾ cup (3 oz.) Gruyère, grated. Spread the mixture on 6 slices of toast and bake them at 400° for 10 minutes, or until the cheese mixture is melted. If desired, add to each toast, in a criss-cross pattern, 2 anchovy filets. Allow one toast per serving.

Cheese Toasts may be given an added interest by a very light sprinkling of dry white wine or kirsch.

Asparagus Toast
Allow 1 slice of toast per serving; on each piece, arrange a slice of cooked ham, a layer of canned asparagus (well drained and lightly salted), and a slice of Reblochon; bake the toasts at 400° for 10 minutes, or until the cheese is melted.

Cheddar Cheese Croquettes: England

12 croquettes · Doubles · Refrigerates
Preparation: 40 minutes · Cooking: 5 minutes

These "Glamorgan Sausages" are a traditional folk dish of the British Isles.

1 cup (4 oz.) Cheddar, grated	In a mixing bowl, blend thoroughly these seven ingredients.
1¼ cups bread crumbs	
3 scallions, finely chopped, with as much green as possible	
¼ cup parsley, finely chopped	
¾ teaspoon dry mustard	
¾ teaspoon salt	
Grinding of pepper	

3 egg yolks	In a mixing bowl, beat together the egg yolks and water. To the dry ingredients, add the liquid and stir the mixture until it forms a ball; more water may be added if the ball crumbles.
3 tablespoons water	

3 egg whites, lightly beaten	Divide the dough into 12 equal parts; roll each part into a cylinder. Dip each "sausage" in the egg white; roll it in bread crumbs.
2 cups bread crumbs (or as needed)	

At this point you may stop and continue later.

⅓ cup vegetable oil	Fry the croquettes in very hot oil, turning them quickly. (More oil may be used as needed.)

Gruyère Fritters: Belgium

Serves 6
Preparation: 30 minutes · Cooking: 3 minutes each
in deep fat at 400°

I first ate this delectable appetizer at the Hôtel Duc de Bourgogne in Bruges. A charming hotel situated on a canal in this lovely, seemingly changeless city, the Duc de Bourgogne offers a first-class dining room.

¾ cup flour ½ teaspoon baking powder ½ teaspoon salt	In a mixing bowl, sift together the dry ingredients.
2 eggs, beaten ½ cup warm beer 2 teaspoons oil	Add the liquid ingredients and blend the mixture well. Allow it to stand for 20 minutes.
½ cup flour 1 lb. Gruyère, cut into pieces the size of dominoes	In the flour, lightly dredge the cheese pieces. Dip them into the batter. Cook them, a few at a time, in deep fat at 400° for 3 minutes, or until they are golden. Drain them on absorbent paper and serve them at once.

Emmenthaler Gebacken (a variant from Switzerland): In a mixing bowl, combine 2 cups (8 oz.) Emmenthaler, shredded, 2 tablespoons flour, and ½ teaspoon salt; fold in 6 egg whites, beaten until they are stiff, and 1 teaspoon Worcestershire sauce. Form the mixture into small balls, roll them in cornflake crumbs, and fry them as directed.

Canapés Horace Gibson

Serves 6 · Doubles
Preparation: 15 minutes · Cooking: 10 minutes

Horace Gibson, co-founder and headmaster of the American School in Florence, is an admirable amateur cook and a warm-hearted host.

12	½-inch rounds of Italian bread	On the bread rounds, arrange, in order, the Mozzarella slices, anchovies, a sprinkling of oregano, salt, and pepper.
12	slices Mozzarella, the size of the bread rounds	
6	anchovy filets, halved	
Oregano		
Salt		
Pepper		

Olive oil

In a skillet, arrange the canapés and over them drizzle olive oil, allowing some extra oil for the skillet. Over medium heat, cook the canapés, uncovered, for 10 minutes, or until the cheese is melted and the bread crisp.

Cheese Ball

Serves 10 to 12 · Refrigerates
Preparation: 20 minutes · Chilling time: 3 hours

2   8-oz. packages cream
    cheese, at room
    temperature
4   scallions, finely chopped,
    with as much green as
    possible
1   small onion, finely chopped
1   8¼-oz. can crushed
    pineapple, pressed dry in a
    sieve
1   3-oz. package chopped
    pecans
Salt

In a mixing bowl, combine the cheese, scallions, onion, pineapple, and one-half of the pecans. Blend the mixture well; season it to taste. Form it into a ball.

Roll the ball in the remaining pecans. In plastic wrap, refrigerate the ball for 3 hours, or until it is firm. (If the cheese ball is too soft to handle easily, refrigerate it before rolling it in the pecans.)

Cheese Log

Serves 6 · Doubles · Refrigerates
Preparation: 15 minutes · Chilling time: 3 hours

2   3-oz. packages cream
    cheese, at room
    temperature
1½ cups (6 oz.) sharp
    Cheddar, grated
2   onions, grated
1   clove garlic, put through
    a press
½   cup walnuts, crushed
2   teaspoons walnuts,
    crushed
¼   cup parsley, chopped
1½ teaspoons dill weed

In a mixing bowl, combine these five ingredients and blend them thoroughly. Chill the mixture for 1 hour.

On waxed paper, form the mixture into a log about one inch in diameter.

Blend these three ingredients and roll the cheese log in the mixture. Wrap the log in waxed paper and chill it for at least 3 hours.

SOUPS

If a soup has been frozen, allow it to thaw fully to room temperature before reheating it in a double-boiler; if it has separated, homogenize it in the container of an electric blender before reheating.

Cheddar Soup

Serves 6 · Doubles · Refrigerates · Freezes
Preparation: 40 minutes

1 large carrot, scraped and very thinly sliced
1 rib celery, finely chopped
1 onion, minced
1 cup boiling water

Cook the vegetables in a covered saucepan in the boiling water until they are very tender; do not drain them. If desired, for a smoother soup, the cooked vegetables may be whirled in the container of an electric blender.

3 tablespoons butter
4 tablespoons flour
2⅓ cups milk

In a large saucepan, melt the butter and in it, over gentle heat, cook the flour for a few minutes. Gradually add the milk, stirring constantly until the mixture is thickened and smooth.

1 10½-oz. can condensed chicken broth, defatted, page 359
1¼ cups (5 oz.) sharp Cheddar, shredded
Worcestershire sauce
Salt

Add the cooled vegetables and their water, the chicken broth, and the cheese to the milk mixture, stirring to melt the cheese. Adjust the seasoning to taste with Worcestershire sauce and salt. Over gentle heat, simmer the soup, covered, for 20 minutes.

Serve now or freeze for later use.

For a heartier soup, 2 cups diced cooked potato and 1 cup diced cooked ham may be added for the final 10 minutes of cooking.

Stracciatella: Italy

Serves 6 · Doubles · Refrigerates
Preparation: 25 minutes

3 eggs ¼ cup semolina flour ¼ cup (1 oz.) Parmesan, grated ½ teaspoon salt	In a mixing bowl, combine these four ingredients and, with a rotary beater, blend them thoroughly.
1 10½-oz. can condensed beef broth	To the egg mixture, gradually add the broth, stirring to blend the ingredients well. Transfer the mixture to a large saucepan.
4 10½-oz. cans condensed beef broth, boiling	Into the contents of the saucepan, stir the additional broth. Simmer the soup for 2 minutes, beating it with a wire whisk. The soup is ready to serve when the egg breaks into strands.

Corn Chowder

Serves 6 · Doubles · Refrigerates
Preparation: 30 minutes

A very different chowder from the preceding one—richer and more elegant.

2 cups water 1 large potato, peeled and diced 2 bay leaves ½ teaspoon cumin seed ½ teaspoon sage 1 teaspoon salt	In a soup kettle, bring the water to the boil. Add the potato and seasonings and cook, covered, for 10 minutes or until the potato dices are tender.
3 tablespoons butter 1 onion, chopped 3 tablespoons flour	In a separate saucepan, heat the butter over low heat and in it cook the onion until translucent. Stir in the flour. Remove the pan from the heat.
1¼ cups heavy cream	To the onion mixture gradually add the cream, stirring constantly until the mixture is thickened and smooth.
1 10-oz. package frozen corn kernels, fully thawed to room temperature 2 tablespoons chives, chopped ¼ cup parsley, chopped Grating of nutmeg Salt Pepper	To the potato mixture in the soup kettle, add the corn and then the cream mixture. Stir in the chives, parsley, and nutmeg. Season with salt and pepper, to taste. Simmer the soup, covered, for 10 minutes. *At this point you may stop and continue later.*
1½ cups (6 oz.) Edam, grated ¾ cup white wine	Over very low heat, add the cheese, stirring constantly until it is melted. Stir in the wine.

A suggestion for Corn Chowder: To your own favorite recipe for corn chowder add, at the time of serving, ½ green and ½ sweet red pepper, diced and sautéed in butter, and ½ cup (2 oz.) Edam or Gouda, shredded.

A suggestion for Fish Chowder: To your own favorite recipe for fish chowder add, at the time of serving, ¾ cup (3 oz.) Edam or Gouda, shredded.

Cold Cucumber Soup

Serves 6 · Doubles · Refrigerates
Preparation: 25 minutes · Chilling time: at least 3 hours

2 tablespoons butter 1½ tablespoons flour 4½ cups milk	In a saucepan, heat the butter and in it, over gentle heat, cook the flour for a few minutes. Gradually add the milk, stirring constantly until the mixture is somewhat thickened and smooth.
2 cups (8 oz.) Edam or Gouda, grated Salt White pepper	Off heat, add the cheese, stirring until it is melted. Season the mixture.
1 cucumber, peeled, seeded, and diced	Stir in the cucumber and chill the soup for at least 3 hours.
Parsley, chopped	Before serving, garnish the soup with the parsley.

Flour Soup: Switzerland

Serves 6 · Doubles · Refrigerates
Preparation: 50 minutes

Mehlsuppe has been known in Switzerland since the Middle Ages. Traditionally served at the famous Basel carnival, it is reputedly an effective remedy for overindulgence in food and drink.

4 tablespoons butter 6 tablespoons flour 2 onions, sliced	In a large saucepan, heat the butter and into it stir the flour. Add the onions and cook them over gentle heat, stirring often, until they are translucent and the flour mixture is a light brown.
4 10½-oz. cans condensed beef broth Salt Pepper	Gradually add the broth and cook the soup, stirring constantly, until it is thickened and smooth. Simmer it, covered, for 30 minutes. Season with salt and pepper to taste.
	At this point you may stop and continue later.
1½ cups (6 oz.) Emmenthaler, grated	Into each warmed soup bowl, spoon ¼ cup of grated cheese. Over it, ladle the hot soup. Serve the dish at once.

In French-speaking Switzerland, the preferred cheese for *potage à la farine* is Gruyère. A little heavy cream or a little red wine may be added at the time of serving.

Minestrone: Italy

Serves 8 generously · Doubles · Refrigerates · Freezes
Preparation: 3 hours

This Piedmontese version of the Italian classic yields an especially good soup.

| 3 | quarts water |
| 1 | lb. dried navy beans |

In a soup kettle, combine the water and beans. Bring the water to the boil and cook the beans, uncovered, for 5 minutes. Remove the kettle from the heat and allow the beans to stand, covered, for 1 hour.

½	lb. salt pork, diced
2	or 3 cloves garlic
¼	cup parsley, chopped
12	fresh basil leaves, or 2 teaspoons dried basil
1	cup (4 oz.) Parmesan, grated

In a mortar, using a pestle, grind the salt pork and garlic to a paste. Add the parsley and basil and grind them into the paste. Add the cheese and sufficient bean water to make the mixture workable; blend it well and reserve it.

Cook the beans for 1 hour, or until they are tender.

1	small head cabbage, shredded
3	medium potatoes, peeled and diced
3	carrots, scraped and diced
4	large ribs celery, diced

To the beans, add the vegetables and simmer them, covered, for 40 minutes.

At this point you may stop and continue later.

| ¾ | lb. *ditalini* noodles |

Add the noodles to the beans; stir and cook for 12 minutes, or until they are *al dente*.

Lentil Soup: Spain

Serves 6 to 8 · Doubles · Refrigerates · Freezes
Preparation: 30 minutes · Cooking: 2 hours

A Catalonian traditional recipe. If desired, it may be served over slices of crusty bread.

6 tablespoons olive oil
3 onions, chopped
1 clove garlic, chopped
2 carrots, thinly sliced
2 tomatoes, peeled,
   seeded,
   and chopped
	In a soup kettle, heat the olive oil and in it cook the vegetables until the onion is translucent.

1 lb. (2 cups) dried lentils, rinsed 1 teaspoon basil 1 bay leaf 8 cups water 1½ tablespoons salt	To the vegetable mixture, add these five ingredients. Simmer the soup, covered, for 2 hours, or until the lentils are tender. *Serve now or freeze for later use.*
Grated cheese of your choice (see page 80)	When serving the soup, offer se'rately a generous amount of gr⍺ cheese.

Reserved pork-cheese mixture	Stir in the reserved pork-cheese mixture. Serve the *minestrone* when it is well blended. (Or you may freeze it for later use.)

Cream of Tomato Soup

Serves 6 · Doubles · Refrigerates
Preparation: 30 minutes

2	tablespoons butter	In a large saucepan, heat the butter and in it cook the onion until it is translucent. Add the flour and cook the mixture over gentle heat, stirring, for a few minutes. Gradually add the milk and then the seasonings, stirring constantly until the mixture is thickened and smooth.
2	onions, finely chopped	
2	tablespoons flour	
2	cups milk	
¾	teaspoon salt	
½	teaspoon pepper	
1	1-lb. can tomatoes, sieved	Stir in the tomatoes and broth. Bring the soup to the boil, lower the heat and simmer it, covered, for 15 minutes.
½	cup condensed chicken broth	
		At this point you may stop and continue later.
½	cup heavy cream	When ready to serve the soup, bring it to the boil, remove it from the heat, and stir in the cream and cheese.
1	cup (4 oz.) Cheddar, grated	

Basic Onion Soup

Serves 6 · Doubles · Refrigerates · Freezes
Preparation: 45 minutes

The traditional favorite from France.

2 tablespoons sweet butter
2 tablespoons olive oil
1½ lbs. onions, thinly sliced

In a soup kettle, heat the butter and oil. Add the onions and cook them over gentle heat, stirring occasionally until they are golden.

3 tablespoons flour
1 teaspoon salt

Stir in the flour and salt and continue to cook the onions for 3 minutes.

6 10½-oz. cans condensed beef broth, heated
Salt
Pepper

Add the broth, stirring. Simmer the soup, partially covered, for 30 minutes. Adjust the seasoning to taste. (At this point, the prepared broth may be frozen for later use.)

12 ¼-inch slices French bread
Olive oil

On a cookie sheet, bake the bread slices at 300° for 20 minutes. Brush both sides with olive oil. Bake them 10 minutes longer.

¾ cup (3 oz.) Parmesan, grated
¾ cup (3 oz.) Gruyère, grated

In a mixing bowl, using a fork, toss together the two cheeses.

At this point you may stop and continue later.

In the bottom of each soup plate, arrange two slices of the bread; top each slice with 2 tablespoons of the cheese. Ladle the soup over the bread.

Customarily, the bread, topped with cheese, is floated on individual servings and browned under a broiler. The average American kitchen has not the proper serving bowls to allow this treatment; the suggested manner of serving works well if the soup is very hot, so that it melts the cheese.

A variation from Auvergne
(the region of Cantal cheese contributes this favorite) To 3 table-spoons melted butter, add 3 large onions, sliced, and cook until golden; add four 10½-oz. cans condensed chicken broth, ½ cup dry white wine, ½ teaspoon thyme, and salt and pepper to taste. Simmer the soup, partially covered, for 30 minutes. In a casserole, put ¼ cup (1 oz.) Cantal, grated. Over the cheese arrange 6 slices of French bread, toasted. Add ¾ cup (3 oz.) Cantal, grated. Pour the soup over the cheese and bake the casserole at 350° for 10 minutes.

A Favorite Soup of Napoleon III
To a large saucepan containing 6 tablespoons melted butter, add 2 lbs. onions, chopped, and cook over medium-low heat until translucent. In the container of an electric blender, reduce them to a puree. In a saucepan, combine the puree, 3 cups dry white wine, and one 10½-oz. can condensed chicken broth. When the soup is hot, season with salt and pepper to taste. Stir in 2 cups (8 oz.) Cantal, grated. When the cheese is melted, serve the soup, garnished with butter-toasted croutons.

As you see, the three preceding soups are close relatives; yet each is distinctive and thus deserving of a place in the cheese chef's repertory. The following soup is also related, but somewhat more distantly.

Creamed Onion Soup
In 5 tablespoons melted butter in a large frying pan, cook 5 large onions, chopped, until translucent. In the container of an electric blender, reduce them to a puree. In a saucepan, combine the puree and two 10½-oz. cans condensed chicken broth; simmer the mixture, covered, for 30 minutes. Add gradually 5 cups of scalded milk; remove the saucepan from the heat. Slowly beat ½ cup of the hot broth into 3 egg yolks, beaten. Then beat the egg-broth mixture back into the contents of the saucepan. Return the saucepan to the stove and, over very gentle heat, cook the soup, stirring constantly, just until it thickens slightly. Add ⅓ cup heavy cream and ¾ cup (3 oz.) Gruyère, grated, stirring until the cheese is melted. Serve the soup garnished with a grating of nutmeg.

Swiss Onion Soup

This onion soup from Switzerland, traditionally made with Gruyère or Appenzeller, may also be made with Emmenthaler or Spalen cheese. The dish improves by being prepared a day in advance of serving; warm it either in the top of a double-boiler over simmering water or over very gentle heat:

6 tablespoons sweet butter
8 large onions, thinly sliced

In a soup kettle, heat the butter and in it cook the onion until lightly golden, but not browned.

2 tablespoons flour
2 cups hot water
4 cups milk, scalded

Stir the flour into the onion. Gradually add the hot water, stirring until the mixture is thickened and smooth. Then stir in the milk. (At this point, the prepared broth may be frozen for later use.)

2 cups (½ lb.) Switzerland cheese, coarsely grated
1 teaspoon salt
Generous grating of nutmeg and pepper
1 tablespoon sugar

Into the broth, stir the cheese. Continue stirring the soup until the cheese is melted. Stir in the seasonings and cook on very low heat, covered, for 20 minutes.

Unflavored croutons
Paprika

When serving the soup, garnish it with croutons and a sprinkling of paprika.

English Onion Soup

3 tablespoons butter
3 large onions, sliced
3 ribs celery, chopped
3 tablespoons flour

In a large saucepan, heat the butter, and in it cook the onion and celery until translucent. Stir in the flour and cook the mixture over gentle heat for a few minutes.

3 cups milk
1 10½-oz. can condensed chicken broth, defatted, page 359
1 teaspoon salt
½ teaspoon white pepper
Generous grating of nutmeg

Gradually add the milk and broth, stirring constantly, until the mixture is thickened and smooth. Stir in the seasonings. Simmer the soup, covered, for 5 minutes. (At this point, the prepared broth may be frozen for use later.)

¾ cup (3 oz.) Cheddar, grated

Bring the soup to serving temperature. Off heat, add the cheese and stir until it is melted.

¾ cup (3 oz.) Cheddar, grated

When serving the soup, offer the additional cheese separately.

Onion Soup with Port Salut: Follow the recipes for any of the Onion Soups, pages 112—115, using 2 cups (8 oz.) Port Salut, coarsely grated, in place of the cheese suggested.

Roquefort Garnish for Onion Soup: Sprinkle 6 slices of toast with crumbled Roquefort; heat them under a broiler until the cheese is melted and golden. Garnish the onion soup of your choice with the toast slices.

Gouda Soup: Holland

Serves 6 · Doubles · Refrigerates
Preparation: 45 minutes

This homely soup from the Netherlands is a substantial one-dish meal. Serve it with a hearty bread and green salad.

6 tablespoons butter
6 onions, sliced
3 carrots, finely diced
3 potatoes, finely diced
1 small cauliflower, cut in flowerets
4 ribs celery, finely diced

In a soup kettle, heat the butter and in it cook the vegetables, stirring, for 8 minutes.

4 10½-oz. cans condensed chicken broth, defatted, page 359

Add the broth and simmer the vegetables, covered, for 10–15 minutes, or until they are just tender.

6 slices bacon
6 slices bread

Render the bacon until crisp; remove and drain it on absorbent paper. In the remaining bacon fat, fry the bread slices on each side until golden.

At this point you may stop and continue later.

6 ⅛-inch slices Gouda

Arrange the fried bread in a baking dish. On each slice, arrange a piece of the bacon, halved, and a slice of cheese. Put the baking dish under a hot broiler for 3 minutes, or until the cheese melts.

To serve the soup, arrange a piece of the cheese-covered toast in individual dishes. Ladle the soup over the toasts.

Potato Soup

Serves 6 generously · Doubles · Refrigerates · Freezes
Preparation: 40 minutes

This soup may be served hot or cold.

3   10½-oz. cans condensed chicken broth

6   scallions, chopped, with as much green as possible

5   medium-sized potatoes, peeled and diced (about 4 cups)

1½ teaspoons salt

½   teaspoon white pepper

In a large saucepan, combine these five ingredients and cook the potatoes, covered, for 20 minutes, or until they are very tender.

1   8-oz. package cream cheese, at room temperature

3   tablespoons chives, chopped

In the container of an electric blender, whirl the potato mixture a little at a time until it is smooth. To one container of the mixture, add the cream cheese. Combine the whirled mixtures and stir in the chives.

Pumpkin and Apple Soup

Serves 6 · Doubles · Refrigerates · Freezes
Preparation: 25 minutes · Cooking: 20 minutes

2	cups canned pumpkin puree
3	tart apples, peeled and grated
4	tablespoons butter
2	teaspoons sugar
1½	teaspoons salt
½	teaspoon white pepper
¼	teaspoon nutmeg

In a saucepan, combine the pumpkin, apple, butter, and seasonings. Over gentle heat, cook the mixture, stirring constantly, for 10 minutes.

1	10½-oz. can condensed chicken broth
3	cups milk, scalded
1	cup (4 oz.) Cheddar, grated

Gradually add the broth and then the milk, stirring constantly. Simmer the soup for 5 minutes. Add the cheese and continue to simmer the soup over low heat, stirring constantly, just until the cheese is melted.

Swiss Cheese Soup

Serves 6 · Doubles · Refrigerates · Freezes
Preparation: 45 minutes

6 slices bacon, diced	In a large saucepan, render the bacon, drain it on absorbent paper, and reserve it. Discard all but 3 tablespoons of the fat.
8 scallions, chopped, with as much green as possible 1 rib celery, finely chopped	In the remaining fat, cook the scallions and celery until they are limp.
½ cup quick-cooking rolled oats 4 10½-oz. cans condensed chicken broth, defatted, page 359 1 teaspoon salt ¼ teaspoon white pepper	Add the rolled oats, broth, salt, and pepper. Simmer the mixture, uncovered, for 40 minutes. In the container of an electric blender whirl it, a little at a time, until it is a smooth puree. Return the mixture to a large saucepan.
	At this point you may stop and continue later. (Or you may freeze the puree for later use.)
½ cup (2 oz.) each: Appenzeller and Gruyère, grated	Add the cheeses and, over gentle heat, stir the soup to melt them.
¼ cup heavy cream ¼ cup dry white wine 4 teaspoons dill weed	Stir in the cream, wine, and dill.
Reserved bacon bits	When serving, garnish the soup with the reserved bacon bits.

MEATS

Beef Patties with Blue Cheese

Serves 6 · Doubles · Refrigerates
Preparation: 1¼ hours · Cooking: 10 minutes

1 cup (4 oz.) blue cheese, finely crumbled
1½ lbs. ground round
1 onion, grated
Dash of Tabasco
1 teaspoon Worcestershire sauce
1 teaspoon salt

In a mixing bowl, combine all the ingredients and, using a fork, cut them in order to blend them well. Allow the mixture to stand for an hour or more in order that the flavors blend.

Form the mixture into six large or twelve smaller patties, depending upon your choice. Arrange them on the rack of a broiling pan.

Broil the beef patties, turning them once, for a few minutes on each side. The time will depend upon your preferred degree of doneness.

Beef Patties with Gouda

Shape ground round into 12 beef cakes somewhat thinner than you usually prepare them and season them to taste. On 6 patties, place a slice of Gouda; top the cheese slices with the remaining 6 meat patties and, using your fingers, seal in the cheese. Cook the patties under a hot broiler or on charcoal. A glorified cheeseburger and very good! (You might also use 6 slices of Port Salut, in place of the Gouda.)

Veal Scallops *Cordon Bleu*

Serves 6 · Doubles · Refrigerates · Freezes
Preparation: 30 minutes · Cooking: 25 minutes

6   large or 12 small veal scallops, pounded flat and thin, seasoned with salt and pepper
6   slices *prosciutto* or other cured ham
6   slices (about ¼-inch thick) Appenzeller, Fontina, or Gruyère

On one side of the large scallops (or on the whole surface of 6 small ones) arrange a ham slice and a slice of cheese (the ham and cheese should be slightly smaller than the veal half, so that the "sandwich" will seal). Fold over the other side of the veal scallop (or top with the remaining 6 small scallops). Press and then gently pound the edges together.

1⅓   cups seasoned flour
2   eggs, beaten with 1 tablespoon milk
1½   cups bread crumbs

Dredge the scallops in the seasoned flour. Dip them in the egg. Dredge them in the bread crumbs.

At this point you may stop and continue later. (Freeze if desired.)

3   tablespoons butter
3   tablespoons olive oil

In a skillet, heat the butter and oil and, over high heat, cook the scallops for 4 minutes, turning them to brown them evenly. Remove them to a serving dish and keep them warm.

1   cup white wine, in which 2 chicken bouillon cubes are dissolved

Discard the excess fat in the skillet. To the skillet, add the wine. Over high heat, deglaze the pan, reducing the wine until it is slightly thickened. Sieve the sauce over the scallops before serving them.

Roquefort Filling: In a mixing bowl, combine and blend 1 cup (4 oz.) Roquefort, crumbled, and 4 tablespoons sweet butter. With this mixture fill the scallops and proceed with the above recipe for *Cordon Bleu*. (This filling may also be used for boneless breast of chicken.)

The *Cordon Bleu* recipe may be given added elegance by adding, *for each scallop,* 2 mushrooms, sliced and sautéed in butter, to the cheese and ham when filling the scallops.

Liver Loaf

Serves 6
Preparation: 25 minutes · Cooking: 45 minutes in a 350° oven

4 slices bacon, diced	In a skillet, render the diced bacon until crisp; drain on absorbent paper and reserve.
2 onions, chopped 3 ribs celery, chopped	In the remaining fat, cook the onion and celery until translucent.
1½ lbs. beef liver, chopped 2 eggs ½ cup tomato juice ½ teaspoon thyme 1 teaspoon salt ¼ teaspoon pepper	In the container of an electric blender, combine the onion mixture and these six ingredients. On medium speed, whirl them for 15 seconds, or until the mixture is smooth.
1 cup bread crumbs	In a mixing bowl, combine the contents of the blender, the bread crumbs, and the reserved bacon bits. Stir to blend the mixture well.
½ lb. Ricotta 6 oz. Mozzarella, sliced	In a lightly buttered loaf pan, arrange a layer of the liver mixture, all of the Ricotta, and the remaining liver mixture. Bake the liver loaf at 350° for 30 minutes; add Mozzarella slices to cover the top and continue to bake the loaf for 15 minutes longer. Serve the loaf with Marinara Sauce, page 355.

Whole Stuffed Cabbage: Italy

Serves 6 · Refrigerates
Preparation: 30 minutes · Cooking: 1 hour

1	2-lb. cabbage	In boiling salted water to cover, parboil the cabbage, whole, for 10 minutes. Drain, plunge it into cold water, and drain it again.
3	tablespoons oil	In a skillet, heat the oil and in it cook the onion and garlic until translucent. Add the meat and brown it.
1	onion, chopped	
1	clove garlic, chopped	
1½	lbs. ground beef	
½	cup (2 oz.) Fontina, shredded	Off heat, stir in the cheese.

Between the leaves of the cabbage, arrange the meat mixture. Tie a string around the cabbage to secure the leaves.

2	1-lb. cans stewed tomatoes	Season the tomatoes with the salt and pepper. Arrange one-half of the tomatoes over the bottom of a flameproof casserole. Set the stuffed cabbage on top of the tomato layer. Over it, pour the remaining tomatoes. Over gentle heat, simmer the cabbage, covered, for 1 hour, or until it is tender. A little water (or white wine) may be added as necessary.
1	teaspoon salt	
½	teaspoon pepper	

To serve the cabbage, cut it into wedges.

Stuffed Green Peppers

Serves 6 · Refrigerates · Freezes
Preparation: 30 minutes · Cooking: 1 hour in a 350° oven

1½ lbs. ground beef
4 slices bread, soaked in milk for 5 minutes and squeezed dry
1 onion, chopped
1 clove garlic, chopped
¼ cup (1 oz.) Bel Paese, Fontina, or Monterey Jack, shredded
1 egg
¼ cup parsley, chopped
1½ teaspoons salt
½ teaspoon pepper

In a mixing bowl, combine these nine ingredients and knead them thoroughly.

6 green peppers
1 1-lb. can tomato sauce
6 cheese slices

Remove just the stem ends from the peppers. Carefully remove the core and seeds. Stuff the peppers with the meat mixture. Stand the peppers in a lightly buttered baking dish. Over them, pour the tomato sauce. Top each pepper with a slice of the cheese you have used in the meat mixture.

At this point, you may stop and continue later. (Also, at this point the dish may be frozen for cooking at your convenience.)

Bake the peppers at 350° for 1 hour.

I suggest that you use, for a snappy flavor, Monterey Jack; for a more delicate dish, Fontina or Bel Paese.

Ground Beef and Eggplant

Serves 6 · Doubles · Refrigerates
Preparation: 25 minutes · Cooking: 30 minutes in a 300° oven

1   large unpeeled eggplant, cut in ½-inch slices

In boiling salted water to cover, cook the eggplant slices for 5 minutes; drain and reserve them.

3   tablespoons olive oil
2   lbs. ground beef
1   onion, chopped
1   green pepper, chopped

In a skillet, heat the olive oil and in it brown the meat, onion, and pepper, stirring and breaking up the meat so that it cooks evenly.

2   tablespoons flour
1   teaspoon oregano
2   teaspoons salt
½   teaspoon pepper
1   1-lb. can tomato sauce

Into the meat mixture, stir the flour and seasonings. Add the tomato sauce, stirring to blend the ingredients well.

1½   cups (6 oz.) Cheddar, grated

In a lightly oiled baking dish, arrange in layers one-half of the eggplant and one-half of the meat. Add one-half of the cheese. Repeat the layers, ending with a layer of cheese.

At this point you may stop and continue later.

Bake the dish, uncovered, at 300° for 30 minutes, or until the cheese topping is melted and bubbly.

Rice with Ground Beef

Serves 6 · Doubles · Refrigerates · Freezes
Preparation: 20 minutes · Cooking: 45 minutes

3 tablespoons olive oil
1½ cups raw natural rice

In a large skillet, heat the oil and in it toast the rice, stirring, until each grain is well coated. Remove and reserve the rice.

4 tablespoons olive oil
1½ lbs. ground beef

To the skillet, add the oil and, when it is heated, brown the beef in it, stirring frequently to cook it evenly.

2 onions, chopped
1 clove garlic, chopped
1 teaspoon sugar
1½ teaspoons salt
⅓ teaspoon pepper

Stir in these five ingredients and simmer the mixture for 5 minutes.

4 ripe tomatoes, peeled, seeded, and chopped (canned tomatoes, drained, will do)
¼ cup parsley, chopped

Stir in the tomatoes and parsley; over gentle heat, simmer the mixture, stirring occasionally, for 30 minutes.

2¼ cups boiling water

Stir in the boiling water and the reserved rice. Simmer the rice, covered, for 15 minutes, or until it is tender and the liquid is absorbed (more water may be added, if necessary).

1 cup (4 oz.) Kashkaval, grated

Remove the skillet from the heat and, using two forks, toss the *pilaf* with the cheese. Cover the dish, allow it to stand for 2 minutes, and serve it.

Moussaka: Greece

Serves 6 to 8 · Doubles · Refrigerates
Preparation: 35 minutes · Cooking: 45 minutes in a 350° oven

This recipe for ground beef and eggplant with cheese was discovered when I took a trip on a 55-foot ketch through the Aegean Islands.

2 medium-sized unpeeled eggplant, cut in ½-inch slices
Olive oil

On a broiling rack, arrange the eggplant slices, brush them with olive oil, and broil them lightly. Turn them and repeat the process.

1½ lbs. ground chuck
2 onions, chopped
3 tomatoes, peeled, seeded, and chopped
1 teaspoon cinnamon
Salt
Pepper

In a skillet, brown the meat and onions. Add the tomatoes and seasonings and cook the mixture until it is still moist but not watery.

¾ cup (3 oz.) Kashkaval (or Cacciocavallo), grated

In an oiled baking dish, arrange a layer of the meat mixture. Add a sprinkling of the cheese. Add a layer of eggplant and a sprinkling of cheese. Repeat until the meat and eggplant are used.

6 tablespoons butter
6 tablespoons flour
1 teaspoon salt
4 cups milk, scalded
4 eggs, beaten
Remaining grated cheese
¼ cup (3 oz.) Kashkaval (or Cacciocavallo)

In a saucepan, heat the butter and in it, over gentle heat, cook the flour for a few minutes. Add the salt. Gradually add the milk, stirring constantly until the mixture is thickened and smooth. Away from the heat, add the beaten eggs, stirring to blend the sauce well. Stir in the grated cheese and, if desired, add more, to taste. Over the contents of the baking dish, pour the sauce.

At this point you may stop and continue later.

Bake the *moussaka* at 350° for 45 minutes, or until it is golden brown.

Ground Beef and Noodles: Greece

Serves 6 to 8 · Doubles · Refrigerates · Freezes
Preparation: 45 minutes · Cooking: 45 minutes in a 350° oven

I first ate *pastitso* at a small *taverna* on the Aegean island of Kea. My enthusiasm for it prompted the cook to act out, in charade fashion, how it was made.

6 quarts salted water
1 lb. macaroni (*mezzani* #3 is recommended)

In a large kettle, bring the water to a rolling boil, add the pasta, stirring to prevent its sticking together. Cook it for 12 minutes, stirring often, until it is just tender. Drain it and rinse it under hot water. Drain again and allow it to cool to lukewarm.

4 tablespoons olive oil
4 onions, chopped
2 lbs. ground round
1 tablespoon cinnamon
Generous grating of nutmeg
2 teaspoons salt
½ teaspoon pepper
¼ cup water

Meanwhile, in a large skillet, heat the olive oil and in it cook the onion until translucent. Add the meat and brown it evenly. Stir in the seasonings and water; simmer the mixture, uncovered, for 10 minutes.

3 eggs, beaten

To the cooled macaroni, add the eggs and, using your hands, toss the mixture gently but thoroughly to blend it well.

1 cup (4 oz.) Kasseri or Kefalotyri, grated (or other grating cheese)

In a 9x13-inch baking pan, arrange a layer of one-half the macaroni; add the meat in an even layer. Sprinkle the meat with one-half of the cheese. Add the remaining pasta; sprinkle it with the remaining cheese.

At this point you may stop and continue later. (Freeze if desired. If refrigerated or frozen, allow it to come fully to room temperature before continuing with the recipe.)

2	tablespoons butter
2	tablespoons flour
1	teaspoon cinnamon
1	teaspoon salt
4	cups milk, scalded

In a saucepan, melt the butter; to it, add the flour, stirring, and, over gentle heat, cook the *roux* for a few minutes. Stir in the seasonings. Gradually add the milk, stirring constantly until the mixture is slightly thickened and smooth. Allow it to cool.

6	eggs, beaten

To the cooled sauce, add the eggs, stirring to blend the mixture well. Pour the custard over the contents of the baking dish.

Bake the *pastitso* at 350° for 45 minutes, or until the custard is set.

Vary the *pastitso* recipe by tossing the cooked macaroni with ¼ cup (1 oz.) Edam, Gouda, or Mimolette, shredded, and the eggs, as indicated. Combine the pasta and the ground meat as directed. Make the custard as directed, using for the cheese ingredient ½ cup (2 oz.) of the same cheese, shredded, as you tossed with the macaroni.

Ground Beef and Peas

Serves 6 · Doubles · Refrigerates
Preparation: 40 minutes · Cooking: 30 minutes in a 325° oven

This recipe is contributed by the artist Edward Giobbi, a near neighbor in the country. The Giobbis and their beautiful children are my *familia in loco* and with them I have enjoyed many handsome meals.

1 cup bread crumbs ½ cup milk	Soak the bread crumbs in the milk for 10 minutes; squeeze them dry and put them in a mixing bowl.

1½ lbs. ground round
3 onions, chopped
½ cup raisins
½ cup (2 oz.) Romano, grated
½ cup parsley, chopped
2 eggs
1 teaspoon thyme
1½ teaspoons salt
½ teaspoon pepper

To the bread crumbs, add these nine ingredients. Knead them thoroughly and form the mixture into 18 meat balls.

Olive oil
½ cup dry white wine

In an oiled skillet, brown the meat balls evenly. When they are brown, pour over them the wine and, over gentle heat, cook them for 5 minutes.

3 tablespoons olive oil
1 onion, chopped
1 clove garlic, chopped

In a separate skillet, heat the oil and in it cook the onion and garlic until translucent.

2 cups tomatoes, peeled, seeded, and chopped
1 teaspoon oregano
1 teaspoon salt
¼ teaspoon pepper
1 9-inch package frozen peas, fully thawed to room temperature

To the onion, add the tomatoes and seasonings. Cook the mixture, covered, for 5 minutes. Add the peas and continue cooking the sauce for 5 minutes.

*At this point you may stop and
continue later.*

½ cup (2 oz.) Romano,
grated

Arrange the meat balls in an oven-proof dish. Pour the sauce over them. Garnish the dish with the grated cheese. Bake the dish at 325° for 30 minutes.

A recipe similar to this one appears in Mr. Giobbi's excellent book, *Italian Family Cooking*. This variation, devised by Edward as I stood watching, shows how flexible recipes can, and should, be.

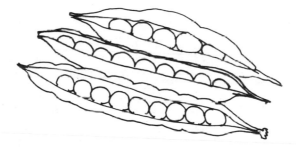

Lamb and Artichoke Hearts

Serves 6 · Doubles · Refrigerates · Freezes
Preparation: 3 hours · Cooking: 35 minutes in a 350° oven

1 quart water, lightly salted ½ cup dried pea beans	In a large saucepan or kettle, combine the water and beans. Bring the liquid to the boil and cook the beans, uncovered, for 5 minutes. Remove them from the heat and allow them to stand for 1 hour. Return them to the heat and simmer them, covered, for 30 minutes, or until they are just tender.
¼ cup olive oil 1½ lbs. lean lamb, trimmed of any excess fat and diced 4 onions, chopped	In a skillet, heat the oil and in it cook the lamb and onion, stirring often, until the lamb is browned and the onion is translucent.
1 bay leaf ½ teaspoon cumin seeds Grinding of pepper	Add the lamb mixture to the beans and their liquid. Add the seasonings. Simmer the mixture, covered, for 1 hour, or until the lamb is tender.
1 10-oz. package frozen artichoke hearts, fully thawed to room temperature ½ cup bread crumbs ½ cup (2 oz.) sharp Cheddar, grated 4 tablespoons butter, melted	Strain the mixture through a colander, reserving 1 cup of the liquid. Return it and the lamb mixture to the saucepan. Add these four ingredients and, using two forks, gently toss the mixture to blend it well.
6 eggs, lightly beaten	Add the eggs and toss the mixture once again.

At this point you may stop and continue later.

Arrange the mixture in a lightly oiled baking dish. Bake it at 350° for 35 minutes, or until a knife inserted at the center comes out clean.

Lamb and Tomato *Risotto*

Serves 6 · Doubles · Refrigerates
Preparation: 30 minutes · Cooking: 1 hour 40 minutes in a 325° oven

Olive oil
2 lbs. lean stewing lamb, cut in bite-sized pieces
Salt
Pepper

In a skillet, heat olive oil as needed and in it evenly brown the lamb; season it. Drain it on absorbent paper. With the remaining oil, lightly grease a casserole.

1½ cups raw natural rice
4 onions, sliced
1 29-oz. can Italian tomatoes, drained (reserve the liquid)
Basil
Marjoram
Thyme
Salt
Pepper

Over the bottom of the casserole, arrange the lamb pieces in an even layer. Over them, arrange the rice, then the onions, and last the tomatoes. Sprinkle the casserole with a pinch each of the seasonings. Pour over this the reserved tomato liquid plus water to equal 2½ cups.

At this point you may stop and continue later.

1 cup (4 oz.) Cacciocavallo, shredded

Bake the casserole, covered, at 325° for 1½ hours. Add the cheese and bake it, uncovered, for 10 minutes, or until the cheese is melted.

Lamb Stew with Blue Cheese

Serves 6 · Doubles · Refrigerates · Freezes
Preparation: 30 minutes · Cooking: 1½ hours in a 300° oven

The dish may also be made with lamb shanks; allow 1 shank per serving. If the recipe is prepared a day in advance of serving and then refrigerated, the excess fat may be easily removed before the casserole is reheated.

1   1-lb. can tomatoes
1   8-oz. can tomato sauce
1   6-oz. can tomato paste
2   cloves garlic
¾   cup dry white wine
1   teaspoon sugar
2   teaspoons salt
Grinding of pepper
1   cup (4 oz.) blue cheese, crumbled
Juice and grated rind of 1 lemon

In the container of an electric blender, combine these eleven ingredients and, on medium speed, whirl them until the mixture is smooth. Reserve the sauce.

2   tablespoons butter
2   tablespoons oil
2½ lbs. lean stewing lamb, cut in bite-sized pieces
Salt
Pepper

In a casserole, heat the butter and oil and brown the lamb; season it. Remove and reserve it. Discard all but 3 tablespoons of the fat.

3   onions, chopped
3   tablespoons flour

In the reserved fat, cook the onion until translucent. Stir in the flour.

2   bay leaves, broken

Add the tomato-cheese sauce to the onion, stirring constantly, until the mixture is thickened and smooth. Add the bay leaves. Replace the meat.

At this point you may stop and continue later.

Bake the casserole, covered, at 300° for 1½ hours, or until the lamb is tender.

To give a new flavor to your favorite meat stew for 6 persons, gently stir in ¾ cup (3 oz.) Cheddar, grated, at the time of serving.

Lamb-stuffed Eggplant: Greece

Serves 6 · Refrigerates
Preparation: 30 minutes · Cooking: 30 minutes in a 350° oven

"Little Shoes"—*papoutsakia*—may be made successfully only with very small eggplant, such as are common in European markets. In this country they are available, if searched for, sometimes under the name of Japanese eggplant.

6 small unpeeled eggplants, halved lengthwise

Scoop out the eggplant pulp to form the "little shoes," taking care not to cut the skin. Chop the pulp and reserve it. In a lightly oiled baking dish, arrange the shells.

3 tablespoons olive oil
2 onions, chopped
¾ lb. ground lamb
½ cup tomato sauce
½ teaspoon ground cumin
½ teaspoon thyme
1 teaspoon salt
Grating of pepper

In a skillet, heat the oil and in it cook the onions until translucent. Add the lamb and brown it. Stir in the reserved eggplant pulp, the tomato sauce, and seasonings. Simmer the mixture, uncovered, for 20 minutes, or until most of the liquid is evaporated.

½ cup (2 oz.) Kefalotyri or other hard cheese of your choice, grated

Into the meat mixture, stir one half of the cheese. Fill the shells with this mixture and over them sprinkle the remaining cheese.

At this point you may stop and continue later.

1 cup hot water

To the baking dish, add the hot water and bake the "little shoes" at 350° for 30 minutes.

Lamb Pie: Greece

Serves 6 to 8 · Refrigerates
Preparation: 1½ hours · Cooking: 1 hour in a 350° oven

Kreatopita is a dish I became acquainted with during a memorable summer when I visited the Aegean islands on a ketch, embattled by the *meltemi,* or Greek mistral.

4 tablespoons butter 4 tablespoons olive oil 3 lbs. lean lamb, trimmed of excess fat and cut into bite-sized pieces Salt Pepper	In a large skillet, heat the butter and oil and brown the lamb. Season it with salt and pepper to taste.

2 large potatoes, peeled and diced
3 onions, chopped
2 cloves garlic, chopped
2 ribs celery, chopped
½ cup parsley, chopped
1½ teaspoons cinnamon
¾ teaspoon dried mint leaves, crumbled

To the lamb, add these seven ingredients, stirring to blend the mixture well. Over gentle heat, simmer the meat and vegetables, covered, for 1 hour. (More olive oil may be added as necessary.)

1 lb. *Phyllo* sheets, page 359
Soft butter
½ lb. Feta, crumbled

In a 9x13-inch baking dish, in an even layer arrange one-half of the *phyllo* sheets, each separately brushed with butter. Over the *phyllo,* arrange the lamb mixture. Over the lamb, arrange the crumbled cheese. Add the second half of the *phyllo* sheets, each separately brushed with butter.

At this point you may stop and continue later.

Bake the pie at 350° for 1 hour.

Baked Pork Chops

Serves 6 · Doubles · Refrigerates
Preparation: 30 minutes · Cooking: 1¼ hours in a 400° oven

½ lb. mushrooms, sliced
4 cooking apples, peeled, cored, and sliced
2 onions, sliced
Salt
Pepper

In a buttered baking dish, arrange layers of the mushrooms, apple, and onion. Sprinkle them with salt and pepper.

6 large loin pork chops
1 cup cider or apple juice

Over the onion, arrange a layer of the pork chops. Over them, pour the cider.

1 cup bread crumbs, toasted with 2 tablespoons butter
1 cup (4 oz.) Cheddar, grated

Combine the bread crumbs and cheese and, using a fork, toss them to blend them well. Sprinkle the mixture over the chops.

Bake the chops, uncovered, at 400° for 1¼ hours, or until they are very tender.

Ham and Banana Rolls

Serves 6 · Doubles · Refrigerates
Preparation: 25 minutes · Cooking: 30 minutes in a 350° oven

2	tablespoons butter
2	tablespoons flour
2	cups milk
½	teaspoon salt
¼	teaspoon pepper
1½	cups (6 oz.) Stilton, finely chopped

In a saucepan, heat the butter and in it, over gentle heat, cook the flour, stirring, for a few minutes. Gradually add the milk and then the seasonings, stirring constantly until the mixture is thickened and smooth. Off heat, add the cheese, stirring until it is melted.

6   slices cooked ham
Mustard
6   ripe bananas, peeled
Melted butter

Lightly spread each ham slice with mustard. Roll a banana in each ham slice. Brush the banana ends with melted butter. Arrange them in a lightly buttered baking dish and over them evenly spoon the cheese sauce.

At this point you may stop and continue later.

Bake the dish at 350° for 30 minutes, or until the sauce is bubbly.

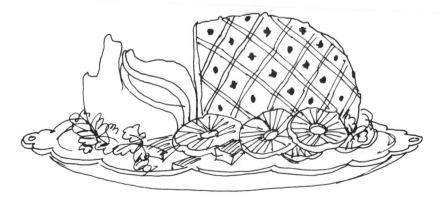

Ham Loaf

Serves 6 · Doubles · Refrigerates
Preparation: 30 minutes · Cooking: 50 minutes in a 350° oven

5	tablespoons butter
3	eggs
¾	teaspoon Dijon-style mustard
¼	cup parsley, chopped

Grating of nutmeg
Salt
Pepper

½	lb. ham, diced
1¼	cups (5 oz.) Emmenthaler, chopped
1¾	cups flour
2	teaspoons baking powder
½	cup light cream

In a mixing bowl, beat the butter and eggs together until light. Add the mustard, parsley, a grating of nutmeg, and salt and pepper to taste.

Into the butter mixture, stir the ham and cheese. Then stir in the flour, baking powder, and cream. The mixture will be thick. Into a lightly buttered 9-inch loaf pan, spoon the mixture.

Bake the ham loaf at 350° for 50 minutes. Serve it, if desired, with a thin pouring sauce, page 345, made with ½ cup (2 oz.) Emmenthaler.

Ham and Eggplant in Custard

Serves 6 to 8 · Doubles · Refrigerates
Preparation: 1 hour · Cooking: 30 minutes in a 375° oven

This dish is a traditional one from the Abruzzese region of Italy.

2	medium-sized unpeeled eggplants, thinly sliced
1	cup seasoned flour (or as needed)
3	tablespoons olive oil

Dust the sliced eggplant with the seasoned flour. In a skillet, heat olive oil and in it brown the eggplant slices on both sides, a few at a time; more olive oil may be added as necessary. Drain the eggplant on absorbent paper.

¼	lb. Italian-style cured ham, thinly sliced
8	oz. Mozzarella, thinly sliced

In a large, lightly oiled baking dish, arrange a layer of one-third of the eggplant. Over it, arrange a layer of one-half the ham. Over the ham, arrange a layer of one-half the cheese. Repeat, ending with a layer of eggplant.

At this point you may stop and continue later.

4	tablespoons butter, melted

Over the contents of the baking dish, evenly pour the butter. Bake the dish at 375° for 15 minutes.

2	eggs
1	cup milk
¼	teaspoon nutmeg
½	teaspoon salt

Meanwhile beat together the eggs, milk, and seasonings in a mixing bowl. Pour the custard over the semi-cooked eggplant and continue baking the dish for an additional 15 minutes, or until the custard is set.

Ham with Endive

Serves 6 · Refrigerates
Preparation: 30 minutes · Cooking: 10 minutes in a 400° oven

1 cup boiling salted water
12 thin endives, the root end trimmed
Light cream

In the water, cook the endive, covered, for 10 minutes. Remove and drain them. Reserve the water and add the cream as necessary to make 1 cup liquid.

12 slices boiled ham

Roll each endive in a piece of ham. Arrange the rolls in a shallow, lightly oiled baking dish.

3 tablespoons butter
4 tablespoons flour
1 cup milk
½ teaspoon salt
¼ teaspoon white pepper
Generous grating of nutmeg
¾ cup (3 oz.) Gruyère, grated
1 egg, beaten

In a saucepan, melt the butter, stir in the flour, and, over gentle heat, cook the *roux* for a few minutes. Add the reserved cup of liquid to the *roux*, stirring. When the mixture is smooth, gradually add the milk; stir the sauce until it is thickened and smooth. Stir in the seasonings. Add the cheese, stirring constantly until it is melted. Off heat, stir in the beaten egg.

Sieve the sauce over the endive rolls.

At this point you may stop and continue later.

Bake the dish at 400° for 10 minutes, or until the sauce is bubbly.

Tongue and Spinach Rolls

Serves 6 · Refrigerates
Preparation: 20 minutes · Cooking: 20 minutes in a 400° oven

2　10-oz. packages frozen chopped spinach, fully thawed to room temperature and pressed dry in a colander
Grated rind of ½ lemon
4　tablespoons butter, melted
Generous grating of nutmeg
¾　teaspoon salt
Grating of pepper

In a mixing bowl, combine these six ingredients and, using two forks, toss them to blend them well.

12　thin slices boiled beef tongue

Over the slices of tongue, spread equal quantities of the spinach mixture. Make rolls of the tongue and secure them with toothpicks. In a buttered baking dish, arrange the tongue rolls.

1　cup sour cream
¼　cup (1 oz.) Gruyère, grated
1　tablespoon prepared horseradish

In a mixing bowl, combine and blend these three ingredients. Over the tongue rolls, evenly spread the sauce.

¼　cup bread crumbs
¼　cup (1 oz.) Gruyère, grated

In a mixing bowl, combine and blend the crumbs and cheese; evenly sprinkle the mixture over the sauce.

At this point you may stop and continue later.

Bake the dish at 400° for 20 minutes, or until the top is browned and the sauce is bubbly.

Sausage in Cheese Sauce

Serves 6 · Doubles · Refrigerates
Preparation: 40 minutes · Cooking: 30 minutes in a 375° oven

4 medium-sized potatoes, scrubbed

In boiling salted water to cover, cook the potatoes for 20 minutes, or until they are tender. Peel and slice them. Over the bottom of a lightly buttered baking dish, arrange a layer of one-half the sliced potatoes; reserve the remainder.

1 lb. sausage meat, rolled into 24 balls

In a skillet, render the sausage balls until they are golden and slightly crusty. With a slotted spoon, remove them to absorbent paper and reserve them. Discard all but 3 tablespoons of the fat.

3 onions, chopped
2 tablespoons flour
½ teaspoon salt
¼ teaspoon pepper

In the remaining fat, cook the onions until translucent. Add the flour and seasonings and, over gentle heat, cook the mixture for a few minutes, stirring.

1½ cups milk

Gradually add the milk, stirring constantly until the mixture is thickened and smooth.

2 cups (8 oz.) Cheddar, grated

Off heat, add the cheese, stirring until it is melted.

Over the potato layer, arrange the 24 sausage balls. Over these, evenly spoon one-half the sauce. Arrange a second layer of the remaining potato slices and over it spread the remaining sauce.

At this point you may stop and continue later.

¼ cup parsley, chopped

Bake the dish, uncovered, at 375° for 30 minutes, or until the sauce is bubbly and slightly browned. Garnish the dish with parsley.

Sausage and Split Peas

Serves 6 · Doubles · Refrigerates · Freezes
Preparation: 35 minutes · Cooking: 30 minutes in a 400° oven

A substantial one-dish meal, kind to the food budget and satisfying to the hungry appetite.

2 cups (1 lb.) dried split green peas, rinsed
5 cups boiling salted water

Cook the peas in the boiling, salted water for 35 minutes, or until just tender; drain them and reserve 1 cup of the water. While the peas are cooking, prepare the remainder of the recipe.

1 lb. sausage meat

In a large skillet, brown the sausage meat, breaking it with a fork to assure its cooking evenly. With a slotted spoon, remove it to absorbent paper. Discard all but 4 tablespoons of the fat.

2 onions, chopped
1 clove garlic, chopped
½ teaspoon celery salt
1 teaspoon dill weed
Grinding of pepper

In the reserved fat, cook the onions and garlic until translucent. Replace the sausage meat. Add the peas and the 1 cup of liquid. Add the seasonings and stir the mixture to blend it well.

1 cup (4 oz.) sharp Cheddar, grated

Into a lightly oiled baking dish, spoon the mixture. Over it, arrange a layer of the cheese.

At this point you may stop and continue later.

Bake the dish at 400° for 30 minutes, or until the cheese is melted and golden.

Brains *en Casserole*

Serves 6 · Refrigerates
Preparation: 25 minutes · Cooking: 30 minutes in a 350° oven

Use calf, beef, or lamb brains. A delicately flavored dish which is complemented by buttered spinach noodles.

1½ quarts water 1½ tablespoons cider vinegar 2½ lbs. brains	In a saucepan, combine the water and vinegar; bring the liquid to the boil. Add the brains and simmer them, uncovered, for 10 minutes. Drain and plunge them into cold water. When they are cool and firm to the touch, remove any membranes and veins and cut the brains into bite-sized pieces.
Grating of nutmeg Salt Grating of pepper Juice of 1 lemon	In a lightly buttered casserole, arrange the brains; season and sprinkle them with the lemon juice.

2 cups Béchamel Sauce,
   page 347
½ cup (2 oz.) Münster,
   shredded
¼ cup (1 oz.) Gruyère,
   shredded
	Into the hot Béchamel Sauce, stir the Münster; continue stirring until the cheese is melted. Pour the sauce over the brains. Over the top, sprinkle the Gruyère.

At this point you may stop and continue later.

Bake the dish, uncovered, at 350° for 30 minutes, or until the sauce is bubbly.

Tripe and Beans: Italy

Serves 6 · Doubles · Refrigerates · Freezes
Preparation: 3 hours · Cooking: 15 minutes

A traditional dish from Lombardy.

3 lbs. honeycomb tripe, cut in bite-sized pieces
2 onions, each stuck with 2 cloves
2 cloves garlic, chopped
1 rib celery
1 bay leaf
6 peppercorns
2 teaspoons salt
2 10½-oz. cans condensed beef or chicken broth (or as needed)

In a soup kettle, combine the tripe, onions, and seasonings; add broth just to cover. Bring the liquid to the boil, reduce the heat, and simmer the tripe, covered, for 2 hours, or until it is fork-tender.

4 tablespoons butter
6 onions, chopped
2 ribs celery, chopped
2 carrots, scraped and diced
1 14-oz. can Italian tomatoes, chopped, and their liquid
1 teaspoon dried sage

In a large saucepan or skillet, heat the butter and in it cook the vegetables until the onion is translucent. Add the tomatoes and sage; cook the mixture, uncovered, for 10 minutes.

When the tripe is tender, drain it. Discard the onions, celery rib, bay leaf, and peppercorns. (Reserve the stock for use in some other dish—excellent for cooking purposes or soup base.) Add the tripe to the vegetables in the skillet.

	Simmer the tripe in the tomato sauce, uncovered, for 30 minutes.
2 20-oz. cans white kidney beans, undrained	To the tripe mixture, add the kidney beans and their liquid; gently stir the ingredients to blend them well.
	At this point you may stop and continue later.
1 cup (4 oz.) Parmesan, grated	Over gentle heat, simmer the dish for 15 minutes, or until it is thoroughly heated. Off heat, gently stir in the grated cheese.

This homely and tasty dish makes companionable fare for wintertime suppers. Serve it with a hearty bread. If desired, additional cheese may be served separately.

To this recipe or the one just below, basil, marjoram, oregano, savory, and thyme may be added, as you feel you wish to use them. Also, parsley, finely chopped, in almost any quantity you desire.

Trippa alla Livornese (a traditional dish from Leghorn): Prepare the tripe as directed in steps 1 and 3, reserving the stock, as suggested; measure the stock. In a large skillet, combine the tripe, 1 cup of the stock, one 1-lb. can tomato sauce, and 1 cup (4 oz.) Parmesan, grated; over gentle heat, simmer the mixture, covered, stirring often for 30 minutes; add additional stock as necessary. Into a baking dish, spoon the mixture. Over the top, sprinkle a mixture of ¼ cup butter-toasted bread crumbs and ¼ cup (1 oz.) Parmesan, grated. Bake the dish, uncovered, at 375° for 30 minutes, or until the top is well browned.

POULTRY

Chicken Breasts
Cordon Bleu

Serves 6 · Doubles · Refrigerates · Freezes
Preparation: 30 minutes · Cooking: 25 minutes in a 350° oven

3 large chicken breasts, skinned, boned, halved, and flattened with a cleaver
6 slices cooked ham
6 slices Gruyère or other cheese of your choice (see suggestions below)

Over the six chicken breast halves, arrange a slice of ham and of cheese; the ham and cheese slices should be slightly smaller than the chicken pieces. Form the chicken into rolls and, if necessary, skewer them.

1 cup flour (or as needed)
1 egg, beaten with 2 tablespoons milk
1 cup bread crumbs (or as needed)

Dredge the chicken rolls in flour, discarding the excess. Dip the rolls in the egg mixture. Dredge the rolls in the bread crumbs.

8 tablespoons sweet butter

In a skillet, heat the butter and in it brown the chicken rolls.

Arrange the rolls in an oven-proof dish and bake them, covered, at 350° for 25 minutes.

2 cups Rich Mornay Sauce, page 347

While the chicken is cooking, prepare the Mornay Sauce.

At this point you may stop and continue later.

Paprika

When the chicken is cooked, pour the sauce over it and sprinkle the dish with paprika.

Place the dish under a hot broiler for 5 minutes, or until it is heated through and the sauce is bubbly.

The dish is excellent made with Liederkranz: use one 4-oz. package cut into 6 lengthwise slices (easily done if the cheese is refrigerated); because Liederkranz has a strong flavor, in place of the Mornay Sauce use Soubise Sauce, page 348.

The dish may be made with slices of Mozzarella: For this variation, a pleasant substitute for the Mornay Sauce should be: 2 tablespoons butter, 1 cup white wine, 2 tomatoes, peeled, seeded, and finely chopped, ¼ cup parsley, finely chopped, and salt and pepper to taste; simmer the sauce, uncovered, for 5 minutes.

Include asparagus: over the bottom of the baking dish, arrange 1½ lbs. fresh asparagus, cooked until barely tender; over the asparagus, arrange the prepared chicken rolls; add the sauce, and bake the dish as directed. If desired, ½ cup butter-toasted bread crumbs may be sprinkled over the sauce for the final 10 minutes of cooking.

If desired, use a bed of 3 or 4 fresh zucchini, sliced and sautéed in butter for 4 minutes; arrange them over the bottom of the baking dish, add the chicken rolls and Mornay Sauce, and proceed as directed.

Chicken with Cream Sauce

Serves 6 · Doubles · Refrigerates
Preparation: 30 minutes · Cooking: 1 hour in a 350° oven

This recipe is contributed by Mary Carver, a long-time friend who is also my father's housekeeper. Mary cooks by intuition and an active tasting-finger. Like other of her recipes I have enjoyed, this one was written down as I watched her make it.

2 tablespoons butter
2 tablespoons oil
Serving pieces of chicken for
    6 persons
Salt
Pepper

In a flameproof casserole, heat the butter and oil and brown the chicken; season it. Remove and reserve it.

3 tablespoons flour
2 cups light cream, scalded
Juice of ½ lemon
Salt
White pepper

To the remaining fat, add the flour and, over gentle heat, cook it, stirring, for a few minutes. Gradually add the cream, stirring constantly until the mixture is thickened and smooth. Stir in the lemon juice and seasonings, to taste. Replace the chicken.

At this point you may stop and continue later.

½ cup (2 oz.) Gruyère or
    Münster, shredded
Grating of nutmeg
¼ cup parsley, chopped

Bake the casserole, covered, at 350° for 1 hour, or until the chicken is tender. Remove the chicken to a serving platter. To the sauce, add the cheese, stirring until it is melted. Spoon the sauce over the chicken, add a grating of nutmeg, and garnish the platter with the parsley.

Chicken *en* Coquilles

Serves 6 · Doubles · Refrigerates · Freezes
Preparation: 25 minutes · Cooking: 15 minutes in a 375° oven

Coquilles de Volaille, well known in French cookery, are a tasty and elegant way of using cooked chicken.

3 tablespoons butter
½ lb. mushrooms, sliced

In a skillet, heat the butter and in it sauté the mushrooms.

4 cups cooked chicken, diced
2 cups Mornay Sauce, page 347
¾ cup (3 oz.) Gruyère or Jarlsberg, grated
1½ tablespoons butter

In a mixing bowl, fold together the mushrooms, chicken, and Mornay Sauce. With the mixture, fill six lightly buttered shells or ramekins. Over the top, sprinkle the cheese and dot with the butter.

At this point you may stop and continue later.

Bake the *coquilles* at 375° for 15 minutes, or until the tops are browned and somewhat crisp.

The recipe may be varied to produce a pleasant *risotto:* with the sliced mushrooms, cook 8 scallions, chopped. In the top of a double-boiler, fold together the mushrooms, scallions, chicken, and Mornay Sauce; keep the mixture warm over hot water. In two 10½-oz. cans condensed chicken broth plus white wine to equal three cups, cook 1½ cups raw natural rice, covered, for 15 minutes, or until the rice is tender and the liquid is absorbed. Using two forks, gently toss the rice with ¼ cup (1 oz.) Parmesan, grated, and ¼ cup parsley, chopped. On a serving platter, arrange the rice in a ring; into the center, spoon the warm chicken mixture and serve immediately.

Chicken with Mushrooms

Serves 6 · Doubles · Refrigerates · Freezes
Preparation: 1 hour · Cooking: 15 minutes in a 400° oven

Truly a delicious dish! Serve it with brown rice and a watercress salad.

2 tablespoons butter 2 tablespoons oil Serving pieces of chicken for 6 persons Salt Pepper	In a large skillet, heat the butter and oil and brown the chicken; season it. Remove and reserve the chicken.
1 lb. mushrooms, sliced	In the remaining fat, cook the mushrooms until they are limp. With a slotted spoon, remove and reserve them.
1 onion, chopped 1 clove garlic, chopped	In the remaining fat, cook the onion and garlic until translucent.
1 10½-oz. can condensed chicken broth 1½ cups white wine Several sprigs of parsley Reserved chicken	Deglaze the skillet with the chicken broth and wine. Add the parsley sprigs and over them arrange the chicken pieces. Poach the chicken in the skillet, covered, for 35 minutes, or until it is fork tender.
Reserved mushrooms	Remove the chicken to an ovenproof serving dish. Over the chicken, arrange the reserved mushrooms. Sieve the stock and reserve it.

2½ tablespoons butter 3 tablespoons flour	In a saucepan, heat the butter and in it, over gentle heat, cook the flour, stirring, for a few minutes. Gradually add the reserved stock, stirring constantly until the mixture is thickened and smooth. Remove the saucepan from the heat.
2 egg yolks ¼ cup heavy cream Juice of ½ lemon ½ teaspoon salt ¼ teaspoon white pepper	In a mixing bowl, beat together the egg yolks and cream; stir them into the sauce. Over gentle heat, cook the sauce until it is creamy; do not let it boil. Stir in the lemon juice and seasonings. Spoon the sauce evenly over the contents of the serving dish.
1¼ cups (5 oz.) Gruyère, grated	Over the top, sprinkle the cheese.
	At this point you may stop and continue later.
	Bake the dish at 400° for 15 minutes, or until it is hot and the cheese is melted.

Poulet à la Reine

In a soup kettle, boil for about 2 hours a 5-lb. stewing fowl in lightly salted water to which a bay leaf is added. When the meat is very tender, allow the chicken to cool in the broth. Reserve the broth. Remove the skin and bones from the chicken and cut the meat into large dices. In butter, sauté ½ lb. mushrooms, halved, until they are barely wilted; add ½ cup of the chicken broth and ½ cup heavy cream; stirring constantly, reduce the liquid to half. Add the diced chicken to the mushroom mixture, and, stirring gently, reheat the mixture. Meanwhile beat together 2 egg yolks, ½ cup (2 oz.) Sbrinz, grated, ½ cup sherry, and ½ cup of the reserved chicken broth. Add this mixture to the chicken and, over very gentle heat, cook the dish, stirring constantly, until the sauce thickens somewhat. Immediately remove it from the heat to prevent the sauce from curdling. Serve the chicken with rice.

Chicken with Corn

Serves 8 to 10 · Refrigerates
Preparation: 2½ hours · Cooking: 40 minutes in a 350° oven

This dish from Costa Rica is a good buffet offering—a kind of pudding, boneless and attractive.

1 5-lb. stewing chicken 1 onion 1 clove garlic, split 1 carrot 1 bay leaf Pinch of thyme 1 teaspoon sugar 1 tablespoon salt 6 peppercorns	In a soup kettle with water just to cover, simmer the chicken and the remaining eight ingredients, covered, for 2 hours, or until the chicken is tender. Allow it to cool in the broth.
	Sieve the broth and reserve the liquid.
	Skin and bone the cooled chicken. Cut the meat into bite-sized pieces.
1 10-oz. package frozen green beans, cooked until just tender and drained 1 10-oz. package frozen peas, fully thawed to room temperature 1 green pepper, seeded and chopped 1 sweet red pepper, seeded and chopped ⅓ cup golden raisins 1 cup reserved broth 1½ teaspoons salt	In a mixing bowl, combine the chicken pieces, vegetables, raisins, broth, and salt. Reserve the mixture.
5 eggs	In a mixing bowl, beat the eggs lightly.

2 1-lb. cans cream-style corn	Into the eggs, stir the corn and then the cheese.
2 cups (8 oz.) Münster, diced	

At this point you may stop and continue later.

In a lightly buttered casserole, arrange a layer of one-third the corn mixture and then a layer of one-half the chicken mixture. Repeat, ending with a layer of the corn. Bake the dish at 350° for 40 minutes, or until the corn has set.

Cheese and Peanut Stuffing for Poultry

Serves 4 · Doubles · Refrigerates
Preparation of the stuffing: 15 minutes

2 cups prepared stuffing	In a mixing bowl, combine these six ingredients.
1 cup (4 oz.) Cheddar, grated	
1 rib celery, finely diced	
½ cup peanuts, crushed	
1 onion, finely chopped	
¼ teaspoon pepper	

4 tablespoons butter, melted	Add the melted butter and, using a fork, toss the mixture to blend it well. If a moister stuffing is desired, add a little warm water.
Warm water, if desired	

1 3½−4 lb. chicken	When stuffing the chicken do not pack the stuffing; skewer the opening. Roast the chicken in your preferred way.

Chicken Breasts and Eggplant

Serves 6 · Doubles · Refrigerates
Preparation: 45 minutes · Cooking: 10 minutes in a 375° oven

1   cup seasoned flour
3   large chicken breasts, skinned, boned, halved, and pounded flat
2   eggs, beaten

In the seasoned flour, lightly dredge the chicken pieces; dip them in the beaten egg. Reserve any unused seasoned flour.

2   tablespoons butter
2   tablespoons olive oil

In a skillet, heat the butter and olive oil and, over high heat, rapidly brown the chicken pieces on each side. Remove them. Discard the fat.

4   tablespoons butter
1   cup white wine

To the skillet, add the butter and wine. Over high heat, deglaze the skillet. Return the chicken pieces to the hot mixture and cook them over medium heat for 10 minutes. Remove them to an oiled baking dish; pour the pan juices into a small bowl and reserve.

½   cup seasoned flour (use reserved flour, if any)
1   large eggplant, peeled and cut in 6 equal slices
¼   cup olive oil

In the seasoned flour, dust the eggplant; in the skillet heat the oil and in it brown the eggplant. Drain it on absorbent paper.

1   8-oz. can tomato sauce
6   slices *prosciutto* or other cured ham
6   ¼-inch slices Mozzarella
¼   cup (1 oz.) Parmesan, grated

Blend the reserved pan juices and the tomato sauce; pour the mixture over the chicken. Top each piece with an eggplant slice. Add a slice of *prosciutto,* a slice of Mozzarella, and a sprinkling of Parmesan.

At this point you may stop and continue later.

Bake the chicken, uncovered, at 375° for 10 minutes, or until the cheese is melted and golden.

Chicken Breasts Fontina: Italy

Serves 6 · Doubles · Refrigerates
Preparation: 40 minutes · Cooking: 35 minutes in a 350° oven

½ cup seasoned flour
2 tablespoons Parmesan, grated
3 large chicken breasts, halved, skinned, and boned

Add the grated Parmesan to the seasoned flour and mix well. Dredge the chicken in this mixture.

2 eggs, beaten

Dip the chicken breast halves in the beaten egg.

8 tablespoons butter

In a skillet, heat the butter and in it sauté the chicken for 10 minutes per side. Arrange the breasts in a lightly buttered baking dish.

½ lb. mushrooms, sliced
½ lb. cooked ham, diced
1 cup (4 oz.) Fontina, shredded

In the remaining butter, sauté the mushrooms. Arrange them evenly over the chicken breasts. Over this, arrange first the ham and then the cheese.

At this point you may stop and continue later.

Bake the dish at 350° for 35 minutes.

Chicken Breasts in Sherry Cream

Serves 6 · Doubles · Refrigerates
Preparation: 25 minutes · Cooking: 10 minutes in a 400° oven

3	chicken breasts, skinned, halved, and boned
1	cup light cream
1½	cups (6 oz.) Pecorino or Romano, grated
Salt	
White pepper	

In a mixing bowl, arrange the chicken breasts and over them pour the cream. Remove and dredge them in the cheese; season them. Reserve the cream and any unused cheese.

4	tablespoons butter

In a skillet, heat the butter and in it, over gentle heat, cook the chicken, about 5 minutes on each side, until it is golden. Arrange the breasts in an ovenproof serving dish.

4	tablespoons butter
1	onion, finely chopped
1	tablespoon flour

To the remaining butter, add the fresh butter and in it cook the onion until translucent, deglazing the skillet as you do so. Stir in the flour.

½	cup sour cream
½	cup dry sherry

To the onion, add the reserved cream and any remaining cheese plus these two ingredients, stirring constantly until the sauce is smooth and slightly thickened.

At this point you may stop and continue later. (Cover the chicken closely to keep it moist.)

Pour the hot sauce over the chicken. Bake the dish at 400° for 10 minutes, or until it is hot.

Chicken Tarragon

Serves 6 · Doubles · Refrigerates
Preparation: 1½ hours · Cooking: 15 minutes in a 350° oven

A delicious and inexpensive party dish.

2 tablespoons butter
2 tablespoons oil
Serving pieces of chicken for
   6 persons
Salt
Pepper

In a flameproof casserole, heat the butter and oil and brown the chicken; season and remove it. Discard all but 1 tablespoon of the fat.

1 onion, chopped
2 cups dry white wine
Several sprigs fresh tarragon,
   tied in a bunch (or 2
   tablespoons dried
   tarragon)

In the remaining fat, cook the onion until translucent. Add the wine and deglaze the casserole. Add the tarragon and replace the chicken. Bake the chicken, covered, at 350° for 1 hour, or until it is tender.

Remove the chicken to an ovenproof serving dish. Discard the tarragon sprigs and sieve the pan juices into a saucepan.

1 8-oz. package cream
   cheese, at room
   temperature
¼ cup fresh tarragon
   leaves, finely chopped
   (or 1 tablespoon dried
   tarragon)

To the pan juices, add the cream cheese and tarragon. Over gentle heat, melt the cheese, stirring constantly. When the sauce is smooth, pour it over the chicken.

At this point you may stop and continue later.

To serve the chicken, reheat it, covered, in a 350° oven for 15 minutes, or until it is hot.

Chicken *Tetrazzini*

Serves 6 · Doubles · Refrigerates
Preparation: 30 minutes · Cooking: 45 minutes in a 300° oven

A festive, elegant way to use cooked chicken meat. The dish may also be made with cooked turkey or ham.

4 tablespoons butter
¾ lb. mushrooms, sliced
1 green pepper, cut in julienne

In a large saucepan, heat the butter and in it cook the mushrooms and green pepper for 5 minutes.

3 tablespoons flour
1 teaspoon salt
¼ teaspoon white pepper

Stir in the flour and seasonings, and cook the *roux* over gentle heat for a few minutes, stirring constantly.

2½ cups light cream

Gradually add the cream, stirring constantly until the mixture is thickened and smooth.

½ cup (2 oz.) Fontina, shredded

Off heat, add the cheese, stirring constantly but gently until it is melted.

4 cups cooked chicken, diced
2 pimientos, chopped
3 tablespoons sherry

Stir in the chicken, pimientos, and sherry.

8 oz. spaghetti, cooked until just tender as directed on the package, drained, rinsed under hot water, and drained again
2 egg yolks, beaten
¼ cup (1 oz.) Parmesan, grated

In a mixing bowl, using two forks, toss together the spaghetti and beaten egg yolks. Fold in the chicken mixture. In a lightly buttered casserole, arrange the chicken *tetrazzini*. Sprinkle it with the grated cheese.

At this point you may stop and continue later.

Bake the dish at 300° for 45 minutes. Then place it under a hot broiler for 2 minutes to brown slightly.

Roast Chicken: Belgium

Serves 4 to 6 · Refrigerates
Preparation: 15 minutes · Cooking: 1½ hours in a 450°/325° oven

1   4-lb. chicken, seasoned and trussed for roasting

On the rack of a roasting pan, arrange the chicken. Put it into the 450° oven; immediately reduce the heat to 325° and roast the chicken, 20 minutes per pound, turning it so that each side is browned. (During the last half hour, grate the cheeses and prepare the bouillon needed for the sauce.)

2   tablespoons flour
⅔   cup hot water, in which 2 chicken bouillon cubes are dissolved
1   cup sour cream
½   cup (2 oz.) Gruyère, grated
½   cup (2 oz.) Romano, grated
Grating of nutmeg
½   teaspoon salt
¼   teaspoon white pepper

Remove the chicken to a baking dish and keep warm. Discard all but 2 tablespoons of the drippings. Into them stir the flour. Gradually add the bouillon, stirring constantly until the mixture is thickened and smooth. Off heat, stir in the sour cream; add the cheeses, stirring until they are melted. Stir in the seasonings.

Spread the sauce evenly over the chicken, and put it under a hot broiler for 4 minutes, or until the sauce is golden.

Chicken- and Ham-filled *Crêpes*

18 crêpes · Doubles · Refrigerates
Preparation: 1 hour · Cooking: 15 minutes in a 375° oven

Make 18 *crêpes* (p. 257) and 2 cups Béchamel Sauce (p. 347).

4 tablespoons butter 4 scallions, chopped 2 teaspoons parsley, chopped ¾ lb. mushrooms, chopped	In a skillet, heat the butter and in it cook briefly the scallions and parsley. Add the mushrooms and, over gentle heat, cook them, stirring occasionally, until any excess moisture has evaporated.
½ cup cooked chicken, diced ½ cup cooked ham, diced ½ cup Béchamel Sauce (reserve the remaining sauce) Juice of ½ lemon Salt Pepper	Into the contents of the skillet, stir the chicken and ham. Add the sauce (½ cup), lemon juice, and salt and pepper to taste; blend the mixture well.
	Onto each *crêpe,* spoon 2 tablespoons of the meat mixture. Roll the *crêpes* and arrange them in a lightly buttered baking dish.
	At this point you may stop and continue later.
1½ cups reserved Béchamel Sauce 1 egg yolk, beaten 1 cup (4 oz.) Gruyère, grated	To the remaining béchamel sauce, add the egg yolk and cheese and, over gentle heat, cook the mixture, stirring constantly until the cheese is melted.

Pour the sauce over the *crêpes* and bake the dish at 375° for 15 minutes, or until the sauce is bubbly. Allow two to three *crêpes* per serving.

Chicken Livers *Risotto:* Italy

Serves 6 · Doubles · Refrigerates
Preparation: 25 minutes

This delicate dish is so rapidly made that there is no need to "stop and continue later."

3 tablespoons butter
1 onion, finely chopped
1½ cups raw natural rice

In a saucepan, heat the butter and in it cook the onion until translucent. Add the rice, stirring to coat it.

2 10½-oz. cans condensed chicken broth
Dry white wine
1 teaspoon salt

To the broth, add wine to equal 3¼ cups. Add the liquid and salt to the rice.

Bring the liquid to the boil, reduce the heat, and simmer the rice, covered, for 15 minutes, or until it is tender but still moist.

4 tablespoons butter
12 or 18 chicken livers, quartered
Salt
Pepper

Meanwhile, in a skillet, heat the butter and in it sauté the chicken livers until they are firm but not hard. Season them to taste.

1 cup (4 oz.) Parmesan cheese, grated
¼ cup parsley, chopped

To the cooked rice, add the livers and their butter, the cheese, and parsley. Using two forks, gently toss the mixture until it is well blended. Serve the *risotto* at once.

FISH AND SEAFOOD

Fish Filets in Cheese Sauce

Serves 6 · Doubles · Refrigerates
Preparation: 20 minutes · Cooking: 10 minutes in a 450° oven

This recipe applies to all lean, white-fleshed fish filets. The cooking time will change slightly, depending upon the thickness and texture of the fish used; fork-testing for easy flaking will indicate when the filets are cooked.

Fish filets for 6 persons (2 lbs.), arranged in serving portions (rolled and skewered, if desired, or cut into pieces of suitable size)

In a lightly buttered baking dish, arrange the filets.

1	onion, finely chopped
2	tablespoons butter
2	tablespoons flour
½	teaspoon salt
¼	teaspoon white pepper
1½	cups milk
1	cup (4 oz.) Fontina or Gruyère, shredded

Juice of ½ lemon

In a saucepan, cook the onion in the butter for 3 minutes. Stir in the flour, salt, and pepper; over gentle heat, cook the mixture for a few minutes. Gradually add the milk, stirring constantly until the mixture is thickened and smooth. Away from the heat, add the cheese and lemon juice; stir the sauce until the cheese is melted.

At this point you may stop and continue later.

Reheat the sauce, if necessary. Pour it over the filets and bake them at 450° for 10 minutes, or until they flake easily and the sauce is bubbly.

Buttered bread crumbs may be sprinkled over the dish before baking it; or a sprinkling of paprika; or a sprinkling of grated cheese (page 80). If desired, ¼ cup parsley, finely chopped, may be added to the sauce.

A variation from Greece: In the baking dish, arrange a layer of half the fish; add 4 potatoes, boiled, peeled, and sliced; dot them with butter and season them with salt and pepper; add a second layer of fish and sprinkle it with oregano. When making the sauce, in place of the onion, use 2 cloves garlic, put through a press; use a Greek cheese of your choice. Bake the dish as directed.

Stuffed Fish Filets

Serves 6 · Doubles · Refrigerates
Preparation: 15 minutes · Cooking: 15 minutes in a 450° oven

4 tablespoons butter 1 onion, finely chopped ½ lb. mushrooms, chopped 1 cup bread crumbs 1 cup (4 oz.) Cheddar, grated ¼ cup parsley, finely chopped ½ teaspoon salt ¼ teaspoon pepper Warm water, if desired	In a saucepan, heat the butter and in it cook the onions until translucent. Add the mushrooms and cook them until just wilted. Off heat, add the remaining ingredients and, using a fork, toss them to blend the mixture well. If a moister stuffing is desired, add a little warm water.
Fish filets for 6 persons	Place equal parts of stuffing on each fish filet. Roll and skewer the filets. *At this point you may stop and continue later.* Bake the filets, covered, at 450° for 15 minutes, or until they flake easily.

Fish Filets with Roquefort Butter

Serves 6 · Doubles · Refrigerates
Preparation: 1¼ hours · Cooking: 10 minutes in a 450° oven

1   cup (4 oz.) Roquefort or
    blue cheese
4   tablespoons soft butter
Juice of 1 lemon
¼   cup parsley, finely
    chopped
1   onion, grated
¼   teaspoon pepper
Salt to taste

In a mixing bowl, using a fork, cream together the cheese and butter until the mixture is smooth. Add the lemon juice, parsley, onion, and pepper. Blend the mixture well and, if desired, season with salt. Allow the Roquefort butter to stand 1 hour so that the flavors meld.

Fish filet for 6 persons (2 lbs., lean, white-fleshed fish), arranged in serving portions (rolled and skewered, if desired, or cut into pieces of suitable size)

Wipe the filets dry with absorbent paper. Arrange them in a lightly buttered baking dish.

Spread the Roquefort butter evenly over the filets.

At this point you may stop and continue later.

Bake the filets, uncovered, at 450° for 10 minutes, or until they flake easily.

A variation from Holland: In 1 tablespoon butter, sauté 1 onion and 8 mushrooms, finely chopped, until the onion is translucent. Put the fish filets in an oiled baking dish and season them with salt and pepper; sprinkle over the filets ½ cup (2 oz.) Edam or Gouda, grated; add the mushroom mixture and the juice of 1 lemon; garnish the filets with ¼ cup parsley, chopped; bake the fish as directed.

Fish Mousse

Serves 8 · Refrigerates
Preparation: 30 minutes · Chilling time: at least 3 hours

½ cup cold water
2 packets unflavored gelatin
½ cup boiling water

In the cold water, soften the gelatin; add the boiling water and stir the mixture to dissolve the gelatin.

2 7¾-oz. cans water-packed salmon or tuna
Juice of 1 lemon
1 onion, coarsely chopped
Dash of Tabasco
2 teaspoons Worcestershire sauce
½ teaspoon paprika
1½ teaspoons salt

In the container of an electric blender, combine the gelatin water with the fish and its liquid, the lemon juice, onion, Tabasco, Worcestershire sauce, paprika, and salt. On medium speed, whirl the ingredients until the mixture is smooth.

⅔ cup mayonnaise

Add the mayonnaise and whirl the mixture until it is homogenous.

2 cups cream-style cottage cheese

In a mixing bowl, combine the fish mixture and cottage cheese, stirring to blend them well. Chill the mixture until it begins to stiffen (about 25 minutes).

1 cup heavy cream, whipped

Fold the whipped cream into the fish mixture. Spoon the mousse into a mold rinsed with cold water, or into a serving bowl. Chill the mousse for at least 3 hours.

Salad greens (optional)

If it has been molded, unmold it on a

bed of salad greens; it may also be served directly from the bowl.

The dish may also be made with two 10½-oz. cans of minced clams. Drain them; measure their liquid. Use ½ cup of the liquid to soften the gelatin; use the remaining clam juice as part of the ½ cup of boiling liquid to dissolve the gelatin. Follow the remainder of the recipe as directed.

Shrimp with Tomato Sauce: Greece

Serves 6 · Refrigerates
Preparation: 50 minutes

6 tablespoons olive oil
2 onions, chopped
1 clove garlic, chopped
6 ripe tomatoes, peeled, seeded, and chopped
½ cup dry white wine
¼ cup parsley, chopped
¾ teaspoon oregano
½ teaspoon salt
Grinding of pepper

In a saucepan, heat the olive oil and in it cook the onion and garlic until translucent. Add the tomatoes, wine, parsley, and seasonings. Over high heat, boil the sauce until it thickens to a light puree (about twenty minutes).

2 lbs. raw shrimp, shelled and deveined
¾ cup (3 oz.) Feta, crumbled

Add the shrimp to the sauce and cook them for 5 minutes, or until they are pink. Off heat, stir in the cheese. Serve the shrimp in soup bowls accompanied by a hearty bread.

Shrimp in Cheese Sauce

Serves 6 · Doubles · Refrigerates
Preparation: 30 minutes

For a dramatic gesture at the dining table, prepare all of the ingredients and cook the recipe in a chafing dish.

6 frozen patty shells, baked according to the directions on the package

While the patty shells are baking or being rewarmed, prepare the shrimp filling.

3 tablespoons butter
3 tablespoons flour
½ teaspoon salt

In a saucepan or chafing dish, heat the butter. Into it, stir the flour and, over gentle heat, cook the mixture for a few minutes. Stir in the salt.

2 cups warm milk
1½ teaspoons Worcestershire sauce
2 drops Tabasco sauce
2 cups (8 oz.) Cantal, grated

Gradually add the milk and cook the mixture, stirring constantly, until it is thickened and smooth. Add the seasonings and cheese, stirring until the cheese is melted.

1½ lbs. raw shrimp, shelled and deveined

To the sauce, add the shrimp, stirring only long enough to heat the mixture through.

Chopped parsley

Spoon the shrimp into and around the hot, baked patty shells. Garnish each serving with a sprinkling of parsley.

Fish Pudding

Serves 6
Preparation: 20 minutes · Cooking: 1 hour in a 325° oven

1 cup sour cream
Juice and grated rind of ½
    lemon
1 tablespoon dill
Salt

First, make the dill sauce, which will accompany the cooked fish pudding: in a mixing bowl, combine the sour cream, lemon juice and rind, dill, and salt to taste. Mix the sauce well and let it stand to "work."

1 lb. white-fleshed fish
    filets, chopped
1 onion, chopped
1 cup milk
2 eggs
2½ tablespoons potato
    flour
½ teaspoon cumin

In the container of an electric blender, combine these six ingredients and, on medium speed, whirl them for 15 seconds, or until the mixture is smooth.

¼ cup milk
¼ cup dry vermouth
1 cup heavy cream
¾ cup (3 oz.) Sbrinz,
    grated

With the motor running, gradually add these four ingredients. When the mixture is homogenous, turn off the motor.

Into a lightly buttered mold, pour the batter. Place the mold in a pan of hot water and bake the pudding at 325° for 1 hour, or until a sharp knife inserted at the center comes out clean.

Serve the pudding with the dill sauce.

Clam Mousse

Serves 6 · Refrigerates
Preparation: 25 minutes · Chilling time: at least 3 hours

2   envelopes unflavored
    gelatin, softened in ½
    cup cold water
½   cup boiling water

To the softened gelatin, add the boiling water, stirring until the gelatin is dissolved. Reserve it.

2   10½-oz. cans minced
    clams
1   onion, coarsely
    chopped
Dash of Tabasco
1   teaspoon
    Worcestershire sauce
1   teaspoon salt

In the container of an electric blender, combine the clams with their liquid, the onion, and seasonings. Whirl them on medium speed for 15 seconds, or until the mixture is smooth.

1   8-oz. package cream
    cheese, at room
    temperature, chopped
½   cup cream-style cottage
    cheese

To the contents of the blender, gradually add the cream cheese and then the cottage cheese, whirling the mixture to maintain its smoothness. With the motor running, add the reserved gelatin.

Spoon the mousse into a serving bowl or into a mold rinsed in cold water. Chill it for at least 3 hours.

Salad greens (optional)

If it has been molded, unmold it on a bed of salad greens; it may also be served directly from the bowl.

Oysters en Casserole

Serves 6 · Refrigerates
Preparation: 20 minutes · Cooking: 35 minutes in a 300° oven

6   tablespoons butter
½   teaspoon anchovy paste
3   cups unseasoned
    croutons

In a saucepan, heat the butter and blend in the anchovy paste. Add the croutons, tossing them with the butter and stirring them so that they will brown evenly.

2   pints oysters, drained
2   tablespoons chives,
    chopped
¼   cup parsley, chopped
1   onion, finely chopped
Juice of 1 lime

In a lightly buttered casserole, arrange one-half of the croutons. Over them, arrange a layer of one-half of the oysters. Sprinkle the oysters with one-half each of the chives, parsley, and onions. Sprinkle with half of the lime juice. Repeat the layers and sprinkle with the remaining lime juice.

¾   cup heavy cream
3   tablespoons sherry
½   cup (2 oz.) Gruyère,
    grated

In a mixing bowl, combine these three ingredients. Over the contents of the casserole, pour the mixture.

Bake the casserole at 300° for 35 minutes.

If desired, butter-toasted bread crumbs may be sprinkled over the top of the dish before baking.

Oyster Pie

Serves 6

Preparation: 25 minutes · Cooking: 30 minutes in a 350° oven

The preparation time does not include readying the pastry.

1 9-inch pastry shell,
   baked at 400° for 10
   minutes

2 pints oysters, drained;
   the liquid reserved

Over the pastry shell, arrange the oysters. Measure and reserve ½ cup of the liquid.

1 cup light cream
1 small onion, sliced
1 bay leaf, broken
½ teaspoon celery seed
½ teaspoon thyme
Salt

In a double-boiler over hot water, combine the cream, onion, and seasonings. Scald the cream (see page 359). Add the reserved oyster liquid and season the mixture with salt to taste. Sieve the cream.

4 eggs
3 tablespoons sherry
½ cup (2 oz.) Gruyère,
   grated

To the cream, add the eggs, one at a time, blending the mixture with a rotary blender after each addition. Stir in the sherry and cheese. Pour the custard over the oysters.

Bake the pie at 350° for 30 minutes, or until it is somewhat puffed and set.

Crab Meat with Noodles

Serves 6 · Refrigerates
Preparation: 30 minutes · Cooking: 35 minutes in a 350° oven

1 8-oz. package noodles, cooked until just tender as directed on the package, drained, rinsed with cold running water, and drained again

While the noodles are cooking, prepare the next step.

4 tablespoons butter
1 onion, finely chopped
1 rib celery, finely chopped
4 tablespoons flour
½ teaspoon dry mustard
1 teaspoon salt
2 cups milk
Juice of ½ lemon

In a saucepan, heat the butter and in it cook the onion and celery until translucent. Stir in the flour, mustard, and salt and, over gentle heat, cook the mixture for a few minutes. Gradually add the milk, stirring constantly until the mixture is thickened and smooth. Stir in the lemon juice.

2 7½-oz. cans crab meat, the tendons removed
2 cups cream-style cottage cheese
⅓ cup parsley, chopped

In a large mixing bowl, combine the sauce, noodles, crab meat, cottage cheese, and parsley; using two forks, gently toss the mixture to blend it well.

½ cup (2 oz.) Parmesan, grated

In a buttered baking dish, arrange the mixture. Sprinkle the top with the cheese.

At this point you may stop and continue later. (Also, at this point the dish may be refrigerated without loss of quality; it should be fully at room temperature before cooking.)

Bake the dish at 350° for 35 minutes, or until the grated cheese is melted and golden.

Coquilles St. Jacques: France

Serves 6 · Refrigerates
Preparation: 30 minutes · Cooking: 10 minutes in a 450° oven

1½   lbs. sea scallops, quartered
¾   cup dry white wine
2   onions, finely chopped
½   lb. mushrooms, thinly sliced
½   teaspoon salt

In a saucepan, combine these five ingredients; bring the liquid to the boil, reduce the heat, and simmer the scallops for 5 minutes. Sieve the scallops, reserving 1 cup of the liquid. Into individual *coquille* shells, evenly divide the scallop mixture.

1   tablespoon butter
1   tablespoon flour
½   cup (2 oz.) Münster, grated

In a saucepan, heat the butter and in it, over gentle heat, cook the flour, stirring, for a few minutes. Gradually add the reserved liquid, stirring constantly until the mixture is thickened and smooth. Off heat, add the cheese, stirring until it is melted. Spoon the sauce over the scallops.

At this point you may stop and continue later.

¾   cup butter-toasted bread crumbs

Sprinkle the bread crumbs over the top of the *coquilles*. Bake them at 450° for 10 minutes.

A variation from Chile: Follow step 1 as directed, reserving only ½ cup liquid; in step 2, use 2 tablespoons butter, 2 tablespoons flour, 1½ cups light cream, scalded, and the reserved liquid; season the sauce with ½ teaspoon chili powder, a grating of nutmeg, ½ teaspoon paprika, and ½ teaspoon salt. Into the sauce, fold the drained scallops. Spoon the mixture into a lightly buttered baking dish. Garnish it with ½ cup bread crumbs tossed with ½ cup (2 oz.) Münster, grated. Bake the scallops at 350° for 20 minutes, or until the top is golden.

Seafood with Pasta

Serves 6 · Doubles · Refrigerates
Preparation: 30 minutes · Cooking: 20 minutes in a 350° oven

¾ cup olive oil
1 onion, chopped
3 cloves garlic, finely chopped
1 small green pepper, finely chopped
1 cup parsley, chopped

In a large saucepan or soup kettle, heat the oil and in it cook the vegetables until the onion is translucent.

1 35-oz. can Italian tomatoes

In the container of an electric blender, reduce one-half of the tomatoes to a puree; repeat with the other half. (Most electric blenders will not accommodate so large a quantity at one time.) Add the pureed tomatoes to the vegetables.

2 teaspoons basil
Grinding of pepper
Salt

Add the basil; salt and pepper to taste. Simmer the sauce for 5 minutes.

1 10-oz. can whole clams, and their liquid
18 raw shrimp, shelled and deveined
½ lb. sea scallops, halved

Add the seafood and simmer the mixture for 10 minutes.

1 lb. *rigatoni*
¾ cup (3 oz.) Fontina, shredded

While the sauce is cooking, boil the *rigatoni,* following the directions on the package, for just 10 minutes. Stir them often. Drain them in a colander and rinse them under cold running water; drain again very well. Add the *rigatoni* and cheese to the seafood, stirring gently to blend the ingredients.

¼　cup (1 oz.) Parmesan, grated

Spoon the mixture into a large, lightly buttered baking dish. Sprinkle it with the cheese and bake it at 350° for 20 minutes.

Seafood *en Casserole*

Serves 6 · Doubles · Refrigerates
Preparation: 25 minutes · Cooking: 15 minutes in a 300° oven

Serve the seafood in patty shells, on toasted English muffins, or with rice.

1　lb. cooked shrimp
1　8-oz. can crab meat, the tendons removed
2　cups (8 oz.) Gouda, shredded
1　onion, finely chopped
½　green pepper, chopped
4　ribs celery, diced
1　cup mayonnaise
¼　cup lemon juice
Grated rind of 1 lemon
¼　cup parsley, chopped
1½　teaspoons Dijon-style mustard
½　teaspoon salt

In a mixing bowl, combine all of the ingredients and gently fold them together to blend them well. Spoon the mixture into a lightly oiled baking dish.

At this point you may stop and continue later.

Bake the casserole at 300° for 15 minutes, or until it is thoroughly heated through.

EGG AND SUPPER DISHES

Croque-Monsieur: France

Serves 6 · Doubles · Refrigerates · Freezes
Preparation: 25 minutes · Cooking: 10 minutes

I first tasted *Croque-Monsieur* at the country home of Mme. Daisy Singer-Dugardin. Her cook, as friendly as "La Domerie" was hospitable, shared the recipe with me. If refrigerated or frozen, the cooked *croques* should be brought fully to room temperature before being heated in a 400° oven for 5 to 8 minutes.

12 slices bread, trimmed of their crusts ("toasting" bread is excellent)
Soft butter

Spread each slice of bread generously with the butter.

12 slices Gruyère, the size of the bread
6 slices boiled ham, the size of the bread
Grating of nutmeg
Pepper

On the buttered side of six of the bread slices, arrange a slice of cheese, a slice of ham, and another slice of cheese. Sprinkle the top piece of cheese with nutmeg and a little pepper. Add the remaining six slices of bread, the buttered side toward the cheese.

3 eggs, beaten with 3 tablespoons water

Pour the egg mixture into a shallow dish and in it dip the outer sides of the six "sandwiches."

3 tablespoons butter
3 tablespoons vegetable oil

In a skillet, heat the butter and oil and brown the *croques* on each side for 5 minutes or until golden. Keep the prepared *croques* warm until all are ready to be served. (More butter and oil may be added, as necessary.)

Pierre Androuët, page 91, the celebrated French authority on cheese, introduced his *Croque-Madame Bel Paese* at the 1932 World's Fair Exposition in Paris. Arranged in layers on toast were Béchamel Sauce, a sprinkling of grated Parmesan, a slice of *prosciutto,* and a slice of Bel Paese—the whole melted under a broiler. If desired, you can make my version of *Croque-Madame* by following the recipe given above, using Bel Paese in place of the Gruyère. When the *croques* are pan-toasted, arrange them in a lightly buttered baking dish, spoon over them 2 cups of Béchamel Sauce, page 347; sprinkle over the sauce ½ cup (2 oz.) grated Parmesan, and place the dish either in a 450° oven or under the broiler for 5 minutes, or until the Parmesan is melted and the sauce is bubbly and golden. A very rich, very good supper dish!

Croque-Monsieur au Port Salut: Follow the recipe for *Croque-Monsieur,* above, using Port Salut in place of Gruyère.

Mozzarella *in Carrozza*

Serves 6 · Doubles
Preparation: 20 minutes · Cooking: 15 minutes

The Italian classic, always tasty and always welcome.

12 pieces thin-sliced bread, the crusts removed Softened butter	Spread one side of each bread slice with the butter.
6 slices Mozzarella, cut slightly smaller than the bread slices	Using the cheese and buttered bread, make six sandwiches with the buttered side in.
3 eggs, lightly beaten ½ teaspoon salt	Season the eggs with the salt and pour them into a flat dish. Soak the sandwiches in the egg mixture, turning them once. Press the edges of the sandwiches together to enclose the cheese.
4 tablespoons butter 4 tablespoons olive oil	Over high heat, combine the butter and olive oil. When the mixture is very hot, quickly fry the sandwiches in it, draining them on absorbent paper as they are cooked. Keep them warm until they are served.

Grandmother's Omelet

Serves 4
Preparation: 15 minutes · Cooking: 15—20 minutes

This recipe of my paternal grandmother's yields a very light omelet—almost a soufflé.

½ cup milk
1½ tablespoons flour
1 cup (4 oz.) Gruyère, grated
¼ teaspoon nutmeg
1 teaspoon salt
¼ teaspoon white pepper
6 egg yolks

In the container of an electric blender, combine these seven ingredients and, on medium speed, whirl them for 10 seconds, or until the mixture is homogenous. Pour the mixture into a large mixing bowl.

6 egg whites, beaten until stiff

Fold the beaten egg whites into the yolk mixture.

In a large buttered skillet, over low heat, cook the omelet, covered, for 15 to 20 minutes, or until it is puffed and the bottom is golden.

Artichoke Omelet

Serves 6
Preparation: 20 minutes · Cooking: 10 minutes

Frittata alla Toscana is a classic Italian dish.

⅓ cup olive oil 2 cloves garlic, split	In a skillet, heat the oil and in it cook the garlic until it is limp and the oil flavored. Discard the garlic.
2 packages frozen artichoke hearts, fully thawed to room temperature Salt Pepper	In the flavored oil, over gentle heat, cook the artichoke hearts, covered, for 7 minutes or until they are tender. Season them to taste and chop them coarsely.
	At this point you may stop and continue later.
3 tablespoons olive oil 9 eggs, well beaten	To the skillet, add the oil. When it is hot, add the eggs. Over them, sprinkle the chopped artichoke hearts.
¼ cup (1 oz.) Fontina, diced	Cook the omelet over low heat, uncovered. When the omelet is half cooked, sprinkle the cheese over it. Turn the omelet and allow it to cook until it has reached the desired doneness.

Omelet with
Buttered Croutons: France

Serves 2
Preparation: 10 minutes · Cooking: 10 minutes

1 cup unflavored croutons
4 tablespoons sweet butter

In a skillet, combine the croutons and butter and, over gentle heat, toast the croutons, stirring them often, until they are golden. Remove and reserve them.

2 tablespoons sweet butter
4 eggs, beaten
Salt
Pepper
¼ cup (1 oz.) Parmesan, grated

In the skillet, melt the butter and add the eggs. Season them with a pinch of salt and a grinding of pepper. Sprinkle over them the reserved croutons and then the grated cheese.

Cook the omelet uncovered over low heat. When the omelet has reached the desired degree of doneness, turn one-half of it over on itself and slip it onto a warm serving plate. Serve the omelet at once.

Roquefort Omelet: Combine ¼ cup (1 oz.) Roquefort, crumbled, and ¼ cup sour cream; when the omelet is almost at the point of being folded, pour the cheese mixture over it; and finish the dish in your usual way.

Bread Pudding with Ham

Serves 6
Preparation: 40 minutes · Cooking: 45 minutes in a 350° oven

12 slices bread, the crusts removed, buttered
6   slices boiled ham

In a baking dish, arrange a layer of 6 slices of the bread, buttered side down. On each, arrange a slice of the ham. Top the ham with the remaining bread slices, buttered side down.

4   eggs
1   cup dry white wine
1   10½-oz. can condensed chicken broth
Pinch of cayenne
¾   teaspoon Dijon-style mustard
¾   teaspoon paprika
1½ teaspoons Worcestershire sauce
½   teaspoon salt
2   cups (8 oz.) Emmenthaler, grated

In a large mixing bowl, beat the eggs and to them add the remaining eight ingredients. Blend the mixture well. Pour it over the bread and allow it to stand for at least 30 minutes.

At this point you may stop and continue later.

Bake the pudding at 350° for 45 minutes, or until it is set and the top is slightly golden.

This simple but tasty recipe is capable of several variations:
(1) A plainer dish omits the ham.
(2) A more flavorful one is possible if the bread is spread with garlic butter.
(3) A nourishing meal for children would omit the wine and broth and substitute 2 cups of milk; in this case, season only with salt, a pinch of pepper, and a generous grating of nutmeg.
(4) A slice of melting cheese may be substituted for the ham.

Cheese Charlotte

Serves 6
Preparation: 25 minutes · Chilling time: at least 3 hours

3 slices each white and whole wheat bread, the crusts removed, buttered, and cut into strips

Along the sides of a buttered charlotte mold or similar utensil of your choice, arrange the bread strips in alternate colors, buttered side in.

3 egg yolks, beaten until thick
½ cup cottage cheese, sieved
½ cup (2 oz.) Cheddar, grated
½ cup heavy cream
¼ teaspoon Dijon-style mustard
½ teaspoon salt
¼ teaspoon white pepper

In a mixing bowl, combine and blend these seven ingredients.

1 packet unflavored gelatin, softened in ¼ cup cold water

In a double-boiler, over simmering water, stir the softened gelatin until it is dissolved. Stir it into the cheese mixture.

3 egg whites, beaten stiff

Fold the egg whites into the cheese mixture.

Spoon the mixture into the prepared mold and chill it for at least 3 hours.

1 bunch watercress, rinsed, well drained, the thick stems removed

Unmold the charlotte onto a bed of watercress and serve.

Ramequin Vaudois: Switzerland

Serves 4
Preparation: 15 minutes · Cooking: 30 minutes in a 350° oven

A tasty hot *hors d'oeuvre* or supper dish from the Canton of Vaud.

8 slices "toasting" bread, the crusts removed
8 slices Bagnes or Gruyère, about ⅛-inch thick

Cover the bread slices with the cheese and, in a lightly buttered shallow baking dish, arrange them in a flat overlapping pattern, as if they were shingles on a roof.

2 eggs
1⅓ cups milk
Grating of nutmeg
½ teaspoon salt

In a mixing bowl, beat together the eggs, milk, and seasonings.

At this point you may stop and continue later.

Pour the egg mixture over the canapés. Set the baking dish in a pan of hot water and bake, uncovered, at 350° for 30 minutes, or until the custard is set and the cheese melted and golden.

Eggs Florentine

Serves 6
Preparation: 30 minutes

2 or 3 packages frozen chopped spinach, fully thawed to room temperature
5 tablespoons sweet butter
Generous grating of nutmeg
Salt
Pepper

In a skillet, sauté for 5 minutes the spinach with the butter; season it to taste. In a lightly buttered ovenproof dish, arrange the spinach in an even layer. Keep the vegetable warm.

12 eggs

Using your preferred method, poach the eggs and arrange them over the spinach.

2 cups hot Mornay Sauce, page 347
1 cup (4 oz.) Gruyère, grated

Over the eggs, pour the Mornay Sauce. Sprinkle the dish with the grated cheese and place it under the broiler for a few minutes to melt the cheese.

Scrambled Eggs with Blue Cheese

Serves 4 · Doubles
Preparation: 15 minutes

An elegant way to serve scrambled eggs.

6 eggs
3 tablespoons heavy cream
4 tablespoons dry white wine
Pinch rosemary, crushed
½ teaspoon salt

In a mixing bowl, beat together these five ingredients.

½ cup (2 oz.) blue cheese, crumbled

Stir in the cheese.

2 tablespoons butter Chopped chives	In a frying pan, heat the butter and add the egg mixture. Scramble the eggs over very gentle heat, stirring them constantly. Garnish them with a sprinkling of chopped chives.

Scrambled Eggs with Cottage Cheese

Serves 4 · Doubles
Preparation: 15 minutes

My favorite scrambled egg recipe.

6 eggs ⅔ cup cottage cheese ½ teaspoon salt White pepper	In a mixing bowl, beat the eggs. Add the cottage cheese and salt; add pepper to taste.
2 tablespoons butter	In a frying pan, heat the butter and add the egg mixture. Scramble the eggs over very gentle heat, stirring them constantly.

Supper Eggs
Hard-cooked eggs, peeled, sliced, topped with Rich Mornay Sauce, page 347, and served on toast, make an excellent supper dish. Garnish the plate with watercress. (I should add that the better the bread, the better the dish—I use homemade bread, trimmed of its crust.)

Eggs en Cocottes
In the lightly buttered bottom of each individual *cocotte* or custard cup, put 2 tablespoons Emmenthaler, grated. Over the cheese, break an egg. Add 2 tablespoons heavy cream and a grating of nutmeg. Garnish the egg with a sprinkling of grated Emmenthaler and a dot or two of butter. Bake the *cocotte* at 450° for 10 minutes, or until the egg is set and the top is golden.

Cheese Ramekins

Serves 6 · Doubles
Preparation: 25 minutes · Cooking: 12 minutes in a 375° oven

3 strips bacon, diced

In a skillet, render the bacon until crisp. Remove it to absorbent paper and reserve it. Discard all but 1 tablespoon of the fat.

1 onion, chopped
2 tomatoes, peeled, seeded, and chopped
6 large mushrooms, chopped
½ teaspoon salt
Generous grating of pepper

In the remaining fat, cook the onion until translucent. Add the tomatoes, mushrooms, and seasonings. Over gentle heat, cook the mixture until most of the liquid has evaporated. Stir in the reserved bacon dice. Divide the mixture evenly among six ramekin dishes.

⅓ cup milk
2 egg yolks, beaten
1½ cups (6 oz.) Cheddar, grated

In a saucepan, combine these three ingredients and cook the mixture over very gentle heat, stirring, until the cheese is melted.

2 egg whites, beaten stiff but not dry

Fold the egg whites into the cheese mixture. Divide the mixture evenly among the ramekin dishes.

Arrange the ramekins on a baking sheet and bake them at 375° for 12 minutes, or until they are well puffed and golden. Serve them at once.

Roquefort Ramekins

In a mixing bowl, combine and blend together smoothly 1 cup (4 oz.) Roquefort, two 3-oz. packages cream cheese, 6 tablespoons sour cream, 6 eggs, all at room temperature, and a grating each of nutmeg and pepper. With this mixture, fill 6 lightly buttered ramekins or custard cups. Arrange them in a pan of hot water and bake them at 400° for 20 minutes, or until the custard is set. Serve them as an appetizer or luncheon dish. (You can also use 1½ cups [6 oz.] Port Salut, finely diced.

Crème Lorraine: France

Serves 6
Preparation: 20 minutes · Cooking: 35 minutes in a 350° oven

A sort of crustless *quiche, Crème Lorraine* goes well with boiled new potatoes and green salad.

8	strips bacon, diced	Render the bacon until crisp and drain on absorbent paper. While the bacon is cooking, prepare the cheese custard.

2	eggs	In a mixing bowl, beat the eggs lightly. Add the cream, salt, and pepper and beat the mixture briefly. Stir in the cheeses.
2	cups heavy cream	
1	teaspoon salt	
¼	teaspoon white pepper	
1½	cups (6 oz.) Gruyère, grated	
1½	cups (6 oz.) Parmesan, grated	

Over the bottom of a lightly buttered 1½-quart baking dish, arrange the bacon. Over the bacon, pour the cheese custard. Bake the *Crème Lorraine* at 350° for 35 minutes, or until the custard is set and lightly browned.

For a more substantial dish, 1½ cups cooked ham, diced, may be used in place of the bacon. For a lighter dish, use half-and-half in place of the heavy cream.

Basic Soufflé Recipe

Serves 4 to 6
Preparation: 15 minutes · Cooking: 30 minutes in a 350° oven

This recipe is a "standard" one which invariably produces good results. It also lends itself to endless variations.

4 tablespoons butter 4 tablespoons flour ½ teaspoon salt Pinch of cayenne Grating of nutmeg 1 cup milk 4 eggs yolks, beaten	In a saucepan, heat the butter and in it, over gentle heat, cook the flour, stirring, for a few minutes. Stir in the seasonings. Gradually add the milk, stirring constantly until the mixture is thickened and smooth. Off heat, stir in the egg yolks.
1 cup (4 oz.) Gruyère, finely diced or shredded	Add the cheese and stir the soufflé batter until the cheese is melted.
4 egg whites, beaten until stiff but not dry	Into the cheese mixture, fold the egg whites. Spoon the batter into a buttered 1½- or 2-quart soufflé dish and bake it at 350° for 30 minutes, or until it is well puffed and golden. Serve it at once.

A *few variations:* Cheese soufflés may be made with almost any cheese except oily cheeses, such as blue cheese; see the list of cheeses suitable for fondues, page 208. Use a smaller quantity of the stronger-tasting cheeses.

If desired, ¼ cup cognac may be stirred into the batter after the addition of the cheese. Warm, ignite, and pour over it 3 tablespoons cognac when serving the soufflé.

For a lighter soufflé, use 6 egg whites.

For a soufflé tasting more heartily of cheese, 2 or 3 tablespoons grated Parmesan may be added to the batter with the Gruyère.

For different flavor accents: add, in place of the nutmeg, 1 teaspoon Dijon-style mustard *or* ½ teaspoon garlic powder *or* the grated rind of ½ lemon.

If desired, hot tomato juice may be used in place of the milk.

For an elegant touch, stir into the batter, following the addition of the cheese, one 7-oz. can of crab or lobster meat (the tendons removed and the meat chopped) or of small shrimp, chopped.

Broccoli or Spinach Soufflé: Follow the Basic Soufflé Recipe, page 202 adding to the milk mixture 1 small onion, grated, and one 9-oz. package frozen chopped broccoli or spinach, fully thawed to room temperature and pressed dry in a colander; instead of Gruyère, use ½ cup (2 oz.) Parmesan, grated.

Corn Soufflé: In the container of an electric blender, combine one 10-oz. package frozen corn kernels, fully thawed to room temperature, and ¾ cup milk; on medium speed, whirl them for 15 seconds, or until the mixture is smooth; use this liquid in place of the milk in step 1 of the Basic Soufflé Recipe, page 202; in place of the Gruyère, use 1 cup (4 oz.) Münster, shredded.

Eggplant Soufflé: Peel and dice 1 medium-sized eggplant; in a small amount of lightly salted boiling water, cook it about 8 minutes, or until it is tender. Drain the eggplant well, press through a sieve, and add it to the butter-flour-milk mixture of the Basic Soufflé Recipe, page 202, made with only ½ cup milk. As the cheese ingredient, use ½ cup (2 oz.) Parmesan, grated.

Roquefort Soufflé: Follow the Basic Soufflé Recipe, page 202, using as the cheese ingredient 1 cup (4 oz.) Roquefort, crumbled.

Tuna Soufflé: In the container of an electric blender, combine one 7-oz. can tuna, drained, with 1 cup of milk. On medium speed, whirl them until the mixture is smooth. Use this mixture in place of the milk in the Basic Soufflé Recipe, page 202. For the cheese, use 1 cup (4 oz.) Emmenthaler, grated.

Soufflé "Gaspero"

Serves 4 to 6
Preparation: 25 minutes · Cooking: 30 minutes in a 325° oven

This recipe is contributed by Gaspero del Corso, owner-director of the Galleria Obelisco, one of the finest showrooms of modern art in Rome. Gaspero offered us this dish, together with other delicacies, following the opening of an exposition of paintings by Edward Giobbi, my close friend and neighbor in the country.

¼ cup water
4 tablespoons butter
Generous grating of
   nutmeg

In a saucepan, combine the water, butter, and nutmeg. Bring the mixture to the boil, stirring.

¼ cup flour

Add the flour, all at one time. Over gentle heat, beat the mixture thoroughly.

4 egg yolks
1 egg
½ cup (2 oz.) Gruyère,
   grated

Off heat, beat in, one at a time, the egg yolks and then the whole egg. Stir in the cheese.

4 egg whites

In a mixing bowl, beat the egg whites until stiff but not dry and fold them into the cheese mixture.

1 egg white (optional)
Generous sprinkling of
   Gruyère, grated

Spoon the batter into a buttered soufflé dish. Paint the surface, if desired, with the optional egg white and garnish the dish with grated cheese.

Bake the soufflé at 325° for 30 minutes, or until it is well puffed and golden.

Although no embellishment is needed, if desired, the soufflé may be served with a tomato, mushroom, or lobster sauce.

Squash Soufflé

Serves 6

Preparation: 20 minutes · Cooking: 30 minutes in a 350° oven

4 tablespoons butter 4 tablespoons flour ½ cup milk ¾ teaspoon salt ½ teaspoon white pepper	In a saucepan, heat the butter and in it, over gentle heat, cook the flour, stirring, for a few minutes. Gradually add the milk, stirring constantly until the mixture is thickened and smooth. Stir in the seasonings.
4 egg yolks, lightly beaten ½ cup (2 oz.) Parmesan, grated	Off heat, add the egg yolks and cheese, stirring until the cheese is melted.
1½ lbs. yellow squash or zucchini, grated and pressed dry in a colander 1 onion, grated	Stir in the squash and onion.
4 egg whites, beaten stiff	Into the squash mixture, fold the egg whites. Spoon the batter into a lightly buttered soufflé dish. Place the dish in a pan of hot water. Bake the soufflé at 350° for 30 minutes, or until it is well puffed and golden.

Cheese Mousse

Serves 6 · Refrigerates
Preparation: 45 minutes · Chilling time: at least 3 hours

Served on a bed of watercress, this is a delightful appetizer or luncheon dish.

2 packets unflavored gelatin, softened in ¼ cup cold water
1 cup milk, scalded

Add the softened gelatin to the milk and stir until it is dissolved. Add the onion, lemon juice, and seasonings.

1 onion, grated
Juice of ½ lemon
½ teaspoon curry powder
½ teaspoon Dijon-style mustard
½ teaspoon paprika
½ teaspoon salt

2 cups (8 oz.) Emmenthaler, grated

Add the cheese and, over gentle heat, stir the mixture until the cheese is melted. Allow the mixture to cool. Chill it until it is the consistency of egg white (about 25 minutes).

1 cup heavy cream, whipped

Into the cheese mixture, fold the whipped cream. Into a mold rinsed with cold water, spoon the mousse. Chill it for at least 3 hours.

1 bunch watercress, rinsed, well drained, the thick stems removed

Unmold the mousse on a bed of watercress and serve at once.

Cucumber Mousse

Serves 6 · Refrigerates
Preparation: 25 minutes · Chilling time: at least 3 hours

2 cups (8 oz.) Cheddar, grated
1 cucumber, peeled, quartered lengthwise, the seeds removed, and finely diced
Dash of cayenne
Generous grating of nutmeg
½ teaspoon salt

In a mixing bowl, combine and blend these five ingredients.

1 packet unflavored gelatin
¼ cup cold water

In the top of a double-boiler, soften the gelatin in the water and, over boiling water, stir it until it is dissolved. Stir it into the cheese mixture.

2 cups heavy cream, whipped but not stiff

Fold the whipped cream into the cheese mixture.

2 egg whites, beaten until stiff

Fold in the egg whites. Spoon the mousse into an 8-inch loaf pan. Chill it in the refrigerator for at least 3 hours, or until it is set.

Salad greens of your choice
Mayonnaise

Unmold the mousse on a bed of salad greens and garnish it with a little mayonnaise.

Fondues

Fondue, that peculiarly Swiss dish so closely associated with the Alps, was popularized outside of Switzerland by Brillat-Savarin, that peculiarly French gourmet and author of *The Physiology of Taste*. Originating as peasant fare for thifty use of cheese and bread too old to serve at table, fondue, now popular world-wide, is considered an elegant dish that is fun, and even dramatic, to prepare at the dinner table. Fondue is indeed a festive and friendly entrée. I can imagine no one who dips his crusty bread into the common pot of golden melted cheese being thereafter socially icy or stiffly formal.

Fondue-making, like summertime outdoor cooking, is often the province of the man of the house. Men enjoy making them (once the ingredients are readied); the process is quick and easy, and the results are virtually guaranteed.

Fondue may be made with almost any cheese mentioned in this book. The following suggestions, used either alone or in combination with Gruyère, may encourage you to experiment: Appenzeller, Bagnes, Bel Paese, Caerphilly (a very delicate fondue), Cantal, Cheddar (a rather robust fondue), Cheshire, Edam, Fontina, Gouda, Jarlsberg, Mimolette, Mozzarella, Münster, and Port Salut. Grated Parmesan or Sapsago may be used as a flavoring. If you use a Dutch cheese, in place of *kirschwasser*, use Genever or, as is often done in Holland, red wine.

Fondue is traditionally flavored with nutmeg, pepper, and, to a lesser degree, *kirschwasser*, but other ingredients may be added to alter or heighten the taste of the dish. I must admit, however, to feeling that fondue is served in order to enjoy the cheese itself and that any other flavor is really unnecessary. For the adventurous cook who would like to experiment, here follows a list of possible flavorings:

> anchovy filets, drained and chopped; bacon, diced, rendered crisp, and added at the time of serving; carraway seed; cayenne; chives, chopped; cumin seed, whole or ground; curry powder; dill weed; garlic, put through a press; ginger; green pepper, seeded and finely chopped; ham, cooked and diced, added at the time of serving; herbs, mixed fresh, finely chopped; mace; marjoram; mushrooms, sliced and sautéed; mus-

tard; onion, finely chopped; oregano; parsley, chopped; sweet red pepper, seeded and finely chopped; tarragon.

There are several substitutes for the bread cubes. The most attractive one I know is a vegetable substitute from Holland: broccoli flowerets and stems (the latter peeled); carrots, scraped and sliced; cherry tomatoes, cucumber slices, sweet gherkins, raw mushrooms, quartered; red onion rings and sweet pepper, cut in julienne; dill or sweet pickle slices; radishes, scallions, zucchini rounds.

You may also offer fresh shrimp, shelled, deveined, and newly cooked—they should be served warm. New potatoes, cooked until just tender, are a pleasant variation. Mix ground beef with bread crumbs and beaten egg; form the mixture into small balls, and brown them until they are somewhat crusty; use them in place of bread.

In place of white wine, *vin rosé* may be used; it gives a more piquant flavor and somewhat changes the color of the melted cheese.

A nonalcoholic fondue is also possible: in place of the white wine and *kirschwasser,* use an equal quantity of hot milk or cider.

For lack of *kirschwasser,* use an equal quantity of any dry *eau-de-vie,* such as brandy or aquavit, or even whisky or gin. (In fondue-cooking, the strong alcohol is used less for flavor and more for the smoothness it imparts to the melted cheese.)

Make a fondue with dry vermouth in which tarragon has been steeped for several days; sieve the vermouth before using it and garnish the completed dish with fresh tarragon leaves, finely chopped.

If you feel very extravagant, make fondue with champagne in place of the white wine. Taste different? Yes, a bit; but in all honesty, the average *amateur de fondue* would not know. More a conversation piece than a culinary triumph.

If demonstrating your culinary flair at table, take one important safety precaution: Be well acquainted with your source of heat. The cooking apparatus (with butane, alcohol, or other source of heat) should be firmly set on the table or—preferably—on a side table (it can be placed in the center of the diners once the recipe is prepared). Also, in all fondue-making, the ingredients should be readied beforehand so that no last-minute concern impedes the cooking.

Fondue is most easily made, I feel, in what the Swiss call a *caquelon* or, in French, a *cocotte à manche,* a ceramic saucepan, fired to assure its being flameproof and glazed on the inside to facilitate its being easily cleaned. *Cocottes à manche* come in several sizes; for fondue, the (approximately) 2-quart size in plain terra cotta serves admirably.

Is the fondue too thick? Add a little lukewarm white wine, stirring constantly.

Is the fondue too thin? Add a little flour well mixed with white wine, stirring constantly.

Traditionally, fondue is accompanied by green salad with a simple oil-and-lemon juice dressing and by a very cold, very dry white wine. If dessert is offered, it should be only ripe fresh fruit. The reason for this unadorned menu lies in the richness of the fondue itself—it is, after all, only melted cheese.

When serving fondue, adjust the source of heat so that the mixture stays hot and cooks evenly during the meal. The fondue should be stirred by each diner as he coats his bread cube; doing so maintains the consistency of the mixture. The bread cubes should have crust on them; the crust tastes good, gives a pleasant texture and "bite," and, most important, prevents the bread from falling to pieces when stirred in the cheese.

The baked-on cheese crust in the empty pan is especially good. Remove the utensil from the heat and, using a knife, lift it from the bottom. With good fortune, you will convince your fellow diners that they will not enjoy it—and then you can eat it yourself!

Basic Fondue Recipe
(Fondue Neufchâteloise)

Serves 4
Preparation: 20 minutes · Cooking: 20 minutes

½ lb. (8 oz.) Gruyère, shredded
½ lb. (8 oz.) Emmenthaler, shredded
3 tablespoons flour

In a mixing bowl, toss together the cheeses and flour.

1 clove garlic, split
2 cups dry white wine
3 tablespoons *kirschwasser*
Nutmeg
Pepper
¼ teaspoon white pepper
2 loaves French bread, cut in bite-sized cubes

Prepare and measure out these seven items. Set each aside separately.

At this point you may stop and continue later.

With the garlic, rub the inside of the 2-quart *cocotte* or other suitable utensil. Add the white wine and bring it nearly to the boil. Gradually add the cheese, stirring constantly until it is melted. Reduce the heat. Stir in the *kirschwasser,* a generous grating of nutmeg, and pepper to taste.

Serve the fondue as soon as it is prepared.

If desired, 1 tablespoon of cornstarch may be tossed with the shredded cheese, in place of flour.

The juice of ½ lemon, sieved, added to the white wine gives a fresh, light taste; the citric acid helps to make a smoother fondue.

Here are four recipes for special fondues:

Fondue au Vacherin Fribourgeois: Follow the Basic Fondue Recipe using, as the cheese ingredient, Vacherin Fribourgeois, and in place of the *kirschwasser,* 1 cup hot water; just before serving, stir in 2 tablespoons sweet butter. While eating this Swiss delicacy, regulate the source of heat to keep the dish warm but to prevent its further cooking.

An Italian fonduta: Follow the Basic Fondue Recipe using, as the cheese ingredient, Fontina, and in place of the *kirschwasser,* hot milk; just before serving, stir in 2 beaten egg yolks and 2 tablespoons sweet butter.

Fondue with Tomatoes: Peel, seed, and chop 4 large ripe tomatoes; cook them until they are very soft with 2 cloves garlic, finely chopped; sieve the tomatoes to yield about 2 cups (add white wine if necessary); use the puree in place of the *kirschwasser* in the Basic Fondue Recipe.

Fondue aux Poires (a superb savory dessert): Follow the Basic Fondue Recipe using, in place of the *kirschwasser,* an equal quantity of pear brandy. In place of the bread cubes, offer firm, ripe fresh pears, peeled, cubed, and tossed with lemon juice to prevent their discoloring.

Liederkranz Fondue

4½ cups
Preparation: 20 minutes

To be served with boiled shrimp or raw vegetables as a cocktail party refreshment.

8   tablespoons butter
8   tablespoons flour
2   cups milk

In a saucepan, heat the butter and in it, over gentle heat, cook the flour, stirring, for a few minutes. Gradually add the milk, stirring constantly until the mixture is thickened and smooth.

1   cup dry white wine
1   10½-oz. can condensed chicken broth, defatted, page 359

Stir in the wine and broth.

2   4-oz. packages Liederkranz, cut in several pieces
Grating of nutmeg

To the contents of the saucepan, add the cheese and nutmeg; stir the mixture constantly until it is melted. The fondue should be kept warm over hot water in a chafing dish.

Raclette: Switzerland

Serves 4 to 6
Preparation: 30 minutes

A simple traditional dish which lends itself to informal cold-weather suppers. Caution your guests against touching the hot plates. (I offer a thick paper napkin to act as a "holder.")

6 medium-sized potatoes, scrubbed	In boiling salted water, cook the potatoes for 20 minutes, or until they are tender. Peel and quarter them. *At this point you may stop and continue later.*
12 oz. Bagnes or Gruyère, cut in 6 equal slices	In the center of each of six small ovenproof plates arrange the slices of cheese. Around the cheese, arrange 4 pieces of warm potato. (If desired, the potatoes may be warmed in the top of a double-boiler over hot water.)
Dill pickle rounds Scallions Sweet gherkins	Under a hot broiler, place the plates, about 4 inches from the heat. When the cheese is partially melted, remove the plates and serve the raclette with the garnishes.

Welsh Rabbits

No one really knows the origin of the name of this simple and satisfying dish. Some say that it substituted for the real rabbit which the poor farmer or inept hunter would like to have had on his supper table. Others suggest that "rabbit" is a perversion of "rarebit." No one really knows—nor should anyone really care. A Welsh rabbit is indeed a rarebit. Well made, it is one of the delights of cheese cookery.

Rabbits, like fondues, can be made with various cheeses (see the list on page 208). They are also amenable to numerous variations. Following is the basic Welsh rabbit recipe, followed by several suggested variations.

Basic Welsh Rabbit

Serves 6 · Doubles
Preparation: 20 minutes

3 cups (12 oz.) Cheddar, finely diced
1 tablespoon butter
Pinch of cayenne
¾ teaspoon dry mustard
½ teaspoon salt

In the top of a double-boiler, combine these five ingredients; toss them together lightly. Over boiling water, cook them, stirring constantly until the cheese begins to melt.

½ cup warm beer
1 egg *or* 2 egg yolks, lightly beaten
1 teaspoon Worcestershire sauce

To the cheese mixture, add these three ingredients. Continue to stir the rabbit until it is smooth.

6 slices toast, buttered

Arrange the toast slices in a lightly buttered baking dish. Over them, spoon the rabbit sauce. Put the rabbits under a hot broiler for 2 minutes, or until they are bubbly.

If desired, the toast may be topped, before the addition of the rabbit sauce, with any of the following: tomato slices; cooked chicken, turkey, or ham, diced; a strip or two of bacon; cooked asparagus, broccoli, or cauliflower; cooked shrimp or crab meat.

Golden Buck: Top each toast slice with a poached egg, add the rabbit sauce and proceed as directed.

Rinktum Ditty: In 2 tablespoons butter, cook 2 onions, chopped, until translucent; stir in 1 tablespoon flour, 1 tablespoon sugar, 1 teaspoon salt, and a grating of pepper. Add one 1-lb. can tomato sauce and bring the mixture to the boil. Add gradually, stirring constantly, the 3 cups cheese. When it is melted, stir in 1 teaspoon Worcestershire sauce and 1 egg, lightly beaten. Serve the sauce over toast, as directed in the Basic Welsh Rabbit recipe. "Rinktum Ditty," or "Rum Tum Tiddy," is a dish from Revolutionary Boston.

Yorkshire Buck: Top each toast slice with 3 strips of crisp bacon, add a poached egg to each, and then the rabbit sauce; proceed as directed.

The Welsh Variation, Caws Bobi (a fine wintertime offering served with substantial bread, sweet butter, and good ale): In a lightly buttered baking dish, arrange 2 lbs. onions, thinly sliced and seasoned with salt and pepper. Cover the onion with 1 lb. Caerphilly, cut in slices. Sprinkle the cheese with paprika and dot it with butter. Bake the dish at 400° for 25 minutes, or until the cheese is melted and bubbly.

Arbolettys

Serves 4 · Doubles
Preparation: 20 minutes

This fifteenth-century dish is probably the precursor of our present-day Welsh rabbit. This particular example of arbolettys is taken from a "cook book" of 1439.

1	tablespoon butter	In a saucepan, melt the butter. Add the cheese and, over gentle heat, stir the mixture until the cheese is melted. Gradually add the milk, stirring constantly.
1½	cups (6 oz.) Cheddar, grated	
½	cup milk	

¼	teaspoon cinnamon	Stir in the seasonings. Over gentle heat, cook the mixture, stirring, for a few minutes.
¼	teaspoon ginger	
1	tablespoon parsley, chopped	
1	teaspoon sage, chopped	

| 2 | egg yolks, beaten | Off heat, stir in the egg yolks. Return the saucepan to gentle heat and cook the arbolettys, stirring, for 3 minutes, or until it thickens. |

| Toast fingers | | Serve the dish accompanied by toast fingers. |

Quiches and Tarts

A *quiche* is any open-faced custard tart. Of time-forgotten origins, it was originally made in France of bread dough, which today is replaced with short pastry. The fillings are usually savory mixtures of fish, onions, spinach, finely chopped meats, or other foods generally associated with an entrée. Historically, *quiche Lorraine* was originally made with eggs, cream, bacon, and *no* cheese, which has evolved as a later addition.

In cheese tarts, the combination of ingredients is almost limitless. The following recipe for *quiche Lorraine* is followed by some variations I have enjoyed. Except for the basic recipe, of course, none pretends to be the classic French dish. But they are all tasty and a fine addition to any cook's repertoire. It is my hope that you will be led to experiment—as I have been—with different ingredients (would not ripe olives, well drained and coarsely chopped, be a fine addition?) and with different cheeses, from mild to piquant to strong (a tart made with Alsatian Münster and accompanied by a well-chilled lager—what a delightful idea!). And how much more exciting to be served a new and unfamiliar dish than to confront time and again a known quantity.

Basic *Quiche Lorraine*

Serves 6 to 8
Preparation: 20 minutes · Cooking: 35 minutes in a 450°/325° oven

The preparation time does not include readying the pastry.

Short pastry for a 9-inch pie shell	With the pastry, line a 9-inch pie plate.
½ lb. bacon (or less, if desired), diced, rendered crisp, and drained on absorbent paper	When the bacon is prepared, discard all but 1½ tablespoons of the fat.

2 onions, chopped	In the reserved fat, cook the onion until translucent.

3 eggs	In a mixing bowl, beat the eggs light-
2 cups light cream	ly. Stir in the cream and seasonings.
Grating of nutmeg	Stir in the cheese.
½ teaspoon salt	
¼ teaspoon white pepper	
2 cups (8 oz.) Gruyère, finely diced	

Over the bottom of the pastry shell, arrange the onions in an even layer; over them, sprinkle the bacon bits. Add the custard mixture. On the lower shelf of the oven, bake the quiche at 450° for 15 minutes; reduce the heat to 325° and continue baking it for 20 minutes, or until the custard is set.

Variations on the Basic Quiche Recipe: There are many cheeses which can be used alone or in combination to yield the requisite 2 cups; consult the list of cheeses which work well in fondue, page 208.

For a firmer custard, use 1 additional egg; for a richer custard, use 2 whole eggs plus 3 egg yolks.

1 cup cooked ham, diced, may be substituted for the bacon.

1 cup mushrooms, sliced and sautéed in butter, may be substituted for the onions. (Try a ham-and-mushroom quiche.)

If desired, use only 1 cup Gruyère plus ¼ cup (1 oz.) Parmesan, grated.

½ lb. sweet or hot Italian sausage links, rendered until crisp, and cut into thin rounds, may be substituted for the bacon.

A 10-oz. package frozen shrimp, cooked and drained, may be substituted for the bacon. Or a 7-oz. can of crab meat, the tendons removed. Or a 7-oz. can of salmon, or tuna (preferably water-packed), well drained and flaked. Or a can of anchovy filets, drained and chopped.

A 10-oz. package frozen asparagus tips, cooked until just tender as directed on the package and well drained, may be arranged over the bacon (or ham). In this case, use only 1 cup each cheese and light cream.

2 10½-oz. cans minced clams, drained, may be added to the Basic *Quiche* Recipe.

Freshly chopped parsley—as much as you want—may be added to the custard. Or a generous sprinkling of dill weed.

A 10-oz. package frozen corn, fully thawed to room temperature, may be arranged evenly over the layer of bacon.

In place of the light cream, use 1 cup of milk combined with one 8-oz. package cream cheese, whirled in the container of an electric blender.

Onion Quiche: Use 6 to 8 onions, sliced and sautéed in butter until translucent; omit the bacon.

Green Onion Quiche (quite a different flavor): use 2 bunches scallions, chopped, with as much green as possible, sautéed in 3 tablespoons butter until wilted; omit the yellow onion and bacon.

Easter Monday Tart (a traditional Swiss dish): Over the bottom of the prepared pastry shell, arrange 2 cups (8 oz.) Emmenthaler, diced and tossed with 1 tablespoon flour; over the cheese, pour the custard, made without the Gruyère; omit the bacon and, if desired, the onion.

Sbrinz Quiche (a variation of the recipe above): In place of the Gruyère, use 1¼ cups (5 oz.) each Sbrinz and Emmenthaler, grated, combined with only 2 eggs, beaten, and 2 cups light cream; omit the bacon and onion; season the custard with nutmeg and salt to taste.

Vegetable Quiche: Over the bottom of the prepared pastry shell, arrange an even layer of finely sliced unpeeled zucchini; add ½ each green and sweet red pepper, chopped, and, if desired, a little eggplant, peeled and diced (in all, 1½ to 2 cups mixed vegetables); add the custard, made with only 1 cup (4 oz.) of cheese, and proceed with the Basic *Quiche* Recipe.

Watercress Quiche: Omit the bacon; in 1½ tablespoons butter, cook 3 cups watercress, chopped, and 1 small onion, finely chopped, until the watercress is wilted. Over the bottom of the prepared pastry shell, arrange the watercress, and proceed with the recipe as directed.

Quiche with a Dutch Flavor: As the cheese ingredient, use Edam or Gouda.

Quiche with a Greek Flavor: As the cheese ingredient, use Feta; in place of the bacon, use ½ lb. boiled ham, chopped; cook the onion in sweet butter; omit the salt.

Quiche with an Italian Flavor: As the cheese ingredient, use equal amounts of Mozzarella, diced, and Parmesan, grated (or Pecorino); in place of the bacon, use *prosciutto crudo,* chopped; cook the onion in a little mild olive oil. Or use equal amounts of Ricotta, Mozzarella, Provolone, and Parmesan.

Quiche au Roquefort: Use as the cheese ingredient, 1½ cups (6 oz.) Roquefort, crumbled; if desired, omit the bacon and/or onions.

Easter *Quiche*

A dish from the Abruzzi-Molese region contributed by Leyna Gabriele, a long-time friend who sang the title role in premiere performances of Douglas Moore's opera, *The Ballad of Baby Doe.*

2½ cups sifted flour
1 teaspoon baking powder
½ teaspoon salt
¾ cup shortening
2 eggs, beaten

Into a mixing bowl, sift twice together the flour, baking powder, and salt. Add the shortening and, using the fingers, blend the mixture thoroughly. Add and blend in the eggs. Line a buttered 10-inch pie pan with one-half the dough. Reserve the remaining dough.

5 eggs
1½ cups (6 oz.) Parmesan, grated
½ cup (2 oz.) Romano, grated
1½ cups (6 oz.) Emmenthaler, grated
1 tablespoon baking powder
¼ teaspoon pepper

In a mixing bowl, beat the eggs until frothy. Add and blend the remaining ingredients.

1 egg yolk

Into the pie shell, evenly spoon the cheese mixture. With the reserved dough, make a top crust and crimp the edges closely; cut a few slits in it and paint it with the egg yolk.

Bake the pie at 350° for 1½ hours; if the pastry browns too rapidly, reduce the heat to 325°.

Spinach *Quiche*

Serves 6 to 8
Preparation: 20 minutes · Cooking: 35 minutes in a 450°/325° oven

Short pastry for a 9-inch pie shell

With the pastry, line a 9-inch pie plate.

3 packages frozen chopped spinach, fully thawed to room temperature and pressed dry in a colander

Prepare the spinach.

½ lb. bacon, diced, rendered crisp and drained on absorbent paper

6 scallions, chopped, with as much green as possible

1 clove garlic, finely chopped

Discard all but 3 tablespoons of the bacon fat. In the reserved fat, cook the scallions and garlic until the scallions are limp.

Nutmeg
Salt
Pepper

To the scallions, add the prepared spinach, season it to taste, and simmer it for five minutes, stirring it often.

3 eggs
1 cup light cream
1 cup (4 oz.) Parmesan, grated

In a mixing bowl, beat the eggs lightly, stir in the cream and cheese.

Over the bottom of the pastry shell, arrange the bacon. Over the bacon arrange the spinach in an even layer. Pour over the custard mixture. On the lower shelf of the oven, bake the spinach tart at 450° for 15 minutes; reduce the heat to 325° and continue baking it for 20 minutes, or until the custard is set.

Spinach Pie: Greece

Serves 6 to 8 · Refrigerates
Preparation: 30 minutes · Cooking: 30 minutes in a 350° oven

Spanakopeta is a classic of Greek cuisine.

4 tablespoons butter
1 onion, chopped
3 10-oz. packages frozen chopped spinach, fully thawed to room temperature and pressed dry in a colander

In a saucepan, heat the butter and in it cook the onion until translucent. Add the spinach and cook it for 5 minutes, stirring often. Allow the vegetable to cool.

1 cup Béchamel Sauce, page 347
5 eggs, lightly beaten
1 cup (4 oz.) Feta, finely chopped
Generous grating of nutmeg
Salt
Pepper

Into the spinach, stir the Béchamel Sauce, eggs, and Feta; season the mixture to taste.

13 sheets *phyllo* pastry
Sweet butter, melted

In an 11x14-inch baking pan, arrange a layer of 6 *phyllo* sheets, each sheet brushed with butter. Over them, in an even layer, spread the spinach mixture. Add the remaining *phyllo* sheets, each sheet brushed with butter.

At this point you may stop and continue later.

Bake the *spanakopeta* at 350° for 30 minutes, or until it is golden. Cut it into serving squares.

Zucchini Tart

Serves 6 to 8
Preparation: 30 minutes · Cooking: 35 minutes in a 450°/325° oven

The preparation time does not include readying the pastry.

Short pastry for a 9-inch pie shell	With the pastry, line a 9-inch pie plate.	

2 lbs. zucchini, cut in ¼-inch rounds

In boiling, salted water, cook the zucchini rounds for 5 minutes. Drain.

¼ cup (1 oz.) Parmesan, grated
¼ cup (1 oz.) Cheddar, grated
½ cup bread crumbs

In a mixing bowl, toss together the two cheeses and bread crumbs. Reserve the mixture for a topping when baking.

2 egg yolks
1½ cups sour cream
4 tablespoons chives, chopped
¼ cup (1 oz.) Cheddar, grated
2 tablespoons flour
Salt
Pepper
2 egg whites, beaten until stiff

In a mixing bowl, beat the egg yolks lightly. Add the sour cream, chives, cheese and flour; salt and pepper to taste. Blend the mixture well. Fold in the egg whites.

Reserved bread crumb mixture

Over the bottom of the pastry shell, arrange a layer of one-half of the zucchini rounds. Over it, spoon one-half of the sour cream mixture. Repeat. Over the top, sprinkle the bread crumb mixture. On the lower shelf of the oven, bake the tart at 450° for 15 minutes; reduce the heat to 325° and continue baking it for 20 minutes or until the custard is set.

VEGETABLES

All vegetables of my acquaintance are capable of an extra gustatory fillip by the addition of cheese, either a *grana,* grated and sprinkled over them, or a melting cheese, shredded and sprinkled over them, or by the addition of simple cheese sauce, page 345, of Mornay Sauce, or of Rich Mornay Sauce, page 347, in each case, the dish is heated for 15 minutes in a 400° oven or put for 5 minutes under a hot broiler.

In preparing the vegetables, use your preferred method of cleaning and cooking them. If you have a microwave cooker, follow the instructions provided by the manufacturer. My favorite method of range-cooking vegetables is to cook them very rapidly in as little water as possible until they are tender-crisp. The drained vegetable is then arranged in an ovenproof dish, the cheese or sauce of my choice is added, and the vegetable finished as described above. One word of caution (no, one suggestion to increase your enjoyment of vegetables): Do *not* overcook them; undercooked vegetables are preferable to the mealy mush often served in the name of vegetable cookery.

I especially enjoy the following vegetables with cheese or cheese sauce:

Artichoke hearts: use frozen ones, cooked as suggested on the package and well drained; two packages yield six servings.

Asparagus: I peel the stalks, arrange them in an ovenproof dish, cover them tightly with foil, and bake them in a 350° oven for 30 to 40 minutes (depending upon the thickness of the stalk); a delicious method of cooking and one with no loss of nutrients.

Beans, green and Lima; and dried beans, too, cooked and drained.

Broccoli

Brussels sprouts

Cabbage: cut the cabbage into six equal wedges, one per serving.

Carrots

Cauliflower: for a particularly attractive presentation, cook the cauliflower whole.

Celery

Corn pudding: add 1 cup (4 oz.) mild cheese, grated, to the recipe before baking the pudding.

Endive: braise it and then add cheese or cheese sauce.

Onions

Peas: add a light, fairly thin cheese sauce.

Spinach

Tomatoes: remove their tops and add cheese before baking or broiling them.

Turnips

Zucchini

In addition to these general suggestions for vegetables with cheese, there follow specific recipes, a bit fancier perhaps and, I hope, pleasant to both eye and taste.

Artichoke Hearts

Serves 6 · Doubles · Refrigerates
Preparation: 25 minutes · Cooking: 15 minutes in a 400° oven

2 9-oz. packages frozen artichoke hearts

Cook the artichoke hearts as directed on the package; drain them, reserving ½ cup of the cooking liquid. While the artichokes are cooking, prepare the sauce.

4 tablespoons butter
4 tablespoons flour
1 onion, grated
¼ teaspoon dry mustard
1 teaspoon salt
¼ teaspoon white pepper

In a saucepan, heat the butter and in it, over gentle heat, cook the flour, stirring, for a few minutes. Stir in the onion and seasonings.

1½ cups milk

Gradually add the reserved ½ cup artichoke water and the milk, stirring constantly until the mixture is thickened and smooth.

1 egg, beaten
¼ cup (1 oz.) Gruyère, grated

Off heat, stir in the beaten egg. Add the cheese, stirring until it is melted.

¼ cup (1 oz.) Gruyère, grated

In a lightly buttered baking dish, arrange the artichoke hearts. Over them, spoon the sauce. Sprinkle them with the cheese.

At this point you may stop and continue later.

Bake the artichoke hearts at 400° for 15 minutes, or until the grated cheese is melted and golden and the sauce is bubbly.

Cabbage

Serves 6 · Refrigerates
Preparation: 25 minutes

4   tablespoons butter
1   small cabbage, shredded
1   onion, chopped
1   small piece ginger root,
     grated
1   teaspoon salt
¼   teaspoon pepper
¾   cup water

In a large skillet, heat the butter and in it cook the cabbage, onion, and ginger root, stirring, for 3 minutes. Add the seasonings and the water. Stir again to blend the ingredients and cook the cabbage, covered, for 8–10 minutes, or until it is tender-crisp. Remove the skillet from the heat.

½   cup sour cream
½   cup (2 oz.) Bel Paese,
     finely diced, at room
     temperature

Into the cabbage, gently stir the sour cream and cheese. Cover the skillet to allow the cheese to melt.

The dish may also be prepared with one 3-oz. package of cream cheese, at room temperature and cut into small pieces to facilitate its melting. Use the cream cheese in place of the sour cream and Bel Paese.

Broccoli in Cheese Custard

Serves 6
Preparation: 25 minutes · Cooking: 30 minutes in a 350° oven

2   bunches broccoli,
    trimmed, rinsed, the
    stalks split for even
    cooking

In boiling salted water to cover, cook the broccoli, uncovered, for 15 minutes, or until it is just barely tender. Drain it.

In a lightly buttered baking dish, arrange the broccoli.

4   eggs
1   cup milk
1½ cups (6 oz.) Cheddar,
    grated
Grating of nutmeg
½   teaspoon salt
¼   teaspoon white pepper

In a mixing bowl, beat the eggs with the milk. Add the cheese and seasonings. Pour the custard over the broccoli.

At this point you may stop and continue later.

Set the baking dish in a pan with 1 inch of hot water. Bake the broccoli at 350° for 30 minutes, or until the custard is set.

Carrots with Honey and Cheese

Serves 6 · Doubles · Refrigerates
Preparation: 25 minutes · Cooking: 10 minutes in a 400° oven

6 large or 12 small carrots, scraped and cut in half crosswise

In boiling salted water to cover, cook the carrots for 15 minutes, or until they are tender.

⅓ cup honey
Pepper
1 cup (4 oz.) Fontina, shredded

In a lightly buttered baking dish, arrange the carrots. Drizzle them with honey and add a grinding of pepper. Sprinkle them with the cheese.

At this point you may stop and continue later.

Bake the carrots, uncovered, at 400° for 10 minutes, or until the cheese is melted and bubbly.

Corn Purée

Serves 6 · Refrigerates
Preparation: 25 minutes

This unusual Latin-American dish is served as a relish accompanying roast meats.

2 10-oz. packages frozen corn kernels, fully thawed to room temperature
⅓ cup milk

In the container of an electric blender, combine the corn and milk and, on high speed, whirl them until they are reduced to a smooth puree.

2 eggs
2 teaspoons paprika
½ teaspoon salt
¼ teaspoon pepper

To the contents of the blender, add the eggs and seasonings. Whirl the mixture again for 15 seconds.

4 tablespoons butter
1 bunch scallions, chopped, with as much green as possible
½ green pepper, chopped

In a skillet, heat the butter and in it cook the vegetables until they are limp.

At this point you may stop and continue later.

To the contents of the hot skillet, add the corn mixture. Over gentle heat, simmer the ingredients, uncovered, stirring constantly until the mixture is somewhat thickened.

½ cup (2 oz.) grating cheese of your choice, page 80

Stir in the cheese, cooking over very low heat; when it is melted, remove the relish from the heat.

Eggplant

Eggplant, like pasta, is especially complemented by being cooked with cheese. It is, moreover—and here I admit to personal bias—a delectable vegetable! The combination of these two circumstances has made a selection of eggplant-cheese recipes difficult; I wanted to include all I know, but have managed to compromise by offering four recipes and two variations.

Incidentally, the regally hued eggplant is not a vegetable at all, but rather a fruit (actually, it is a berry). And its botanical family is allied to the potato. This gratuitous bit of information should not prejudice you against eggplant, however, for it is one of our great (albeit, often ignored) delicacies.

Baked Eggplant Slices

Serves 6 · Doubles · Refrigerates
Preparation: 30 minutes · Cooking: 30 minutes in a 400° oven

1 large unpeeled eggplant, cut in ½-inch slices	In a shallow dish, marinate the eggplant in the vinaigrette sauce for 30 minutes; turn the slices and repeat. Drain the slices, reserving the dressing. Pat the slices dry with absorbent paper.
½ cup Vinaigrette Sauce*	

In a lightly buttered baking dish, bake the eggplant at 450° for 15 minutes, or until it is tender. While the eggplant is baking, make the sauce.

1	onion, grated
2	tablespoons flour
1½	cups milk, scalded
¾	cup (3 oz.) cheese of your choice, grated (Bel Paese, Fontina, Münster)

In a saucepan, heat the reserved vinaigrette sauce. Stir in the onion and then the flour. When the mixture is well blended, gradually add the milk, stirring constantly until the sauce is thickened and smooth. Off heat, add the cheese, stirring until it is melted. Pour the sauce over the eggplant.

At this point you may stop and continue later.

Bake the eggplant at 400° for an additional 15 minutes, or until the sauce is bubbly.

Vinaigrette Sauce: In a jar with a tight-fitting lid, combine 1 teaspoon salt, 1 teaspoon sugar, ½ teaspoon dry mustard, and a pinch of pepper. Add 2 tablespoons water and 4 tablespoons wine vinegar. Cover the jar and shake it vigorously to dissolve the salt and sugar. Add 1 cup mild olive oil and shake the sauce once again. Yield: 1¼ cups.

Eggplant *en Casserole*

Serves 6 · Doubles · Refrigerates
Preparation: 45 minutes · Cooking: 40 minutes in a 350° oven (plus 5 minutes broiling)

Olive oil
2 small, unpeeled eggplant, each cut in 6 slices

In a skillet, heat enough oil to cover the bottom. In it, brown the eggplant slices on each side, a few at a time. Drain them on absorbent paper.

12 anchovy filets
1 Bermuda onion, cut into 6 slices
6 slices cooked ham
3 cloves garlic, finely chopped
1 green pepper, finely chopped
Salt
Pepper
6 slices Provolone

In a lightly oiled baking dish, arrange six of the eggplant slices. Over each slice, arrange 2 anchovy filets, an onion slice, a piece of ham, and a sprinkling of garlic and green pepper. Add a sprinkling of salt and pepper. Add a slice of Provolone. Top the "sandwiches" with the remaining six slices of eggplant.

1 20-oz. can stewed tomatoes
2 bay leaves
2 whole cloves
¼ cup olive oil

Over the eggplant, pour the tomatoes; tuck in the bay leaves and cloves. Cover the baking dish with foil wrap.

At this point you may stop and continue later.

Bake the eggplant, covered, at 350° for 40 minutes.

½ cup bread crumbs
½ cup Emmenthaler, grated

Combine the bread crumbs and cheese. Remove and discard the foil wrap. Over the top of the eggplant, sprinkle the crumb mixture and set the dish under a hot broiler for 5 minutes, or until the crumbs are browned and the cheese melted.

Eggplant and Zucchini in Custard

Serves 6 to 8 · Doubles · Refrigerates
Preparation: 1 hour · Cooking: 40 minutes in a 350° oven

A Neapolitan delicacy.

½ cup seasoned flour
2 small, unpeeled eggplant, thinly sliced
3 medium-sized zucchini, sliced
Olive oil

Dust the eggplant and zucchini slices with the seasoned flour. In a skillet, heat olive oil and in it brown the vegetables on both sides, a few slices at a time; olive oil may be added as necessary. Drain the vegetables on absorbent paper.

¼ cup parsley, chopped
½ teaspoon basil
3 tomatoes, sliced
2 onions, chopped

In a large, lightly oiled baking dish, arrange one-half of the eggplant; over it, sprinkle the parsley and basil; add all of the zucchini in an even layer; then the tomatoes and onion; top with a layer of eggplant.

2 eggs
1 cup milk
¼ teaspoon nutmeg
½ teaspoon salt
½ cup (2 oz.) Parmesan, grated
8 oz. Mozzarella, sliced

In a mixing bowl, beat together the eggs, milk, seasonings, and Parmesan. Pour the custard over the contents of the baking dish. Garnish the dish with the Mozzarella slices. Bake the eggplant at 350° for 40 minutes, or until the custard is set and the top is lightly browned.

If desired, the zucchini may be omitted; light cream may be substituted for the milk; the cooked dish may be garnished with a mixture of ¼ cup each bread crumbs, Parmesan, grated, and parsley; put the dish under a hot broiler for 3 minutes, or until the top is browned.

Add to your favorite recipe for *ratatouille*, ½ cup (2 oz.) Edam, Gouda, or Mimolette, in small dices.

Eggplant Parmigiana

Serves 6 · Doubles · Refrigerates
Preparation: 1 hour · Cooking: 40 minutes in a 375° oven

This dish is contributed by Teresa Carducci, the housekeeper of a friend living in Rome. Her recipe is simpler than some and, I feel, very good indeed.

Olive oil
2 small, unpeeled eggplant, thinly sliced, seasoned with salt

In a skillet, heat olive oil to cover the bottom. In it, brown the eggplant slices on both sides, a few at a time. Drain them on absorbent paper. More oil may be added as necessary.

5 tablespoons olive oil
2½ lbs. ripe tomatoes, peeled, seeded, and chopped (*or* one 35-oz. can, drained and chopped)
1½ teaspoons basil
Salt
Pepper

To the oil remaining in the skillet, add the additional 5 tablespoons of oil. Add the tomatoes and basil and simmer them, uncovered, stirring occasionally, until the sauce is thickened. Season it with salt and pepper to taste.

1¼ cups (5 oz.) Parmesan, grated
8 oz. Mozzarella, thinly sliced

In a lightly oiled baking dish, arrange a layer of one-third of the eggplant. Sprinkle it with one-third of the Parmesan and add one-half of the Mozzarella slices. Spoon over one-half of the tomato sauce. Repeat, using the final one-third eggplant for a top layer; sprinkle with the final third of cheese.

At this point you may stop and continue later.

Bake the eggplant, uncovered, at 375° for 40 minutes.

Signorina Carducci cooks her eggplant parmigiana, covered, in a *bain-marie;* the completed dish is then put briefly under a broiler to brown.

A *variant from France:* In both steps 1 and 2, use butter in place of olive oil. In step 2, cook 6 onions, sliced, until translucent, before adding the tomatoes: add ⅓ cup parsley, chopped, and 3 cloves garlic, finely chopped, when cooking the tomatoes. In step 3, in place of the Parmesan, use 1½ cups (6 oz.) Gruyère, grated. Assemble and bake the dish as directed.

A *variant from Romania:* Follow step 1 as directed. In step 2, cook 2 onions, chopped, until translucent, before adding and cooking the tomatoes; in place of the basil, use 1 teaspoon thyme and 1 teaspoon sugar. In step 3, in place of the Parmesan, grate 4 oz. (1 cup) of Kashkaval and, in place of the Mozzarella, cut 4 oz. of Kashkaval into thin slices; assemble the dish and bake it as directed.

Green Onions with Cheese Sauce

Serves 6 · Doubles · Refrigerates
Preparation: 25 minutes

1 chicken bouillon cube dissolved in 1½ cups water
6 bunches scallions, trimmed

In a saucepan, combine the bouillon and scallions; bring the liquid to the boil and cook the scallions, covered, until they are just tender (about 10 minutes). Drain them, reserving the liquid. Keep the scallions warm.

3 tablespoons butter
3 tablespoons flour
½ cup milk
Grating of nutmeg
Salt

In the saucepan, heat the butter; stir in the flour and, over gentle heat, cook it for a few minutes. Gradually add the reserved scallion liquid and then the milk, stirring constantly until the mixture is thickened and smooth. Season it.

1 cup (4 oz.) cheese of your choice, shredded (Cheddar, Fontina, Taleggio)

Off heat, add the cheese, stirring until it is melted.

6 slices toast

Arrange the scallions on the toast slices. Over them, pour the hot sauce.

A variation from Alsace uses leeks: In lightly salted water, poach 12 leeks, trimmed and thoroughly rinsed, for 20 minutes, or until they are tender. Drain (reserving 1 cup of the water) and arrange them in a lightly buttered baking dish. Using the reserved 1 cup leek water and 1 cup of light cream, make Béchamel Sauce, page 347, adding ½ cup (2 oz.) Münster, grated. Over the leeks, pour the sauce and sprinkle the dish with ½ cup (2 oz.) Münster, grated. Bake the dish at 400° for 15 minutes, or until the sauce is bubbly and the cheese melted and golden.

Hominy Grits

Serves 6 · Doubles
Preparation: 20 minutes · Cooking: 30 minutes in a 350° oven

This recipe is contributed by Mrs. Donald B. Percy, a neighbor in the country, whose beautiful home and warm graciousness make dinner with her a pleasure long to be remembered.

7 cups water 1½ cups quick-cooking hominy grits 1 tablespoon salt	Combine these three ingredients, bring to a simmer, and cook for 15 minutes, or until the mixture is the consistency of thick pudding.
2 cups (8 oz.) Cheddar, shredded	Off heat, add the cheese, stirring until it is melted.
1 egg, beaten	Stir in the egg.
3 tablespoons Cheddar, grated	Into a lightly buttered baking dish, spoon the hominy. Sprinkle it with the cheese. Bake the dish, uncovered, at 350° for 30 minutes.

Lima Beans

Serves 6 · Doubles · Refrigerates · Freezes
Preparation: 15 minutes · Cooking: 15 minutes in a 350° oven

2   10-oz. packages
    Fordhook Lima beans,
    cooked as directed on
    the package and drained
    (1½ lbs. fresh Lima
    beans may be used, if
    desired)
½   cup light cream
½   cup (2 oz.) Cheddar,
    shredded
½   teaspoon celery salt
¼   teaspoon pepper

In a mixing bowl, combine the beans and the other ingredients. Using a fork, toss them gently to blend the mixture well.

In a lightly buttered 1½-quart casserole, arrange the beans.

At this point you may stop and continue later.

Bake the beans at 350° for 15 minutes, or until the cheese is melted and the sauce is bubbly.

Curried Lima Beans and Cheese

Serves 6 · Doubles · Refrigerates
Preparation: 1½ hours · Cooking: 2 hours in a 300° oven

A delightful main course which may be made with all easily melted cheeses—Cheddars or Swiss cheeses, for example. Using the Welsh Caerphilly produces a delicately flavored entrée.

1   lb. dried baby Lima beans
6   cups water

In a large saucepan, combine the beans and water. Bring the liquid to the boil; remove the saucepan from the heat and allow the beans to stand, covered, for 1 hour. Drain the beans and reserve the water.

2   onions, minced
4   tablespoons butter, softened
1   cup seedless raisins
2   teaspoons curry powder (or more, to taste)
1   teaspoon salt

In a casserole, combine the beans, onions, butter, raisins, curry powder, and salt. Add enough reserved bean liquid just to cover the beans. Bake the casserole covered, at 300° for 2 hours; stir the beans occasionally and add more bean liquid, if necessary.

At this point you may stop and continue later.

1   cup Caerphilly cheese, finely chopped

Stir in the cheese and allow the dish to stand for 5 minutes before serving it.

Mushrooms Mornay

Serves 6 · Doubles · Refrigerates
Preparation: 30 minutes · Cooking: 10 minutes in a 400° oven

4   tablespoons butter
½   teaspoon each: basil, dill, oregano, and thyme
2   lbs. mushrooms, the stems trimmed
Salt
Pepper

In a skillet, heat the butter and to it add the herbs. Add the mushrooms and cook, uncovered, for 10 minutes, or until they are tender. Stir them often to coat them with the butter. Season to taste.

¼   cup parsley, chopped
2   cups Mornay Sauce, page 347

In a lightly buttered baking dish, arrange the mushrooms. Sprinkle them with the parsley. Over them, spoon the Mornay Sauce.

At this point you may stop and continue later.

Bake the dish at 400° for 10 minutes, or until the sauce is bubbly.

Mushrooms with Green Peas

Serves 6 · Refrigerates
Preparation: 30 minutes · Cooking: 10 minutes in a 400° oven

2 10-oz. packages frozen peas
¾ teaspoon basil
1 teaspoon salt

In a saucepan, combine the peas, basil, and salt; add sufficient water to cover; cook the peas, following the directions on the package, until they are thoroughly tender. Drain and reserve them.

1 tablespoon butter
1 onion, chopped

In a saucepan, heat the butter and in it cook the onion until translucent. In a mixing bowl, combine the cooked peas and onion, and, using a fork, toss them lightly to blend them.

18 large mushroom caps
8 tablespoons butter, melted
½ cup (2 oz.) Emmenthaler, grated
¼ cup (1 oz.) Parmesan, grated

Dip the mushroom caps into the melted butter. In a baking dish, arrange them, their smooth side down. To the peas, add any remaining butter and the Emmenthaler. With this mixture, mound the mushroom caps. Sprinkle them with the Parmesan.

At this point you may stop and continue later.

Bake the mushrooms at 400° for 10 minutes, or until the cheese is melted.

Stuffed Green Peppers

Serves 6 · Doubles · Refrigerates
Preparation: 25 minutes · Cooking: 35 minutes in a 350° oven

1   cup raw natural rice
1   10½-oz. can condensed chicken broth, plus water to equal 2 cups

In a saucepan, combine the rice and broth. Bring the liquid to the boil, reduce the heat, and simmer the rice, covered, for 15 minutes, or until it is tender and the liquid is absorbed.

6   slices bacon, diced

While the rice is cooking, render the bacon in a skillet until it is crisp. Remove it to absorbent paper and reserve it; discard all but 2 tablespoons of the fat.

1   onion, chopped

In the reserved fat, cook the onion until translucent.

1   cup (4 oz.) Cheddar, grated
2   tomatoes, peeled, seeded and chopped
½   teaspoon thyme
½   teaspoon salt
¼   teaspoon pepper

To the cooked rice, add the reserved bacon bits, cooked onion, cheese, tomatoes, and seasonings. Using a fork, toss the mixture to blend it well.

6   firm green peppers

Slice off just the stem ends from each pepper and carefully remove the core and seeds. Stuff the pepper shells with the rice mixture.

At this point you may stop and continue later.

Bake the peppers at 350° for 35 minutes, or until they are tender.

Asparagus *en Casserole*

Serves 6 · Doubles · Refrigerates
Preparation: 30 minutes · Cooking: 15 minutes in a 400° oven

3   lbs. fresh asparagus, trimmed and rinsed

In 3 quarts boiling, salted water, cook the asparagus for 10 minutes. Drain the asparagus, reserving 1½ cups of the water. Arrange the asparagus in a lightly buttered baking dish.

3   tablespoons butter
1   onion, chopped
3   tablespoons flour

In a saucepan, heat the butter and in it cook the onion until translucent. Stir in the flour and, over gentle heat, cook it for a few minutes. Gradually add the reserved asparagus water, stirring constantly until the mixture is thickened and smooth.

½   cup (2 oz.) Fontina, shredded
⅓   cup (1½ oz.) Parmesan, grated
½   teaspoon rosemary, crushed
Grating of pepper

Off heat, add the cheeses, stirring until they are melted. Stir in the seasonings.

½   cup (2 oz.) Provolone, shredded

Over the asparagus, pour the sauce. Over the top, sprinkle the Provolone.

At this point you may stop and continue later.

Bake the asparagus at 400° for 15 minutes, or until the Provolone is melted and the sauce is bubbly.

Spinach with Cheese Sauce

Serves 6 · Doubles · Refrigerates
Preparation: 15 minutes · Cooking: 10 minutes in a 400° oven

3 10-oz. packages frozen chopped spinach, cooked as directed on the package

While the spinach is cooking, prepare the sauce.

1 tablespoon butter
1½ tablespoons flour
½ teaspoon salt
¼ teaspoon white pepper
Grating of nutmeg
1 cup milk
1 onion, grated

In a saucepan, heat the butter and in it, over gentle heat, cook the flour, stirring, for a few minutes. Add the seasonings. Gradually add the milk, stirring constantly until the mixture is thickened and smooth. Stir in the onion.

1 cup (4 oz.) Gruyère, shredded

Off heat, add the cheese, stirring until it is dissolved.

¼ cup (1 oz.) Gruyère, shredded

In a colander, drain the cooked spinach and, using a large spoon, press it as dry as possible. Add the spinach to the cheese sauce, stirring the mixture to blend it well. Spoon it into an ovenproof dish. Sprinkle the mixture with the shredded cheese.

At this point you may stop and continue later.

Bake the spinach, uncovered, at 400° for 10 minutes, or until it is thoroughly heated and the cheese is melted.

Spinach with Cheese Custard

Serves 6 · Doubles · Refrigerates
Preparation: 15 minutes · Cooking: 20 minutes in a 350° oven

3 10-oz. packages frozen chopped spinach, fully thawed to room temperature and pressed dry in a colander
Grating of nutmeg
Salt
Pepper

In a lightly buttered casserole, arrange the spinach in an even layer. Season it to taste.

1 8-oz. package cream cheese, at room temperature
½ cup milk
1 egg

In the container of an electric blender, whirl these three ingredients until the mixture is smooth. Pour it over the spinach.

½ cup (2 oz.) Gruyère, grated

Over the top, sprinkle the grated cheese.

At this point you may stop and continue later.

Bake the dish at 350° for 20 minutes, or until the custard is set.

Spinach with Bacon and Cheese

Serves 6
Preparation: 20 minutes · Cooking: 15 minutes in a 400° oven

6 slices thick-cut bacon, diced

Render the bacon dices until crisp; drain them on absorbent paper.

4 cloves garlic, finely chopped

3 10-oz. packages fresh spinach, the heavy stems removed, rinsed, and drained

Toss the bacon dice and garlic with the spinach.

In a soup kettle, cook the spinach without adding water; when it is just wilted, remove it from the heat and discard any excess water. Arrange the vegetable in a lightly buttered baking dish.

½ cup (2 oz.) Sbrinz, grated

2 eggs

⅓ cup light cream

In a mixing bowl, beat together these three ingredients. Pour the sauce over the spinach.

6 strips Emmenthaler

Garnish the dish with the cheese strips.

At this point you may stop and continue later.

Bake the dish at 400° for 15 minutes, or until the cheese strips are melted and golden.

Zucchini Parmesan

Serves 6 · Doubles · Refrigerates
Preparation: 20 minutes · Cooking: 15 minutes in a 350° oven

6 tablespoons olive oil 2 cloves garlic, split	In a saucepan, heat the oil and in it cook the garlic until it is browned; discard the garlic.
6 to 8 small zucchini, thinly sliced	In a mixing bowl, combine the zucchini and flavored oil; toss them to blend them well.
½ cup (2 oz.) Parmesan, grated Salt Pepper	Add the cheese, season to taste, and toss the zucchini again.
¼ cup (1 oz.) Parmesan, grated	In a lightly buttered baking dish, arrange the zucchini. Sprinkle them with the grated cheese. *At this point you may stop and continue later.* Bake the zucchini, covered, at 350° for 15 minutes, or until they are tender-crisp.

A variant from Greece: follow step 1 as directed, reserving the oil; in step 2, cut the zucchini into lengthwise halves and arrange them in a lightly oiled baking dish. Combine the reserved oil, 2 tablespoons tomato paste, 1 cup water, ⅓ cup (1½ oz.) Kashkaval, grated, ½ cup (2 oz.) Feta, crumbled, 1 teaspoon oregano, and ¼ cup parsley, chopped. Pour this mixture over the zucchini. Sprinkle the top with ¼ cup (1 oz.) Kashkaval, grated. Bake the dish at 375° for 20 minutes, or until the zucchini are tender-crisp.

FARINACEOUS FOODS

Basic Recipe for *Crêpes:* France

18 crêpes · Doubles · Refrigerates · Freezes
Preparation: 2¼ hours · Cooking: 40 minutes

Crêpes, properly stored with plastic wrap separating them, keep almost indefinitely in the freezer. They must be fully thawed to room temperature before being used.

1½ cups flour	In the container of an electric
½ teaspoon salt	blender, combine all of the ingre-
2 eggs	dients. On medium speed, whirl
¾ cup milk	them, using a rubber spatula to in-
¾ cup water	corporate all the flour, until the mix-
3 tablespoons cognac (optional)	ture is smooth. The batter will be thin. Allow it to stand for 2 hours
5 tablespoons butter, melted	before making the *crêpes.*

Soft butter

Using a pastry brush, "paint" a hot 5-inch *crêpe* pan or small skillet with the butter. Add just enough batter to coat the bottom of the pan (about 3 tablespoons). Cook each *crêpe* quickly, turning once, until it is golden. Drain on absorbent paper while cooking the next one.

For Cheese-Flavored Crêpes: Add ½ cup (2 oz.) Parmesan, grated, to the batter when preparing it in the blender. This is a delightful way to serve creamed chicken or avocado or other filling not made with cheese.

Here follow several fillings for plain *crêpes;* in reality, however, the possibilities are virtually numberless: small shrimp in cheese sauce, scallops in cheese sauce, minced ham in cheese sauce, spinach in cheese sauce, etc.

Cheese Filling for Crêpes: In a saucepan, melt 6 tablespoons butter; into it stir 8 tablespoons flour; gradually add 2 cups warm milk, stirring. When the mixture is thickened and smooth, add ¾ cup (3 oz.) Gruyère, grated, and ¼ cup (1 oz.) Parmesan or Sapsago, grated. Stir until the cheese is melted and add 3 egg yolks, beaten; season the mixture to taste with a grating of nutmeg, salt, and pepper. Spoon the filling into a lightly oiled shallow rectangular pan and chill it for 3 hours. Cut it into eighteen 3-inch oblongs. Roll the *crêpes* around the cheese "sticks," tucking in the sides as you do so. In a lightly buttered baking dish, arrange the *crêpes* and cook them in a 400° oven for 20 minutes. Serve them with a thin Soubise Sauce, page 348.

Sausage and Spinach Filling for Crêpes: In a skillet, crumble and brown 1 lb. sweet Italian or American breakfast sausage meat; drain it on absorbent paper. Press dry in a colander one 10-oz. package frozen chopped spinach, fully thawed to room temperature. In a mixing bowl, combine the sausage meat, spinach, ¼ cup (1 oz.) Romano (grated), ¼ teaspoon thyme, and pepper, to taste. Blend the ingredients well. Onto each *crêpe,* spoon a little of the sausage mixture; roll the *crêpes,* tucking in the sides as you do so. In a lightly buttered baking dish, arrange the *crêpes.* Over them, spoon 2 cups Mornay Sauce, page 347, sprinkle the sauce with a little paprika, and bake the dish, uncovered, at 400° for 20 minutes, or until the sauce is bubbly.

Ham and Raisin Filling for Crêpes: Make 2 cups basic cheese sauce, page 345. Into 1 cup of the sauce, stir ½ cup cooked ham, chopped, and ¾ cup golden raisins. Fill the *crêpes* with this mixture, arrange them in a buttered baking dish, and over them spoon the remaining sauce. Heat them as directed.

Port Salut Crêpes: To 1 cup panada, page 345, add 2 cups (8 oz.) Port Salut, shredded, and 2 tablespoons tomato puree; stir the mixture until the cheese is melted and adjust the seasoning with salt and pepper to taste. Using this filling, complete the Basic Recipe for *Crêpes,* page 257.

Roquefort Crêpes: Allowing 2 *crêpes* per serving, make a Béchamel Sauce with 2 tablespoons butter, 2 tablespoons flour, and 1⅓ cups milk. Add 1½ cups (6 oz.) Roquefort, crumbled, and a grating of nutmeg. Over gentle heat, stir the mixture until it is smooth. Fill and roll the 12 *crêpes* and arrange them in a lightly buttered baking dish. Brush them with melted butter and bake them at 400° for 20 minutes, or until they are thoroughly heated and golden.

Cheese Dumplings

Serves 6 · Doubles
Preparation: 10 minutes · Cooking: 15 minutes

For meat and poultry stews. And for clear soups.

1   cup flour
2   teaspoons baking powder
½   teaspoon salt

Begin preparing the dumplings about 30 minutes before the stew or soup will be finished. (Or, if reheating, bring to a good, hot simmer before adding the dumplings.)

In a mixing bowl, sift together the three dry ingredients.

½   cup milk

Gradually add the milk.

¾   cup (3 oz.) cheese of your choice, shredded (Bel Paese, Cheddar, Münster)

With the flour mixture, using two forks, toss the cheese.

½   cup milk

Gradually add the milk, stirring constantly. The batter should be stiff but smooth.

Drop the batter from a spoon onto the simmering liquid of the stew or directly into the soup. Cook the dumplings, covered, for 15 minutes.

The size of spoon used to drop the dough will determine the size of the dumplings. For stews, I like one large dumpling per person (use a big spoon); for soups, I prefer small dumplings (use a teaspoon).

Blintzes

12 blintzes · Doubles · Refrigerates
Preparation: 45 minutes · Cooking: 15 minutes

For appetizers, main course, or dessert. The final cooking may be done in a chafing dish at the dining table—always an *effective gesture.*

1 cup flour 1½ teaspoons baking powder ½ teaspoon salt 2 eggs 1¼ cups milk 3 tablespoons melted butter, cooled	In the container of an electric blender, combine these six ingredients and, on medium speed, whirl them until the mixture is smooth.
Soft butter	Into a hot, well-buttered 6-inch frying or *crêpe* pan, pour 3 tablespoons of batter. Brown only one side of the blintz; let them drain on absorbent paper. Make 12 blintzes in all.
1 cup small-curd creamed cottage cheese 1 3-oz. package cream cheese, at room temperature ½ teaspoon salt	In a mixing bowl, blend the cheeses and salt. Spoon an equal amount of the mixture across the center of the *cooked* side of the blintzes. Fold the two opposite edges over the filling and roll the blintzes.
	At this point you may stop and continue later.
2 tablespoons butter	In a skillet, heat the butter. Add the blintzes and brown them, turning them carefully as necessary.
Sour cream	Serve them hot, accompanied by sour cream.

For a main course: To the cheese mixture, add herbs of your choice, diced ham, diced cooked chicken, or chopped cooked vegetables.

For dessert blintzes: Add to the batter 2 tablespoons sugar; add to the cheese mixture 4 tablespoons sugar, 1 teaspoon vanilla or orange extract, and ½ teaspoon (or to taste) grated orange or lemon rind.

Pancakes

About 24 pancakes · Doubles
Preparation: 10 minutes · Cooking: 15 minutes

6 eggs	
2 cups cottage cheese	
⅔ cup flour	
1 teaspoon salt	

In the container of an electric blender, combine these four ingredients. On medium speed, whirl them until the batter is smooth.

Cook the pancakes in your preferred manner. Serve them with honey, syrup, a fruit conserve of your choice, or sweetened and flavored sour cream.

If desired, the 6 eggs may be separated: add a pinch of cream of tartar to the 6 whites and beat them until stiff. Make the batter, using the 6 egg yolks in place of the whole eggs; pour the batter from the blender container into a mixing bowl; fold in the whites and cook as directed. Delightfully light and airy for dessert pancakes.

For dessert pancakes: Add to the ingredients in the container of the blender 3 tablespoons honey and ¾ teaspoon cinnamon.

Cheddar-flavored pancakes: Add to this or to your favorite pancake recipe ½ cup (2 oz.) Cheddar, grated.

Poached Dumplings

18 dumplings
Preparation: 1½ hours · Cooking: 15 minutes

This recipe from Poland may be served either as a light main course or as a dessert—with entirely different seasonings, of course.

¾   lb. Farmer Cheese, sieved

In a mixing bowl, beat the egg yolks, one at a time, into the cheese. Beat in the butter and the dill weed *or* sugar. Gradually add the flour, beating each addition until the mixture is smooth.

3   egg yolks
2   tablespoons soft butter
1   tablespoon dill weed (if dumplings are to serve as a main course)

or

2   tablespoons sugar (if dumplings are to serve as a dessert)
⅔   cup flour

3   egg whites, beaten stiff

Fold the egg whites into the cheese mixture. Using your hands, roll the dough into three balls of the same size. Roll each ball into a 2-inch roll. Wrap the rolls in waxed paper and refrigerate them for at least 1 hour.

Cut each roll into six pieces.

3   quarts water
1½   teaspoons salt

In a soup kettle, bring the salted water to a boil. In the boiling water, poach the dumplings, six at a time, for 5 minutes, or until they are firm. Drain them on absorbent paper, arrange them on a serving dish, and keep them warm.

8   tablespoons butter
½   cup bread crumbs

In a skillet, heat the butter and in it toast the bread crumbs until they are crisp. Over the dumplings, sprinkle the bread crumbs and serve them.

Pasta with Egg and Garlic

(a smooth and delectable pasta dish, that is easy to prepare and suitable as a main course.) For 4 servings, cook 1 lb. pasta al dente in boiling salted water according to the directions on the package; drain well; toss the pasta, using two forks, with 4 tablespoons soft sweet butter, 4 eggs, beaten, 4 cloves garlic, put through a press, ½ cup (2 oz.) Parmesan, grated, and ½ cup (2 oz.) Gruyère, grated. Serve it accompanied by a well-functioning pepper mill.

Fettucini in Cream

Serves 6
Preparation: 20 minutes

A very rich, very good pasta dish.

1 lb. fettucini, cooked al dente as directed on the package and drained well	In a large serving bowl, combine all the ingredients and, using two forks, gently toss the pasta until it is well coated. Serve the dish at once, garnished with the parsley.
1 cup whipped sweet butter, at room temperature	
1 cup heavy cream, heated	
1 cup (4 oz.) Parmesan, grated	
½ cup parsley, finely chopped	

If desired, the cream may be omitted.

Fettucini alla Romana: Add one 10-oz. package frozen peas, cooked as directed on the package, and ⅔ cup prosciutto, cut in fine julienne.

Pasta with Roquefort: To hot, cooked pasta of your choice for 6 persons, add soft butter, to taste, and ¾ cup (3 oz.) Roquefort, finely chopped; using two forks, toss the mixture. Add a generous grating of pepper.

Basic Recipe for Macaroni and Cheese

Serves 6 · Doubles · Refrigerates · Freezes
Preparation: 20 minutes · Cooking: 30 minutes in a 375° oven

This dish may also be made with spinach noodles.

6 quarts boiling salted water
1 8-oz. package elbow macaroni

In the water, cook the macaroni, uncovered, for 8 to 10 minutes, or until it is just tender. Drain it in a colander and rinse it under running hot water; drain again well. In a baking dish, arrange the pasta.

4 tablespoons butter
4 tablespoons flour
½ teaspoon dry mustard
3 cups milk
Salt
Pepper
Worcestershire sauce
1 onion, grated
2 cups (8 oz.) sharp Cheddar, grated

Heat the butter in a saucepan and in it, over gentle heat, cook the flour, stirring, for a few minutes. Stir in the mustard. Gradually add the milk, stirring constantly until the mixture is thickened and smooth. Season the sauce to taste with salt, pepper, and Worcestershire sauce; add the onion and then the cheese, stirring until the cheese is melted.

⅓ cup bread crumbs, toasted in butter (optional)

Pour the sauce over the pasta. With a fork, stir the ingredients gently. If desired, sprinkle the dish with the bread crumbs.

At this point you may stop and continue later.

Bake the macaroni at 375° for 30 minutes.

Macaroni and Cheese with Ham: For a more festive recipe, follow the Basic Recipe for Macaroni and Cheese, above, adding ½ to ¾ cup cooked ham, diced, to the cooked pasta just before the cheese sauce is added. Proceed with the recipe as directed.

Macaroni and Cheese with Sausage: Roll 1 lb. sausage meat into small balls; in a skillet, evenly brown them. Drain them on absorbent paper and reserve them. Discard all but 2 tablespoons of the fat; in the fat, cook 2 onions, chopped, until translucent. Prepare the macaroni as in the basic recipe, page 264. In the baking dish, arrange one-half of the prepared pasta, then a layer of all of the sausage balls, top them with the onion, and add a layer of the remaining macaroni. Prepare the sauce and proceed with the recipe as directed.

Macaroni Greek Style

Serves 6 · Doubles · Refrigerates
Preparation: 20 minutes

To be served as an accompaniment to a roast or stew.

1   1-lb. box macaroni, cooked *al dente* in lightly salted water, according to the directions on the package, rinsed in a colander under running hot water, and drained well

½   lb. Feta, crumbled

8   tablespoons sweet butter, melted and cooked until golden over gentle heat

In a large mixing bowl, using 2 forks, toss together the macaroni, Feta, and butter.

1   cup (4 oz.) Kefalotyri, grated

On a large, deep-sided serving platter, arrange a ring of the macaroni. (Into the center, ladle the hot stew; or serve the macaroni separately.) Offer the grated cheese in a side dish.

Macaroni or Noodles
with Ricotta Sauce I

Serves 6 · Doubles · Refrigerates
Preparation: 25 minutes

An agreeable luncheon dish from the Rome-Lazio area, popular with children.

1   1-lb. package macaroni, cooked *al dente* in boiling salted water according to the directions on the package

While the pasta is cooking, prepare the sauce.

1   cup (4 oz.) Ricotta, at room temperature
⅓   cup hot milk
2   tablespoons honey
½   teaspoon cinnamon or nutmeg
½   teaspoon salt

In the container of an electric blender, combine these five ingredients and, on medium speed, whirl them until the mixture is homogenous.

Drain the macaroni, rinse under hot running water, and drain again well. In a large heated serving bowl, combine the pasta and the sauce; using two forks, gently toss them until the macaroni is well coated.

Ricotta Sauce II: in place of step 2 as directed, combine ½ cup (2 oz.) Parmesan, grated, ½ cup parsley, chopped; reserve the mixture. In the top of a double-boiler, combine and heat over hot water 8 oz. Ricotta and 1 cup heavy cream. Toss the cooked pasta with the reserved Parmesan mixture and the Ricotta mixture; add a generous grating of pepper.

Macaroni or Noodles with Feta: follow step 1 as directed; in step 2, omit all the ingredients and substitute with 2 cups (8 oz.) Feta, crumbled, and cooked for 2 minutes in 4 tablespoons melted sweet butter. In step 3, add 1 teaspoon paprika before tossing the pasta with the Feta.

Macaroni or Noodles with Cottage Cheese: follow step 1 as directed; in step 2, combine and blend well 6 scallions, chopped, with as much green as possible, 1½ cups cottage cheese (not cream-style), 2 cups sour cream, 1 teaspoon salt, and a generous grating of pepper; with this sauce, toss the cooked pasta; into a lightly buttered baking dish, spoon the mixture, top it with 1 cup butter-toasted bread crumbs mixed with ½ cup (2 oz.) Parmesan, grated; bake the dish at 350° for 30 minutes, or until the crumb mixture is browned.

Edward Giobbi's Macaroni with Ricotta

Serves 6 to 8 · Refrigerates
Preparation: 25 minutes · Cooking: 25 minutes in a 350° oven

The preparation time does not include readying the marinara sauce, which is always a pleasant adjunct to Italian cheese dishes.

2 10-oz. packages frozen chopped spinach, fully thawed to room temperature and pressed dry in a colander 1 lb. Ricotta, at room temperature ½ cup (2 oz.) Parmesan, crumbled ⅓ cup parsley, chopped 2 tablespoons salt Generous grating of pepper	In a large mixing bowl, combine and blend well these six ingredients.
3 to 4 cups Marinara Sauce, page 355	To the Ricotta mixture, add the marinara sauce and blend well.
1 1-lb. package macaroni or other tubular pasta cooked for 3 minutes in boiling salted water, drained, rinsed in a colander under running hot water, and drained again well	Add the Ricotta mixture to the pasta and, using two forks, toss the mixture.
¼ cup (1 oz.) Parmesan, grated	In a baking dish, arrange the pasta and its sauce. Over the top, sprinkle the grated cheese.

*At this point you may stop and con-
tinue later.*

Bake the dish, uncovered, at 350° for
25 minutes.

Spinach Lasagne: Follow step 1 as directed; in step 2, prepare and
reserve the sauce. In step 3, use 1 lb. *lasagne*, cooked, in a lightly oiled
baking dish, arrange a layer of one-third of the *lasagne* and over it spread
one-half of the Ricotta mixture; repeat, ending with a layer of *lasagne*.
Over the top, spread 1 cup Marinara Sauce, page 355, and a sprinkling
of Parmesan, grated. Bake the dish at 400° for 15 minutes, or until it is
thoroughly heated.

Sausage Lasagne (a Neapolitan specialty): Follow step 1 as directed,
substituting 2 eggs, lightly beaten, in place of the spinach. Prepare Marinara Sauce, page 355, but do not add it to the Ricotta mixture. Brown ½
lb. Italian sweet sausage meat; drain it on absorbent paper. In step 3, use
1 lb. *lasagne*, cooked; with a little of the sausage fat, grease a 12x14-inch
baking dish; in it, arrange one-third of the *lasagne*. Over the *lasagne*,
arrange one-half of the sausage meat. Over it, spread one-half of the
Ricotta mixture. Repeat the layers, ending with a layer of *lasagne*. Over
the top, spoon 3 cups Marinara Sauce. Add a layer of ½ lb. Mozzarella,
sliced. Bake the dish at 375° for 45 minutes.

Green Noodles with Cottage Cheese

Serves 6 · Doubles · Refrigerates
Preparation: 30 minutes · Cooking: 30 minutes in a 350° oven

The original recipe from Russia uses white noodles. I find green, or spinach, noodles visually more appealing.

6 slices bacon, diced, rendered until crisp, and drained on absorbent paper (reserve the bacon fat)

8 oz. green noodles, cooked *al dente* in boiling salted water and drained well in a colander

While the bacon and noodles are cooking, prepare the sauce.

2 eggs
2 cups cottage cheese
¼ cup milk
1 onion, grated
1 teaspoon salt
¼ teaspoon white pepper

In a mixing bowl, beat the eggs lightly. Add the remaining five ingredients and blend them well.

2 tablespoons bacon fat

In a large mixing bowl, combine the drained noodles and the bacon fat. Using two forks, gently toss the noodles.

To the noodles, add the cottage cheese mixture and the cooked bacon. Using two forks, gently toss the mixture once again.

Bread crumbs toasted in butter (optional)

In a buttered 2-quart casserole, arrange the noodles. If desired, garnish them with bread crumbs.

At this point you may stop and continue later.

Bake the noodles, uncovered, at 350° for 30 minutes.

Spaghetti *Carbonara*

Serves 6 · Doubles
Preparation: 30 minutes

½ lb. thick-sliced bacon, diced

In a skillet, render the bacon until crisp. With a slotted spoon, remove it to absorbent paper and reserve it. Discard all but 3 tablespoons of the fat.

2 onions, chopped
½ cup *prosciutto* or cooked ham, finely chopped
½ cup parsley, chopped
2 cups (8 oz.) Fontina, diced
Generous grinding of pepper

In the reserved fat, cook the onion until translucent. Replace the bacon and add the *prosciutto*, parsley, cheese, and pepper. Over gentle heat, cook the mixture, stirring constantly, for 5 minutes, or until the cheese is nearly melted.

1 1-lb. package spaghetti, cooked *al dente* in salted water as directed on the package, rinsed in a colander under running hot water, and drained well
4 eggs, lightly beaten

In a large serving bowl, using two forks, gently toss the pasta and eggs. Add the meat mixture and toss the pasta again.

Grated Parmesan cheese

Serve the dish at once accompanied by a generous bowl of the grated cheese.

Polenta

Serves 6 · Doubles · Refrigerates · Freezes
Preparation: 1 hour · Cooking: 25 minutes in a 400° oven

Polenta, known to Caesar's legions, is a healthy and delicious dish, enhanced by the addition of cheese.

2½ cups water 1 teaspoon salt	In the top of a double-boiler, over direct heat, bring the water to the boil. Add the salt.
1 cup yellow cornmeal 1½ cups cold water	Mix together the cornmeal and cold water. Add the mixture to the boiling water, stirring. When the water returns to the boil, place the double-boiler over simmering water and cook the *polenta,* stirring it occasionally, for 45 minutes.
2 cups (8 oz.) Fontina, shredded, *or* 1 cup (4 oz.) Gorgonzola, crumbled *or* ¾ cup (3 oz.) Parmesan, grated 4 tablespoons butter, melted	Into a lightly buttered 9-inch baking dish, evenly spoon the *polenta.* Over it, sprinkle the cheese and melted butter.
	At this point you may stop and continue later.
	Bake the dish at 400° for 25 minutes, or until the cheese is melted and the *polenta* is golden.

Polenta with Sausage: brown 1 lb. sweet Italian sausage meat, crumbling it so that it cooks evenly; with a slotted spoon, remove it to absorbent paper and reserve it. Discard all but 2 tablespoons of the fat. In the fat, cook 2 onions, chopped, until translucent. To the onion, add 1 clove garlic, finely chopped, one 1-lb. can Italian tomatoes, one 1-lb. can tomato sauce, 1 bay leaf, ¼ teaspoon pepper, and ¾ teaspoon salt. Simmer the sauce, uncovered, for 1 hour; add the reserved sausage and continue to cook the sauce for 30 minutes. Over the prepared *polenta*, spoon the sausage mixture, sprinkle the dish with either Fontina or Parmesan; omit the melted butter. Bake the *polenta* as directed above.

Linguine with Four Cheeses: Italy

Serves 6 · Doubles
Preparation: 30 minutes

I first ate this delectable dish at one of Capri's enchanting restaurants, having just visited Anacapri and St. Michele; the dish and the sojourn are experiences I shall never forget.

1   cup milk
1   teaspoon cornstarch
8   oz. sweet butter
¼   cup (1 oz.) Fontina, diced
¼   cup (1 oz.) Gruyère, diced
¼   cup (1 oz.) Provolone, diced

Add the milk to the cornstarch and stir until smooth. In a saucepan, heat the butter and to it add the cornstarch mixture, stirring constantly until the mixture is smooth and slightly thickened. Off heat or over very low heat, add the cheeses, and stir constantly until they are nearly melted.

1   lb. *linguine,* cooked *al dente* according to the directions on the package, rinsed in a colander under hot running water, and drained well
4   tablespoons soft sweet butter
1   cup (4 oz.) Cacciocavallo, grated

In a warmed serving bowl, combine the pasta and the butter. Using two forks, toss the *linguine* until the butter is melted. Pour over the cheese sauce and toss the mixture again. Serve the *linguine* accompanied by the Cacciocavallo and a pepper grinder.

The dish may also be made with macaroni—and with any combination of cheeses that strikes your fancy.

Linguine Toasted with Cheese

Serves 6
Preparation: 20 minutes · Cooking: 10 minutes

A contribution from Gaspero del Corso, the epicure director—owner of Rome's modern art gallery, the Galleria Obelisco.

1   lb. *linguine,* cooked according to the package directions and drained well

6   tablespoons soft butter

½   cup (2 oz.) Parmesan, grated

In a large mixing bowl, using two forks, gently toss the *linguine* with the butter and cheese.

Divide the pasta into two equal portions. In an ovenproof serving dish, keep one-half warm.

3   tablespoons butter

3   tablespoons olive oil

In a skillet, over high heat, combine the butter and olive oil and, when the mixture smokes slightly, toast the second portion of *linguine.* As they become crisp, chop them small to make "croutons."

Parmesan cheese, grated

Toss the toasted *linguine* with the reserved pasta and serve at once with additional cheese.

Pasta *alla* Caprese

Serves 6 · Doubles · Refrigerates
Preparation: 30 minutes

A dish from Capri.

¼ cup olive oil
3 large ripe tomatoes, peeled, seeded, and chopped
½ teaspoon salt

In a skillet, heat the oil and in it simmer the tomatoes, seasoned, for 15 minutes, uncovered.

1 lb. pasta, cooked *al dente* according to the directions on the package, rinsed in a colander under hot running water, and drained again well.

While the tomatoes are simmering, cook the pasta and prepare the fish mixture.

3 teaspoons anchovy paste
1 3½-oz. can tuna, drained
8 black, seedless olives
Olive oil

In a mortar, combine the anchovy paste and tuna and grind them until they are well blended. Add the olives and grind them into the fish. Force the mixture through a sieve to assure its smoothness and add sufficient olive oil to yield a paste.

1 cup (4 oz.) Mozzarella, diced

To the tomatoes, add the fish mixture and the cheese. Over gentle heat, cook the sauce, stirring, until the cheese is nearly melted.

In a large warm serving bowl, combine the pasta and the sauce. Using two forks, gently toss the pasta to coat it well. Serve the dish accompanied by a well-disciplined pepper grinder.

Pasta with Cheese

Serves 6
Preparation: 15 minutes · Cooking: 12 minutes

6 quarts rapidly boiling salted water
1 lb. pasta of your choice (spaghetti, *linguine*, noodles, green noodles, etc.)

In the boiling water, cook the pasta, stirring it often with a fork to prevent its sticking together. Follow the directions on the package; do not overcook the pasta. Drain the pasta in a colander and rinse off the excess starch with very hot (preferably boiling) water and drain again very well. While the pasta is cooking, grate the cheese.

8 tablespoons sweet butter, at room temperature (very soft) *or* ½ cup fine olive oil
1½ cups (6 oz.) freshly grated Parmesan, Romano, or other hard grating cheese of your choice

Add the butter or olive oil to the pasta and, using two forks, gently toss. Add the cheese and toss gently. Serve the pasta at once, accompanied by additional grated cheese and a well-filled pepper mill.

There are more complicated cheese and pasta dishes, but there is none better. For a main dish serving, increase the pasta to 1½ lbs. for 6 persons; augment the other ingredients proportionately.

The dish may be varied without loss of its genial simplicity:
(1) cook 9 cloves of garlic, peeled and chopped, for 5 minutes in the butter or oil; proceed as directed, including the cooked garlic as an ingredient of the sauce. This variation is perhaps my favorite.
(2) for those who want only a hint of garlic, cook 4 cloves of garlic, quartered, in the water with the pasta; remove the garlic quarters and proceed as directed.
(3) in the butter or oil, cook for 5 minutes 8 scallions, chopped, with as much green as possible; proceed as directed.

(4) for those who want a stronger taste of cheese, increase the quantity to 2 cups (8 oz.).

(5) for a mild but pleasant dish, melt 8 tablespoons butter and, in the container of an electric blender, combine it with 1 cup Ricotta or cottage cheese, whirling the ingredients on medium speed to homogenize them. Pour the sauce over the rinsed pasta and toss it gently. A generous grating of nutmeg enhances this dish.

Potatoes *Dauphinois:* France

Serves 6 · Refrigerates
Preparation: 25 minutes · Cooking: 30 minutes in a 425° oven

This classic from French cuisine is very rich and very good. Not for calorie-counters, however!

6   medium-sized "boiling" potatoes, pared and cut into ⅛-inch rounds
2   cloves garlic, finely chopped
Nutmeg
Salt
Pepper
Butter
2   cups light cream
1   cup (4 oz.) Gruyère, grated

In a buttered casserole, arrange the potatoes in layers; season each layer with a little garlic, nutmeg, salt, and pepper; dot each layer with butter. Over the layers, pour the cream; allow it to settle (it should reach just to the top of the layers). Add the cheese.

At this point you may stop and continue later.

Bake the potatoes at 425° for 30 minutes, or until they are tender.

Potatoes with Provolone: Prepare the potatoes as directed. Prepare 1 cup of Béchamel Sauce, page 347; to it, add 1 cup white wine, a pinch of oregano, and 1 cup (4 oz.) smoked Provolone, diced; stir the sauce until the cheese is melted. Layer the potatoes as directed; over each layer, spread a little of the sauce; top with any remaining sauce. Bake the potatoes as directed.

Potatoes with Cottage Cheese or Ricotta: Prepare the potatoes as directed. In the container of an electric blender, combine 2 cups large-curd cottage cheese (or Ricotta), 1 cup milk, 2 cloves garlic, chopped, 6 scallions, chopped, and 1 teaspoon salt; on medium speed, whirl the mixture until it is smooth. Layer the potatoes as directed; over each layer pour a little of the cheese mixture; top with any remaining sauce. Over all, sprinkle 1 cup (4 oz.) Cheddar, grated. Bake the potatoes as directed.

Potato Dumplings Parmesan

Serves 6 · Refrigerates
Preparation: 3 hours · Cooking: 10 minutes

Gnocchi di patate Parmigiano is a delicious Italian dish which I like to serve as a first course. This recipe is my version of one given me by my neighbor Edward Giobbi, the painter and author of *Italian Family Cooking*.

4 large baking potatoes, unpeeled
Boiling salted water

Cook the potatoes in the water to cover for 40 minutes, or until they are very tender. Drain, cool, peel, and mash them until they are of very smooth consistency.

2 eggs
1 small onion, grated

To the potatoes, add the eggs and onion; beat the mixture thoroughly.

2 cups flour
1 teaspoon salt
1 teaspoon baking powder
½ cup (2 oz.) Parmesan, grated

In a mixing bowl, sift together the dry ingredients. Gradually add them to the potato mixture, blending well.

On a floured surface, knead the dough until smooth (it will be sticky). Form it into a ball, wrap it in plastic wrap, and refrigerate it for at least 2 hours.

At this point you may stop and continue later.

4 quarts gently boiling salted water	With a teaspoon form little dumplings of the dough. Drop them into the boiling water; take care that the water does not stop boiling. Cook the *gnocchi* for 4 minutes; they will float to the surface when done. With a slotted spoon remove them to absorbent paper; then arrange them in an ovenproof dish and keep them warm.
4 to 8 tablespoons sweet butter, melted Freshly grated Parmesan	When all the dumplings are cooked, pour the melted butter over them and sprinkle them generously with the cheese. When serving, accompany them with additional grated cheese.

Ricotta and Spinach Dumplings (a variation of the recipe above, this one is a specialty of Teresa Carducci, a good friend in Rome): in a mixing bowl, blend 1 lb. Ricotta with one 10-oz. package frozen chopped spinach, fully thawed to room temperature and pressed dry in a colander, 1 small onion, grated, 2 eggs, well beaten, 1 cup (4 oz.) Parmesan, grated, ½ teaspoon salt, and ¼ teaspoon pepper. Add and blend in 1¼ cups flour (the dough will be sticky). On a floured board, pat out the dough to a thickness of ½ inch and cut it into 1-inch rounds. In lightly salted, gently boiling water, cook the dumplings for 4 minutes; they will float to the surface when done. With a slotted spoon, remove them to absorbent paper; then arrange them in a warm ovenproof dish. Over them, pour sweet butter, melted, and serve them with additional grated Parmesan.

Potato Pie

Serves 6 · Doubles · Refrigerates
Preparation: 50 minutes · Cooking: 25 minutes in a 400° oven

6 medium-sized potatoes, cooked in boiling water for 20 minutes, or until tender, peeled, and mashed
4 tablespoons butter, softened
2 eggs, well beaten
¼ cup parsley, finely chopped
Salt
Pepper

Into the mashed potatoes, stir the butter; add the eggs and parsley. Season the potatoes to taste.

½ lb. Mozzarella, sliced

Into a buttered baking dish, evenly spoon the mashed potatoes. Over them, arrange one-half of the Mozzarella slices.

3 large ripe tomatoes, peeled, seeded, and chopped
Oregano
Salt
Pepper
¼ cup (1 oz.) Parmesan, grated

Over the cheese, spread the tomato. Season the dish to taste. Add the remaining Mozzarella slices. Over the top, sprinkle the Parmesan.

At this point you may stop and continue later.

Bake the dish at 400° for 25 minutes, or until the cheese is melted and the top is golden.

Potato Puff: Follow step 1 as directed, using only 2 egg yolks in place of the whole eggs and adding to the potatoes ¼ cup heavy cream and ½ cup cottage cheese; beat the potatoes until they are light. Beat 2 egg whites until they are stiff; fold them into the potato mixture. Omit steps 2 and 3. Bake the potato puff as directed.

Baked Potatoes with Cheese

Serves 6 · Doubles · Refrigerates
Preparation: 1 hour · Cooking: 15 minutes in a 400° oven

3   large baking potatoes, scrubbed, rubbed with soft butter, and baked at 450° for 40 minutes, or until they are fork-tender

Cut the baked potatoes in lengthwise halves. Remove the pulp and reserve the shells. In a mixing bowl, using a potato masher, mash the pulp until it is smooth.

2   cups (8 oz.) Cheddar, grated
½   cup sour cream
1   teaspoon salt
½   teaspoon pepper

To the potato pulp, add these four ingredients and beat the mixture until it is smooth.

½   cup (2 oz.) Cheddar, grated

Mound the reserved potato shells with the potato-cheese mixture. Sprinkle them with the grated cheese. Arrange them in a lightly buttered baking dish.

At this point you may stop and continue later.

Cook the potatoes at 400° for 15 minutes, or until they are golden brown.

If desired, 1 cup (4 oz.) crumbled blue cheese may be used in place of the Cheddar; or 2 cups (8 oz.) grated Gruyère or Jarlsberg; or 1 cup (4 oz.) grated Parmesan.

Cream-style cottage cheese may be used in place of the sour cream.

Six scallions, finely minced, may be added to the potato stuffing.

Scalloped Potatoes

Serves 6 to 8 · Doubles · Refrigerates · Freezes
Preparation: 30 minutes · Cooking: 45 minutes in a 350° oven

¼ cup milk
2 cups cream-style cottage cheese
1 onion, coarsely chopped
1 clove garlic, coarsely chopped
½ teaspoon celery salt
¾ teaspoon salt

In the container of an electric blender, combine these six ingredients. On medium speed, whirl them until the mixture is smooth.

½ cup parsley, finely chopped
1 cup (4 oz.) cheese of your choice (Baronet, Monterey), shredded

In a mixing bowl, combine the parsley and cheese. Add the contents of the blender container and stir to blend the sauce well.

12 "new" potatoes (about 2¼ lbs.), peeled, quartered lengthwise, and sliced

As you prepare the potatoes, add them to the sauce to prevent their darkening.

Into a lightly buttered casserole, spoon the potatoes. Bake them, covered, at 350° for 15 minutes; remove the cover and continue to bake them for 30 minutes, or until they are tender.

This dish may be made with 6 medium-sized boiling potatoes. Cook them in their skins for 20 minutes, or until they are just tender. While they are cooking, prepare the sauce. Peel and cut the potatoes as directed. Follow the remaining steps of the recipe as directed; bake the dish for 30 minutes, uncovered, in a 350° oven.

Rice

Rice, that most nutritious, least fattening of the farinaceous foods, lends itself willingly and delectably to the addition of cheese. Everyone has his favorite method of cooking rice; in my case, I "toast" briefly 1½ cups raw natural rice in 1½ tablespoons melted butter and then add 3 cups water in which 3 chicken bouillon cubes are dissolved. The toasting tends to keep the grains separate while cooking. Raw natural rice requires about 15 minutes to cook, covered, at the simmer; when the grains are tender and the liquid is absorbed, the rise is done. Brown rice will require about 50 minutes to cook.

Cheese goes equally well with brown rice. No, it goes better—because brown rice, in my opinion, *is* better than polished white rice. In *risottos* it holds its texture, has a more distinctive flavor, *and* it is more nutritious. Brown rice is, of course, only unpolished white rice. Or, to state the matter another way, white rice is only brown rice with its coat removed. For better-tasting rice dishes, with a more pleasing texture and greater nutritive value, use brown rice; I believe you will enjoy it.

Rice with Gorgonzola: To 1½ cups cooked rice, add ¾ cup (3 oz.) Gorgonzola which has been crumbled and melted in ¼ cup hot milk; using two forks, gently toss the rice.

Rice with Swiss Cheese (one of my favorites): In a saucepan, combine 2 tablespoons butter, ¼ cup milk, and ½ cup (2 oz.) Emmenthaler or Gruyère; over gentle heat, cook the mixture, stirring constantly, until the cheese is melted; pour the sauce over the cooked rice and, using two forks, toss the mixture to blend it well. For an added fillip, offer grated Parmesan separately.

Rice with Four Cheeses: Follow the directions for *Linguine* with Four Cheeses, page 273; in step 1, use only 4 tablespoons butter and only ½ cup milk; omit the cornstarch altogether. In step 2, omit the butter.

Rice with Cheese and Lemon: Over the hot cooked rice in its cooking utensil, pour 3 tablespoons melted butter; in a separate mixing bowl, beat 3 eggs lightly; to them add 1 cup (4 oz.) Parmesan, grated, the juice of 1 lemon, and a generous grinding of pepper. Add this mixture to the rice and, using two forks, gently toss the ingredients to blend them well. Over gentle heat, heat the rice, stirring constantly, for 3 minutes, or until the egg just begins to cook.

Risotto Milanese (a classic Italian dish): Cook the rice in chicken broth; when it is cooked, add ¼ teaspoon saffron (which has been crumbled into 1 tablespoon hot water), 4 tablespoons soft butter, and ¼ cup (1 oz.) Parmesan, grated; using two forks, gently toss the rice.

Risotto Italiano (more flavorful): When toasting the rice, use equal parts butter and olive oil to which are added 1 onion, finely chopped, 1 clove garlic, finely chopped, ¼ cup parsley, chopped, and 6 anchovy filets, finely chopped; as the cooking liquid, use equal parts chicken broth and white wine. Using two forks, toss the cooked rice with ¾ cup (3 oz.) Parmesan, grated.

Chicken Giblet Risotto (with a generous salad, a one-dish meal): Use brown rice; add to the rice while cooking, 1 lb. chicken giblets, trimmed of any fat and gristle and diced; as the cooking liquid, use equal parts chicken broth and white wine. While the rice is cooking, sauté 2 onions, chopped, in 2 tablespoons butter. When the rice is cooked, using two forks, toss it with the onion, ½ cup (2 oz.) Parmesan, grated, and a generous grinding of pepper.

Mushroom Risotto: In ¼ cup olive oil, cook 1 clove garlic, split, until the oil is flavored; discard the garlic. To the oil, add ½ lb. mushrooms, sliced, and ¼ cup parsley, chopped, and cook them for 5 minutes. In a flame-proof casserole, heat 4 tablespoons butter and in it cook 1 onion, chopped, until it is translucent. Add 1½ cups raw natural rice and toast it, stirring to coat each grain. Cook the rice as suggested on page 284. When it is readied, using two forks, toss it with the mushrooms and ½ cup (2 oz.) Parmesan, grated.

Riso Arrosto alla Genovese (another Italian *risotto*): Roll into small balls 1 lb. sweet Italian sausage meat; render them until they are golden; drain them on absorbent paper. Discard all but 2 tablespoons of the fat; in it, cook 2 onions, chopped, until translucent. Add ½ lb. mushrooms, sliced, and cook them until they are wilted. In a large mixing bowl, toss together 1½ cups raw natural rice, cooked, the sausage balls, the onion and mushroom mixture, one 9-oz. package frozen small peas, one 9-oz. package artichoke hearts, both thawed to room temperature, and 1 cup (4 oz.) *grana* of your choice. Spoon the mixture into a lightly oiled casserole or large ovenproof dish and bake the *risotto,* covered, at 350° for 30 minutes. This recipe serves 8 to 10 persons and is especially good for buffet suppers.

Risotto Neapolitan: Toss the cooked rice with ½ lb. veal scallops, diced, ½ lb. chicken livers, coarsely chopped, 3 tomatoes, peeled, seeded, and chopped, ½ lb. mushrooms, coarsely chopped, and ½ lb. Mozzarella, diced. Season the mixture to taste with a little oregano, salt and pepper; spoon it into a lightly oiled ovenproof dish, and bake the *risotto,* covered, at 350° for 30 minutes. Like *Riso Arrosto alla Genovese,* above, this dish serves 8 to 10 persons and is very practical for buffet suppers.

Baked Rice in Swiss Style: Cook 1½ cups raw natural rice in salted water for 8 minutes; drain it and toss it with ¾ cup (3 oz.) Sbrinz, grated. In a mixing bowl, beat together 2 eggs, 1 cup milk, and 1 cup white wine; season to taste with salt and pepper and fold the mixture into the rice. Spoon the mixture into a deep, lightly buttered baking dish. Over the top, sprinkle additional grated Sbrinz. Bake the dish at 300° for 40 minutes, or until the rice is tender.

Rice and Peas: Italy

Serves 6 · Doubles · Refrigerates · Freezes
Preparation: 25 minutes

Risi e bisi was traditionally served at the Venetian Doges' Feast of St. Mark.

1   cup raw natural rice
2   tablespoons butter
1   10½-oz. can condensed chicken broth, plus water to equal 2 cups

In a saucepan, combine the rice and butter and, over gentle heat, stir the rice until the butter is melted and each grain is coated. Add the chicken broth mixture, bring the liquid to the boil, reduce the heat, and simmer the rice, covered, for 15 minutes, or until the rice is tender and the liquid is absorbed.

3   strips bacon, diced
3   scallions, chopped, with as much green as possible (1 onion, chopped, may be used, if desired)

Meanwhile, in a skillet, render the bacon until it is crisp; remove it to absorbent paper and reserve it. In the bacon fat, cook the scallions until they are limp.

1   10-oz. package frozen small peas, thawed
¼   cup water

To the scallions, add the peas and water. Bring the liquid to the boil, reduce the heat, and simmer the peas for 5 minutes, or until they are just tender.

½   cup (2 oz.) Parmesan, grated

In a large serving bowl, combine the hot rice, the reserved bacon, the contents of the skillet, and the cheese. Using two forks, gently toss the ingredients until they are well blended.

To vary your favorite recipe for *paella Valenciana:* just before serving sprinkle the dish with ¾ cup (3 oz.) Edam or Gouda, shredded.

SALADS

Apple and Orange Salad

Serves 6 · Doubles · Refrigerates
Preparation: 25 minutes

4 apples, peeled, cored, and diced
Juice of 1 lemon

Pour the lemon juice into a container with a tight-fitting lid. As each apple is diced, add the pieces to the covered container and shake well so that the dices will be coated with the lemon juice.

2 oranges, sliced paper thin, seeded, and quartered

Prepare the oranges and reserve them.

⅓ cup mayonnaise
⅓ cup plain yogurt

In a mixing bowl, blend together the mayonnaise and yogurt.

8-oz. Gouda, diced
Salad greens

To the mayonnaise mixture, add the apples and lemon juice, the oranges, and the cheese. Gently stir the salad to blend it well. Serve it on greens of your choice.

Avocado and Watercress Ring

Serves 6 · Doubles · Refrigerates
Preparation: 30 minutes · Chilling time: at least 3 hours

The recipe may also be made with arugola (rocket), trimmed of its heavy stems, in place of the watercress.

1 packet unflavored gelatin ¼ cup cold water	In the top of a double-boiler, sprinkle the gelatin over the cold water. Set it aside while you prepare the next step.
2 3-oz. packages cream cheese, at room temperature 1 cup milk ½ cup cream-style cottage cheese 1 teaspoon salt	In the container of an electric blender, combine the cream cheese, milk, cottage cheese, and salt. Whirl them on medium speed until the mixture is smooth.
2 large ripe avocados, peeled and coarsely chopped ¼ cup lemon juice	To the contents of the blender container, add the avocado and whirl it until the mixture is smooth. Add the lemon juice and whirl the mixture once more. Over boiling water, dissolve the gelatin. Add it to the contents of the blender and whirl the mixture to homogenize it.
1 bunch watercress, washed, the woody stems removed	To the contents of the blender, add the watercress and, on low speed, whirl it only enough to chop it. Pour the mixture into an oiled ring mold. Chill it for at least 3 hours.
Salad greens	Unmold the ring on a bed of salad greens.

Suggested filling

Fill the center with chicken salad to which seedless grapes, stemmed, rinsed, and halved lengthwise, have been added. Or with tuna fish salad. Or fruit salad. Or shrimp salad.

Caesar Salad

Serves 6 · Doubles · Refrigerates
Preparation: 20 minutes

Juice of 1 lemon
1   egg
1   clove garlic
¼   cup olive oil
½   teaspoon oregano
½   teaspoon salt
Grinding of pepper

In the container of an electric blender, combine these seven ingredients and, on medium speed, whirl them for 15 seconds, or until the mixture is smooth.

¼   cup (1 oz.) Parmesan, grated

Add the cheese and whirl it to homogenize the mixture.

6   strips bacon, diced

In a skillet, render the bacon until crisp; remove it to absorbent paper and reserve it.

2   large heads romaine, cut in 1-inch slices
½   cup unflavored croutons

In a large salad bowl, combine the romaine and the cheese dressing. Toss the salad. Garnish it with the reserved bacon and croutons.

If desired, 1 can anchovy filets may be used in place of the bacon. Add the anchovies and their oil to the ingredients of step 1; omit the salt. Their stronger taste will make a totally different kind of Caesar salad. I prefer the bacon, but sometimes a change is pleasant. Also, more cheese may be added, to taste.

Kidney Bean Salad

Serves 6 to 8 · Doubles · Refrigerates
Preparation: 15 minutes

1   20-oz. can white
    kidney beans, rinsed
    and drained
1   20-oz. can red kidney
    beans, rinsed and
    drained
1   red onion, chopped
½   green pepper,
    chopped
1½ cups celery, chopped
2   cups (8 oz.) sharp
    Cheddar, diced

In a salad bowl, combine these six ingredients.

¾   cup mayonnaise
2   tablespoons lemon
    juice
1   teaspoon Dijon-style
    mustard
Salt
Grinding of pepper

In a mixing bowl, combine the mayonnaise, lemon juice, and mustard. Blend the ingredients well; adjust the seasoning to taste with salt and pepper.

Pour the dressing over the contents of the salad bowl and, using two forks, toss the salad gently.

Green Bean Salad

Serves 6 · Doubles · Refrigerates
Preparation: 30 minutes · Chilling time: 2 hours

The addition of *fresh* summer savory is a delightful accent.

1½ lbs. green beans, trimmed, rinsed, and cooked until just tender in boiling salted water (about 10 minutes)

As soon as the beans are tender-crisp, drain them through a colander and plunge them into cold water. When they have cooled, drain them thoroughly and chill them for at least 2 hours.

1 onion, grated
⅓ cup olive oil
3 tablespoons lemon juice
½ cup (2 oz.) Parmesan, grated
½ teaspoon salt
Grinding of pepper

Meanwhile, make the dressing: In a jar with a tight-fitting lid, combine these six ingredients and shake them vigorously.

In a salad bowl, arrange the beans, over them pour the dressing, and toss them gently.

If desired, to the dressing may be added 1 clove garlic, put through a press. More cheese may be added, depending upon your taste. Also, lemon juice may be added, to taste.

Chickpea Salad

Serves 6 · Doubles · Refrigerates
Preparation: 15 minutes

Served with good pumpernickel and cold beer, this dish makes a fine summer supper.

2   20-oz. cans chickpeas, rinsed and drained

½   lb. sharp cheese of your choice, diced

2   large red onions, thinly sliced and separated into rings

In a salad bowl, combine these three ingredients.

⅔   cup olive oil

⅓   cup lemon juice

1   teaspoon ground coriander

1   teaspoon sugar

1¼   teaspoons salt

Grinding of pepper

In the container of an electric blender, combine these six ingredients and, on medium speed, whirl them for 15 seconds (or combine the ingredients in a jar with a tight-fitting lid and shake them vigorously until the mixture is homogenous).

Pour the dressing over the contents of the bowl and toss the salad.

Salad Mold

Serves 6 · Doubles · Refrigerates
Preparation: 35 minutes · Chilling time: at least 3 hours

½ cup cold water
1 envelope unflavored gelatin

In the top of a double-boiler, sprinkle the gelatin over the cold water; allow it to soften and, over boiling water, dissolve it.

1 8-oz. package cream cheese, at room temperature
¼ cup light cream
½ cup (2 oz.) mild Cheddar, grated
Salt

In a mixing bowl, using a fork, whip the cream cheese and the cream until the mixture is homogenous. Stir in the Cheddar. Add salt to taste.

1 cup heavy cream, whipped

Into the cheese mixture, stir the dissolved gelatin; fold in the whipped cream. Into a ring mold, pour the mixture and chill it for at least 3 hours.

Salad greens

Unmold the salad onto salad greens of your choice. Serve the salad with vinaigrette dressing.

Potato Salad

Serves 6 · Doubles · Refrigerates
Preparation: 40 minutes

4 large potatoes, boiled until tender, peeled, cooled, and diced

While the potatoes are cooking, prepare the other ingredients.

½ lb. bacon, diced
6 hard-cooked eggs
1 cup mayonnaise
Lemon juice

In a skillet, render the bacon until crisp; drain it on absorbent paper. Peel and chop the eggs. Season the mayonnaise with lemon juice to taste.

At this point you may stop and continue later.

6 large ribs celery, diced
1 bunch scallions, chopped
2 cups (8 oz.) Emmenthaler, diced
½ cup parsley, chopped
Salt
Pepper

In a large mixing bowl, combine the first four ingredients. Add the dressing and, using two forks, gently toss the mixture to blend it well. Adjust the seasoning with salt and pepper, to taste.

Salad greens of your choice
3 tomatoes, cut into wedges

On a serving platter, arrange a bed of salad greens. On them, spoon six equal portions of the potato mixture. Garnish the salad with tomato wedges.

Greek Salad

Serves 6 · Doubles · Refrigerates
Preparation: 20 minutes

This traditional salad was my daily lunch when I sailed from Greek island to island on an old-fashioned ketch. Greek tomatoes are, I feel, unequaled anywhere, and Feta has ever since been a favorite.

3 tomatoes, each cut into eight wedges 1 cucumber, peeled and cut in ¼-inch slices 1 green pepper, cut in ¼-inch julienne 2 sweet onions, thinly sliced and separated into rings 12 radishes Anchovies (optional) 12 to 18 oil-cured olives	On a serving platter, arrange all of the ingredients.
1½ cups (6 oz.) Feta cheese ¼ cup olive oil Lemon juice Oregano	Over the salad, crumble the cheese. Sprinkle over the olive oil; add lemon juice to taste. Garnish the salad with a sprinkling of oregano.

If desired, hard-boiled eggs may be added to the serving platter as a garnish.

For an unusual lunch for two or three persons: combine 2 cups (8 oz.) Tilsiter, cubed, 8 oz. cooked ham, diced, and one 9-oz. package frozen small peas, fully thawed to room temperature. Toss the mixture with 6 tablespoons mayonnaise and 2 tablespoons lemon juice. Serve the salad on greens of your choice.

A very pleasant summertime salad: alternate slices of fresh ripe tomato with slices of Mozzarella. Dress the salad with a sprinkling of fresh basil, chopped, lemon juice, olive oil, salt, and pepper.

Tomato and Cucumber Salad

Serves 6 · Doubles · Refrigerates
Preparation: 20 minutes

4 tablespoons mayonnaise
½ cup sour cream
1 onion, grated
½ teaspoon Dijon-style mustard
½ teaspoon curry powder
Juice of ½ lemon

In a mixing bowl, combine and blend these six ingredients.

1 cup (4 oz.) cheese of your choice, diced
½ cup cooked ham, diced
2 ripe tomatoes, peeled, seeded, chopped coarsely, and drained
1 cucumber, peeled, seeded, and diced

Fold together the dressing and these four ingredients.

Salad greens

Serve the salad on greens of your choice.

BREADS

Yeast Bread

Two 8-inch loaves · Doubles · Refrigerates · Freezes
Preparation: 2¼ hours · Cooking: 50 minutes in a 375° oven

The quantity of cheese will depend upon the strength of its flavor; the suggested 1 cup is an average measure.

2   packets dry yeast
2   cups warm milk
3   tablespoons butter, melted
2   tablespoons sugar
2   teaspoons salt

In a large mixing bowl, dissolve the yeast in the milk. Add the butter, sugar, and salt.

1   cup (4 oz.) cheese of your choice, grated

Stir in the cheese.

4   cups unbleached flour

Add the flour, one cup at a time, mixing the dough thoroughly after each addition. The dough will be sticky.

Cover the bowl with a damp cloth and allow the dough to rise in the middle of an unheated oven until it has doubled in bulk (about 1 hour).

Stir the dough down and spoon it into two well-buttered 8-inch loaf pans. Cover the pans with a damp cloth and allow the dough to rise until it reaches the top of the pans (about 40 minutes).

Put the pans in an unheated oven. Turn the oven on to 375° and bake the loaves for 50 minutes, or until the bread sounds hollow when tapped.

Remove the loaves from the pans
and allow them to cool on a rack.

Peppered Cheese Bread: Add ¾ teaspoon freshly ground pepper to the
dry ingredients; add 1 egg, lightly beaten, to the liquid ingredients, and, if
desired, a dash of Tabasco sauce. Proceed with the recipe as directed.

Cheese Muffins

12 large or 18 small muffins · Doubles · Refrigerates · Freezes
Preparation: 15 minutes · Baking: 15 minutes in a 400° oven

2 cups sifted flour 1 tablespoon baking powder ½ teaspoon salt	In a mixing bowl, combine and blend these dry ingredients.
½ cup (2 oz.) sharp Cheddar, or Roquefort, or other cheese of your choice	To the dry ingredients, add the cheese.
2 eggs 1 cup milk 2 tablespoons melted butter	In a mixing bowl, combine these liquid ingredients. Using a rotary beater, blend them well.

Add the liquid mixture to the
cheese-flour mixture and, using a
fork, stir the mixture only enough to
dampen the flour.

Fill lightly buttered muffin cups two-
thirds full. Bake the muffins at 400°
for 15 minutes, or until they are
golden.

Gougère: France

Serves 6

Preparation: 15 minutes · Baking: 45 minutes in a 375° oven

The classic Burgundian cheese pastry may be served hot or cold, albeit I prefer it hot.

1 cup flour 1 teaspoon dry mustard ½ teaspoon sugar 1 teaspoon salt ¼ teaspoon white pepper	In a mixing bowl, sift together the dry ingredients.
1 cup water 6 tablespoons butter	In a saucepan, heat the water and melt the butter. Bring it to a rolling boil. Add all the flour mixture at one time, and cook the mixture, stirring constantly, until a ball forms away from the sides of the pan. Remove the pan from the heat.
4 eggs ⅔ cup (3 oz.) Gruyère or Münster, shredded	To the dough, add the eggs separately, thoroughly beating in each addition. Add the cheese and blend.
Additional shredded cheese, if desired	Spoon the dough in a ring around the sides of a lightly buttered pie tin (or drop the dough in separate spoonsful on a lightly buttered baking sheet). Sprinkle the dough with the additional shredded cheese, if desired.
	Bake the *gougère* at 375° for 40 minutes, or until it is well puffed and golden. Turn off the heat and allow the pastry to "dry" for an additional 5 minutes. Serve it in place of bread or muffins.

Apple Muffins with Cheddar

12 to 15 large muffins · Doubles · Refrigerates · Freezes
Preparation: 25 minutes · Cooking: 25 minutes in a 400° oven

8	tablespoons butter	In a mixing bowl, beat together the butter, sugar, and eggs until the mixture is light yellow and satiny.
½	cup sugar	
2	eggs	

1½ cups flour
¾ cup quick oats
1 teaspoon baking powder
1 teaspoon soda
½ teaspoon salt

In a mixing bowl, sift together the dry ingredients.

2 apples, finely diced, sprinkled with lemon juice
¾ cup (4 oz.) Cheddar, grated
¾ cup milk

Ready the apples, cheese, and milk.

At this point you may stop and continue later.

Combine the egg mixture, dry ingredients, apples, and cheese. Gradually add the milk, stirring the batter only sufficiently to moisten the flour.

Fill buttered muffin cups two-thirds full. Bake the muffins at 400° for 25 minutes, or until they are well risen and golden.

Spoon Bread

Serves 6 · Doubles
Preparation: 25 minutes · Cooking: 35 minutes in a 375° oven

1 cup yellow cornmeal
2 cups milk

In the top of a double-boiler, over boiling water, combine the cornmeal and milk and cook the mixture, stirring, until it is thickened.

1 cup (4 oz.) "store" cheese, shredded
2 tablespoons butter
1 tablespoon sugar
1 teaspoon salt

To the cornmeal, add these four ingredients, stirring until the cheese is melted. Remove the top of the double-boiler from the heat.

3 egg yolks
½ cup milk

In a mixing bowl, combine the egg yolks and milk and beat the mixture well; stir the liquid into the cornmeal mixture.

At this point you may stop and continue later.

1 teaspoon baking powder
3 egg whites, beaten until stiff

Into the cheese mixture, stir the baking powder. Fold in the egg whites.

Into a buttered casserole or baking dish, pour the batter. Bake the spoon bread at 375° for 35 minutes, or until it is risen.

Bacon Spoon Bread: Follow step 1 as directed; in step 2, add 2 cloves garlic, put through a press, ½ lb. bacon, diced, rendered until crisp and drained on absorbent paper, and 2 tablespoons of the bacon fat. Follow steps 3 and 4 as directed. In step 5, use some of the bacon fat to grease the baking dish. The addition of the bacon makes the recipe sufficiently substantial to serve as a main dish for supper.

Swiss Toast
(a fine, crisp accompaniment to salad luncheons): Prepare *crêpe* batter,

page 257, adding to it 1 cup (4 oz.) Emmenthaler, grated. Remove the crusts from 12 slices of "toasting" bread, sprinkle them lightly with dry white wine, dip them in the *crêpe* batter and, in a little butter, fry them until they are golden brown. Keep the prepared toasts crisp in a warm oven.

Cheese Yorkshire Pudding

For a delicious variation, to your favorite recipe for Yorkshire pudding for 6 persons, add ½ cup (2 oz.) sharp cheese, grated; cook the Yorkshire pudding in your usual way.

Cottage Cheese Muffins

12 large or 18 small muffins · Doubles · Refrigerates · Freezes
Preparation: 20 minutes · Cooking: 20 minutes in a 400° oven

1 cup flour ¼ cup whole wheat flour ⅓ cup yellow cornmeal 3¼ teaspoons baking powder Grating of nutmeg ½ teaspoon salt	In a mixing bowl, sift together the dry ingredients.
2 eggs ⅔ cup cottage cheese ⅔ cup buttermilk 5 tablespoons oil 2 tablespoons honey	In a mixing bowl, beat the eggs lightly. Add the cottage cheese, buttermilk, oil, and honey. Using a rotary beater, blend the ingredients well. *At this point you may stop and continue later.* Combine the dry and liquid ingredients, mixing them only sufficiently to dampen the flour. Fill lightly buttered muffin cups two-thirds full. Bake the muffins at 400° for 20 minutes, or until they are well risen and golden.

Onion Bread

One 9-inch loaf · Refrigerates · Freezes
Preparation: 2¼ hours · Cooking: 35 minutes in a 350° oven

1 cup hot water, in which 1 beef bouillon cube is dissolved
1 packet dry yeast
2 tablespoons honey
1 egg, lightly beaten
1 teaspoon salt

In a mixing bowl, when the water is lukewarm, combine it with the yeast; stir the mixture until the yeast is dissolved. Add the honey, egg, and salt; stir to dissolve the salt.

1 cup (4 oz.) Emmenthaler, grated
2 onions, finely chopped

Stir in the cheese and onion.

3 cups flour (or more as needed)
1½ feaspoons dill weed

Combine the flour and dill and add it, a cupful at a time, to the liquid ingredients, blending the mixture thoroughly with each addition. The dough should be sufficiently stiff to knead; add more flour, if necessary. In a lightly buttered bowl, arrange the ball of dough; cover it with a damp cloth and, in a warm draft-free place, allow it to rise until doubled in bulk (about 1 hour).

Punch the dough down and knead it briefly. In a lightly buttered 9-inch loaf pan arrange the dough. Allow it to rise once again (about 45 minutes). Bake the loaf at 350° for 35 minutes, or until it is golden and sounds hollow when tapped. Remove the loaf from the pan and cool on a wire rack.

Scones: England

12 scones · Doubles · Refrigerates · Freezes
Preparation: 15 minutes · Cooking: 10 minutes in a 450° oven

1¾	cups flour	In a mixing bowl, sift together these dry ingredients.
3	teaspoons baking powder	
½	teaspoon dry mustard	
½	teaspoon salt	

2 tablespoons soft butter
1 cup (4 oz.) Cheddar, grated

Add the butter and, using your fingers, rapidly blend the mixture. Using a fork, stir in the cheese.

At this point you may stop and continue later.

½ cup milk

Add the milk, stirring. On a floured surface, knead the dough lightly and roll it out to ½-inch thickness. Cut out the scones (about 2 inches in diameter). Arrange them on a buttered baking sheet and bake them at 450° for 10 minutes, or until they are golden brown.

The recipe may also be made with 1½ cups (6 oz.) Caerphilly, grated; bake the scones at 425° for 15 minutes, or until they are golden brown.

DESSERTS

Fresh fruit, accompanied by cheese, is one of the most pleasant desserts I know—light, satisfying, comparatively innocent of calories. The following combinations are a few I have enjoyed; in reality, virtually all cheeses are complementary to fresh fruit.

Apples	Blue-veined cheeses
	Cheddar
	Port Salut
Apricots	Cantal
	Fontina
Bananas	Blue-veined cheeses
	Edam
	Gouda
Figs	Blue-veined cheeses
	Reblochon

Grapes	Brie
	Camembert
Melons	Parmigiana
	Ricotta
Peaches	Blue-veined cheeses
	Mimolette
Pears	Provolone
	Parmigiana
Pineapple	Brie
	Camembert
	Cream
	Münster
Strawberries	Cream
	Gervais
	Neufchâtel

Baked Apple Slices

Serves 6 · Refrigerates
Preparation: 25 minutes · Cooking: 35 minutes in a 350° oven

A dessert, served hot, with cream, or, if desired, a warm side dish to accompany roast meats.

6 apples, peeled, cored, and sliced
Juice of 1 lemon

In a lightly buttered baking dish, arrange the apple slices. Over them, sprinkle the lemon juice.

½ cup brown sugar
½ cup flour
¾ teaspoon cinnamon
¼ teaspoon salt

In a mixing bowl, sift together these dry ingredients.

4 tablespoons butter, softened
1 cup (4 oz.) mild Cheddar, grated

Using a fork, cut the butter into the flour; the mixture should be crumbly. Add the cheese and toss the mixture to blend it well. Spread it lightly over the apples.

At this point you may stop and continue later.

Bake the apples at 350° for 35 minutes, or until they are tender and the crust is golden.

Cheesecake and Cheese Tarts

Cheesecake and cheese tarts are among the oldest "made" desserts. They are mentioned in Plato. The Romans ate them. In Tudor England, the little cakes—called "Maids of Honor," a recipe traditionally invented by Anne Boleyn for the delectation of Henry VIII—were originally made with cheese. Czar Alexander, traveling in France with a large retinue (including a pastry chef), is reputed to have introduced the delicacy to Paris, where it was called *Coeur à la Crème,* a far cry from the dessert of that name as it is known today, and which may be found on page 327. Because cheesecake is capable of many variations, we start with a basic recipe followed by some favorite variations.

Basic Recipe for Cheesecake

Serves 6 · Refrigerates
Preparation: 25 minutes · Cooking: 20 minutes in a 350° oven
Chilling time: at least 3 hours

1¾ cups graham cracker crumbs 6 tablespoons butter, melted	In a mixing bowl, combine the crumbs and butter and, using a fork, stir the mixture until it is well blended. With it, cover the bottom and sides of a 9-inch pie plate, pressing the crumbs with the fingers to form a crust. Bake the shell at 400° for 6 minutes; allow it to cool. Turn the oven down to 350°.
2 8-oz. packages cream cheese, at room temperature 2 eggs, beaten ½ cup sugar 1 teaspoon vanilla (*or* grated rind of 1 lemon)	In a mixing bowl, combine these four ingredients and, using a fork, beat them until they are thoroughly blended.

Fill the crust with the cheese mixture. Bake the dessert at 350° for 20 minutes. While the cake is baking, prepare the topping.

1 cup sour cream
4 tablespoons sugar
1 teaspoon vanilla

In a mixing bowl, combine these three ingredients and blend them well.

Over the top of the cheesecake, spread the mixture. Turn off the oven and return the cake to the oven for 5 minutes.

Allow the dessert to cool and then chill it for at least 3 hours.

If desired, the chilled cake may be topped with fresh strawberries, hulled, rinsed, and thoroughly drained.

Butter-and-Cheese Tart: Follow step 1 as directed in the basic recipe (or use short pastry, prebaked at 425° for 10 minutes). For the filling: cream together until light one 8-oz. package cream cheese, at room temperature, 6 tablespoons sweet butter, softened, and ½ cup sugar; add 2 beaten eggs and a generous grating of nutmeg; beat the mixture for 2 minutes. Spoon the mixture into the shell. Bake the dessert as directed. Omit the topping. Serve the tart hot or cold.

Ginger Cheesecake: Follow step 1 as directed in the basic recipe (or use short pastry, baked at 425° for 10 minutes). For the filling: combine two 8-oz. packages cream cheese, at room temperature, ⅔ cup sugar, 2 beaten eggs, the juice and grated rind of 1 lemon, and 1 piece fresh ginger root the size of a walnut, grated. (If you prefer, you may use, in place of the fresh ginger, several small pieces of candied ginger, finely chopped.) Beat the mixture until it is smooth; spoon it into the prepared shell and bake the cake as directed. If desired, add the topping. Serve the dessert chilled or at room temperature.

Lemon-Orange Cheesecake: Follow step 1 as directed in the basic recipe. For the filling: combine and blend thoroughly one 8-oz. package cream cheese, 3 egg yolks, beaten, ¼ cup cream, ¼ cup sugar, and the grated rind of 1 lemon and 1 orange. Fold in 3 egg whites, beaten stiff. Spoon the filling into the pie shell. Bake the dessert at 350° for 20 minutes, or until it is well puffed and golden. (It will settle as it cools, but will retain a lightness.) Omit the topping. Serve it hot or at room temperature.

Molded Cheesecake (a French recipe): Using softened sweet butter, generously grease a 2-quart soufflé dish; coat the dish with ½ cup graham cracker crumbs and discard the excess. For the filling: combine three 8-oz. packages cream cheese at room temperature, 1 cup heavy cream, 1½ cups sugar, and the grated rind and juice of 2 lemons; beat the mixture until it is smooth. Add 6 eggs, beaten, and 1½ teaspoons vanilla; blend the mixture thoroughly. Pour the batter into the prepared soufflé dish; place the dish in a pan of hot water; bake the dessert at 325° for 1½ hours; turn off the heat and allow the cake to remain in the oven for 30 minutes. Cool the dish on a rack before unmolding the cake; serve it chilled or at room temperature.

Pineapple Cheesecake (This dessert is especially good made with ½ to ¾ cup ripe fresh pineapple, grated and pressed dry in a colander.): Follow step 1 as directed in the basic recipe. Over the crust, arrange one 8¼-oz. can crushed pineapple, drained and pressed dry in a colander. For the filling: sift together ¾ cup sugar, 1 tablespoon flour, and ¼ teaspoon salt; add two 8-oz. packages cream cheese, at room temperature, and beat the mixture until it is smooth. Add 4 eggs, beaten, ½ cup light cream, and 1 teaspoon vanilla and blend well. Pour the mixture over the pineapple. Bake the cake at 350° for 30 minutes. Cool and chill the dessert.

Ricotta Pie: Follow step 1 as directed in the basic recipe. For the filling: sieve 1½ lbs. Ricotta. In a separate bowl, beat 4 eggs with ⅓ cup sugar until they are foamy; to the eggs, add the juice and grated rind of 1 lemon; combine the Ricotta and egg mixture and beat them until they are thoroughly blended. Pour the filling into the prepared shell and bake the dessert as directed for 35 minutes, or until the filling is firm. Allow it to cool to room temperature before serving.

Roquefort Cheesecake: Prepare the crust as directed in the basic recipe. For the filling: add to the basic recipe, 1½ cups (6 oz.) Roquefort, crumbled; beat the filling until smooth and light; flavor it with the grated rind of 1 lemon. Proceed with the recipe as directed. Serve the dessert chilled.

Spiced Cheesecake (a recipe from seventeenth-century England): Follow step 1 as directed in the basic recipe (or use short pastry baked at 425° for 10 minutes). For the filling: in a mixing bowl, beat 3 whole eggs and 2 additional egg yolks with ¼ cup sugar. Add 1 cup cottage cheese, ¼ teaspoon each cinnamon, mace, and nutmeg, a pinch of powdered clove, and ½ teaspoon salt; beat the mixture until it is smooth. Add in a steady stream, beating constantly, 1 cup heavy cream and ¼ cup cream sherry that have been warmed together. Pour the mixture into the prepared pastry shell and bake it as directed. Omit the topping. Serve the dessert chilled.

Three-Cheese Cheesecake (an adaptation of a Greek recipe): Follow step 1 as directed in the basic recipe (or use short pastry, baked at 425° for 10 minutes). For the filling: combine 1 cup (4 oz.) each cottage cheese, Feta, and Fontina, grated; beat the mixture to blend it thoroughly. Add ½ cup honey, ½ teaspoon cinnamon, and a pinch of salt; beat the mixture again. Add, one at a time, 5 eggs, beating in each one thoroughly. Spoon the mixture into the prepared crust. Omit the topping. Bake the dessert as directed for 30 to 35 minutes, or until it is firm. Serve it at room temperature.

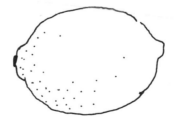

Ricotta Fillings for Cheesecake

In Italy, cheesecake often consists of layers of *pan' d'Ispagna* (literally, "Spanish bread"), a pastry closely resembling our sponge cake. The following two fillings may be used with either American sponge cake, the French *genoise,* or (of course) *pan' d'Ispagna.*

Torta di Ricotta "Carlo"

This first filling appeared as a menu item I espied—and enjoyed—at Carlo Fiori's "Carlo in Trastevere" restaurant on the via Cardinale Merry del Val in Rome. A fine restaurant, noted for its fish and seafood, as well as for the warm hospitality of its owner-host. *The filling:* beat until satiny and thick 8 egg yolks with 1 cup extra-fine granulated sugar; add ½ cup finely pounded blanched almonds, 1 lb. Ricotta, 1 cup softened sweet butter, and ½ teaspoon salt. Beat the mixture until it is light and smooth. Fold in 8 egg whites beaten until stiff. Spread the mixture between cooled layers of sponge cake and, over the top layer of the cake, drizzle ⅓ cup dark rum. Chill the dessert for at least 3 hours.

Orange-flavored Filling

Add the grated rind of 1 orange to the above filling; over the composed cake, drizzle ¼ cup Cointreau or Grand Marnier. Complete the recipe as directed.

Cheddar Cheesecake: England

Serves 6 · Doubles · Refrigerates · Freezes
Preparation: 30 minutes · Cooking: 45 minutes in a 425°/325° oven

1 cup flour
1 teaspoon baking powder
⅓ cup confectioners' sugar
5 tablespoons butter, softened

In a mixing bowl, sift together the flour, baking powder, and sugar. Add the butter and, using your finger tips, blend the mixture until it resembles bread crumbs.

1 egg yolk
2 tablespoons milk

Blend in the egg yolk and milk to yield a stiff dough.

Roll out the pastry and with it line a 9-inch pie tin. Bake the pastry for 10 minutes at 425°, or until it is just golden. (Do not turn down the heat.) Allow the pastry to cool.

1½ cups (6 oz.) Cheddar, grated
1 egg yolk
½ cup unflavored yogurt
2 tablespoons flour
3 oz. granulated sugar
Juice and grated rind of 1 lemon

In a mixing bowl, combine and blend the cheese, egg yolk, yogurt, flour, sugar, and lemon rind and juice. Beat the mixture well.

2 egg whites, beaten stiff but not dry

Into the cheese mixture, fold the egg whites. Spoon the batter into the cooked pastry.

Place the cheesecake in the 425° oven; immediately reduce the heat to 325°. Bake the dessert for 45 minutes, or until it is firm and golden. Allow it to cool to room temperature before serving.

Apple Crisp

Serves 6

Preparation: 25 minutes · Cooking: 30 minutes in a 350° oven

1   cup flour
1   cup dark brown sugar, packed
½   cup (2 oz.) sharp Cheddar, shredded
½   cup butter, melted

With a fork, mix together the flour, brown sugar, and cheese until there are no lumps; add the butter, stirring only enough to moisten the flour.

8   large apples, peeled, cored, and sliced
Cinnamon

Butter a flat baking dish and in it arrange a layer of one-half of the apples, season with a sprinkling of cinnamon, and add one-half of the flour mixture; repeat.

Heavy cream, whipped cream, or vanilla ice cream (optional)

Bake the dessert at 350° for 30 minutes. Serve it warm or at room temperature with the cream, whipped cream, or vanilla ice cream, if desired.

Apple or Berry Pancakes: Norway

24 pancakes
Preparation: 30 minutes · Cooking: 20 minutes

1 cup sour cream
1 cup cream-style cottage cheese
4 eggs
¾ cup flour
1 tablespoon sugar
¾ teaspoon salt

In the container of an electric blender, combine these six ingredients and, on medium speed, whirl them until the mixture is smooth.

½ cup apple, grated (*or* 1 cup blueberries, picked over, rinsed, and drained)

Into the batter, fold the fruit. Allow the mixture to stand for 20 minutes.

1 cup cream-style cottage cheese
2 tablespoons sugar
1 teaspoon vanilla

For the sauce: in the container of an electric blender, on medium speed, whirl the cottage cheese, sugar, and vanilla until the mixture is smooth.

At this point you may stop and continue later.

Soft butter

Wipe a *crêpe* pan or small skillet with a little butter. Drop the batter by large tablespoons, forming 4-inch pancakes, and cook the pancakes quickly on each side. Keep them warm until ready to serve them. Accompany them with the prepared sauce.

Apricot Pudding

Serves 6 · Doubles · Refrigerates
Preparation: 25 minutes · Chilling time: at least 2 hours

12   large lady fingers, split

With the lady fingers, line the bottom and sides of a glass or porcelain bowl.

1   20-oz. can apricot halves
3   tablespoons cream sherry

Drain the liquid from the apricots and combine the liquid with the sherry. Pour the mixture evenly over the lady fingers and refrigerate them.

2   cups cottage cheese

In the container of an electric blender, combine the drained fruit and cottage cheese. On medium speed, whirl them for 15 seconds, or until the mixture is smooth. Refrigerate the mixture for 2 hours or more.

½   cup heavy cream, whipped

Whip and refrigerate the heavy cream.

At this point you may stop and continue later.

¼   cup preserved ginger, finely diced

To serve the dessert, spoon the apricot-cottage cheese mixture over the lady fingers. Add the whipped cream in an even layer. Sprinkle the dessert with the diced ginger.

Coeur à la Crème

Serves 6 · Doubles · Refrigerates
Preparation: 20 minutes · Chilling time: at least 2 hours

A French country classic, made here with ingredients readily available to us.

1   cup cottage cheese at room temperature
1   8-oz. package cream cheese, at room temperature

Into a mixing bowl, sieve the cottage cheese. Add the cream cheese and, using a fork, beat the mixture until it is light and smooth.

½   cup sour cream
1   teaspoon confectioners' sugar

Add the sour cream and sugar and blend the mixture well.

In a heart-shaped, cheesecloth-lined mold, pack the mixture. Chill it for at least 2 hours.

Cream and sugar (*or* strawberry preserves)

On a serving platter, unmold the *Coeur à la Crème* and serve it with either cream and sugar or strawberry preserves.

Petit Suisse

Serves 6 · Doubles · Refrigerates
Preparation: 15 minutes · Chilling time: at least 2 hours

In France, unripened *Petit Suisse* cheese is used as a bland but satisfying dessert. The cheese is unavailable in this country, but a comparable substitute is easily made.

2 8-oz. packages cream cheese, at room temperature 1½ teaspoons sugar 2 tablespoons heavy cream (more as needed)	In a mixing bowl, combine the cheese and sugar. Using a fork, whip the mixture until it is light. A little at a time, add heavy cream, beating constantly, until the cheese is soft but still holds its shape.
	In waxed paper, roll it into a cylinder 1¼ inches in diameter. Chill the cylinder for at least 2 hours.
1 quart strawberries ¼ cup sugar	Hull, rinse, and drain the strawberries. Put them in a bowl and sprinkle the sugar over them. Chill for 2 hours.
	At this point you may stop and continue later.
	Cut the cylinder into equal rounds and serve them surrounded by the strawberries.

Pears with Roquefort

Peel, core, slice lengthwise, and brush with lemon juice 6 firm ripe fresh pears (or use 12 canned pear halves). In a mixing bowl, combine and blend ¾ cup (3 oz.) Roquefort, crumbled, one 8-oz. package cream cheese at room temperature, 2 tablespoons milk, the grated rind of ½ lemon, and 1 teaspoon sugar. With this mixture, mound the cavities of the pear halves; arrange them in an ovenproof serving dish, and bake them at 450° for 10 minutes. Serve the pears hot.

Gougère, page 306, may be used as a dessert pastry: allow the baked *gougère* to cool, cut it in half horizontally, top the lower half with prepared fruit of your choice, add slightly sweetened whipped cream, to taste, and replace the top of the pastry ring. Serve the dessert as you would a pie, cutting the *gougère* into wedge-shaped pieces.

Rich Custard Cream

About 3 cups
Preparation time: 15 minutes · Chilling time: at least 2 hours

This *crème anglaise*, called in the seventeenth century *"mon ami,"* is delicious served over fruit.

2 cups heavy cream, scalded
1 cup (8 oz.) cottage cheese
¼ cup sugar
¼ cup honey
1 teaspoon vanilla
Few grains of salt
4 egg yolks, lightly beaten

In the container of an electric blender, combine all the ingredients, and, on high speed, whirl them until the mixture is smooth.

Pour the custard into the top of a double-boiler and, over boiling water, cook it, stirring constantly, until it thickens and coats the spoon. Into a serving bowl or pitcher, sieve the custard; allow it to cool before chilling it.

Bananas Baked with Cream Cheese: Nicaragua

Serves 6 · Doubles · Refrigerates
Preparation: 25 minutes · Cooking: 20 minutes in a 375° oven

8   tablespoons butter
6   firm bananas, halved lengthwise

In a skillet, heat the butter and in it brown the banana halves; drain them on absorbent paper.

1   8-oz. package cream cheese, at room temperature
3   tablespoons dark rum
2   tablespoons dark brown sugar
1   teaspoon cinnamon
6   pieces candied ginger, finely chopped

In a mixing bowl, combine these five ingredients and beat them until the mixture is smooth.

In a lightly buttered baking dish, arrange a layer of one-half the bananas; over them, spread one-half the cheese mixture. Repeat the layers.

At this point you may stop and continue later.

⅔   cup heavy cream

Over the top, pour the cream. Bake the dessert at 375° for 20 minutes, or until the cream is absorbed and the top is golden.

Fruit with Whipped Cheese

Serves 6 · Doubles · Refrigerates
Preparation: 20 minutes · Chilling time: 1 hour

This topping is a pleasant accompaniment to stewed apricots, berries, canned cherries, orange segments, fresh pineapple, stewed prunes, and stewed rhubarb.

1 8-oz. package cream cheese, at room temperature ½ cup milk 3 tablespoons honey Grated rind of 1 lemon	In a mixing bowl, combine these four ingredients and, using a fork, beat them together until they are light.
1 cup heavy cream 2 tablespoons confectioners' sugar Grated rind of 1 lemon	In a mixing bowl, beat the cream until thick, add the sugar, and continue beating it until it is whipped stiff. Fold the whipped cream into the cheese mixture. Arrange it in a serving bowl and sprinkle it with the lemon rind. Chill the mixture for 1 hour.
Fruit of your choice	Serve the whipped cheese as a topping for the fruit of your choice.

A Variant Using Cottage Cheese: In the container of an electric blender, combine 2 cups cream-style cottage cheese, ½ cup sugar, the juice of ½ lemon, and the grated rind of 1 orange; on medium speed, whirl the mixture until it is smooth. (If desired, the cottage cheese may be sieved and blended with the other ingredients in a mixing bowl.)

Cottage Cheese and Orange Pie

Serves 6 · Refrigerates
Preparation: 15 minutes · Cooking: 45 minutes in a 325° oven
Chilling time: at least 3 hours

The preparation time does not include readying the pastry.

1   9-inch pie shell, baked
      at 425° for 12 minutes

1½   cups (12 oz.) cottage cheese

In the container of an electric blender, combine these seven ingredients and, on medium speed, whirl them until the mixture is smooth.

1   6-oz. can frozen orange juice concentrate, thawed
4   eggs
2   tablespoons flour
⅓   cup sugar or honey
¾   teaspoon salt
Grated rind of 1 orange

Pour the custard into the prepared pie shell and bake the dessert at 325° for 45 minutes. Allow the pie to cool on a rack before chilling it. Chill the pie for at least 3 hours.

If desired, the pie may be topped with strawberries.

The recipe may also be made with the juice and grated rind of 1 — 2 lemons or limes (depending upon how strong a flavor of fruit is desired); in this case, omit the orange juice concentrate and orange rind and increase the sugar to a generous ½ cup.

Lemon Cheese Pie

Serves 6 · Doubles · Refrigerates
Preparation: 20 minutes · Cooking: 30 minutes in a 350° oven
Chilling time: at least 3 hours

4 tablespoons butter, softened
1 4-oz. can shredded coconut

Using all of the butter, grease evenly but heavily a 9-inch pie plate. In a bowl, using two forks, toss the coconut until the shreds are separated. Press the coconut evenly but firmly into the butter to form a "crust."

1½ cups (12 oz.) cream cheese, at room temperature
3 eggs
⅔ cup sugar
¼ teaspoon salt
Grated rind and sieved juice of 1−2 lemons (I prefer 2)

In a mixing bowl, beat the cream cheese until it is light. Add singly the eggs, beating the mixture well after each addition. Then beat in the sugar, salt, and lemon rind and juice.

Spoon the cream cheese mixture over the coconut crust. Bake the dessert at 350° for 30 minutes. Allow it to cool before chilling it for at least 3 hours.

Note: The pie will lose some of its puffiness as it cools. The chilled dessert, however, will be light in texture.

Cheddar Pastry for Fruit Pies

Two 9-inch crusts · Refrigerates · Freezes
Preparation: 20 minutes · Chilling time: 2 hours

2½ cups flour
½   teaspoon salt

In a mixing bowl, sift together the flour and salt.

⅔   cup (11 tablespoons) sweet butter, softened
1¼ cups (5 oz.) sharp Cheddar, grated

To the flour, add the butter and cheese and, with the fingers, rapidly work the ingredients until the mixture forms crumbs the size of peas.

¼   cup ice water (approximately)

A tablespoon at a time, sprinkle the water over the flour mixture and work it in with a fork. When the dough forms a compact ball, sufficient water has been added. Do not knead the dough.

Wrap the dough in waxed paper and chill it for 2 hours.

Roll out the dough and proceed with the recipe of your choice.

Topping for Open Fruit Pies

Topping for 1 pie
Preparation: 15 minutes

½ cup flour
½ cup sugar
4 tablespoons butter, melted

In a mixing bowl, combine the flour, sugar, and butter. Using a fork, blend the mixture until it is crumbly.

⅓ cup Parmesan, grated

Add the cheese and stir the mixture until it is well mixed.

Sprinkle the mixture over the fruit and bake the pie as your recipe directs.

Ricotta Pudding

Serves 6 · Refrigerates
Preparation: 25 minutes · Cooking: 1 hour in a 375° oven

A version of *Budino Toscano,* a dessert popular in Italy.

2⅔ cups lightly salted
      boiling water
½   cup fine farina
1⅓ cups milk, scalded

Over the water, sprinkle the farina. Stir the mixture and cook it, uncovered, for 5 minutes. Stir in the milk and continue to cook the mixture, uncovered, for 5 minutes. Allow it to cool.

1   lb. Ricotta, sieved
4   egg yolks, well beaten
½   cup sugar
½   cup glacéed fruit peel,
      diced
½   cup golden raisins
1   teaspoon vanilla (*or*
      orange extract)
Grated rind of 1 lemon

To the cooled farina, add the cheese, egg yolks, sugar, fruit peel, raisins, flavorings, and grated rind. Stir the mixture to blend it well.

4   egg whites, beaten stiff

Fold in the egg whites.

Spoon the mixture into a buttered soufflé dish and bake it at 375° for 1 hour, or until it is well puffed and golden. Serve the pudding at once.

Ricotta Balls

Serves 6 · Doubles
Preparation: 15 minutes · Cooking: 5 minutes in deep fat at 350°

A contribution of Leyna Gabriele.

1 lb. Ricotta 3 eggs 4 teaspoons baking powder 3 tablespoons sugar ½ teaspoon salt	In a mixing bowl, combine and blend these five ingredients.
1 cup confectioners' sugar (or as needed)	Into deep fat at 350°, drop teaspoonsful of the mixture. It will form into little balls. Cook them, a few at a time, for 5 minutes, or until they are lightly browned. With a slotted spoon, remove them to absorbent paper and keep them warm. Sprinkle the Ricotta balls with confectioners' sugar and serve them warm.

Cold Cheddar Soufflé

Serves 6 · Refrigerates · Freezes
Preparation: 30 minutes · Chilling time: at least 3 hours

3 egg yolks, beaten
⅓ cup sugar
¼ cup orange juice

In the top of a double-boiler, combine the egg yolks, sugar, and orange juice. Over hot but not boiling water, cook the mixture, stirring constantly, until it is thickened.

¼ cup orange juice
1 packet unflavored gelatin

In the orange juice, soften the gelatin and, over simmering water, stir to dissolve it. Add the gelatin to the custard mixture and stir well. Remove the pan from the heat.

2 cups (8 oz.) Cheddar, grated
½ cup milk
1 cup heavy cream, whipped but not stiff

In a mixing bowl, combine the cheese and milk; fold in the whipped cream. Combine this mixture with the custard.

3 egg whites, beaten until stiff

Into the mixture, fold the egg whites. Spoon the mixture into a mold, lightly rinsed with cold water. Chill the dessert for at least 3 hours, or until it is set.

To serve, unmold the soufflé onto a serving plate.

Chocolate Soufflé

Serves 6
Preparation: 25 minutes · Cooking: 45 minutes in a 350° oven

2 tablespoons butter 2 tablespoons flour 1 cup milk ¼ teaspoon salt	In a saucepan, heat the butter and in it, over gentle heat, cook the flour for a few minutes. Gradually add the milk, stirring constantly until the mixture is thickened and smooth. Stir in the salt.
1 8-oz. package cream cheese, at room temperature 2 1-oz. squares unsweetened chocolate 1 teaspoon vanilla	Add the cheese and chocolate and stir the mixture until they are melted. Stir in the vanilla. Remove the saucepan from the heat.
4 egg yolks ⅔ cup sugar	In a mixing bowl, beat the egg yolks lightly. Add the sugar and beat the mixture until it is thick and satiny. Stir the yolks into the cooled chocolate mixture.
5 egg whites, beaten stiff	Fold a little of the chocolate mixture into the egg whites. Then fold the egg whites back into the chocolate. Spoon the soufflé batter into a lightly buttered soufflé dish. Place the dish in a pan of hot water. Bake the soufflé at 350° for 45 minutes, or until it is well puffed. Serve immediately.

Cream Cheese Soufflé

Serves 6
Preparation: 20 minutes · Cooking: 35 minutes in a 350° oven

1	8-oz. package cream cheese, at room temperature	In the container of an electric blender, combine these five ingredients and, on medium speed, whirl them until smooth. Pour the mixture into a mixing bowl.
1	cup heavy cream, at room temperature	
3	tablespoons honey	
4	egg yolks	
¼	teaspoon salt	

4	egg whites, beaten stiff	Into the cream cheese mixture, fold the egg whites. Spoon the batter into a lightly buttered soufflé dish and bake the dessert at 350° for 35 minutes, or until it is well puffed.

1	pint strawberries, hulled, rinsed, drained, halved, and tossed with ¼ cup sugar	Serve the soufflé immediately, accompanied by the strawberries.

Cream Cheese Frosting for Cake

For a 2-layer cake
Preparation: 15 minutes

1 8-oz. package cream cheese, at room temperature

In a mixing bowl, beat the cream cheese until it is light.

1 egg
1 teaspoon almond, lemon, orange, *or* vanilla extract
¼ teaspoon salt

Add the egg, flavoring, and salt. Beat the mixture until it is light.

2½ cups confectioners' sugar

Add, a little at a time, the sugar, beating in thoroughly each addition. With a spatula, spread the frosting evenly over the bottom of each layer; put the two layers together, the frosted bottoms facing each other. Spread the remaining frosting on the top and sides of the cake.

If desired, the finely grated rind of ½ orange may be added.

Also, in place of the extract, 1 or 2 tablespoons orange-flavored liqueur may be used.

SAUCES AND DRESSINGS

Basic White Sauces

In cheese cookery, there are four basic white sauces (*roux* and milk) which may be used for different purposes. They are all made alike save for the quantity of milk used, which determines their consistency, and hence their function. The four sauces and their quantities are:

(1) *thin pouring sauce* (the basis of soups): 2 tablespoons butter, 2 tablespoons flour, 3 cups milk;
(2) *normal pouring sauce* (for use with pasta and vegetables): 2 tablespoons butter, 2 tablespoons flour, 2 cups milk;
(3) *coating sauce* (used to cover meats, poultry, fish, and vegetables): 2 tablespoons butter, 2 tablespoons flour, 1 to 1¼ cups milk;
(4) *panada* (the basis of soufflés): 2 tablespoons butter, 2 tablespoons flour, ½ cup milk.

The cooking technique for all is the same:

(1) in a saucepan, melt the butter;

(2) add the flour and, over gentle heat, cook the mixture *(roux)*, stirring, for a few minutes;

(3) gradually add the required amount of milk and salt and pepper, to taste, stirring constantly until the mixture is thickened and smooth;

(4) off heat, add, if the recipe calls for it, grated or shredded cheese; stir the sauce until the cheese is melted. (The quantity of cheese depends upon your choice and your palate: 1 cup [4 oz.] for a mild sauce to 2 cups [8 oz.] for a highly flavored one.)

Béchamel Sauce

2 cups
Preparation: 10 minutes

4 tablespoons butter 4 tablespoons flour ½ teaspoon salt ¼ teaspoon white pepper Grating of nutmeg (optional)	In a saucepan, melt the butter. Add the flour and, over gentle heat, cook it, stirring, for a few minutes. Stir in the seasonings.
2 cups milk	Gradually add the milk, stirring constantly until the sauce is thickened and smooth.

Mornay Sauce

About 2½ cups
Preparation: 15 minutes

Make 2 cups hot Béchamel Sauce, as above, add ¼ cup (1 oz.) each Gruyère and Parmesan, grated, and 2 tablespoons softened sweet butter. Stir the mixture until the cheese is melted.

Rich Mornay Sauce: stir into the 2 cups Béchamel sauce 2 egg yolks, lightly beaten, and ½ cup heavy cream, heated; add the cheeses and butter, as described above.

There are, of course, numerous ways of making the same sauce, and Mornay sauce is no exception. For those who would like to try yet another recipe, I offer this typically French manner of making it: prepare a *roux* of 4 tablespoons sweet butter and 4 tablespoons flour; add 2 cups light cream, scalded; when the mixture is thickened and smooth, season it with ½ teaspoon salt and ¼ teaspoon white pepper; stir in ¾ cup homemade chicken stock and ¾ cup (3 oz.) Gruyère, grated.

Soubise Sauce

2½ cups
Preparation: 45 minutes

6 tablespoons butter
4 cups onion, chopped

In a saucepan, heat the butter and in it, over gentle heat, cook the onions, covered, for 25 minutes, or until they are very tender but not browned.

4 tablespoons flour

Add the flour and cook the mixture, stirring, for a few minutes.

2 cups milk, scalded
Generous grating of nutmeg
¾ teaspoon salt
¼ teaspoon white pepper

Gradually add the milk, stirring constantly until the mixture is thickened and smooth. Stir in the seasonings. Over gentle heat, cook the sauce, stirring occasionally, for 10 minutes.

In the container of an electric blender, whirl the sauce on medium speed until it is smooth. (Or, if desired, it may be sieved.) In the top of a double-boiler, over hot water, reheat the sauce before serving it.

Cheese Butters

Cheese butters are flavorful and pleasant variations to use on toast, hot rolls, or other breads. The following recipes will spread 12 slices of bread. They may be prepared ahead and refrigerated; allow them to come to room temperature before using, when they should have the consistency of soft dairy butter.

Emmenthaler Butter
Beat until well blended ¾ cup (3 oz.) each Emmenthaler, grated, and softened butter, 2 tablespoons heavy cream, 2 teaspoons Dijon-style mustard, and 1 egg yolk.

Gruyère Butter
Beat until well blended, ¾ cup (3 oz.) each Gruyère, grated, and soft butter, 2 tablespoons mayonnaise, 1½ teaspoons Dijon-style mustard, the juice of ½ lemon, a grating of nutmeg, and white pepper, to taste.

Sbrinz Butter
Beat until well blended ¾ cup (3 oz.) Sbrinz, grated, 3 tablespoons softened butter, 1½ teaspoons Dijon-style mustard, 3 tablespoons white wine, a grating of nutmeg, and pepper to taste.

Sapsago Butter
Beat until well blended 2 tablespoons Sapsago cheese, grated, 3 tablespoons softened butter, and ⅓ cup heavy cream, whipped until thick but not stiff.

Roquefort Butter for Steak
In a mixing bowl, combine and blend ¾ cup (3 oz.) Roquefort, 3 tablespoons softened sweet butter, 1 tablespoon cognac, and ¼ cup parsley, finely chopped. Shape the mixture into six equal portions and refrigerate them until they are firm. At the time of serving, garnish six individual steaks or one large cut of your choice with the Roquefort butter.

Cheddar Mayonnaise

1 cup · Refrigerates
Preparation: 10 minutes

1 egg
1 tablespoon cider vinegar
½ teaspoon salt
Pinch of cayenne

In the container of an electric blender, combine these four ingredients and, on medium speed, whirl them briefly.

½ cup (2 oz.) Cheddar, grated

Add the cheese and whirl it briefly with the other ingredients.

½ cup olive oil

With the motor running on medium speed, slowly add the olive oil in a thin, steady stream. As soon as the oil has been poured, turn off the motor.

Blue Cheese Salad Dressing

1 cup · Doubles · Refrigerates
Preparation: 15 minutes

½ cup olive oil
¼ cup cider vinegar
¼ teaspoon salt
¼ teaspoon white pepper

In the container of an electric blender, combine these four ingredients and, on medium speed, whirl them briefly.

3 tablespoons heavy cream
¼ cup (1 oz.) blue cheese of your choice
Juice of ½ lemon

With the motor running, add, in order, the cream, cheese, and lemon juice. When the mixture is smooth, turn off the motor.

Cheddar Salad Dressing

2 cups · Doubles · Refrigerates
Preparation: 15 minutes

1 cup unflavored yogurt ⅓ cup (1½ oz.) Cheddar, finely diced 1 small onion, grated	In a mixing bowl, combine the yogurt, cheese, and onion.
1 apple, peeled and grated Juice of 1 lemon	Grate the apple into the lemon juice, stir it well, and sieve off the excess juice.
Salt White pepper	Into the yogurt mixture, stir the apple. Adjust the seasoning to taste.

If desired, 1 teaspoon tomato puree may be added with the apple.

For a smoother dressing, combine all the ingredients in the container of an electric blender and, on medium speed, whirl them for 15 seconds, or until the mixture is smooth.

Camembert Salad Dressing

Using a fork, mash a 1⅓-oz. section of Camembert. To it, add 4 tablespoons light olive oil, 2 tablespoons wine vinegar, and freshly ground pepper to taste. Blend the mixture well.

Dill Salad Dressing

Using a fork, whip together one 3-oz. package cream cheese, at room temperature, 2 tablespoons light olive oil, 2 tablespoons milk, 2 tablespoons unflavored yogurt, and the juice of ½ lemon. Season the mixture with salt and white pepper. Add, to taste, a generous amount of fresh or dried dill weed. Allow the dressing to "work" for 1 hour before using it.

Orange Salad Dressing

1 ½ cups · Refrigerates
Preparation: 15 minutes

For fruit salads and "peppery" greens, such as watercress or arugola.

1   8-oz. package cream cheese, at room temperature
Grated rind and juice of 1 orange
2   tablespoons lemon juice
2   teaspoons sugar
½   teaspoon salt
¼   teaspoon white pepper

In the container of an electric blender, combine all the ingredients and, on medium speed, whirl them until the mixture is homogenous.

Sapsago Salad Dressing

Using a fork, blend 1 tablespoon Sapsago, grated, 3 tablespoons white wine vinegar, 4 tablespoons light olive oil, 2 tablespoons cream, and ½ teaspoon Worcestershire sauce.

Stilton Salad Dressing

1 ½ cups · Doubles · Refrigerates
Preparation: 10 minutes

1   cup sour cream
3   tablespoons mayonnaise
2   tablespoons lemon juice
½   teaspoon sugar
¼   teaspoon salt

In the container of an electric blender, combine these five ingredients and, on medium speed, whirl them for 15 seconds, or until the mixture is homogenous.

1   cup (4 oz.) Stilton, crumbled

Add the cheese and, on medium speed, whirl the dressing for 15 seconds, or until it is smooth.

Cheese Sauce for Cooked Vegetables

In a double-boiler, over hot but not boiling water, cook 1 cup milk that has been mixed with 2 beaten egg yolks. When the mixture thickens slightly and coats the spoon, remove it from the heat and add ½ cup (2 oz.) Edam or Gouda, shredded; fold in 2 egg whites beaten until stiff. Pour the sauce over the vegetables which have been arranged in a lightly buttered baking dish. Bake the dish at 350° for 15 minutes, or until the top is golden.

Pesto Genovese: Italy

Serves 6 · Refrigerates
Preparation: 15 minutes

The supreme sauce, I feel, for spaghetti; this recipe must be made with fresh basil leaves.

½ cup olive oil
3 tablespoons water
2 cloves garlic
2 tablespoons butter, softened

In the container of an electric blender, on medium speed, whirl these four ingredients until the garlic is thoroughly chopped.

2 cups (or to taste) fresh basil leaves
3 tablespoons pine nuts
4 tablespoons Parmesan, grated

With the motor running, add the basil leaves a little at a time. When they are thoroughly blended with the oil mixture, add the pine nuts and cheese.

Serve the sauce on hot spaghetti or *linguine* with a side dish of grated cheese. (If the sauce has been refrigerated or left standing for over 15 minutes, it may darken on top. In this case, simply whirl for a few seconds in an electric blender before using.)

Meat Sauce for Pasta

Serves 6 · Doubles · Refrigerates
Preparation: 30 minutes

A simple and tasty sauce from Greece.

4 tablespoons olive oil 2 lbs. ground round 1 teaspoon salt ½ teaspoon pepper	In a skillet, heat the oil and in it brown the meat. Season it.
1 10½-oz. can condensed chicken broth	Add the broth and, over gentle heat, simmer the meat, covered, for 15 minutes. *At this point you may stop and continue later.*
2 cups (8 oz.) Kefalotyri or Romano, grated	Off heat, stir in the cheese. Serve the hot sauce at once over pasta of your choice.

Cottage Cheese Dressing

1 ¾ cups · Refrigerates
Preparation: 15 minutes

For salads and cooked vegetables.

½ cup buttermilk ¾ cup cream-style cottage cheese ¼ cup white malt vinegar 1½ teaspoons soy sauce ½ bunch watercress, coarsely chopped 4 scallions, coarsely chopped	In the container of an electric blender, combine all the ingredients and, on medium speed, whirl them until the mixture is homogenous.

Edward Giobbi's Marinara Sauce

3 to 4 cups · Doubles · Refrigerates · Freezes
Preparation: 1 hour

Happily and gratefully acknowledged, for it is the best marinara I know.

¼ cup olive oil
3 onions, chopped
2 cloves garlic, chopped
2 carrots, scraped and diced

In a skillet, heat the oil and in it cook the vegetables until translucent.

1 35-oz. can Italian tomatoes, drained and sieved
Salt
Pepper

To the onion, add the tomatoes and blend the mixture; season it to taste. Simmer it, partially covered, for 15 minutes. Sieve the sauce, forcing the solids through. Return the sauce to the skillet.

4 tablespoons butter
1 teaspoon basil
1 teaspoon oregano

To the sauce, add the butter and herbs. Simmer the sauce, uncovered, for 30 minutes; it will thicken somewhat.

A GLOSSARY OF COOKING TERMS

Butter: Because one wants the flavor of cheese to be dominant in these recipes and also because certain cheeses are salty, I recommend using sweet (unsalted) butter.

Chicken broth, canned, to defat: Place the can of chicken broth in the refrigerator overnight; when ready to use the broth, remove the lid and spoon off the solidified fat.

Freezing: When it is possible to freeze a dish, indication is made to that effect. It is suggested, however, that freezing be done only for leftovers, not for the meal you intend serving to your guests. Cheese dishes frequently do not freeze well—while their flavor is unimpaired, their appearance and consistency often are. It is important that frozen dishes be allowed to thaw fully to room temperature before being reheated for serving. Do not allow thawed precooked dishes to overcook when reheating.

Phyllo pastry: The remarkably thin sheets of pastry used in Middle Eastern cooking can be obtained (also available as strudel leaves) in specialty food shops; they keep almost indefinitely in the refrigerator.

Preparation time: The times suggested cover a coordinated readying of the ingredients for cooking. Most recipes indicate the time necessary for preparation plus any additional time required for chilling, marination, and so on. However, you are advised to read each recipe through carefully to see that you have on hand any ingredients requiring advance preparation as well as to ensure that you have allowed enough time to prepare the recipe before you intend to serve it. Because many people keep on hand frozen pie pastry, preparation times for pies and tarts do not include readying the pastry.

Refrigeration: Prepared dishes so indicated in the recipe itself may be refrigerated without loss of flavor or, often, of consistency. Before heating them for serving, allow them to come fully to room temperature. Do not allow refrigerated dishes to overcook when reheating them.

Scalding: It is not necessary to boil milk to scald it; doing so changes its flavor and makes the pan difficult to clean. Scalding may be done over direct heat or over boiling water. In either case, heat the milk until the thinnest film forms on the surface and the milk itself shimmers; remove it from the heat.

Seasoned flour: ⅔ cup flour, 1½ teaspoons salt, ½ teaspoon pepper, shaken together in a waxed paper bag. Any remaining seasoned flour may be used in making the sauce for the dish.

Wines: In this book, dry wines are used unless specific indication is made to the contrary. The quality of a dish cooked with wine depends upon the quality of the wine itself. While it is unnecessary to cook with wines of rare vintage, it *is* advisable to use good, if not expensive, table wine.

APPENDIX

Cheese-Tastings and
a Few Hints
on Serving Cheese

Cheese-tastings are a fine way to entertain after dinner. There was a time when "dessert parties" were popular. Now, cheese-tastings seem to be the *après-dîner* vogue, perhaps because "made" desserts, often heavy, are somewhat less in culinary fashion and also because cheese follows almost any dinner so easily and complementarily. When giving an after-dinner cheese-tasting, tell your guests the kind of evening it will be so they will know how to plan their meal.

A feeling of warm informality characterizes such parties. The cheeses themselves and your guests' reactions to them stimulate conversation, and a good accompanying wine further enhances the feeling of compatibility.

In keeping with the atmosphere of informality, the table should be arranged attractively but simply. A white cloth or one which enhances the décor of the room or simply the unadorned wooden surface of the table will provide the most effective background for the cheeses, their accompaniments, and the beverages. A bowl of attractively arranged fresh fruit, for both visual and tangible consumption, will decorate the table nicely without making it look ornate. The focal point, however, should be the cheeses. For this reason, too, offer the cheeses in the simplest fashion, on a large board where they are well separated one from the other, on individual boards, or on plain, undecorated plates. Sharp knives should accompany hard cheeses; spreaders should be offered for soft ones. Supply napkins, of course, preferably cloth ones, which will not tear and disintegrate as paper ones do. Candlelight will enhance your table, glinting against wine bottles and glasses (I recom-mend the traditional "tulip" glass which works well for all wines). Above all, let there be "breathing room" on the table; no display of food can rise above overcrowding, and this is particularly true of cheese, each having its special quality. If your table cannot accommodate the entire spread, find a second place for wines and glasses; but do allow the feeling of unclutter to prevail.

In arranging the table, place the cheeses in progressive order from the mildest to the strongest (it is interesting to guests if cheeses are labeled); the wines should also be arranged from the lightest to the most robust. This arrangement, from mild to strong flavors in cheese and beverage, ensures against deadening the sense of taste.

For easy reference, here is a checklist of eight "do's" and two "do-not's" to enhance your cheese-tasting:

DO
1) Do provide an attractive but simple setting.
2) Do serve all cheeses at room temperature. (Hard cheeses need only about one hour, depending upon the size of the cheese. Soft cheeses require two hours.)
3) Do allow sufficient cutting room. (A cheese resting on a surface nearly its own size prevents people from serving themselves easily.)
4) Do offer a plate of *sweet* butter with the cheese. (Many people find this a delightful accompaniment to cheese-tasting.)
5) Do keep the flavors of the cheeses separate.
6) Do offer sufficient knives (one for each cheese and at least one for each guest—with a few extras).
7) Do offer enough napkins.
8) Do offer breads and biscuits which complement the taste of the cheese. (For example, thin-sliced French bread or water biscuits with Brie, Camembert, or Roquefort; a good dark pumpernickel with Limburger or Livarot. If you are in doubt, stay with bland breads and unsalted biscuits, thus letting the cheese speak for itself.)

DO NOT
1) Do not pour wine glasses so full that the *bouquet* is lost.
2) Do not offer too strong a wine for the types of cheeses that you are serving.

The question often arises, whether for cheese-tastings or for daily serving of table cheese, what wines go with what cheeses? I know of only one rule: robust wines with pungent cheeses, light wines with delicately flavored ones. Beyond this, I feel, the choice is a matter of taste based on your experimentation. To facilitate your adventures in trying different wine and cheese combinations, here follow suggestions for your guidance; but they are only that—suggestions:

Full-bodied, robust red wines—Blue cheeses, Edam, Gruyère, Livarot, Münster.

Light-bodied red wines—Brie, Camembert, soft-running cheeses.

Dry white wines—Edam, Emmenthaler, Gruyère.

Light, dry, and fruity red, white, or rosé wines—Appenzeller, Port Salut, goat's-milk cheeses.

Semi-dry white wines—fresh, unripened cheeses.

Wines from the same area as the cheeses themselves, if available, are almost invariably complementary.

For those who would enjoy giving a "United States" cheese-tasting (a good beginning in the appreciation of cheese), offer New York Cheddar, Vermont Sage, Ohio Liederkranz, California Monterey Jack, Minnesota Blue, and perhaps Kentucky Trappist. An American claret or well-chilled beer will go well with these, as will rye bread and any bland, crisp cracker. Nothing very complicated here. Nothing very subtle, either; but one starts somewhere and this selection, simple as it is, will prove satisfying and pleasant.

On a more sophisticated level, an "international" cheese-tasting might include: Dutch Gouda, English Cheshire, French Brie, German Münster, Italian Gorgonzola, and Swiss Appenzeller. A good but moderately priced Burgundy will enhance these cheeses. French bread, Melba toast rounds, and water biscuits will also complement them.

The following suggestions are made for an inexpensive, a moderately priced, and a gala cheese-tasting of eight to ten guests each. Allow ¼ pound of cheese per guest (total, that is—not of each cheese).

An Inexpensive Cheese-Tasting

American Cheddar, Danish Blue, French Camembert, Danish Tilsiter (Havarti). Plain biscuits (crackers); French or black bread. Well-chilled beer or homemade sangria. Total cost for cheeses, about $7.00.

A Moderately Priced Cheese-Tasting

Italian Fontina, French Brie and Cantal, Italian Gorgonzola, Swiss Gruyère. Whole-wheat biscuits, French bread, pumpernickel. Moderately-priced, light red wine (Bordeaux) or homemade sangria (only semi-sweet). Total cost for cheeses, about $10.00.

A Gala Cheese-Tasting

French Camembert, Port Salut, Reblochon, Roquefort, and a goat cheese. Unsalted biscuits or Melba toast, French bread. Good (not necessarily costly) Burgundies, both red and white. Total cost for cheeses, about $15.00.

In these instances, the cost for cheese is modest. Breadstuff and beverages can be similarly moderate in price. For example, the total cost of the "Gala," purposely made "French" to show just one "national" possibility open to you (it could as easily have been American, German, Italian, or what you will) would be approximately $30.00 for an evening's entertainment of ten persons, a very reasonable expenditure.

Cheese-tasting, like cheese recipes, need only your inventiveness and originality to make them unusually delightful occasions: inventiveness and originality in terms of the cheeses selected, their arrangement, the beverages offered, the hospitality of your table and—of course—the combinations of people you invite. Carefully planned cheese-tastings provide evenings of delicious and unusual refreshment, of good conversation, and of warm and friendly companionship. Little wonder that they are rapidly growing in popularity!

Disconnected Thoughts on Serving Cheese

When serving cheese, allow, for dessert, 2 to 4 ounces per person and, for a cheese course, 3 to 5 ounces a serving.

When serving Emmenthaler as a dessert, offer also a mild cream cheese as a contrast; apples and fresh nuts are companionable accompaniments, as are sweet gherkins, sweet butter, crusty bread, and the pepper mill.

The sizes and shapes of cheeses should contrast on a serving tray, making them more appealing to both eye and appetite.

Portions of cheese uneaten at table, if too dried to serve again, should be wrapped and saved for use in a cooked dish of your choice.

Cheeses arranged on vine or tree leaves, which have been rinsed under cold water and dried with absorbent paper, are particularly attractive. Grape-vine leaves have been traditional garnishes since antiquity; any leaves, however, from the fresh greens of spring to the tawny golds and brilliant reds of fall will enhance the appeal of cheeses.

Why serve cheese on wood? It is easily cut supported by wood. And the wood will not break. Cutting hard cheese on a ceramic platter may result in the cracking of the plate itself.

Decorate your cheese tray with cherry tomatoes, radishes, sweet gherkins, parsley sprigs. Or offer cheese with ripe pears, melon slices, apples, cherries, grapes. In autumn, serve fresh nuts and an accompanying nutcracker, together with seasonal fruits.

INDEX

GENERAL INDEX

RECIPE INDEX

STAYING ALIVE!

The true story of Kaqun water and its effectiveness in improving health and lives

Martha Tailor

STAYING ALIVE!

The true story of Kaqun water and its
effectiveness in improving health and lives

Martha Tailor

First Edition

ISBN 978-963-7146-39-8

RADNAI Publisher
Production manager in charge: Radnai Gábor
Press: Csaba-Könyv Bt., Békéscsaba
Production manager in charge: Somogyi Attila
Typeset, cover and layout design: Tonetograph

www.marthatailor.hu • www.radnaikiado.hu

Attention

This book was born out of a decision made by József B. who recovered from a terminal illness. His intention with this book was to provide guidance for others who suffer from various diseases; his story inspires the reader never to give up hope, not even when all seems lost. He offers a way to stay alive that helped him to survive. After reading the story the reader will have a chance to overcome death by way of an alternative therapy available to all.

He recommends the book to everyone who wishes to make a conscious decision concerning their health while calling our attention to the importance of using the remedy alongside with a therapy prescribed by a physician and not instead of it.

I wish to note here that everything conveyed in this book is based solely on the experiences of Joseph B. which he gained during the course of his illness and subsequent recovery. All stories published in the book were compiled by József B. All the photos and data were collected by him and provided to the author who gave the book its final form and who cannot be held responsible for the contents of this publication.

Foreword

You have to want to live!

It is the foremost responsibility of a medical professional to examine all the aspects of necessary treatments in order to improve the patient's condition or achieve full recovery of the patient. Many a times we do not have the faintest idea what to make of a medical certificate. Diagnosis based on medical tests will accurately determine the condition of the patient's blood and the type of the illness that they suffer from. Then it is the job of the physician to prescribe the necessary therapy for the patient. Options are rather limited at this point because not every illness has a cure. Modern medicine will place priority on eliminating the problem as soon as possible even if considerable side effects are expected.

I believe that we all agree on is that the source of many illnesses is our attitude to life and is the result of our actions. Anyone who is a smoker or lives a stressful, sedentary lifestyle or has alcohol problems cannot expect to stay fit and healthy in the long run and may have to face an early exit from life.

Health-conscious modern people anticipate things and plan accordingly. Nowadays more emphasis is put on disease prevention such as a healthy diet, regular exercise, stress avoidance, abstaining from toxic substances as well as doing self-detoxication on a regular basis.

In my practical experience I have found that it is a widespread phenomenon that patients, after receiving a cancer diagnosis, fall into a depression and the fear of death follows close by. Anger comes soon after. Most frequently questions surface such as: Why is this happening to me? Why now?

Great differences are seen in how patients react to the disease. Based on modern knowledge, much depends on successful cooperation and that is why it is very important to be aware of the precursors which foreshadow positive or negative adaptation to the illness.

It is a fact that false beliefs and outdated information about cancer are difficult to change. For instance, a patient with cancer cannot recover or cancer equals death. This is, however, not true for all cases. Cancer research recognizes the instances of spontaneous remission. Such cases are well documented and numerous cancer survivors represent the chances for staying alive.

I would like to share the story of a good friend of mine with my esteemed readers. The story of James Sorenson from California may provide an explanation of recovery and hope for many of us.

James was 71 years old when he made the decision to change his lifestyle and start a new life by leaving behind old habits and opting for a different path for the rest of his remaining life. Six years earlier James went home one day with the feeling of sadness after a diagnosis of advanced prostate cancer. He immediately got a start on his cancer therapy, and like a good patient who wants to recover, he followed the advice of his oncologist to the letter. He tolerated the first series of treatments very well and received positive results. He lived cancer free for three years and perceived himself to be cured and done with it all. But life intervened and the tumor recidivated (returned) – this time with metastatic cancer, malignant cells evident in his brain, lungs, and prostrate.

James was facing a difficult two-year-long battle. He knew he had to give it all to survive. Unfortunately, however, his superhuman effort and trials ended in failure. As a last resort, James moved into a hospice. By that time the cancer cells in his lungs had spread and his brain tumor grew to become the size of a golf ball. His pain increased to the point of preventing him from performing basic living functions.

But James did not give up, not even at the age of 71. He spent his spare time looking for a solution and when the morphine patches decreased his headache, he was diligently searching the internet to find a way out of his predicament.

One day our mutual friends called to ask me to find a dignified way for James to die. Then I recalled a new method that a Hungarian therapist had shown me. I have to admit the procedure was rather surprising to me, too. It seemed very simple and I was expecting some "abracadabra" but the deeper my knowledge concerning this therapy became, the more devoted I felt. It was logical and scientific at the same time.

Then I tried it myself just to see how I feel! I thought that strong faith or concentration will bring about the miracle but neither was needed. I fell asleep. Then I woke up refreshed and full of energy.

I advised James to travel to Budapest to see the miracle for himself. He took my advice and with his last effort he spent two months in the Hungarian capital. Time wore on and one day I received a newspaper clipping showing James with a smile and noticeable happiness on his countenance. After having read the article I understood what really happened. James' CT scan and lung scan spoke for themselves. According to his doctor, a miracle had taken place because neither the brain nor the lungs showed any traces of cancer! Modern diagnostic equipment failed to recognize any anomalies.

As for me, I am certain that many cases like this exist and not only in Budapest. We often hear of miraculous recoveries from terminal diseases, cancer being one of them. It is my hope that many will learn from James' story and will be able to gain strength to fight their own illnesses. Life should never be given up because it will find a way if it wants to go on! (James' detailed story can be found in the *South County News July, 2000 edition pp. 4-9.*)

Dr. Richard Y. T. Chen

Table of Contents

Martha Tailor

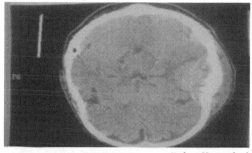

Before Kaqun bath

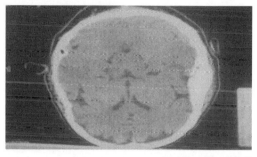

After Kaqun bath

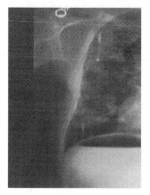

Before Kaqun bath

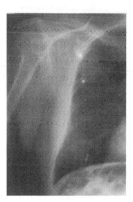

After Kaqun bath

THE ANTHEM OF LIFE

By Mother Theresa

Life is a single chance, take it seriously!
Life is beauty, look upon it with wonder!
Life is happiness, taste it!
Life is a dream, make it happen!
Life is a challenge, accept it!
Life is duty, fulfill it!
Life is a game, play it!
Life is wealth, use it!
Life is love, surrender to it!
Life is a secret, unravel it!
Life is a promise, fulfill it!
Life is sadness, overcome it!
Life is a melody, sing it!
Life is a battle, fight it!
Life is an adventure, accept it!
Life is a reward, earn it!
Life is life? Live it!

THE TRAGEDY OF A YOUNG GIRL

A light came on during the darkness of the night. A thin shadow passed by the drawn curtains. A young, newly graduated girl tossed and turned sleeplessly in her bed. It was the night before her very first job interview. She had a 10 a.m. appointment and the excitement would not let her rest. And there was something else! She felt a sharp pain every time she inhaled. She was holding her breath just to delay the pain. She had been sick with a fever for the past; she had had a terrible cold. She had taken her medicine and felt better but now once again became weak and lethargic. The pain worsened and felt intolerable. She was upset about being ill when she should look her best in order to get the job!

She could not remain in bed anymore. She got up and walked unsteadily to the bathroom. She turned on all the lights to see how much her face reflected her ill state.

Suddenly, a strong cough attack came upon her. She leaned over the sink to splash water on her face but when she glanced into the mirror she nearly fainted. Her entire face was covered in blood!

Her eyes dilated, her heart began racing, and she felt out of breath. Her legs were trembling and she had to hold onto the edge of the sink to keep herself from collapsing. Her tears mixed with blood as they fell into the white basin.

"Oh, God! What is happening to me? Where is all this blood coming from?" she whispered in dismay, while leaning nearer to the mirror. She did not need to get any closer – even through her tears she saw that the blood was coming from her mouth. Every breath brought an even more intense pain.

She pressed her palms to her chest when a strong spell of nausea hit her. She started to get dizzy. She knew that within seconds she would lose consciousness and would not be able to return to her room. Her legs started to tremble. She held her arms out and touched the tile on the wall, slowly sliding down and leaving streaks of blood.

Finally she sank down to the cool tiled floor. She leaned her back to the wall and hung her head down when another cough attack consumed her. Her chest and back were enveloped in a terrible pain while blood was streaming out of her mouth staining her white pajamas.

She wiped her mouth and tried to take deep breaths because the taste of blood brought more nausea but deep breathing caused her to experience intolerable pain. Tears were shedding from her eyes without a stop. She tried to stand up to hold the sink's edge but she was so weak that she was unable to do that either.

She felt the dizziness and the oncoming unconsciousness. She was not concerned about herself but about her parents. What is going to happen when she is found covered in blood? Her parents would die of fright. No! She cannot let that happen, somehow she must stand up, wash her face, and return to her room to change her clothes. She tried again but failed. She was unable to move her arms and the dreadful weakness took over her.

She was terrified! She did not understand what was happening to her. It seemed she could not spare her parents from the spectacle; she had to yell to wake them up because she was not able to stand up on her own. She could not stay on the tile because of her susceptibility to colds and she did not want another bout with fever.

She opened her mouth and shouted but she only had strength for a quiet whisper. Horrible pain has overtaken her chest and back but she tried a few times to shout loud enough to summon her parents' help.

Slowly, she gave up. She realized that she would not succeed. Things seemed to be shaking around her and her teeth were rattling. She was that cold.

She sat motionlessly for a half an hour. The stream of blood stopped and she felt better. She pulled her legs underneath her and got on her knees. With her arms stretched out, she gathered up all her strength and slowly got up.

She took a towel and she pressed it to her mouth, and step by step, holding onto various things, she managed to get into her bed. She fell onto her pillow and sobbed loudly. Her shaking from the cold worsened and she covered herself completely with her blanket. She tried to sleep and squeezed her eyes closed but could not fall asleep.

Fear was taking her thoughts over. She had no idea what was happening to her but she felt that it was something very serious. She wished her parents could be with her but she had no strength to walk over to them. She was glad to have made it to her own bed.

Since there was nothing she could do and she was trapped by her fears she let her tears flow freely. She sobbed bitterly and while dawn was nearing outside, her room only gave home to fears.

When she calmed down a little, she sat up in her bed. She licked her dry lips and touched her mouth with her fingers but there was no blood to be found. She thought that the force of the cough might have ruptured a blood vessel in her throat. She had heard of such things happening. Of course! That is what must have happened to her, too! There is no other explanation why blood should be coming out of her mouth while coughing or throwing up.

But then what is this intolerable pain? Every time she inhaled, she felt as if her lungs were just ripped out and breathing was still very laborious for her. She felt as if a great amount of weight had been placed on her chest. She had pain in her face, throat, jaw, and ears, too. She had difficulty swallowing which she understood to be the symptom of the ruptured blood vessel in her throat.

This thought calmed her down a little but when she turned to her side, she had another spell of cough and she felt warm blood flooding her mouth. She pressed the towel to her mouth in full panic.

"What is this? What is happening to me?" she thought and fell to her pillow crying.

The door opened and her mother appeared.

"Why aren't you sleeping, my dear?" she asked as she came closer and then she noticed her crying. The mother, scared to death, embraced her daughter.

"Darling, what is wrong? You know you can tell me everything!" she said as she lifted her daughter's head with her hand. When she looked the girl in the face she noticed the blood that had stained everything around and she screamed. There was blood on the towel, on the pillow, and on the pajamas.

"Oh, Lord! What is happening to you?" her mother screamed. Her father just arrived. "For God's sake, what is all this screaming so early in the morning? I can't even..." his words froze in his mouth as he stepped closer and noticed all the blood.

"Sweetie! What is happening?" he said as his face turned fearful and he kneeled down next to his daughter.

"I don't know! My chest and back hurt awfully. I have felt sick for the past few days." She whispered as she struggled for breath. Her mother placed her hand on her forehead.

"Oh, dear! You have a high fever! You have another bad cold!" she said as she looked towards her husband.

"I don't know what is wrong with me. I feel very weak and when I take a breath my chest and my back hurt terribly. That is why I couldn't sleep. I just tossed and turned throughout the night, I tried to hold back my breath as long as I could so that I didn't have to breathe so frequently. Then I went to the bathroom to see how bad I looked, you know, because of the job interview...

That is when I started coughing and then I looked into the mirror and saw all the blood. I was so scared!" cried the daughter.

"But sweetie! Why didn't you tell us?" said the father while holding his daughter's thin fingers.

"I didn't want to frighten you. I thought that I had busted a blood vessel in my throat while coughing but then I got nauseous and started vomiting blood. I held a towel to my mouth and held onto things to get back to bed." she said while pain distorted her face.

"I have such a terrible pain!" she said while holding her chest.

"Calm down, dear. I will take you to my doctor friend immediately and he will tell us what is wrong and he can help you with the pain, too," offered the father while kissing his daughter on the forehead. He stood up but the girl pulled him back down.

"Dad! I am so scared!" she said while hugging his neck. The father embraced her and looked at his wife who was staring at him with teary eyes full of fear.

"Everything is going to be all right! Don't worry, my love! Nothing bad is going to happen! I am calling my friend right now and I am taking you to him to the hospital. I was talking to him yesterday afternoon, he said he was on duty and he should still be there. He will find out what is wrong with you, darling." He said as he caressed her feverish face.

"And… and what about my job interview?" whispered the girl.

"Of course we will call them and ask them to give you another appointment. They will understand the reason for the delay. Don't worry about that, dear. If they don't understand then there will be other job opportunities. The most important thing is to get you to a doctor immediately." He said and turned to his wife.

"Get ready while I make that phone call. OK?"

"All right!" answered the mother and helped her daughter get up. She hugged the girl and they stepped into the bathroom.

* * *

The doctor was waiting for them in the hospital. He e-scorted the daughter into a room and asked the parents to wait outside. After a long time, the door opened. The doctor stepped out. He was pale and solemn.

"What is wrong with our daughter?" they asked almost simultaneously.

"I am sorry but I believe we have a very serious problem. I have talked to my colleagues and based on the X-rays, I can only conclude that she has a malignant tumor in her lungs...

"No!" shouted the mother and she collapsed into her husband's trembling arms.

"Oh God! You can do surgery, right? She can recover, right?" asked the father as he looked on his friend with an ashen expression.

The doctor looked over the father's shoulder as he spoke to him.

"I promise to do everything possible to help her." said the doctor as he placed a reassuring hand on the shoulder of the concerned father.

* * *

The young woman was treated surgically and with aggressive chemotherapy but after three months of suffering she passed away...

SOME ALARMING STATISTICS

The data concerning cancer-related deaths in Hungary have been showing appalling figures for a long time. Currently, 300,000 patients are suffering from cancer in this country.

Every year nearly 40,000 people die of cancer related diseases. When compared with the cancer data of thirty other European countries, combining all cancer deaths, concerning men, Hungarians are first on the list, and concerning women, Hungarians are second on the list to die from all types of cancers.

When considering all European countries, it can be concluded that in smoking-related lung and mouth cancer deaths Hungarian men lead all statistics. When we compare cancer deaths among European females, Hungarian women are first in the statistics of colon cancer and leukemia-related deaths and they are ninth on the list in death related to breast cancer.

According to the most recent data, 2.6 million Europeans have died of cancer and while the statistics vary greatly, cancer deaths are disproportionately higher in Eastern Europe, and especially in Hungary.

The European cancer death list is led by lung cancer – 20% of all cancer deaths –, followed by colon cancer, stomach cancer, and breast cancer. Among men, lung cancer is the leading type of cancer responsible for most deaths, and among women it is breast cancer. Western Europe is the leading region where most men die from cancer – except for Austria –, followed by Eastern Europe, with the lowest rate in Northern Europe.

THE STORY OF JOSEPH

Near death...

I had always been known to be the guy full of energy, the one who never rests. 24 hours a day was not enough for me; I was never tired. I worked because my family was the most important aspect of my life and I wanted to provide everything possible for them. I knew very well that I did not spend a lot of time with my wife and three children even though I tried to give them all my free time.

All that work resulted in a home and a vacation house at the "Hungarian Sea", Lake Balaton. We looked forward to our vacation time at the lake every year. We tanned to a bronze color; we enjoyed the sun and the water. We had a wonderful time together.

It happened to be another beautiful summer day on that fateful day when we arrived at the lake house. I discovered a small, strange spot on my chest, near my neck. It slightly emerged from my skin and had a different color. I did not think much of it concluding that it had been caused by a naturally increasing pigment material as a way of protection from the sun. My neighbor also noticed it and I explained it to him that it was a result of tanning. Suddenly I lost my voice and I had to clear my throat. I remarked that this had happened before, cleared my throat again and everything was all right again. I did not give it much thought.

My neighbor gave me a serious look.

Staying Alive!

"Listen, József. Have a doctor to take a look at you. The spot and your vocal cords, too. It is better to be safe than sorry!" he advised me but I shooed the warning away with a joke because I was the jokester, the always happy and fun loving guy...

After our vacation ended and we went back to Budapest, I returned to my job in the car part store where I always had to talk. That was not a problem for me: I loved to chat but my voice gave out on me more and more frequently, and the spot did not want to disappear either. I recalled the kindly warning words of my lakeside neighbor more and more often. Finally I decided to see a doctor because the spot had not disappeared even though I stopped tanning and my voice was giving me a hard time.

One morning I went to see my general practitioner, who looked me over. He listened to my symptoms and handed me a prescription. I took the medicine regularly but my condition did not improve. I went back and he told me that I needed to see a specialist. I was a little surprised to see a throat specialist but that is the doctor to see if someone has a throat problem.

I went to see the specialist thinking I needed to settle this matter because there is too much work waiting for me at the store. I went to the hospital and found the doctor's office. I sat down outside and waited for my turn and when I looked up I noticed a man sitting right across me. He was about my age. The sight was too horrible not to look at: he had a hole in his throat with a tube sticking out of it.

When I realized that he noticed me looking at him, I turned my head thinking that if this happened to me my life would be over. If I could not talk anymore, my life and my work would just end. I recalled that I had had customers before who could not talk for the same reason. I had a strange feeling and served them with special attention...

The sight had a significant effect on me and I could not wait to get away from that waiting room. It was a relief when I was finally called into the doctor's office. When the examination was over the doctor gave me a serious look and told me that he had found an anomaly in five little places on my vocal cords; altogether they were about the size of a half a lentil.

I was just staring at the doctor, too dumbfounded – or scared – to ask anything. I was thinking of that man outside in the waiting room. That hole in his throat was all that my eyes could see... What if that is going to happen also to me? I felt a drop of sweat trickle down on my back but I calmed down when the doctor gave me a prescription. He told me to take my medicine and do steam treatments on my throat.

I was relieved when I left the hospital. I convinced myself that if something had been seriously wrong they would have treated me through surgery and not with pills.

I started to take my medicine exactly as prescribed and did my home remedy steam treatments regularly. Unfortunately, I had to realize that I was not getting any better.

I went back to the throat specialist who examined me and advised me to have a biopsy taken, so he could give me a more accurate diagnosis. I froze when I heard his words. A biopsy? Why? He would have answered me if I had asked those questions out loud but my throat strangely tensed up and all I could do was to nod in agreement.

* * *

I had a bad feeling but the next day I was in hospital, trying to keep the negative thoughts away that had taken up hold in my mind and tried to keep a brave face. I attempted to convince myself that nothing could be wrong with me. I feel fine, I don't feel any pain. I lose my voice once in a while, so what? And after all, I was just too cool to be sick!

I have to admit that, for the first time in my life, I had a hard time keeping negative thoughts away. My great sense of humor had left me.

* * *

I had always been healthy; my only reason to go to a hospital was to visit others. And now... doctors in white coats, busy nurses, all the beds, and that strange, typical hospital smell... I was at the end of my rope. I could barely wait until the procedure had been done and I could finally go home.

After the biopsy was taken, every minute seemed like eternity while I had to wait for my results. My moods were changing according to how I was feeling. Sometimes I was totally depressed because I was sure that I had a terrible disease and I would probably have to have a hole cut into my throat. At other times I was laughing at the whole thing because I believed that I was this strong healthy person who could not possibly have a disease!

Then the moment came when the doctor was standing in front of me with the results in his hand. I was watching his face but I did not feel any better from what his expression reflected. He was very serious and there was something in his eyes that made my throat close up. It was as if he was trying to calm me with his eyes.

"Please, doctor, tell me the results! I feel as if I was sitting on needles and my legs want to run home! My pigeons are waiting! That is my hobby, you know," I said, trying to cover for my nerves.

The doctor then took a seat next to me and got a hold of my hand.

"It is a malignant squamous cell," he said quietly and squeezed my hand gently. When he told me I was just looking at him wondering why he was so serious instead of smiling. This isn't cancer! It is a squamous cell, even if it is malignant. Not cancer, not what I was afraid of! I was relieved.

He probably read my expression and knew that I had not understood because he repeated himself in more details.

"I am so sorry, but the result is alarming. This is a type of cancer that is most difficult to treat. There is no other option. I have to perform surgery."

I don't know what happened to me in the next moment. It was as if the world had ceased to exist and I was just hovering between the heavens and earth. I felt that I had no body and that I didn't even exist and it was only the fear that overwhelmed my soul.

The doctor placed the results on my nightstand and then touched my shoulder. He rested his hand there to calm me down because he knew that I took a hard hit.

"I have to do the surgery as soon as possible! You know, as with any disease, the sooner we get to it, the better the chances are for recovery," he explained but I only heard him from a distance. First I did not even hear him mention surgery; I did not even remember it because there was a single word echoing in my mind: Cancer! Cancer! Cancer!

This whole thing – like a lightning bolt from clear skies – just hit me. I felt so strange as if something had snapped inside me. I was looking at the doctor, I saw his mouth and hands move but I did not comprehend him because my mind was somewhere else. I was somewhere else! Far, far, far away… I was struggling not to cry. I am strong, I could not be crying because of such a minor thing!

The doctor was called away in an emergency. He left immediately leaving the results behind.

I wanted to be sure I was alone, so I looked around the hospital room. That is when I lifted up the biopsy results and only God knows how many times I read it again and again.

No, I was not ashamed to admit to the uncontrollable crying that came over me. I fell onto my pillow and let out the tears of frustration and fear. Death hovered in front of my eyes and I saw it slash at me with a bloody reaper.

Then my family appeared in front of me! My wife with her eyes full of tears and sadness. My children who held unto me and looked at me with no comprehension of what was happening. I felt as if my life had ended. I am my family's security, the bread-winner! What is going to happen to them? Then my family suddenly disappeared and I ceased to see anything but that hole on that man's neck.

Suddenly I raised my hand to my throat as in fear that the hole had already been there. I swallowed while my whole body was trembling. I tried to gather my strength in order to think clearly and to convince myself that I did not need a hole on my throat. That patient probably had another kind of disease!

What can I say, I failed.

I always ended up going back to that fear; I was unable to shake off the thought. Maybe that hole will become part of my life from now on? If I have a life at all from now on… since how could that be called living? Without a voice, without speaking, given the sentence of eternal silence. No! That cannot be! I could never settle for that!

My heart leaped into my throat and continued to beat there strong enough to almost prevent me from breathing. I walked unsteadily towards the bathroom and washed my face with cold water. I remembered my lakeside neighbor and suddenly felt angry with him. His nonchalant advice about seeing a doctor! The squawking crow!

Well, here I am! Of course!

"Better safe than sorry!" he said so smartly. Well, he can have his day because I am scared now; in fact, I have never been so terrified in my life!

I turned my face to the mirror and looked into my own eyes and started to feel ashamed. Why do I blame my neighbor? It was not him who gave me this disease. If he had not urged me to see a doctor, who knows, maybe I would be beyond all help at some point!

Staying Alive!

As a matter of fact, can they help me at all? My head was reeling from fear.

There was a knock on the door. I quickly gathered my strength to look calm because I thought my wife had come to visit me. I did not want her to see me falling apart. I even forced a small smile on my face and looked at the door. I was relieved when another doctor friend of mine stepped in instead of my wife. We had known each other for a long time; I did not have to hide my feelings from him.

"Well, what's going on? Do you have the results?" he asked while walking towards me but when he looked into my face, his mouth trembled. We were old friends and he could read me very well.

"There is something wrong, isn't there?" he inquired. I could not talk; sobbing has closed up my throat, so I just nodded towards the papers.

He lifted up the medical results and read them. He stared at the papers, turned towards me with tears running down his face.

"Oh, God! József! A squamous cell carcinoma! I am so sorry, I cannot lie to you: this is the worst kind of cancer. It hurts me to tell you but you must prepare for the worst!" he said. He held my hand and embraced me. We cried together.

When he left, I really crashed. Instead of encouraging me he confirmed that the end was here! How could anyone prepare for the worst? How can I accept that I have to die? I am a strong guy, barely older than fifty and I have so much more to accomplish in this life! My children need me! No squamous cell is going to have the best of me! It is only a size of a half a lentil.

"I am much stronger than that!" I told myself trying to regain my typical cool but it did not go too well.

It was as if I was at the edge of insanity. Kneading my own hands, I was running around in the room trying to figure out who I could ask to help me deal with all this. It would be great to talk to someone who had been through this and had been able to convince himself about the reason for all this. He could tell me how to do it!

Of course, in front of my family I did not reveal my fears. I was laughing, joking, and… crying inside. If they had not been supporting me, I would not have wanted to go on living.

* * *

Drawing from the strength of my family, I tried to live day by day. I made it a point not to show what is going on inside me. I wanted to spare them from the worries and the pain. I knew that my wife knew very well what was going on inside me. But she also knew my strength and my way of trying to protect them from getting hurt.

What can I say? I have never felt so bad. I was weak, sick, and useless! Many times I thought: what am I going to be good for from now on? Is there even a *from now on*…?

I had terrible days but the nights were even worse. The daily routine made me forget my predicament for a short time but at night I had nothing to keep me busy. Thoughts were whirling around in my head and I could almost feel the ice cold breath of death on my face.

Staying Alive!

I don't know how I lasted for a month, but a month later, in the August of 2001 I had my surgery. I was so very nervous and scared. What happens if I do not make it through the surgery, or if I die right after? If I pass away…? If I can never see my children again, or my grandkids? What if I can never hear my wife's voice again?

I still have so much to do, so many things to take care of! I cannot just die!

I have to admit I was terrified but I believe that my family was even more scared. My beloved wife – with her eyes red and swollen – held my hand trembling, the children were sobbing… They were asking what was happening to dad and why he could not come home.

I will never forget their fearful eyes as I will never forget a dream I had before the surgery. I saw an altar and I had been laid down dead in front of it. I saw myself from outside. Then I woke up. I was sweating rivers and was saying aloud: "No! No! I am not going to die! I want to live and I am going to live!"

Then an unexplainable, strange thing happened to me because I felt an unbelievable amount of emerging will power which I used to have before. Since my youth I had been independent, I made my own decisions which were usually the right ones, and I was my own man. This will to live; this great strength swept away all my fears. I completely changed.

* * *

The surgery was a success. My newly found strength made me walk the next day. Doctors and nurses could not believe their eyes when they saw it.

I was sitting in front of my window and I was thinking about that incredible amount of strength that I had received before my surgery and it was still with me. This strength and my love for my family pushed me to get well. I believe that since this great "love-force" helped me, I was on my way to recover and soon I could be leaving hospital…

* * *

Naturally, I went back to the hospital for regular check-ups and I received radiation therapy to prevent a reoccurrence. It seemed that I could hope that I had escaped and triumphed over cancer!

After that, when given the chance, I tried to inform myself about cancer prevention methods. Can a change of diet or a change in the lifestyle help? I was scared that the cancer might return and that the throat of a person was not a great oak tree that can be trimmed every week. The size is limited and that is what's needed: I have to pay attention to my health.

Unfortunately, no one could answer my inquiries about cancer prevention and therefore I concluded that there was nothing that I could do. I could only hope that I fully recovered and that was the impression given at the hospital where I was told that the amount of radiation therapy I had received took care of the problem for at least another thirty years.

I went home a happy man. I was well and my zest for life started to return. There were less and less instances when I was thinking about the reoccurrence of cancer. My family also started to relax a little because they saw my old self again. I was joking and laughing again.

Then the happy and fun times ended because soon it became evident that my hopes were in vain and the doctors' encouragement was in vain as well. Six months later, in the March of 2002, the right side of my neck started to swell up.

Another lightning bolt from a clear sky! The shock was quickly replaced by fear of reality. What else could I have been thinking? The cancer has returned and my sad story continues... or even ends.

I have never considered that this could happen to me. Why me? Why is it me who has to face this horrible disease? While others live a happy life, I have to live through hell! I was angry because I was helpless and I could not solve my problem the way I had been able find solutions before. I was going mad because of that helpless feeling.

Slowly, I got past the self-pity. I realized that it does not help if I always cry and feel sorry for myself. I am strong and I can win against cancer! I was sure I had to face the dreadful disease again. I had to be stronger once again because I did not want to burden my family as they had been through enough already.

As soon as I had noticed the new symptoms, I went back to my doctor, to the one who performed my first surgery. I knew that the sooner the treatment starts the better the chances are for survival. As much as I would have liked to, I knew I could not avoid surgery. It proved to be effective once; why could it not work again? I was hopeful that I would get another chance to stay with my family.

The doctors could not believe that despite the great amount of radiation therapy, the cancer had returned. They performed the various examinations and tests, scans, MRI which all turned out to be worse than expected. I thought I knew what to get ready for; still it was difficult to face reality. I believed that nothing could surprise me now but the shock was once again hard to bear. Somewhere in the deep recesses of my mind and heart I dared to hope that the tumor was not malignant...

In the meantime the tumor in my neck swelled with water and an edema occurred.

The doctors tried injecting it but that brought no relief and another life saving procedure became necessary. It was feared that the edema could cause asphyxiation.

I was trembling when I asked what that life saving operation really means. The doctor described that there would be an incision across my larynx to keep my trachea (windpipe) open.

My heart jumped up into my throat and kept beating there. I could barely utter the words:

"Does that mean that I will have a hole in my throat for the rest of my life?"

I was looking at my doctor with hope but he placed his hand on my arm and said:

"I am sorry, that is exactly what it means. We have no other option to save you. If we choose not to go ahead with the procedure, you will choke to death."

This was the moment when I feared like never before. Since I had seen that poor patient with the hole in his throat, I was petrified that this could happen to me. And here it was!

Staying Alive!

It first occurred to me that I would not want to undergo the surgery. I would rather choke to death than live without a voice and without the ability to talk. No one will stare at me on the street or at the store when I can only point and talk without making sounds…

I told the doctor to forget about the whole thing because there was going to be no surgery. He kindly and patiently explained that many people would have gladly accepted this option but were not given the chance. People could still live a normal life like that! He advised me not throw away my life because my family needs me.

The doctor talked about my future with such conviction that he also convinced me not to give up. He is right, I should not quit. I have to accept the fact, no matter how bitter or painful, that I would not be able to talk anymore and I would have a hole in my throat.

The procedure was done without anesthesia and even though I did not feel anything, I did hear the crunching noises when the cartilaginous organ was removed. I will never ever forget that! I was swallowing my tears while I was telling myself I had to get through this; I had to get through this!

Then the first glance into a mirror! I thought I was prepared but I really wasn't. I had to face cold reality, it was shocking. I am at loss for words when it comes to trying to explain how I felt when I saw the hole in my throat and the tube sticking out of it. I thought I was not going to survive, I was so depressed. I cried like a child.

When I cried myself out, I sagged onto my bed and just stared into nothing. I did not understand how this was all possible. How could cancer develop in my body? I do not smoke, I do not drink and those risk factors are continually mentioned as primary causes of cancer. So, how did I get it? How?

Since the beginning of my disease, I had hit several low points but it was as if hell had opened up! I thought I was much stronger and I would be able to cope with the circumstances but I could not. I regretted choosing the surgery and contemplated that death would have been a better option. I did not want to live not being able to make a sound! I will be silent like a fish, I will just move my mouth but no one will understand me because I cannot speak.

"I cannot speak!" I would have screamed but only my lips were moving and my tears were flowing.

I lived through some real hard times and if it wasn't for my family my dear readers would never have come across my story. In the end, I decided to live life. Even though I lost the battle, I did win the war. My life did not end; I was able to live on with my family and my loved ones. They accepted me the way I was and I had a reason to live for because they mean the most to me.

I recalled an event that happened while staying at Lake Balaton. I was sitting in the garden just enjoying nature. I always loved the outdoors, I always enjoyed looking at the clouds floating across the sky; listening to the birds chirping and hearing the cricket's night music. Then I observed a tiny little ant that was carrying something far larger and a lot heavier than itself. I attempted to block its way but it kept trying to get through, it did not give up, it wanted to break through the obstacle. I placed my finger on the ant and forced it to stop. It was amazing to me how it wiggled and squirmed, how it wanted to live! The ant gathered all its strength to get free and it tried without ever giving up! I let it go and I marveled at how small it was and yet how tirelessly it struggled! Such a will to survive!

It did not occur to me at the time that someday I will remember that minuscule episode and will gain strength from it! I was ashamed but I had to admit that the little ant had taught me a lesson!

* * *

Slowly I reconciled myself to what could not be changed and I accepted what fate had dealt to me. I have to say it was not easy! I went through difficult times but I kept repeating to myself that I have to bear it and I have to give thanks to my Savior that I was still alive!

Of course, not all my medical problems were resolved. The malignant tumor between my chin and shoulder was still growing. I found out that every nine days it doubled in size.

My doctors told me that the tumor had to be removed as soon as possible and they reminded me that I could not receive any more radiation treatments because I had been given the maximum dosage already.

That was the defining moment when I truly realized that the end has surely come. I was so depressed about being silenced forever that I did not even think about the tumor and that it was malignant.

I finally understood that my death sentence has been issued... If the cancer comes back – and it did because the evidence was clearly bulging out of my neck. No, there is nothing else left; this is the end!

I believe that I really felt the nearness of death. I knew that after the surgery there would be no chances left because I could not receive any more treatment. And cancer patients cannot heal just by themselves. I was practically declared cancer-free after the 30 doses of radiation therapy and I thought I could go on living – if not for thirty years but at least a while longer. I was hopelessly being ravaged by a deadly disease and there was nothing anybody could do about it!

Once again, I completely lost it and I did not see reason to continue the struggle. I have to give up and admit that the cancer has won! It was stronger! And then I remembered the little ant... No! I cannot give up that easy! I said a hundred times, a thousand times that I am stronger and I will not lose hope! My willpower was getting stronger and stronger and I decided not to surrender to death. I would continue the struggle until I triumphed! I had no idea how to go on but I wanted to live for another few years...

* * *

I was given the possibility of choosing the date of the surgery but I was warned not to take too long. I knew that myself, too but I wanted to delay the moment when I had to go under the knife again. Not just because I was scared but because I was hoping to find a miracle that would save me from surgery.

I spent my days looking for a solution. I was searching the internet, the newspapers, the media and any other place where health issues were discussed.

I tried out everything. I drank wine essence because I heard it helps slow down the progress of cancer. I took some newly-discovered medicine, 30 pills a day; I took supplements that were supposed to destroy cancer cells. I drank different mineral waters, herbal teas, and tried other alternative treatments but none brought results.

By that time I was so depressed that I was about to agree to the surgery but then again my anger and my survival instincts took over. I had never had such will to live and I pulled myself together like never before, ready to buck the world if I had to. I could not believe that there was no help and so I could not give up. My mind's eye saw the scared faces of my three children, my smiling grandchildren and the crying face of my wife. That gave me power to go on searching further and further even though I tried everything that I could get my hands on.

I sat in my armchair one day struggling with sadness and frustration when my son-in-law came in. He put his hand on my shoulder and said:

"There is hope for recovery!"

I thought I heard him wrong. I jumped out of the chair as if a snake had bitten me.

"What is it? Please, just say it already!" I urged him excitedly.

"An acquaintance told me about a type of water that can do miracles."

"A kind of water that can do miracles?" I asked him with a puzzled expression.

"Please, stop kidding me! My life depends on this, so do not mess around!" I said with disappointment because I thought he was playing a joke on me.

"No! I am not joking! How could you think I could joke with something this important?" he said looking at me very seriously.

"I really did hear about a certain kind of water from a friend, some kind of oxygenated water, if I remember correctly. It worked for him; he is doing much better."

"Why? What is wrong with him?" I asked because he got me interested.

"He has cancer. Leukemia." he answered.

I think my heart stopped at this point. I felt better already. It was as if a colossal boulder rolled off my soul, and I did not even know what this treatment was all about. I recalled the previous methods of healing and their taste. If this was only water then it would be a blessing because some of the tastes I endured were horrible. I swear that if I had breathed on a camel (and they don't smell all that great either) it would have just keeled over.

I thought this oxygenated water could only be beneficial.

"Please, tell me about this water! What does it mean that it's oxygenated? Why would that be different from other mineral waters?" I asked.

"No, I am not talking about mineral water, I know that much. But I don't know how it heals. I know that there are treatments when you drink it and there are other treatments when you bathe in it. My friend suggested that you should go to Dobogókő where there is a special place: a Shaolin village where the bath club is. That is where you get answers to your questions."

"A Shaolin village? Oxygenated water that heals?" I said staring at my son-in-law with my eyes wide open.

"Well? My friend swears by it!" he shrugged his shoulders. "You can't harm yourself if you go and take a look for yourself." he said.

"Of course, I will go to see it." I said with a smile – something that had not been on my face for a long while.

* * *

As soon as I stayed alone, I got on my computer and I tried to find information about the Shaolin village. I found it and more. I found out that the oxygenated water does exist and it is being used as a drinking and bathing treatment.

I got even more excited. I went to my wife and explained to her what I was going to do. I thought she was going to be as skeptical as me about the oxygenated water but I was wrong. She was all for it, she encouraged me with tears in her eyes because she wanted me to be with her for some more time as much as I did.

She immediately packed all the necessary things and sat next to me on the bed holding my hand. She leaned onto my shoulder and we sat in silence while the pale shadow of hope fluttered in our hearts.

I barely slept that night. I was thinking about the water that healed a cancer patient. Even though I did not have leukemia, it could also help me. My hope for the future passed before my eyes. Maybe there is a chance for me to survive? Maybe I can see my children and grandchildren grow up to be decent adults?

Dawn was upon me when I finally fell asleep. I slept for about 3-4 hours but I did not feel tired. As soon as I had opened my eyes, I jumped out of bed. Curiosity and excitement propelled me so much that I could have flown right over to Dobogókő. There was a single thought in my head: I do not have to die and the miraculous water will heal me, too.

Hope...

When I arrived in Dobogókő and got out of my car, I just had a great experience. I had been to the Pilis Mountains before, I knew that the scenery was beautiful but I had no idea that I would encounter the wonders of the Far East there, so far away from the hustle and bustle of the city, in such a pristine mountain environment.

Dobogókő - the entrance of the Kaqun Bath at the Recreational Center

Staying Alive!

First I thought that I had entered a world that only exists in fairy tales. In the most spectacular part of the Pilis Mountains, not far from the Rám Ravine, there was a small village that appeared out of nowhere. I just stood there taking in the sight as many other vacationers must have done, since this place was well known as a paradise for nature lovers. I could hardly believe what I saw. Nature revealed so many aspects of itself and that is what made this place so unique.

My heart was about to stop so I took a deep breath. I felt the air go through my body and my soul. A few yards from me a group of tourists gathered as the guide started his presentation. I listened to that guide with my ears and heart all opened.

"This place is not just beautiful but it is also shrouded in mystery. According to legend, we are 25 kilometers from Budapest and this place here just happens to be the exact point where the earth's heart chakra lies. Supposedly the entire mountain is charged with energy because this peak is the point of interception for the lines of power." he said.

His words had a great influence on me. I could almost feel the energy that passed through all my cells.

"How did I end up here?" I thought to myself and I looked around as if I had never been there before. Yes! That is how I felt. Everything was so different. Even the air! I made my way towards my destination: life giving hope.

I stood before the finely carved gate and read the inscription:

"He who enters, prepare for the unexpected!"

The entrance of the Shaolin village at Dobogókő

My heart bounced all over inside and leaped into my throat when I walked through the gate because the next few yards led me into a truly different world.

I wanted to jump into the water, I wanted to taste it, I wanted to start the therapy immediately but I did not even know where to start.

"Where is the water that is going to heal me?" I thought while I was turning around and I started to feel lost.

I stood there hesitantly for a few seconds then I took off straight forward.

"Would this be the Shaolin village? No, this can't be it; I can't see any signs leading me to the oxygenated water. Did I take the wrong entrance? Was there another gate somewhere?" I was asking myself while doubts surfaced in my mind. My excitement changed to disappointment.

I was taking in the sights while asking myself where I was but there was no answer. So I was taking careful steps forward when I came close enough to hear a conversation between two men. I was hoping that they were talking about the oxygenated water and they would lead me where I needed to go.

I really started paying attention to them and felt stranger by the minute. My legs felt as if I had sprung roots into the ground – I could not move. What I heard completely awed me even though I knew it was not polite to eavesdrop.

The men suddenly stopped talking and I looked around with wonder.

"I did not get lost. I am standing in Europe's only Shaolin village. I have arrived. This place is truly special. I will have a chance to get to learn about *shaolin kung-fu*." I thought because the things I overheard piqued my interest. Then I suddenly came to realize... But I came here for treatments and not for sports! But the conversation picked up again:

"People get stronger here in body and in spirit. China, the cradle of Far Eastern martial arts, is the model and that is why this Shaolin village is built the way it is. Shaolin has a 1,500 year old history and it is the foundation for other martial arts but whoever enters through the gates may use the training facilities and could practice any martial art he or she chooses. Of course they can learn the basic martial art moves but more than that they can learn meditation and breathing exercises with the help of expert instructors. Recreation is given here but not just recreation but recovery for those who would like to regain their health, their well-being and all of that is based on life giving oxygen."

Of course, I was in the right place! I calmed down after my initial confusion. The place, the environment was all new and strange to me.

Then I relaxed from one second to another. I remembered the patient who was helped by the oxygenated water and there was no place left in me for negative thoughts.

"I have to look forward and I have to believe!" I told myself and turning to the side I noticed a sign on one of the buildings. My whole body was enveloped with sudden heat because I was standing on the threshold of my much hoped recovery.

My legs were shaking with excitement when I walked into the office and I received a very friendly welcome. The employees introduced themselves and an assistant started working with me and during our conversation it became evident that she herself used the oxygenated water even though she was not ill. So did the others.

The friendly welcome put me at an ease and gave me strength to hope and to believe. I talked about my illness and that all traditional treatments had been exhausted. I told the assistant that doctors could not do anything more for me but I heard about the healing water and I wanted to try it out. My assistant took my detailed medical history and then we covered the specifics of the drinking and bathing treatments.

I can't even begin to describe the amount of hope I had even though my fellow patients overheard the assistants' conversation in which they estimated my survival chances to be at 10%. That did not cause me any alarm, I looked at it as better than no chance. If the healing power of the oxygenated water is real than I should be feeling it soon! Maybe the surgery can wait a little while longer! The tumor on my neck continued its growth and I knew the time soon will come for decision making. I was literally playing with my life if the operation was delayed much longer.

* * *

It came as a surprise that lodging was conveniently provided while I was taking treatments. I had a place that was comfortable and clean.

I was excited and hopeful to begin the treatments. I was bathing three times a day and I drank far more water than suggested because after the first sip I realized that never in my life did I encounter such a silky, smooth and refreshing drink. I did not just quench my thirst but it was exhilarating. My body and my soul felt better!

During my stay, I had the opportunity to observe people. It was incredible to see the changes they went through after the bath treatments. Visible changes were easier to notice on women. After taking a bath in this special water their skin glowed and became more beautiful. They truly blossomed!

Of course, I was observing myself with great intensity eager to see improvement concerning the tumor on my neck. I really depended on this to be able to avoid another surgical procedure and to see that the tumor disappears for good!

It was not difficult to keep up with the treatment because there were no side effects to the water: it did not hurt, I was not getting sick, I had no nausea or vomiting, there was no diarrhea and I felt better. I could hardly believe my eyes: my skin was becoming younger and healthier!

Days went by and my anticipation grew because the water was healing me in a spectacular way. When I arrived in Dobogókő the tumor on my neck was 6 cm (2 inches) long and 2 cm (nearly 1 inch) wide. It was solid as a rock and it was unmovable. Now, six weeks later, the tumor shrank to one third of its size and the skin over it was not stretched but it became loose! My face regained its original, healthy color and it possessed a new youthful quality. This was not quite evident first but it became very apparent later on. Not that I could complain, I'd always had healthy skin.

I remember that I had grey skin on my face after the first surgery –it may have been used to scare naughty kids. The skin on my hand loosened and stayed that way. It looked as if it had belonged to a very aged person. It looked horrifying to me… I was not planning on becoming a mummy. I have to admit that the water had blessed effects on me.

I decided to recommend it to everyone, especially to ladies who would like to have smoother and tighter skin. Bathing is a pleasant experience; you will love every minute of it.

I thought back to the time when I first heard about the water many times. I have to admit I did not really believe in it but now, after experiencing it, I know the effects of it on the human body! Everything about the water was true; it is really capable of performing miracles!

* * *

Staying Alive!

I gladly went back to the hospital where the doctors were shocked by the gigantic improvement. They still decided to perform the surgery, saying that even though the tumor had decreased in size, there were cancerous cells present in the body which could spread if not removed.

I did not agree with the doctors because they could see the improvement for themselves. I thought that if I continue the drinking and bathing treatments, the tumor would disappear. But then again, I did agree with them because metastasis could occur if cancer cells are left in the body. And who knows how much time is necessary for all the cancer cells to completely die out. I knew very well that I could not receive anymore radiation treatments. Therefore I could not whine nor could I run risks.

I was very disappointed and sad. I had been so sure that no more surgeries would be necessary. I wanted to be left alone and I had no desire to do anything.

The surgery was a serious procedure. I had to sign papers declaring that I had been being treated for cancer. I guess they wanted to make sure that I would not complain after the operation. I do not think that this would be a good way to lose weight, to have parts of the body taken out.

I was sitting on my bed just before the surgery and my head was full of concerns when my wife entered the room. I could see immediately that something had happened. I knew her well: when her eyes sparkled and her lips had a tiny smile hiding in the corners she always had great news. I was almost certain that the surgery was cancelled. I intently gazed at her lips looking for the words that meant the escape from the "knife" and from further suffering.

"Your fourth grandchild has been born! It is a little girl!" she finally said. My eyes teared up. I have never felt like that before: I was happy and disappointed at the same time. With all my heart I rejoiced at the birth of my grandbaby but this news also meant that surgery would take place.

My wife was only allowed to stay for a few minutes; as I later found out, the intent was for me to receive such really positive news before the procedure, so I would gather strength to withstand the newest hurdle.

After I stayed alone, I lied down and closed my eyes. I was contemplating how unpredictable fate was – or was it in fact logical? Maybe my life will be extinguished and in my place a new life will begin. My fourth grandchild…

I imagined her little face and in my mind I touched her rosy cheeks and then a very strange thing happened. It was as if she had opened her pearly eyes and I could hear her sweet little voice. She said: "I love you!" I just sat there with tears in my eyes and answered her: "I love you, too, sweetie!"

* * *

And then, there I was in the operating room again. My tiny grandbaby's voice echoed in my ear: "I love you!" Then I heard the assistant's voice from Dobogókő in my mind:

"I trust in the healing power of the water, you can trust it, too!" I think that gave me the strength to pull through the surgery.

When the doctors opened the tumor on my neck, they could barely believe their own eyes. They discovered that the small cancer cells were covered by tiny white pearly spheres which prevented any spreading. All that because of the effects of oxygen!

After the surgery, I was thinking about my new grandbaby and I could hardly wait to hold her in my arms and thank her for helping me. I wanted to thank my assistant from Dobogókő for supporting me. She knew what the water could do!

I was rather surprised at the precise quality of the surgery. The doctors were careful to preserve the natural look of my neck. If not for the hole, no one could have guessed that I had had surgery performed on my neck. I can live with this, I just have to get used to it. There are others who are missing a leg; I have an extra hole on my body, so what...

"What do I have to complain about?" I told myself maintaining my positive attitude.

I asked my wife to bring in oxygenated water and while I was in the Intensive Care Unit, I was drinking my special water to aid my recovery. My assistant from Dobogókő paid me several visits. She encouraged me with everything she said, she emphasized positive thinking, and I took and kept her advice. An important part of recovery was that the surgeons had to have been successful in removing all the cancer cells to prevent reoccurrence.

After I was released from the hospital, I continued my drinking and bathing treatments and I started to feel stronger and healthier.

The sword of death...

A whole year went by after my surgery. Every day passing I believed more that I could make it. I was not sick and my zeal for life had returned. I could not describe how relieved I was that I was doing that well. Cautiously, but with increasing expectation, I dared to hope that the sword dangling above my head would slowly retreat... I was not allowed to have any radiation treatments and I still survived even though I had not given myself more than a month...

I was drinking the water gladly and bathed in it and slowly I regained my enthusiasm for life. I forgot about my operations and I did not think of cancer so often anymore.

I went back to work. Surely, it was not the same anymore because I lost my own voice but at least I had a chance to communicate even through the phone. It was not easy to accept the circumstances, especially when during phone calls I was laughed at for my mechanical voice. I had to get used to it and had to live with it.

Months went by and I was feeling well. I went back to the hospital for a follow up visit without worries. I was not scared because I felt completely healthy.

When the tests and examinations were finished I was grinning at the physician but he was not smiling back.

My blood froze! "It can't be happening again...?" Fright raced through my body.

I saw the CAT scan results which indicated that the disease might have returned but the outcome was not all that clear. Experience was on the medical professionals' side; my secret hopes for full recovery were all in vain?

"I am sorry but we found an anomaly on your trachea (windpipe) which will need to be removed." said the doctor but I was not paying any attention to him. It took one single second to have chaos around me. I collapsed as a castle made of cards. I was not strong anymore.

"What did I gain by not giving up? What did I gain by drinking that special water and bathing in it when the cancer had returned? Why did it not work for me? How many people did I see get healed? Why did others recover while I did not? It was all a lie! Why did I believe in what the assistant said?" I was outraged when I recalled what my fellow patients said: 10% chance. I did not even have that much...

At the same time I did not understand why I was pain free. "Why I do not feel the weakness and why don't I feel bad? I feel perfectly well! Why do I have a healthy color?

I can work and I am not tired! How is this all possible?" I had all these questions surfacing in me which I immediately answered. I only think that I am healthy and strong. That is what I want and believe but in reality I am fooling myself. The results of the tests prove that I am exactly at the same spot where I started from. The cancer took a stronghold in my body and I will never be free from it.

I had to be called back to reality and I finally understood the words the doctor was saying:

"I know it is terrifying to realize that the cancer had reoccurred, and I am truly sorry. My colleagues and I believed in your complete recovery. It hurts me to say that we have no other option but to operate."

My soul rebelled. I didn't want another surgery; it didn't matter anymore but I did not possess the strength to reply. I bowed my head and tried to hold my tears back. Suddenly, from one second to another I became furious and I could barely hold myself back from attacking the doctor. I was mad at him and at myself. I was mad at the wondrous water and the whole cursed world!

"Surgeries like that are performed in the city of Szeged. You have to travel there!" said the doctor while placing a hand on my shoulder. After I looked up at him he gave me all the details.

I remember that I did not feel any anger when I left the hospital. As if I was not even myself. My legs were taking me somewhere but they were moving independently from my will. Weakness and frustration filled my soul and I felt even worse for them. Since my youth, I had been my own man, solving my own problems; I had been standing on the ground with both feet and now it was all over! I had lost my voice for nothing, I had a huge hole on my throat for nothing which I had been so petrified of... I accepted this situation... all for nothing.

I have to admit that all my effort, all my strength and all my willpower was for nothing...

The statement that the doctors told me after the first surgery echoed in my head:

"Don't worry, cancer will definitely not return for the next thirty years." And now, not even two years later, I was back at the starting point for the third time.

I had no strength or desire to go home. How could I stand in front of my family and tell them that I had cancer again? No, I did not have the courage! They had suffered so much because of me and for me, and now I should ask them once more to stand by me and encourage me. But where do they get the strength from?

I got into my car and started driving with no purpose or destination. Then I was standing at the bank of the river Danube. This is where I ended up, at a place that was so precious for us because this is the place where I met my wife. So many times we sat at the water's edge, on the stairs, planning our future…

"I did not think that my future would be like this!" I thought as I plopped down onto the stone. I just stared at the water and I had an increasing obsession to jump in. That would solve all my problems. The depth would swallow me, I would not have to suffer anymore, and I could spare my family from what is waiting for them.

At that precise moment my phone rang. The indicator showed that it was my wife. At first I did not want to talk to her because I knew if I did then I would not have the strength to do what I was preparing for. But she kept ringing and ringing – very stubbornly, so I answered it.

My wife's voice was shaking and I sensed her worry. I calmed her down and promised to head for home.

I stood up and looked at the water for a long time, then – like someone who had just woken up – I ran for my car. Covered in sweat and trembling, I sat in my car for a long time, silently thanking my wife for preventing me from doing something tragic. I wanted to throw my life away but I did not figure that a suicide would have caused even greater pain to my family.

I recalled that since my disease was discovered there had been times when I possessed strength beyond what I could imagine and other times I got weaker than a small child. I don't think I should be ashamed of that. Humans were created with emotions and sometimes that causes us to soar and other times we just sink into the deepest depths. We also possess the ability to control our emotions! There are instances when we must have control in order to avoid fatal mistakes. For that I needed my wife's voice. She always knew when I needed her the most... Even when I was far away from her.

As I was sitting in my car leaning on the steering wheel, thoughts like that were occupying me. My teeth started to chatter from the chill when I realized that I almost went through something insane caused by bitter pain and frustration. I did not do it though because of my wife's timely intervention.

When I stepped into my home, my wife ran over to me and hugged me while whispering in my ear how worried she was about me being late. She loved me and she had proved it to me many times.

I admit that telling her about the cancer's return and another surgery was very difficult. I saw that she almost fainted. She had a deep conviction that I was healed!

She did not say a word; she just silently embraced me, while our tears rolled down our faces and mixed together.

* * *

Yes, I made it; I did not commit suicide but I was very disappointed and my assistant at the bath club tried in vain to convince me that there had to be a mistake because my body does not contain any cancer cells – I did not believe her.

Anger and fear took over my body and soul. What is she talking about? What misunderstanding? The examination clearly indicated that I have tumors on my trachea. That was not a misunderstanding; that was a fact!

I fell apart again. At that moment I did not believe in the positive power of the oxygenated water. I thought that the recovered patients were just lucky but my wife and kids insisted that I continue the treatments, so I kept drinking the water and bathing in it while I was completely against the whole thing.

I believed it to be useless but I did not want to cause more pain to my loved ones, so I did what I was expected to do.

One time I was relaxing in a waiting room after my bath when a very beautiful young woman plopped down on a chair next to mine. She started a conversation and even though I did not feel up to it, as I was not going to be impolite, I joined in. She introduced herself; her name was Csilla. I mumbled my name but I don't think she understood me.

She told me how happy she was to have found this healing water and she could never be thankful enough to her neighbor who had brought her here.

I just swallowed but I did not have enough guts to tell her that there I was – the living negative example.

When she asked what was wrong with me, I almost lost it. I just wanted to jump up and run for it. I did not want to talk about it! I did not want to hear her boasting about the water when I was disappointed with it. I was wondering whether she was still very enthusiastic and happy if I told her that in fact nothing was true of what she was preaching about the water since it had brought me no relief even though I had been a regular user of it for a long time. She was expecting a response, so I summed it up in a single sentence.

Her face saddened for a moment but then started smiling again.

"Please, believe me; you are at the right place. You will get well. I should know!" she exclaimed with her eyes sparkling. Then she continued: "If you listen to my story, you will believe me! Three months ago a miracle took place in my life. I am twenty-three years old. A year and a half ago I married the sweetest man in the world. We had gone out for a year before we decided to join our lives. Our parents accepted and supported our decision. I had earned my degree and my husband had had a secure job. He had inherited a small home from his grandmother, so we decided to get married…

(I could hardly hold myself back from yelling at her that I was not interested in her story. I did not care that she got married and her husband is the sweetest man in the world. I cared for absolutely nothing, I wanted to stay alone but this young lady just kept on talking.)

"I was at the gynecologist that day and during the examination he told me that I was six-week pregnant. I thought I was going pass out from the shock because as a young girl I had had a serious infection and supposedly I was infertile. I could not do a thing but lean onto my doctor and cry.

He was trying to console me and told me that I could have an abortion. The doctor thought I did not want a child."

"I could barely utter that I was crying because I was happy since the sweet miracle no one counted on had taken place anyway and I now could become a mother!"

"We talked about the things that needed attention and then I was on my way home. I decided to surprise my husband and I wanted to prepare a special dinner. I decided to make his favorite dish: layered potatoes. That's something I can actually make because I am still a beginner when it comes to cooking. I wanted to make sure that everything got done on time so I used a pressure cooker to cook the potatoes since my mother had told me that it was faster than conventional pots. While the potatoes were being prepared I could take the time to choose a sexy dress to wear while making the incredible announcement to my husband."

"I went to the closet and starting rummaging through my dresses and then took out three for the final selection. I could not decide so I chose to try them on one by one to select the right one."

"I was just taking off the second dress when I heard strange noises from the kitchen. I got concerned because I realized that there was something wrong with the pressure cooker. Wearing only my lingerie, I rushed to the kitchen. I got to the stove and I wanted to turn the heat down a bit but then I heard an explosion and I felt steaming hot water scalding my body. I could not have imagined such pain. Everything got dark before me and I fainted…"

(I lifted up my head. No matter how depressed I was, this part of her story shook me to the core. I looked at her expectantly and she continued.)

"My husband called me but could not get through because I was unconscious and I was lying on the kitchen floor. So he tried calling our friend, our next door neighbor, to ask him to look in on me since I was not picking up the phone."

"Imre knocked and banged on the door but there was no answer. Apparently, he came home at the same time as me; I just did not notice him. I was too happy and I did not see or hear him. He was sure I was home. He went around to the kitchen window, as he usually did to let me know it was him, and peeped in. That is when he noticed me."

"He broke the window and climbed in. He was very frightened when he realized that the pressure cooker had blown up and the scalding water caused serious injuries. I was just starting to come around and I began to feel the burns which were so severe that I could only whimper. Imre quickly opened my front door from the inside, picked me up and ran to his car while trying to calm me down by telling me everything was going to be all right. He covered me with something. As later I found out, he used his shirt to drape me over since I was not dressed."

"He sat me down on the back seat and took off. I was barely conscious because of the intolerable pain. My right arm, my torso, and both of my legs were burned. I only heard it from a distance that Imre called my husband while he was driving. I don't know what he told him because I was slipping in and out of consciousness."

"When I woke up, I was sitting in a bathtub. I would be lying if I said that I was feeling well but I was not nearly in as much pain as I had felt earlier. Slowly, my head cleared and I cautiously lifted my arm out of the water, then my legs and my body. As I looked myself over, I screamed. I was scared to death because what I saw was awful. My body was covered in giant blisters where the hot water had splashed on it. My skin around the blisters was scarlet red, just like a lobster's. Beside the bathtub sat a middle-aged woman who kindly asked me to take the cup from her and drink its contents."

"I drank it quickly and I was surprised for it was just clear water. I thought it was going to be some kind of medicine or a pain killer but the taste was unmistakable. My throat felt better from it so I drank the whole cup and asked for another one. Then I asked which hospital I was at but I found out that I was not in a hospital but at a bath club."

"A bath club? What I am doing at a bath club? I did not understand anything. A large part of my body had burned and I should have been at hospital. I was just going to mention that I know of burn units where I could receive treatment when my husband stepped in the room and ran to me. He kneeled down next to me and he looked very worried. I started sobbing loudly. I think the shock finally set in."

"My poor darling!" He was so scared because he thought that I was crying out in pain, so he kissed me and jumped up. He said he would call an ambulance and he would have me taken to a hospital. He ran out but then he soon returned. He told me that Imre suggested that we should stay here because the kind of care I receive should have me recovered very quickly. According to him, the water had an incredibly beneficial effect! Imre brought me here because his mother had been treated here at the bath club after receiving burn injuries from hot cooking oil. She did not have to do anything but drink the water and bathe in it and she also received a cream to apply. Her injuries were healed and were barely visible now. My husband let me decide. It was my decision."

"Strangely enough, I said I would prefer staying a while because the water felt really good. My husband's face turned sad. I could tell he was surprised."

"Later, when my 50-minute bathing time was up, I was escorted here, to this waiting room and my injuries were treated with a cooling gel. I was told to take another two baths and to drink the water continuously for another ten days. The employees in the club were so nice that they stayed very late so I could take the other two baths. That really made an impression on me."

"You know, between two baths I suddenly realized that I had forgotten about the little life I was now carrying under my heart. I was thinking what kind of mother I would make if I could just forget about my baby who was conceived so miraculously. I had an increasingly bad feeling that I did not deserve to be a mother because I was irresponsible. If I had not left the stove on full power, the pressure cooker would not have blown up and this accident would not have happened. Even at the very beginning I was not taking good care of my baby."

Staying Alive!

"I had never been so scared in my life. I started sobbing again. My husband did not know why I was crying so suddenly again. He kept asking me until I told him that we were going to be parents but I had already risked our baby's life. I felt so guilty because I did not even know if the baby survived the shock or the fall I had when I collapsed. My side was hurting pretty badly; I must have fallen on it…"

* * *

The young woman stopped her story and I unwittingly assured her that she was going to be a wonderful mother and I could tell that the baby was going to be fine. Her story got me so involved that I almost forgot about my misery.

Csilla was crying quietly, she was under the spell of her memories but then she spoke:

"You know, I will never forget the expression on my husband's face when he found out that he was going to be a dad. He just looked at me smiling through his tears and did not know how to hug me. I felt his whole body was trembling…"

"I am only taking control baths now and I will be on my way to the hospital after this for an ultrasound examination. Soon we will know if the baby is a boy or a girl!"

She placed her hand on her tummy and then she looked at me. She whispered: "I have to tell you. I did not believe in this water for one single second! But now I am a believer! I took a vow to always have this pleasant and beneficial water as my drink and now whenever I have the chance I come to take baths. This water is a miracle in itself! I think it works very well for the healthy as well as for the ill. I tell everyone about it so that more people know about it and experience its positive effects. When the baby is born, I will give it to my little one also because this water is so good it can be given to children!"

She was quiet for a while and then looked into my eyes.

"I researched it and found out quite a bit about this water. Don't worry! It will heal you. Do you want to bet?" she said as she extended her hand towards me. "Let's bet in a box of water that you will recover!"

"I thought we could meet here in six months after my baby is born. Well? Are you up for it?" she asked.

I shook her soft thin hand and agreed to the terms but my throat closed shut on me. She was about to leave but she stopped and stepped back to me.

"I still can't believe what has happened to me. For ten days, I was bathing in this 34-35 °C warm water, I drank two quarts and I used the recommended gel. Look at my arms and legs!" she said. "I had third degree burns on my arms, first degree burns on my stomach and second degree burns on my legs. Can you believe that it looks like this in less than three months? You don't believe it, do you? Neither did the doctors who saw it. My husband insisted that I should see a doctor. All my thanks go to this water. I had never thought that I could recover. So don't you give up! I'll see you right here in six months!"

Staying Alive!

As soon as I remained alone, my bad mood returned. I regretted taking on the bet. I was almost certain that I could not even last that long!

"Come on! Where am I going to be in six months?" I told myself sadly.

* * *

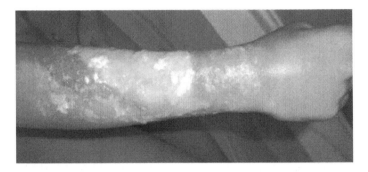

Before Kaqun bath

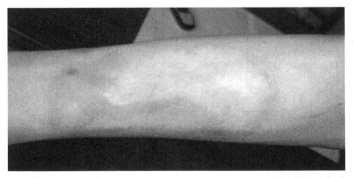

After Kaqun bath

Then the dreaded moment came. Once again, there I was in the operating room. I was thoroughly convinced that my luck had run out. I only wished to die during the surgery, so my family and I would not have to suffer for months to come. I could not stand the thought of lying in agony while they were also dying with me of sadness.

With tears in my eyes and with great sorrow in my heart, I silently said my good byes and gave myself over to fate...

* * *

When I opened my eyes, I was lying on a bed surrounded by many. At first I was just staring at them thinking I was on the other side...

Then I realized: "I am alive!" I felt better, my head was clearing, and I had survived the surgery. My joy did not last long because I soon remembered everything that I was considering before I had gone under the operation. Yes, I was alive but for how long? I couldn't have radiation and did not have any other options if the cancer attacked again. How would I live if I stayed alive? In constant fear, dreading the return of the cancer?

Then I remembered a remark I had heard from a doctor: "Whoever passed the five-year-mark may have hope to have beaten cancer." Yes, but what about the quality of those five years? I had lived through nearly two... I believed, I hoped but I could not forget for one second that death was just around the corner, waiting to strike! I couldn't know when the reoccurrence will happen but I could almost count on it! No one can live knowing this!

I felt that all my strength had left me and not even the example of that little ant helped. I got mad at it and wished that I had stepped on it right then and there!

My bitter thoughts were interrupted by the entrance of the surgeon who had performed the procedure.

"I have to tell you something!" he said as he looked at me and placed his hand on my blanket. I just knew: here comes the "this is the end" speech! I have to accept it… it is over. My heart was beating so hard that my chest nearly started hurting. I thought I could not live for another moment.

"We have to apologize to you… the biopsy did not confirm the presence of cancer. What you had was calcified saliva deposits on your trachea and we should not have operated on you! Please, believe me, we are profoundly sorry!"

I had no idea what was happening to me. I did not comprehend what he was telling me. My wife cried and hugged me; my sobbing children were grasping my hand.

A very strange thing happened to me then. For a few moments I felt that it was not even me who was on that bed. A very special melody filtered in from somewhere and infinite peace descended upon me – it was beyond my capacity to describe it. I felt as if I was hovering and I had bright light around me. I enjoyed the warmth and the peace that surrounded me.

The music stopped and I returned to reality. I felt tears rushing into my eyes. Who cared that I had had to suffer through surgery? I was flooded with indescribable happiness, relief and hope that I could live on and that I would survive! At the same time I was ashamed. I felt bad that my trust in the oxygenated water had been shaken and I did not trust the employees either. They believed in the benefits of the water and I almost quit.

I made it my first priority to apologize to them. I could barely wait to meet them again and to sink into that water which had proven its wonderful powers since the cancer did not return. Actually, the water protected my body from the disease!

* * *

Many times I recall that period in my life and I feel ashamed of myself having been such a doubter. I cried more often then than at any other time in my life. Crying is something that I would usually keep a secret but I decided to reveal it. I am doing that to be able to be of help to those who are suffering from serious diseases. I would like to provide an example on how not to give up. Do not let fear and frustration take over you, no matter what! Believe me! You have to fight against the disease and you can overcome if you want to and if you believe. Your family and friends – who support you – can be a great source of energy. If you have no one to stand by you, let me be your support and take strength from my story.

(I would like to emphasize at this point that I am not pitching any products or services and I am not campaigning against any. I just want to help others with good intentions and tell them about my own experiences.)

The healing...

After leaving the hospital my first priority was to see my helpers at the bath club. They welcomed me back with love and rejoiced with me. I was so overwhelmed that I could barely whisper my apology for having doubted them and the effects of the water, and I thanked them for what they had given me back: my life!

And when finally I could sit in the bathtub again, I touched the surface of the water with my lips and planted a kiss on the water. I thanked the water for my wondrous healing, thus expressing my gratitude without words.

My second trip took me to my pigeons. Yes, I have 350 birds. This is my hobby and my love and I have been continually at it since 1956. When I found out about my illness and fell apart, even then I did not forget about my pigeons. I am sure today that they were of great help in my recovery. They would have perished without me. My family needed me and so did my birds.

I remember when I had to stay at the hospital, I always took my binoculars. You can just imagine what people were thinking of me. A patient on the cancer wards walking towards the balcony with binoculars in his neck...

Since the hospital was very close to my home, I watched my house when I could. Sometimes I was put into a room where I could actually see my home from the windows, but when I did not manage to, then, after the morning rounds I took off to a place where I could see my birdies fly. Maybe you think that there are not many peculiar people like me in the world but to me it was a joy to see my pigeons. During my hard times they made me forget about my illness and suffering.

I recall that when I felt that I could go on no more, my life was over and I was lying on my death bed, I was still watching my pigeons through the window. I watched as they flew as tiny white spots in the infinite blue. I longed to be with them.

Maybe many will laugh at me or think me weird but I know what my birds meant and still mean to me. They helped me to think positively and when I watched them or thought about them they chased away depression and I did not think about my illness.

I remembered some of their races. I always got excited about races. How many times I had a chance to be really proud when they won awards! Possibly, the birds were the ones who helped me realize that cancer may be respected but it has to be defeated.

Tracking the healing water...

A hundred and a thousand times I thought that a great miracle had been bestowed on me but every time I had to realize that this miracle is very tangible because it is the oxygenated water! But how does it differ from other types of waters? There are so many clear, great tasting, glacier based waters sold in Hungary and all over the world. Why and how is this water different? How can it heal patients who have terminal diseases, who have nowhere else to turn to and no other help? I wanted to know everything about this water!

I started doing some research. I was glad to hear that besides Dobogókő there are other bath clubs in Budapest (in Zugló), in Budakeszi, Budafok, Kerepes, and in Veszprém, operating under the same name: Kaqun Clubs. The official commercial name of the oxygenated water is Kaqun water and it is known by this name by consumers.

* * *

I could not sleep at night; I was so excited about the incredible power of the water. When I had time I was sitting in front of the computer, looking for information about this special water. I read everything about it that could be found on the Internet and that is how I traced it to Italy. I found where the factory is, where the water is made and that the source of the water is there as well.

I had no peace after that. I told my wife that I had to travel and I would not return until I had seen the source with my own eyes and tasted it. I had to know how it was processed, why it was so different because it was the water that had helped me!

My wife just smiled mysteriously. She knew me well and did not try to talk me out of it because she understood how important this trip was to me. She packed up my luggage and I got into my car and I left to find out more about the water. The drive should have lasted about six hours – however, having a smooth and efficient trip was not my style.

I was halfway between my home and the border when my back tire blew up. There was not much traffic and luckily I did not cause an accident. I limped off to the hard shoulder and changed the punctured tire.

I put my briefcase on the top of the car and slipped my cell phone in there so that I could hear it if someone called while I was working on changing the tire.

It was a warm day and I had sweated through by the time I was done. I had a big jar of water in the trunk so I washed my hands and my face thoroughly. Then I popped back into my car and took off. I had to make up for the lost time!

I drove for about 3 miles when my blood froze. That is when I realized that I had left my briefcase on the top of the car. I had to drive another mile or so to be able to make a U turn. Just about that time I called myself everything but a smart handsome guy. How could I be such an idiot?

I got back to the place where I had changed the tire. I stopped the car and ran across the road to the other lane. I was certain that quite a few cars had driven across my important papers and my phone by then but I did not see a thing. My briefcase's zipper had not even been closed so my documents and money should have been scattered all around the place. I was turning in every direction so that I could spot my belongings. Nothing. By then I knew that someone obviously had seen my briefcase and its contents and picked it up.

I felt hopeless and stopped after a few yards. I was done and finished. I can't go anywhere without a passport, documents, and money! I have to turn back!

I lifted my head towards the sky and almost said something very inappropriate when I suddenly heard my phone ringing.

I turned around in a snap and finally spotted my briefcase stuck in a gap between two panels of the guardrail. It probably flew and landed there when I took off with a considerable speed. Quickly, I thanked my Redeemer for protecting my belongings and keeping them safe then I took out the phone. My wife was calling me.

I ran over to my car, sat down and put the receiver to my ear. I did not mention to her my recent adventure; I did not want her to worry about me. I think she was worried enough already; she sounded as if she had been crying.

I calmed her down by telling her that everything was all right and I was nearing the border and I would call her again later. We were both a lot more at peace after that.

I was holding the phone and heaven only knows how many times I thanked my wife that she exists. If she had not called me I might have not found my briefcase at all and I would have had to turn back without reaching my destination.

The rest of the trip was not that exciting. I finally arrived in Italy, not in six hours as it had been planned but in ten hours. I stopped at a small town and asked about the factory. The local people enthusiastically explained which way to go but either they were wrong or I misunderstood – all in all, I got lost.

What can I say? I was not troubled with that because I would have missed out on so many beautiful places. What an adventure! I can tell you not many places could be compared to what I saw there. I admired the high mountains, the deep valleys and the little hidden lakes that sparkled like jewelry. I was awed by the blue skies that were bluer than anywhere else; I reverenced the green fields, the forests, the springs breaking forth from the bowels of the mountains. My soul was filled with positive feelings. It had been a long time since I felt that good. I was calmly asking around for directions and the local people were kindly giving me information and guidance.

When I first saw the Dolomite Mountains of Northern Italy, my heart fluttered. I had arrived and soon I would know everything about that wondrous water!

I just stood there looking up on 7000 feet tall Pasubio Peak where the water breaks to the surface and flows down to the Valley of Posina which is located at 1800 feet height. The villagers gave me a lot of useful information such as the spring being 100 years old. People used to transport the cool clear water in buckets. And now I can see it! I loved the beauty of the surrounding scenery.

I drove down to the valley through a tunnel. Between two mountains I saw a majestic castle and some mist-covered peaks and I stood under a bridge next to a multi-leveled waterfall that made me feel like an insignificant sapling. At last, I had arrived at the factory.

I stated where I came from and why. I received a warm welcome; the director of the processing plant nodded with a smile and although he did not disclose how the water is processed, he did provide rubber boots, flashlights and two guides, who led me into a five-foot-high tunnel. We bent over while we were making our way in the bowels of the mountain where water was flowing through some holes. We were trekking 4 °C degrees cold crystal clear water and if I wanted I could bend down and touch it (which I did). I was so happy I was almost in tears.

The water processing plant in Italy

As we were making our way in the belly of the mountain, the sound of falling water became very apparent; sometimes quietly whispering and other times roaring like thunder. I had never had such an experience before and I doubt I will ever forget it.

Spring water in the cave

Through a large glass window I could see that the water was cascading down through 4800-foot-high cracks into natural reservoirs. I found out that there is enough crystal clear water falling down daily to fill 300 tanker trucks.

I leaned down several times and touched it. Every time I had the same sensation: the water was incredibly soft, silky and refreshing.

When we returned, the director of the plant explained to me that the water is beneficial and pleasant because it is naturally clean and it is nearly void of minerals which characteristic makes the oxygenation process much easier.

I felt fantastic. I satisfied my curiosity; I touched and tasted the water in its natural environment and that translated into an uplifting feeling. I took a lot of pictures of the beautiful scenery and I started for home. I accomplished my goal: I was assured that the water I was drinking was of the highest quality, some clearest, original, mountain spring water whose special benefits I could witness to with my recovery.

When I arrived home I recalled the entire return trip. I found it interesting that on the way back, on the long drive I did not feel tired and I did not have the need for sleep. All thanks to the Kaqun water because – as it goes without saying – I was drinking it on the way home.

Lying down on my bed I was thinking about something I had not elaborated on yet: what a great role water and oxygen have in my life!

Water and Oxygen...

The travail is lengthy. After the pain, shouting, perspiration, and sighs, finally the sweet little voice fills a mother's soul. A tiny human is born! Life is the greatest gift which is unrepeatable and unique. We have to preserve it so we can enjoy it for a long time!

As we know, the fetus safely develops in the amniotic fluid inside the uterus. It could not survive without that environment. But what happens to the baby after making its painful, long way into an unknown and frightening world? The baby breathes in OXYGEN because that is the only way for them to stay alive...

* * *

Water! One of the most important preconditions of life! When we say the word what do we associate it with? Is it a refreshing drink in the summer heat? Do we imagine a pool, a lake, a river, or perhaps the ocean that is inviting us for a splash or a swim? Is it a soothing bath that relaxes? Do we see when the sky opens up and covers the earth with a flood of tears? Do we imagine a devastating tidal wave that swallows and destroys everything in its wake?

It is thought-provoking to contemplate that the single most abundant element on earth is the rarest in other places in the Solar System. The immense oceans and seas that cover our earth provided an optimal environment to many forms of life; our planet develops and refreshes with the help of water, and the cycle of life would not continue without the presence of it either.

I read an old inscription which perfectly illustrates and explains the continual interrelationship between life, water, and the earth: *"The blood of the earth is the river of the body."*

Among inorganic chemicals that make up a living cell, water – with its various roles – is the first on the list of importance. Babies have the highest water content in their bodies – 98%, while the body of an adult carries 60-70% water which decreases as the individual ages.

Water content varies in different organs as well. Bones or tooth enamel contains the least amount of water, only 1%. There are organs which are made mostly of water such as the body of the eye which is composed of 99% water; the kidneys are made of 83% water, while the brain has 79%, the muscle has 75%, the liver has 70% and fatty tissues contain 30% water.

Staying Alive!

During an average lifespan an individual consumes 40,000 liters of water. An average person could live without food for weeks whereas without water an individual may last but for some days. The pain of thirst is very well illustrated by a Greek legend according to which the gods punished King Tantalus by having him stand up to his chin in cool water but he was not allowed to drink from it. As soon as the king's lips neared the surface of the water, it disappeared. He was sentenced to eternal thirst. The image is so enduring that it was incorporated into our language: the English word "tantalize" originates from the name of Tantalus meaning the action of placing an object of desire beyond someone's reach.

* * *

Oxygen! Even children know that oxygen is an essential element and most forms of life could not exist without it. Life can only be sustained for a very limited amount of time without oxygen. The exchange of oxygen is critical to the body throughout the life of most organisms.

Recently, I have read an interesting article. It was about the decrease of the oxygen levels since the beginning of time. Scientists agree that earth's oxygen quantities are only one third of what it is used to be during ancient times and the amount of oxygen is continually decreasing at an alarming speed. Due to global pollution and declining natural resources, less and less oxygen is recycled into the air and less carbon dioxide is broken down. Our modern technological processes use up to twenty times more oxygen than six billion breathing human beings...

The result is that the proportion of oxygen is decreasing compared to other components of air and our bodies become oxygen deficient. This inadequacy is on such a large scale that it creates stress on the human body which struggles to intake enough oxygen for optimal functioning. As the oxygen level of the body declines, the individual becomes more vulnerable to complex health issues and less resistant to diseases.

Thus the correlation between oxygen, oxygen-deficiency, and disease is unquestionable.

* * *

Not long ago, I had the opportunity to read some notes of Professor Otto Wartburg M.D., who realized back in the early 1900's that oxygen has a healing capacity. He made a statement about oxygen being an "essential detoxifying agent" and pointed out that oxygen deficiency is the cause of degenerative diseases and ultimately the true cause of the death of cells. His statements are the result of lengthy research and experiments. For his scientific contribution, Professor Wartburg was awarded the Nobel Prize in 1931.

Professor Wartburg's research also supported the theory that the over-acidifying of the body is the basis and precondition for the development of cancer cells. In his experiments, he made forty-two different species of animals develop cancer just by lowering the pH factor in their blood and decreasing the oxygen level in the cells. He observed that even a mild acid increase drastically decreased the oxygen content of the blood.

Each one of us has cancer cells developing in our bodies at any given day but a healthy immune system recognizes and removes the diseased cells. Cancer cells can only grow in over acidified bodies. Oxidation or festering plays a crucial role in this process.

Healthy cells burn up sugar into carbon dioxide, while cancer cells produce lactic acid furthering the body's over-acidified state thus creating the acidic environment they need.

A cancer cell is a type of cell well-adapted to the body's over-acidic condition and – in theory – it is IMMORTAL!

The acidified body and the acid production of cancer cells produce a state of irreversible acidity. Under such conditions normal cells lose their vitality and cancer cells flourish, and the body system eventually crashes. Since this process affects the whole body, surgical procedures or radiation treatments, at best, can only have a delaying effect.

Professor Wartburg's experiments concluded that cancer cells – similarly to bacteria – prefer oxygen deficient environments. Anytime he decreased the oxygen level in a healthy cell by 35%, cancer appeared. Professor Wartburg discovered that the increase of oxygen prevented cancer cells from growing and ultimately, similarly to the alkaloid environment, it became able to destroy cancer cells.

"There is no opportunity for tumor growth in an environment where the alkaloid – acid balance exists and where there is an abundance of oxygen." – stated Professor Wartburg which would also explain why heart cancer does not exist. The blood that flows from the lungs into

the heart is the blood of highest oxygen content with the highest pH value. While the blood flows through the lungs, the toxic acid byproducts are taken out to be replaced with plenty of oxygen and a high pH value. Cancer cells have extreme pH levels and they are oxygen deficient, while healthy cells are mildly alkaloid with a high level of oxygen content.

* * *

I read the following excerpt from the works of Dr. W. Spencer Way:

"Deficient oxygen equals deficient biological energy which causes anything between mild fatigue and life threatening illness. The relationship between inadequate oxygen levels and diseases has thus been established."

According to Dr. Arthur Guyton's observations: *"All chronic illnesses are the result of oxygen deficiency on the cellular level."*

Dr. Paris Kid also shares this opinion when he states: *"We can consider oxygen deficiency to be the single reason for all diseases."*

Scientists like Dr. Way and many others theorize that the initial symptoms of oxygen deficiency – which could lead to the eventual destruction of all seventy trillion cells in the body – are as follows: fatigue, memory loss, circulatory problems, inadequate metabolism, and acidic stomach, insufficient immune reaction to colds or the flu, bronchitis and various bacterial, fungal, parasitic and viral infections.

Staying Alive!

Thus oxygen is an *essential* element which gives the body its necessary oxidizing power. With the help of oxygen, the body is capable of resisting microorganisms, illnesses, and, furthermore, it is enabled to produce the energy to better assist life functions and oxygen also facilitates easier breathing.

* * *

I do not need to give further evidence to prove that oxygen is an essential necessity for most life forms and what a blessing WATER is, neither do I need to attest further that these two elements together can heal. I escaped from suffering, pain, depression, and death, thanks to willpower, perseverance, and the Kaqun water's healing power. Let my story be an example to you, dear reader, in hopes that it may alleviate the pain, the suffering brought by terminal illness; let it be a source of strength to triumph over the most fearful/terrifying disease: cancer. Please, do not forget that this water is accessible to all and many others prove with their recoveries that it *saves lives!*

The blessed effects of Kaqun water

Obviously, I am not laid back about everything going well with me. Far from it!

I am still taking baths and I am drinking the water – but I am not doing it for being sick with disease. I am watching out for myself and I am guarding my health!

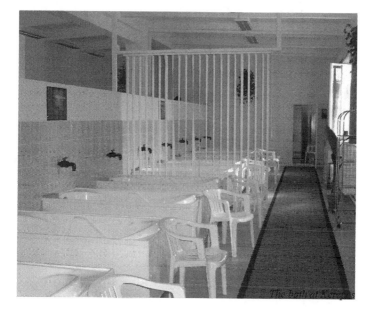

As I mentioned earlier, many other bath clubs have been established, giving more chances for the recovery of the ill and more opportunity for the strong to preserve their health, to improve their well-being...

One day I was at the bath in Kerepes just enjoying the silky touch of the Kaqun water when I got to thinking about stories that I had heard from my fellow club members. They have all recovered and today I may belong in their ranks...

I remember a man in his forties. His face was glowing as he told me how thankful he was to the club for having changed his life. He had received a serious infection on his leg at a public pool a few years ago. It was painful and brought along many difficulties. One of his friends had many good things to say about the Kaqun water and he decided to give it a try. He could barely believe his eyes when he became asymptomatic within a short amount of time. He is still healthy. He returns to the club as a member now...

A young, thirty-year-old woman suffered from allergies. She was allergic to many things and that really made her life hard to bear. She was taking a lot of medicine and had to endure many unpleasant side effects. She heard about the water and started taking it and bathing in it. Her health has improved, her fatigue diminished, and most importantly, she was able to discontinue taking all of her allergy medicines, and she moved on to a more complete life. She told me with tears in her eyes that she will be thankful to the Kaqun water forever!

I recalled another woman who had suffered from the adverse effects of frequent asthma attacks. She had had asthma since her childhood and the disease took over her life as the years progressed. She could not have survived without her inhaler.

She had read about the Kaqun water on the web and that is how she found her way to the club. She started drinking the water as part of her therapy and took baths. Within a few weeks she achieved remarkable improvements. When we last met, she was not carrying her inhaler anymore...

* * *

Yes, I feel cured and I contemplate many times what could have happened to me without the water. What if I had not heard about it, drunk it and bathed in it? I can admit now that I believed that there was a trick and thus at least some belief or a strong effort of concentration was needed for the miracle to happen, but I had to accept that I was wrong.

Through the course of my illness I realized that the water is not a medicine even though it can perform real miracles. It does not substitute the remedies used by traditional medicine but the water has remarkably positive effects when used together with traditional healing therapies.

If I had not had surgeries to remove the growths, I would not be alive today but at the same time the surgery would not have prevented the return of cancer. This incredibly effective water halted and destroyed the disease for which I will be grateful for the rest of my life…

* * *

I was thinking about it for days: *"How is it that other oxygenated waters cannot provide such spectacular results as the Kaqun water can?"* I was working and I did not have a lot of free time and when I did, I tried to spend it with my family. But at the same time I seized every opportunity to continue my search to satisfy my curiosity. I was questioning my doctor friends, I browsed web pages, and I read every article about the Kaqun water to learn about it as much as I could. I did discover many interesting things.

I found that the Kaqun water is special; it is the product of a revolutionary new procedure. The Kaqun water's oxygen content surpasses that of mineral water or tap water. In that aspect, it is already very different from other kinds of water. It absorbs through the skin and also through the digestive system. When consumed, the Kaqun water dramatically increases the body's oxygen level and –according to my personal experience – it is essentially important to health, it may even save a life.

There is something else that is crucial: I know it from my own experience that it has no side effects! I had had another health problem I had struggled with for years. I had a stubborn fungal infection on my elbow. I had tried all kinds of creams and every therapy but it did not heal. My dermatologist was unable to help me because while the symptoms temporarily disappeared and the itching stopped, if I missed applications for a day or two, it was back all over again.

The infection and the cream therapy caused some unpleasant problems such as leaving unsightly spots when I was wearing a long-sleeved shirt.

It was my wife who noticed that I was not using the cream. I suddenly realized that I forgot about it since the itching had stopped and I could see no trace of the repulsive-looking skin disease. I could not believe my own eyes! I had to realize that the water had completely healed my fungal infection as well.

* * *

My neighbor was a young lady and we talked a lot about my recovery. She told me that her facial skin had been attacked by a virus and since then her entire body was covered with small lesions and the daily medicine dosage made her sick and had stomach ache. She suffered a lot; she wore long sleeves and long dresses even in the very heat of summer to cover herself. Her skin hurt and itched terribly. I recommended that she try the Kaqun therapy since it had been really helpful for my fungal infection. She just gave me a defeated smile and said that her wounds were open and they could not touch water. She was not willing to try the Kaqun water in fear of making her problem become worse. But I did not let up; I kept on trying to convince her until she accompanied me to the Kaqun club. She started a ten-day drinking and bathing therapy.

I will never forget her face when I met her in the court-yard after the first treatment. Her eyes sparkled and she proclaimed that she had never felt better. Most remarkably, her skin lesions did not hurt. The effects were similar to taking a pain killer.

A week went by and her wounds started healing and ten days later they were nothing but just little red spots. My young neighbor healed up and one day she came over with her eyes in tears and holding a huge flower basket to thank me for my help. I kissed her on the cheek and told her to take the gift over to Kerepes to the employees of the bath club because they are the ones who deserve gratitude.

All in all, I was shocked because even though I recommended her to try the water, I really did not expect that it would be so very effective. She healed up completely.

That was only one more proof for the beneficial effect of the water concerning so many different kinds of maladies…

* * *

Staying Alive!

One does not have to be a doctor or a medical professional to draw the conclusion: the increase of oxygen level in the body halts terminal diseases. I know it from my experience that the Kaqun water destroys cancer cells! Of course, to achieve such results, a carefully designed series of therapies was needed as well having the expert input from the employees of the bath and beyond all it was essential to follow meticulously their instructions.

I was glad to find out that many other European countries also have Kaqun baths – and not only for the sick. I realized that taking care of myself and pursuing proactive things to maintain my health would save me from countless diseases and spare me from the suffering that comes with illness. That is the purpose of having Kaqun bath clubs. During bath therapy the skin is in contact with the highly oxygenated water which absorbs into the skin. If one cannot devote the time to take Kaqun baths then it is highly recommended that they should consume the bottled version.

We do not really realize how much we contribute to our illnesses. Besides environmental pollution, we ourselves pollute our bodies with alcohol, smoking, and stress. If such factors become a regular part of our daily lives then we can expect the disease to be chronic and serious in nature.

The Kaqun water is a defensive agent for the healthy and a therapy for the ill. It will help to maintain health and it will accelerate the speed of recovery. We cannot hear it enough times from the experts to increase water intake; at least 2 liters a day. If we take this much Kaqun water; we also receive a cleansing therapy on top of other benefits!

I remember having had a lot of problems with my digestion. My intestines had constantly been inflamed but the drink therapy took care of that. I cannot emphasize it enough: it is incredible how many health problems the Kaqun water is designed to help with!

One day I was just resting outdoors and next to me sat a very thin woman. I could not help but notice her sunken face and her nicotine-stained fingers.

She was on her second course of ten-day treatments. She had lung cancer. She had been smoking two to three packs of cigarettes a day for many years and now that she became ill, she stopped...

She was so sorry for not having listened to the warnings but then she added with a smile:

"I should have been drinking Kaqun water..."

* * *

As soon as I was sure of the beneficial effects of the Kaqun water, I insisted on my whole family's drinking it. Since the consumption of Kaqun water is beneficial to all – age and gender notwithstanding – I recommend drinking it every four months for 15 – 20 days.

I hope my story constitutes a good example why it is worth to maintain our health!

The water itself is easy to find; it can be bought in any natural health stores or pharmacies. The Kaqun water is also beneficial when taken internally. It quenches thirst, increases the amount of water passing through the kidneys which is very important since insufficient liquid intake results in acidic and concentrated urine.

Staying Alive!

If you have any remaining doubts even after hearing about the effectiveness of the Kaqun water, please be assured that the Kaqun water adheres to Hungarian food safety standards both as a drink and as a bathing agent. Testing and licensing was conducted by the National Public Health Institute. The bath club is licensed by the Hungarian National Public Health and Medical Officer Service and it falls under the category of "physical fitness therapy".

* * *

One Sunday my family gathered together at my house. Since my recovery, all of my family members have been using the Kaqun water. They do not take it as a therapy but rather as a defensive measure since beyond its refreshing, pleasant taste and thirst quenching effects this water has proven to be really useful for the body, which adds to its benefits.

My oldest grandchild held a bottle of water in his hand and shook it vigorously. He looked at me with surprise because the water did not burst forth from the opened bottle; the bubbles disappeared instantly without the dramatic effects that soft drinks would have produced.

I smiled and I was happy because I was ready to provide an answer. I knew a lot about the Kaqun water. I told him that it does not contain absorbed oxygen but a special oxygen molecule and it cannot be compared to other types of oxygenated waters that contain absorbed oxygen which quickly escapes after opening the bottle. The oxygen is part of the molecular structure and this characteristic is a revolutionary new invention that is unique in the world.

I could not believe that my grandson comprehended what I told him but he said:

"This is special, Grandpa. It is not surprising that it healed you."

I went to my room and got my thick notebook containing all my notes and opened it at the section where the molecular structure of the Kaqun water was depicted.

I explained to him what that was all about.

Compared with regular water, the difference is rather striking. The pH level of regular water is 6.0 – 6.5, while Kaqun water has the pH level at 8.9 – 9.2 at the temperature of 37 – 38 degrees Celsius. The Kaqun water feels soft and silky and its color ranges from light blue to light green.

My grandson listened intently and then asked how the water could be changing color from blue to green. That was a great question and it only showed that he was paying attention and understood the important points. My answer was prepared:

"The color of the water depends on what kinds of oxygen structures are present. This water holds its oxygen content for 14 months without change but it must not be boiled for the same reason."

When I asked him if he understood, he quickly nodded his head. Our conversation must have been interesting because the adults also joined in. One of my daughters gently touched my hand and noted:

"Dad, you have become a Kaqun expert!"

I looked at her proudly and explained to her that my interest in the Kaqun water was mainly due to the fact that it had saved my life. I added that it is my hope that the water will save other lives as well since today's polluted world and stressed lifestyles result in numerous diseases.

It was my own experience that when I was under stress and depression during the period of my illness I had no strength. I was too tired to move but after taking a bath in Kaqun water I felt renewed. I felt stronger and better. Not to mention recovering from the fungal infection and the itching that I had suffered from for years.

I was an eye witness to recoveries from allergies, liver and urological problems, burns and I saw my neighbor's incredible recuperation from a serious viral infection.

I can also be thankful to the water for my own rehabilitation from a terminal disease. That is why I tell all my family members to let everyone know about this wondrous water that can save lives! Only God knows how many people we can help by bringing their attention to this special water and its healing effects.

I can tell you with confidence what the Kaqun water means to me: LIFE!

* * *

I give thanks everyday that my family is healthy because during my illness had to face to face with the fact that people in all walks of life can become sick; the young, the old, women, children and men. Diseases do not differentiate...

I know I am not alone when I say that seeing children sick breaks my heart. During my years of taking Kaqun baths I saw many parents with teary eyes who were told by doctors that their children are beyond help.

I particularly recall a mother and her son, Botond. She brought her child for the treatments diligently. We started talking and I got to know their tragic story. Little Botond was born on March 6, 2007 as a second child in the family. The delivery was quick although he was born with the umbilical cord twice wrapped around his neck. He was of average size and weight and the APGAR score – 10/10 – indicated that everything was all right. The parents took their beautiful child home happily.

In the first weeks of his life, he only slept and ate but had no other times of activity. When he was five or six weeks old, he started looking around and the parents realized that Botond suffered from a severe case of crossed eyes. He was sticking his tongue out and took up the guard position. "Since Botond is not my first child, I knew something was wrong," said the mother. "At the same time, I really did not understand because he was released from the hospital in perfect health."

"At the six week examination, the pediatrician sent us to a neurologist who recommended some exercises to be administered at home three to four times a day. I exactly followed the instructions for three months and took Botond in for an examination. The exercise yielded good results because in less than a month my son was able to turn from his stomach to his back. I can't tell you how happy I was because I thought that we had taken a giant step forward."

"I was enthusiastically telling the doctor about the progress we made but the neurologist was more pessimistic about my son's condition than a month before. He found that

Botond's left side was gaining more muscle tone and ability of movement than his right side. I do not wish that feeling on anyone. My heart was thrusting through my throat. I did not understand this whole thing because my son's improvement was obvious. But I kept up with the doctor's recommendations and did what he asked me to do."

"He prescribed regular exercise under expert supervision. He sent Botond to have an MRI done on his brain which indicated no stroke or signs of brain damage. You can only imagine how I felt during the week and a half between the exam and the brain scan. I was petrified. What if the test shows brain damage? How do we go on after that? I could not imagine a worse diagnosis than that. How could I possibly go on knowing that I had been carrying a healthy child under my heart but once I held him in my arms instead of beaming with happiness and pride, I look on him with sadness and fear? Perhaps my child will never be able to live a normal life."

"The waiting for the test was dragging on and felt like years went by until the day of the exam finally arrived. Each moment of the brain scan felt like an eternety. I was full of fear… but at the bottom of my soul I had some hope left and I could barely wait to find out the test results."

"When the doctor told me that the scan yielded negative results, all tension and stress just surfaced as I broke down in sobs and cuddled my son. There were no signs of stroke and no indication of structural anomalies. I was holding him in my arms and felt that I was the happiest mother in the world."

"Of course, we knew as those serious illnesses were ruled out, that not everything was well, even though the exams showed that it should have been. My husband and I took the situation very seriously and kept searching for a solution. We asked for a second opinion from another neurologist who recommended more exercise. This meant more commitment from us as the "Dévény" method required exercises for several times a week.

We participated in group exercise at a local public pool. Our days were spent with more and more exercise under constant doctor's supervision."

"Whoever experienced this, knows how it feels; who has not – may consider themselves blessed… The exercise performed at home lasted for 25-30 minutes, accompanied by the bitter cries of my son. Later he took it a little better because I found a playful way of doing the exercises. He gradually accepted the necessity of the movements and enjoyed the extra attention and love. We ended up both loving the time spent together."

"The only thing my baby could not accept and always fought against was the "Dévény" method. The first time we had to do it I cried together with Botond. It was a terrible feeling to watch him suffer but the effectiveness of that therapy was beyond all doubt and this fact really encouraged me. Many times, when my son started crying, I felt my heart breaking and if it had been up to me I would have scooped him up into my arms and would have run for it. Oftentimes I felt that I would give up, whereas I was only an assistant while the physical therapist and my son did all the hard work. But then I persevered. I knew I had to be strong because every painful movement served the interest of my son.

One day all the work started to pay off and it became obvious that it was all worth it. From one session to the other, his progress was observable and evident. He reached all movement development stages on time, his tight muscle tone started to relax and even his crossed eye condition showed improvement. According to the doctors, the eyes would be the last to get better in the process of advancement.

My son's body responded so well to the Dévény method especially during the initial sessions that we almost believed that there was nothing wrong with him, except for maybe having taken an awkward position while in the uterus.

We were ecstatic but it did not last long because differences in the muscle tone indicated that a mild oxygen deficiency might have occurred. However, this could not be proven by an ultrasound examination. Oxygen deficiency could have been the reason why Botond was not walking on his own.

After many days and many minutes and hours of hard effort, my child was still not walking. His so far encouraging development stopped at this point. The legs of my little darling spread out like those of Charlie Chaplin.

It was a terrible feeling to face failure after so many positive milestones. I felt that I would die of the sorrow because three months of therapy just failed to yield the desired results. While we were on a scheduled break from the Dévény method, a lifestyle advisor talked to us about the beneficial effects of Kaqun water and suggested that we visit a nearby Kaqun bath club.

We immediately agreed and made an appointment for the next day. We received a warm welcome and we were told that everything possible would be attempted to help Botond. We discussed all the difficulties and Botond started a ten-day bathing session while drinking about a pint of water a day.

The first ten-day course had not even come to an end when Botond's foot position started to show improvement. His feet were not parallel yet but they have certainly straightened out to some extent. Furthermore, his eye-muscles had improved as well! I was hesitant to believe…

After a week of bath therapy my son took two or three independent steps; something he had not been able to do before. I cannot describe how that felt! We did not dare trust our eyes, we did not dare believe. We were crying and laughing at the same time when we hugged our son. After a ten-day rest from the bath therapy we started the new course and that brought the result we had been so hopeful for. We were a week into the second course when one night – before going to bed – Botond stood up from all fours and did not just walk but almost ran a full circle around the living room! We were trembling as we watched his every move but my little boy did not show any more willingness for walking until the next morning. Our happy expectations were almost tumbling into despair when my son finally stood up again and started walking – shouting with happiness and we just joined in with him.

I still get the chills from the feeling and tears fill my eyes when I recall that my son had to be carried to the bath club one day, and he just walked in, all by himself, with no one holding his hand on the other.

The Kaqun bath therapy was an excellent supplement to the Dévény movement therapy. It proved to be helpful when Botond's advancement halted; it helped to give him momentum and enhanced the effects of the Dévény method.

A month later Botond's walk stabilized; he was almost running. Today he can spin around, count to three with his little fingers, spin on his heel and change his direction quickly. He can walk up the stairs while holding the rails and shows an all around rapid improvement in all areas of life. I cannot be thankful enough to the lifestyle advisor for recommending the Kaqun bath and I just wish we had known about it sooner, and had started our child's therapy sooner...

* * *

I cannot emphasize enough how much strength and faith I myself get from hearing about such cases. Botond's story is a living proof! A child who could not walk before – runs around all happy and healthy today...

After hearing about Botond, I started thinking. Since I started going to the bath club, I heard the term "oxygen deficiency" many times but – truthfully – I did not know what that exactly meant. I just knew it caused a lot of problems. Since I was curious I asked my doctor friend to explain to me what exactly oxygen deficiency is.

Hypoxia

I have to say, I was right; hypoxia does cause some very serious diseases and I decided to pass on this information in the hope of informing people about it.

I learnt that *hypoxia* is a condition that accompanies the lack of oxygen in living tissues as a result of a decrease in the blood oxygen levels. If the oxygen supply becomes inadequate, all the body functions are affected but the one to suffer the most is the central nervous system. In Botond's case, for example, as soon as the oxygen deficiency was eliminated, his movements became coordinated and his muscles worked sufficiently.

There are many types of oxygen deficiency. A condition like that may occur on many levels. It can occur in the brain, in the tissues, in the kidneys, in the liver, or even on the cellular level. That type of condition is actually called *hypoxia.*

Other diseases may bring on *hypoxia,* such as a decline in the functioning of the lungs, bronchial obstructions, emphysema, anemia, or circulatory dysfunctions. Unfortunately, permanent damage may occur if the brain suffers *hypoxia* even for a short period of time.

When the body reaches an oxygen-deficient state, it is unable to maintain the oxygen-carbon dioxide exchange and as a result it will be incapable of sustaining the metabolism necessary for life functions. Many groups were formed in order to learn more about *hypoxia.*

We can encounter *hypoxia* during air travel, or experience it at heights above 9000 feet and even at the bottom of the ocean. Divers are well acquainted with *hypoxia.*

Types of re-oxygenation processes are also well known, but the most frequently mentioned one is something that is called ozone therapy.

I found all this information very intriguing and I searched further. I discovered that ozone therapy is a way of healing with the use of a machine (creating ozone) operated by doctors.

The first medicinal ozone therapy equipment was invented by Dr. Hansler in 1957. The oxygen – ozone mixture (95% oxygen/ 0.5–5% ozone) created by the machine is used for medicinal purposes. When reaching the blood stream, the mixture would break down into oxygen and would be absorbed by the body.

Ozone is a very unstable gas – made up of three oxygen molecules – which has a very typical smell. In its natural state, it exists 20-30 km up in the mesosphere forming a 2-3 mm thick layer around our globe. As the rays of the sun bombard the ozone layer, some of it changes into oxygen while filtering out the sun's harmful UV rays. Ozone, unfortunately, is also a pollutant and thus a potential health threat, being a by-product of industrialization and car exhaust. It can be found in urban environments but after rain it is also present in rural areas. If inhaled, it acts as a radical aggressive substance. At higher concentrations, ozone is an excellent virus, bacterium, and fungus eliminator. In lower doses, ozone stimulates the immune system and helps the circulatory system. Its industrial uses, among others, include water cleaning and acting as a whitening agent as well as a disinfectant.

In healing, a 95.5/5% or 99.5/0.5% oxygen-ozone mixture is used, applied into arteries and veins, or into joints, under the skin, or onto the skin, and into the anus. Such applications can only be administered by doctors. Being well-trained is a crucial element of risk-free treatments. Ozone therapy is being currently used in Germany, Switzerland, Austria, Bulgaria and Italy.

During ozone therapy, patients inhale rich oxygen that stimulates metabolism and has beneficial effects on the protein molecules of the blood. This is only one form of breathing therapy but it also plays an important role in pediatric dentistry where its painkilling effects are applied. Ozone therapy is also used in treating serious ailments such as circulatory diseases, diabetes, different types of dermatological illnesses, dizziness, memory loss, and liver diseases.

Ozone therapy may play a leading role in treating allergy related illnesses that do not respond well to other healing methods, such as allergic diseases like hay fever and asthma. During my research I found another interesting detail. Another oxygen-related therapy would be the high oxygen content rectal suppository which is inserted into the anus where it is absorbed and circulates through the digestive system.

It should be known about the suppository that while it is very rarely used by doctors, it has a beneficial effect on improving the quality of life. It reoxygenates, refreshes, and regenerates the body which directly helps the patient to recover. It is recommended for use by patients participating in chemotherapy. The suppository can be used before, during, and after chemotherapy courses. As a side effect, the use of suppositories may cause headaches or flatulence.

Ozone therapy is a very effective supplemental method of helping patients suffering from colon, liver, prostrate and ovarian cancer. It may also be beneficial in some cases of leukemia.

The oxygen suppository was invented by Dr. Hermann in 1980. His child was suffering from AIDS. Dr. Hermann put all his energy and talent into finding a way to save and heal his son. The well-known researcher invented the technology because he wanted to stop the HIV virus and he knew that large amounts of oxygen absorbed by the body tissues and cells would kill off the virus. He worked towards finding a way to introduce a safe way to get the oxygen into the bloodstream and thus he would have been able to help millions of patients.

The introduction of the medicine was delayed for six months and Dr. Hermann's son died in 1983. Grief-stricken, Dr. Hermann was unable to continue his work and all experiments were abandoned. It took a long time for him to recover from his mourning but he restarted his research in hope of helping countless others.

The oxygen suppository was officially accepted as a supplement with healing properties and its use is widespread in the US, Canada and the Far East. Many in Austria also started to work with the suppository, especially health professionals who were already familiar with the ozone therapy. They tried to formulate a solution in which oxygen would be bonded with the use of pressure...

* * *

My thoughts were leading me away from *hypoxia* when I heard my phone ringing. After I talked into it I heard the sound of laughter. I quickly turned off the phone and nervously walked around. I got used to having a mechanical voice and sometimes I forgot about it all together but at times like that I got into a bad mood.

I remember the first time my grandchildren heard my artificial voice – they ran from me crying. I thought I would die from a broken heart but they adapted to hearing grandpa talk through a microphone. They came to accept it and never made remarks about it but others, unfortunately, liked making fun of it...

I was having flashbacks about the nights when I could not sleep and I was asking myself: what have I done to have such a devastating disease ransack my body? Today, I know that the development of illnesses is influenced by our lifestyles and by the environment we live in. Our immune systems are overtaxed and regeneration takes longer to happen or it does not happen at all. Everyone who survived a serious illness, like me, will come to this realization after examining our own lives. Every person is a prisoner of their circumstances therefore modifying lifestyles and circumstances is most difficult to achieve –

however, it is essential! Lots of suffering, pain, and hard times have made me wiser, if I can phrase it that way. I would like all, especially my readers, to pay more attention to things that would help us preserve our health.

On some days when I stayed late at the bath club I had two hours of rest between two sessions and I had a chance to talk to other patients and the assistants. I heard it from them that the body's oxygen supplementary system declines during the development of the disease, the tissues will acidify and the ability to regenerate diminishes. This condition can be helped by taking Kaqun baths! The improving physical and emotional regeneration will be helpful to steer a patient towards a healthier lifestyle which would further bolster the condition of the individual and would reduce the chances of other illnesses to develop.

I was told that the clean bath water contains 40% absorbed oxygen. (The pleasant feeling of well-being after taking a bath was recognized by the ancient Romans).

Kaqun water contains 98 – 99% absorbed oxygen; it is stable and will not bubble because of the special process mentioned earlier. It will not evaporate from the bathtub and its pH value is alkaloid. An immersed body will absorb the oxygen from the water by way of diffusion through the skin and the capillaries. The pores will open in the pleasantly warm water and the oxygen content of the water will enter into the body while the oxygen content of the water will decrease and it will start to acidify. That is how the gas exchange works.

One time I was in the bath club and was sitting in the bathtub talking to an athlete who was also enjoying a treatment. We started talking and he was telling me how much he liked coming to the club at Kerepes. He had done some research on this matter and found that through going to the bath his body received more oxygen than as if he had been involved in a sport activity or had performed more intense breathing.

The applied oxygen which quickly absorbs into the tissues and cells will prevent acidification. A beneficial pH factor improvement takes place which helps to enhance vital bodily functions.

* * *

I still admire the positive effects of the Kaqun water. In countless cases, I have witnessed with my own eyes the effects of the water in quickly healing wounds, how the mood of cancer patients improved and how dramatically the tumors were reduced in size. In my own case, the tumor on my neck significantly decreased in just six weeks. That was due to the improvement in my own body's regenerative capacity. All thanks to the bath water which proved to be an effective therapy by introducing absorbed stabilized oxygen to my body. Consequently, the normal physiological processes of the body could be positively influenced. Not to mention another personal benefit: the relaxing and refreshing feeling of the bath therapy!

It is hard to believe that the body produces cancer cells all the time but a healthy immune system will destroy such cells. This is why it is so crucially important to pay attention to disease prevention! We do not think about all the ways that our immune systems can be affected. Most causes are toxin or pollutant related. When we get into a bathtub and we take out the most fragrant soaps – and ladies: all those cosmetic products which clog up the skin and prevent the skin from performing its unique function!

The breathing of the skin improves when all the remaining make-up layers – full of toxins – get cleaned off the skin so that it become able to breathe in oxygen through the water. When taking a bath in Kaqun water, the layer under the epidermis gets refreshed by the water while it also increases its water content. The stimulated metabolic function supports the breakdown of fats, resulting in weight loss. We can call that a pleasant diet!

That reminds me of an opportunity that many would like to take advantage of, especially those who would like to achieve weight loss and would like to do it without overstressing their bodies. My wife and my daughters all tried this and they succeeded in losing some extra weight without overburdening their bodies.

The Kaqun diet

The above mentioned diet makes losing weight easy; if someone would like to get thinner, the diet will bring about painless weight loss with no suffering.

Unlike other very effective diets which cause tiredness and lethargy, the Kaqun diet does not "rob" the body. The specially processed, oxygen-enhanced water increases the oxygen content of the cells, it helps the body to de-acidify and that is why it is remarkably refreshing. The Kaqun diet merges the recipes of traditional, mild weight-loss programs with de-acidifying diets.

Consuming the Kaqun water ensures that metabolism accelerates and the diet provides an energetic, pleasant feeling of well-being and the effect of it can be felt after the very first day. A faster metabolism results in good weight loss but it also helps to keep the extra weight off since metabolism works faster even during the breaks between the dieting days.

For optimal results, one should only stay on the diet plan for three consecutive days and then take a two-day break – and then start again. The phases can be repeated until the desired goal is achieved. Another advantage of a two-day break is that a larger weekend meal will fit into the schedule but, similarly to other diets, the Kaqun diet also advises moderation in eating during the breaks.

The quantity of Kaqun water taken with the diet is not limited but if one drinks no other type of liquids, the minerals need to be supplied from another source, since Kaqun water is not mineral water and its mineral content is low.

The diet plan described below covers the food for all three days and the two-day-break provides an opportunity to vary meals and to avoid boredom with the food. After the three main meals, it is recommended to drink half a liter (approx. 1 pint) of Kaqun water.

– *Breakfast* – two oranges, a large grapefruit, 2 small slices of toast thinly buttered (no margarine). A thin slice of turkey or chicken may be added to the toast.

- *Midday snack* - a few fresh celery stalks dipped into yoghurt or Rockfort cheese sauce (no mayonnaise or fatty salad dressings),
- *Lunch* – ½ pound of grilled or boiled fish with fresh salad or steamed vegetables,
- *Afternoon snack* – (strictly before 4 p.m.!) a banana and half a pint of milk,
- *Dinner* – (strictly before 7:30 p.m.!) a cup (not bigger than half a pint) of plain yoghurt with 100 grams of fresh fruit added (no bananas, coconut or papaya!).

It is very important to keep drinking a liter and a half of Kaqun water with the meals during the diet because it provides the necessary liquids for optimal body functions and it also has a detoxifying effect.

A weight loss group consists of 8 – 10 men and women who follow the diet for 6 days and adhere to the following – rather pleasant program:

– the dinner is followed by *chi-kung* or *tai-chi* breathing exercises, then a relaxing bath with candle lights combined with a facial gel treatment which uses a Kaqun water based gel and has all the benefits of the Kaqun water. The product has a hydrating effect and it carries the water to the deepest layers of the skin. With the use of the Kaqun gel, the skin cells receive plenty of oxygen, cell metabolism regenerates and the skin regains its collagen content and becomes more flexible.

The skin will be energized and refreshed enabling women to feel and look younger.

The gel is recommended for all skin types and comes in two varieties: fragrance and non-fragrance. There is a soft, relaxing music playing during the bath…

The bath

I still enjoy every minute of the bath treatment. The 50 minutes I spend in the bathtub is incredible. The water is at a temperature of 37 – 38 (85 – 88 F) degrees Celsius, it is soft and silky as it caresses me. I relax in it, there is no pain, and I think of nothing but relaxing. The fact that the water does not cool off by more than a negligible 0.5 – 0.6 degrees (1F) always amazes me. It's fantastic! Not to mention that the attendants on duty come in now and then to ask how I am feeling. It's good to know that I am being cared for as well as all the other guests and patients are.

After completing the bath treatment, I can relax in a separate lounge where I can measure the oxygen level of my blood with a special instrument called OXICARD.

* * *

I remember that when I started the treatments I was worried. I had no idea how I was going to feel sitting in a bathtub with others in the room. I needn't have worried since all the tubs are separated by curtains and even though there are others taking a bath as well I still had my privacy. I could dip under the water without being watched or I could cry, or enjoy the bath and relax. If I wanted to talk to someone, I could open the curtain and have a conversation.

I recall that at the beginning of my illness when I was mostly preoccupied with my own illness, I did not want to be in the company of other people and it bothered me when others wanted to talk to me. Nowadays, I feel better when I can have conversation with a fellow bather. We can discuss each other's problems and we can rejoice together when someone is cured.

When I step out of the bathtub I always have the sense of being regenerated: my face is rosy, my mood lifts and I feel great. That has not only been this way since I healed but that was the way I felt during the worst and darkest hours of my illness, too. Even now, after taking bath treatment three times a day, the feeling is the same! Bathing in this remarkable water is not only beneficial for the ill but also for people who do a lot of mental work. They will quickly refresh and can return to work.

That is why I asked my family to drink the water and go to take bath treatments.

The result is that they are all healthy and that is of utmost importance to me.

Essential preconditions of life...

My wife went to sleep but I could not settle down and rest. A concept had been developing in my mind for days and I finally felt that it was ready to be written down on paper. I created this diagram and named it "*the essential*

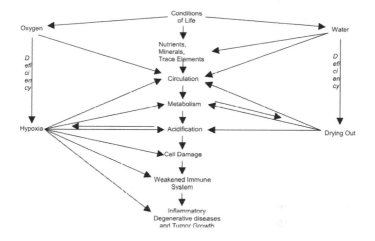

preconditions *of life*" to have it in front of me to remind me how to live a long life. I would love that very much!

Meals and supplements

The Kaqun water, both in the form of bathing and drinking, became part of my life. I had not been able to rest until I found more ways to keep me healthy. I listened to a lecture where the importance of choosing and following an appropriate diet was emphasized, more specifically, the types of food which are harmful and those that are vital for a weakened body when it is trying to regenerate and heal.

Since I listened to that presentation, I have been especially careful **in avoiding sugar and sweets in any form,** and I have also found out how **adverse pickled foods, vinegar, yeast and alcohol can be.** I stay away from such kinds of food even though I am healthy!

During my illness it was especially important for me to consume steamed vegetables, especially broccoli and Brussels sprouts. They have very beneficial effects when fighting cancer. There is bread that is prepared without yeast. It is harder to find and it does not taste the same as regular bread but it is worth the trouble and one can get used to it!

Naturally, I had tried naturopathic nutritional supplements before but when I realized how important it was to have an effectively functioning immune system I searched even further for products that help my body to stay healthy.

D-LENOLATE

I found one of the products that the Kaqun club recommended on the web by the name of D-Lenolate (500 milligrams per capsule), and it is a very effective, natural substance that destroys bacteria, viruses and fungi and has no side effects whatsoever.

I wanted to know more about this product. I guess I am just a very curious person! Since I regained my health I have become very conscious of what my body takes in. That's why I kept up the search and succeeded. I found that famous institutions were involved in research, like Upjohn Pharmaceuticals. They have been doing a research on whether the *oleuropein* extracted from the olive leaf granulate, in a dry state, indeed has its anti-bacterial and fungi-eliminating properties. The Upjohn experiments have been continuously going on for the past eight years.

They maintained the extracts in an alcohol preparation which enabled the substance to be stored in large quantities but made it impossible to market the product to children and pregnant women. There was a real need to have the olive leaf granulate in a dry extract and East Park Research Corporation succeeded in formulating the olive leaf in such a way. They were first to make this food supplement available in the global market as a capsule and maintain their prestigious status by having a high quality product. D-Lenolate is being produced in thirty-two countries using East Park's patented formula. Many large companies have tried to copy the original recipe but were unsuccessful.

What is the real issue here? The Bible talks about the olive leaf and we know a lot about it from this ancient source. When I read it I realized that the olive leaf is one of the most important healing substances mentioned: there are thirty-seven entries in the holy scriptures that discuss the healing effects of olive branches, olive leaves, and the "fruit" of the olive tree. The olive trees growing for the past 2000 years on the banks of the river Jordan have been dated and proved to be two millennia old and they survived with having no bacterial or viral infections. There were no traces of parasitic infections either.

I believe that to be very thought-provoking! What can be the explanation for this? I think the reason is very obvious: these trees have been producing a defensive agent which resides in the leaves and not in the root or in the olive itself.

Olives are well known nowadays and Mediterranean countries have many dishes that include olives and they are a part of the daily diet. Olives are beneficial for heart and circulatory problems and reduce cholesterol. But it is not that well-known that olives also possess antiseptic properties.

I read recently that, according to scientists, antibiotics are designed to destroy a specific group of pathogens, i.e. infectious agents. Most of these antibiotics are designed to be leathal for a certain type or group of pathogens; however, by their very nature, most man-made antibiotics weaken the immune system. When injuries or excessive physical or mental stress weaken the immune system, harmful organisms become stronger and spread out to glands, organs, and tissues causing functional difficulties, otherwise known as diseases.

The indications of a diminishing immune system include allergies, intestinal problems, large lymph nodes, fatigue, joint pain, loss of appetite, nasal blockage, bronchial problems, skin eruptions, wounds, insomnia, general weakness and susceptibility to infectious diseases.

It is essential to strengthen the immune system. It is more important than most people (and health professionals) think. Today we know that *healing is the result of the efforts of the immune system* and not of medicine or herbs; it does not occur because of the use of vitamins or minerals.

The most recent test results indicated that olive leaf extract helps to strengthen the immune system. I bought some D-Lenolate and started taking it and the sudden change was remarkable. I became more energetic and I did not get sick even during the worst flu. The fungal infection from under my nails disappeared. It changed my life.

Since my purpose is to help others I would like to recommend the D-Lenolate capsules. Licensing for the D-Lenolate has been approved in Hungary; the product can be purchased in any pharmacy or at any Kaqun club.

INDIUM

I love to go to the Kaqun Club because I can gather important information that concern both healthy and ill people and we can share experiences as well. For example, I was glad when one of my fellow club members brought a special little book to my attention that was written about a mineral called INDIUM. (I was really interested in it since I had already been familiar with it as a supplement used at the Kaqun Club.) He had so many positive things to say about the book that I went out the next day and bought it...

It was a small book and I finished it quickly. While I was reading it I realized that there were many important points emphasized in the book. I recommend it to everyone!

I would like to share a few interesting and significant details with my readers in the hope of getting you interested in the book and in indium itself.

The indium supplement is an important factor in preventive health. This trace element received distribution license as a food supplement and many users claim it has changed their lives.

It is a proven fact that indium can have very remarkable effects. I can definitely support that because I experienced the benefits of indium. I think many of us can safely say that we have certain health problems that we cannot get relief for, no matter what we try. Thank God I know the answer now and I would like to share it with you: the solution to your problem is indium.

Since I have been regularly taking it, I have had so much more energy; I feel younger and experience other health-related benefits. Indium had been used in the field of healthcare for many years now; however, the wide-range role of it as a food supplement is a relatively new development. Indium has been a homeopathic medicine for the last seventy years used for symptoms such as tooth pain, migraine, throat pain, and for aching neck and shoulder muscles. It is also used as therapy for the following ailments: depression, headaches, attention deficit disorder, dizziness, eye pain, eye irritation, nasal discharge, sneezing, nasal stuffiness, mouth ulcers, loss of appetite, nausea, flatulence, stomachache, intestinal complaints, urinary problems, trembling of arms and legs, weakness of the legs, general pains, sleepiness, fever, weakness, irritation and menstrual problems. According to a research paper, taking indium reduced the number of cancer illnesses as well!

The results of researches and end experiments proved that indium is a safe food supplement to take for anyone! Some researchers conducted studies to show that indium exists in the human body; however, because of its very low concentration, they were not able to trace it. Certainly, that does not necessarily mean that we do not need it! On the contrary!

Despite that, indium helps people live a more active life. More energy means more physical exercise and more cal-

ories burned. More exercise results in more mus
Since muscle tissues use four times the calories compared
to fatty tissues, metabolism accelerates even during resting. Active people burn more calories during their sleep
than inactive people do. However surprising it sounds, one
may lose weight while sleeping!

If someone pays close attention to the rate of metabolic
functions, this goal may become reality. Athletes involved
in body building are familiar with this fact. They work
out for hours each day to add muscle mass to their bodies.
They have to eat thousands of calories every day merely
to supply their basic body functions with "fuel". For those
not wishing to engage in such a great daily commitment,
indium provides them with similar benefits.

The most promising research relating to indium is the
one involved in reducing pain that accompanies inflamma-
tory diseases such as *arthritis* and ailments alike. There is
research being conducted to prove whether a certain amino
acid that is found in the brain – named P-material – does
contain indium which would explain its positive benefits.

According to Dr. Hunt – a British researcher – the
P-material can prove helpful treating depression, anxiety,
stress, and chemical addiction. He studied the effects of
the P-material on people with drug addiction and he found
the P-material to have positive effects on patients wishing
to give up the use of drugs. This supports the accounts
of drug addicted patients whose withdrawal process was
eased with the use of indium.

It has been known to the consumers of indium for the
past two decades that this substance provides a feeling of

well-being and euphoria after having taken it for just a few days.

The measure of pressure within the eye ball increases from the range of 8/8 in childhood to the tens in teenage years and by the time of retirement the pressure range is up to 20/20. The pressure within the eye is also measured during a general eye exam. A result that shows 20/20 is a reason for concern and if the range of numbers reaches 25/25, the doctor will be writing a prescription, but the medicine prescribed can also constitute a source of side effects. If a patient takes indium long enough, such numbers will dip back into safer value zones.

People suffering from hypertension (blood pressure above 160) will most likely experience their rates diminish as well. It also works for low blood pressure.

Many people suffer from diabetes. Indium maybe the solution for that ailment also! Patients who have type II diabetes may have to readjust their insulin dosage because in some cases the indium makes that a necessary step to take – for some people it was necessary on the very first day they took indium! There were a number of patients who were able to discontinue insulin intake after a few weeks of taking indium. Why that happens is not entirely clear at this time but it is conceivable that indium enables the glands to send a more accurate signal to the pancreas and the level of insulin stabilizes.

Indium is found – in minute quantities – in the earth's crust and therefore it is considered a micro-mineral. Minerals are, by their very nature, inorganic substances and thus the body cannot utilize them in such form.

Most frequently, our body gets minerals from the food we digest since vegetables absorb inorganic minerals from the soil and convert them to organic substances through photosynthesis and these organic substances can be utilized by our organs.

Researchers have been aware from the beginning that if indium was to be used as a food supplement, it had to be transformed into a water soluble, organic form. If indium was water soluble, it could still bond with food molecules into a useless substance. Indium does not absorb if there is food present in the digestive tract. Maybe that was one reason why nutrition experts finally gave up on indium. Fortunately, one scientist, by the name of Dr. Henry Schroeder, did not retreat and he did find a solution. After dozens of experiments he discovered that indium sulfate has a hydroscopic quality which makes it water-soluble.

If we wish to use indium as a food supplement, we have to take it in a liquid form.

Indium is capable of stimulating the body to utilize nutrients in a more optimal way and helps to increase the life expectancy of red blood cells from ninety days to one hundred and twenty days.

Unfortunately, however, it is a fact that unless we replenish indium, it will not form part of our diet and we will have to do without the benefits of it.

The assistants at Kaqun Club realized that the inaccessibility of indium makes it difficult for the human body to have that micro-mineral even though it is necessary for a healthy body. So much so that the indium became a food supplement component of their treatments.

The daily recommended dose is 10 milligrams – a single drop of indium which absorbs in the mouth and in the stomach. Indium is to be taken on an empty stomach. Ideally, indium can be taken first thing in the morning by dropping it onto the tip of the tongue.

While taking indium I realized that I needed less sleep and I woke up more rested. I was full of energy; I started my day refreshed and in a good mood. I think this supplement is a necessity in order to accomplish everything that needs to be done during the day.

The Club

By the way, the Club is not for bathing only. Guests who visit the club to refresh and regenerate may become members of the club. There are many members, I am one of them. We organize meetings for the afternoons or for the weekends and they are always fun.

I particularly enjoy the kind of get-togethers where club members share the stories of their recovery. I have shared my experience with others many times and tried to put a lighthearted spin on it in order to relax others who were facing similar circumstances. This is how we get to know and support each other. Such hope-raising conversations are essential because they build a foundation of strength and faith to carry us through difficult times. We bear our burdens a little easier and we become role models for others. "If he can do it with a smile on his face, so can I!"

It is essential to mention that whatever was said at the meeting it had not been rehearsed but, they were honest answers to numerous questions, according to the particular situation. This was not a fake show full of tricks. It warmed my heart to watch my friends being touched by what I said and to see a shadow of hope on their pale faces. It helped their hope grow.

Many a times, my fellow club members came to visit me to have a private conservation. You could see the fear of future on their faces. I always tried to fill them with hope. I talked about my experiences of when I used to face the same fears. I realized that one must not focus on what is negative and on something that cannot be turned back, i.e. the destination of which is not our Creator but the cemetery…

Every time I kept emphasizing the same thought, the one I learned so well and will never forget: it is not only the oxygen that has to do its job but the patient as well! Old habits that were regimen practiced on a daily basis or had great importance must be left behind. I mentioned my consumption of sugar, not necessarily the kind you eat as candy but the one you put into coffee, tea or hot chocolate. I used to put a minimum of five spoonful of sugar into each of them. Then I have not even talked about cakes, pastries and ice cream yet.

I remember eating ice cream after my first surgery; and that is a staple for cancer! When that became evident for me, I quit eating it and started consuming greens, such as Brussels sprouts and broccoli which did not use to be my favorite foods. I eat yeastless bread, the taste of which was nothing like bread. I did that *for me* because I wanted to live!

Such things are not all that big of a deal but changing them is difficult but I do think our lives are worth it…

I was happy when other club members came to me and told me that they had taken the first steps towards making changes. It was good to know that my efforts had not been in vain and they were on their way towards recovery.

I believe *that it is very important that people get to know the Kaqun water, its beneficial effect and the whole process. This should not be kept as a secret because it is not a privilege* (even though in our times we tend to be more against each other than for one another).

Many do not believe in the positive effects of this water. There have been so many remarkable events in the world that scientists denied and later recanted their ideas knowing they made a mistake.

This water causes no harm and results in no pain, it only helps. If it was up to me, and providing I had sufficient financial background, I would supply it to everyone in the country, a cup in the morning and another cupful at night. I know and believe many would feel better drinking the water.

Visiting the Club

I was very curious so I decided to visit all the other Kaqun Clubs. After having visited the club at Dobogókő for a time, I started going to the one in Kerepes. I still wanted to know how things are going on at the other clubs.

It was not easy but I took time out to fulfill my desire in seeing the other clubs. First I went to visit the one in

Budafok. I was excited: What is social life like there? Nowadays I frequent the bath club at Kerepes where we socialize in the afternoons and at the weekends and always have fun. But what about the other clubs? Do they have the same positive attitude? If they do, then people go there gladly and what happened to me may also happen to others...

I have to tell you that the clubs are neither hospitals nor clinics. Not even close! Club members are interested in ways to improve their own life quality. The club is essentially different from hospitals where – in my experience – patients receive their therapies, they are told what medicines to take, how to help themselves at home and what kind of antibiotics to take.

I think I am not alone when I say that a patient who is going through difficult times requires a little more than that, a little positivity. We all know that we like to belong somewhere and we like to find a place where we are accepted and loved. Usually the family fulfills this need but it is totally different to meet up with people who have the same problems as we do. It is not just about me, of course. I am convinced that other patients, the ones with leg sores, the ones with burns, as well as patients undergoing chemotherapy and radiation therapy are also the same. People like us want company around us who do not pity us.

I remember how many times my throat closed up and my eyes teared up while I balled my hand in a fist when people were staring at the hole on my throat and then they whispered among themselves behind my back. Many times I could hardly stand not to express my feelings but I knew that my mechanical voice would just make things worse. We need a community, a group of people where we can look each other in the eye and feel that we are in the same boat.

* * *

As I was parking at the Budafok Kaqun Club I observed the building from the outside. I expected a similar structure as in Kerepes but I was wrong. It looked more like a giant detached house.

I was excited but I was not surprised: I was welcomed into a clean, beautiful facility with family-like atmosphere. I thought my supposition was right that all the clubs operate in the same way everywhere in the country – and I liked that very much!

It turned out that in the Budafok Kaqun Club, just like in the one in Kerepes, there were regular club meetings where the members could spend a few pleasant hours together on a monthly basis. When I got there, the club meeting was already in full swing with about 25 members attending. It is hard to believe that patients can create such a close-knit group. The subject of the discussion was the ways of supplying essential oxygen to the body. They were enthusiastically involved in the group conversation.

They discussed that oxygen can be introduced to the body through sports, exercise, *tai chi, chi kung* or other series of movements based on Chinese philosophy.

Kaqun water bath therapy and drinking the water was, of course, also listed as a method of oxygen introduction.

It was interesting to meet several athletes in Budafok. They were glad to be members of the club where rehabilitation was also taking place. The Kaqun weight loss program was also very successful because visitors could receive advice on dieting and take part in exercises with the use of personally designed plans. There were massage and sauna facilities available in the basement. Candle light bathing was part of the routine from 7 p.m. – 10 p.m. and the weight loss group could take their time until 11 p.m. There was a fitness club available on the premises, making scheduling and exercise a lot easier.

* * *

I left Budafok Kaqun Club with a good feeling. I had a lot of pleasant thoughts going around in my head on my way home. I recalled the time when I became a club member many years ago in Kerepes. I went there every day to refresh myself but no one ever pressured me to become a member, I was never forced into anything. That left me with a very positive feeling. The membership is totally voluntary, anyone can join who would like to see his family members and himself become healthier. There is a one-time, lifetime membership fee and one card can be used for the whole family. A card comes with two free baths at the club where the sign-up was paid. I thought that was very generous.

During meetings it was always emphasized to think of each other with compassion. Positive thinking was essential! Many times we were told about the importance of preventive health measures. My health problems, or, more accurately, escaping from the shadows of death propelled me towards the decision to do everything to prevent my family from having such suffering.

The membership card is issued under the member's name but I can take any family member with me or even a friend. At the time of singing up, the new member will have two free baths and can enjoy the other bath visits at half price.

The plastic card may be used at any club in the country but setting up an appointment is still necessary.

There was another important point that had a positive effect on me: I could check on my own oxygen level. I could actually do that at any Kaqun Club. I had never had that type of test anywhere in my life. That was a significant problem because a body that is deprived of oxygen may develop many kinds of serious diseases. Assistants, club members and volunteers are very helpful in solving all kinds of problems.

I have to say that the family atmosphere at the club is very important to me and to other club members as well. Our friendships are open and honest and we can discuss all types of subjects, including health problems. We also inform the new members of what happens during the treatments and tell them to make sure that they have a preset appointment.

I really liked the amount of flexibility displayed by the bath club employees; how accommodating and flexible they were even during evening times when I and other members came late. Such flexible and "user-friendly" attitude is true for all the other clubs as well.

I was also impressed by the free lifestyle advice. That was a really important factor.

The club organizes social programs that I gladly participate in because we can talk about many subjects freely; first of all about our problems. We do not have to be ashamed; we do not have to talk in flowery language. We can just truly tell each other what we observe on ourselves and what kind of improvement is taking place in our health. Of course, the greatest joy is to hear when someone is able to announce a positive change.

We can talk about things we do not like, such as the water being too hot to our liking (has not happened yet), or the club closed too early. We can mention things that are important in the life of the Kaqun community. Positive and constructive presentations always have a great effect on me. I have given my testimony several times...

I went back in thought to that afternoon in Budafok where I also spoke during the meeting. I told others that I belonged to the Kerepes Kaqun Club; I told them about the ordeals I went through during my illness and what kind of therapies I had received. I went into details when discussing the numbers of baths taken, the amounts of water I consumed and the kinds of supplements I took.

It was a satisfying feeling to talk about all that among ourselves and that we were able to give advice to each other. Many of the pieces of advice were accepted by the membership. If it was not accepted then at least they listened to the options...

Thinking about this, I realized that only Heaven knows how grateful I am for belonging to the club. There is a familiar and calm environment to discuss the future. We exchange experiences and there is an opportunity for individual consultation.

Every club provides classes to learn breathing and movement techniques that have been used in Chinese healing arts for many centuries. In Europe such old techniques have only been available for the past two decades. I came to realize that such breathing techniques increase the blood's oxygen level by 20 % and help the circulatory system. Besides all that, such methods provide mental relaxation as well.

The Club is a place of warm welcome where one can refresh and relax after the bath therapy, have conservations and may use other equipment at a discounted price such as foot massage machines, massage tables and saunas. Every bath club has a sauna. All this equipment was useful in helping my immune system function, giving me the greatest gift: health.

* * *

I kept my promise and visited every bath club in the country. I went to Veszprém where I was welcomed just as warmly as at Budafok. I visited Budakeszi, Zugló and similar pleasant experiences awaited me as everywhere else. I was assured that patients could use the bath clubs no matter where they live and they will always be treated well. When the clients leave they will feel like a new person.

* * *

The Kaqun Clubs have an annual meeting where members from all parts of the country come together.

Dobogókő has hosted two of the annual gatherings. I am always happy to participate. We spent three days together and had bonfires at night and had great talks. There were seminars to increase our knowledge on how the Kaqun system works.

Days like that are especially memorable and important for me because we have them each year and we can meet with the same people every year. It is especially exciting to see the members who were not supposed to make it or their doctors told them they only had a year or two to live. It is a great feeling to sit and talk with them three or four years later. We share our stories. Some have already forgotten that they were ever ill. For me, it is different. Everyday I wake up in the morning I know that I have received another new day as a gift...

* * *

Vis Vitalis Health Preventive and Rehabilitation Institute

Staying Alive!

I am always excited to go to the bath club at Kerepes. It feels like going home. I calm down and rest there and I always get a recharge. I could not have imagined how this could be made even better; but it can!

I found out about an adjoining complex under construction in Kerepes next to the bath that will surely be mentioned as a unique wonder of the world. The Vis Vitalis Prevention and Rehabilitation Institute will be a high class hotel that gives home to the largest Kaqun Bath Facility in the world.

I cannot even describe how happy I was to be able to visit the hotel. This complex houses a bath club with thirty-six bathtubs and all the branches of traditional Chinese medicine will be represented under the supervision of Chinese doctors. Acupuncture, *tina, chi-kung and tai chi* will all be offered. A pharmacy will also be part of the facility.

On the upper floors more than fifty double rooms will be waiting for the guests and I found seven apartments as well. Expanded infrastructure will serve the guests where phone lines, web access, and cable TV will be available throughout the 5000 m² hotel building. Several different types of massage services, cosmetics and a hair salon will be available for the ladies who will most likely want to become more beautiful while relaxing. The hotel has its own laundry facilities.

The hotel will have a restaurant, a bar and a coffee house as well. There will be facilities for conferences with three auditoriums that accommodate forty to fifty people. The conference rooms will have state-of-the-art projectors, lights and computers.

Parking place is provided around the building, the size of the parking lot is 25,000 m².

I believe that visitors will come from all parts of the world to enjoy the wonders awaiting them, here at Kerepes. The hotel is opening soon to serve the comfort of the guests. The location reveals careful planning since the hotel is easily accessible on Road No. 3 and it is a "stone's throw" away from the light rail station. Buses and cars can easily reach this location.

A large garden surrounds the hotel which will be used for the exercises that the guests perform. Visitors will be able to choose between active or passive resting. Thus there will be three parts to the garden: a relaxation park, a small fishing-lake and sport fields.

The relaxation park will provide a place for all kinds of pleasant activities. One will be able to hide from problems and the world and may meditate in peace. I am not an expert of the tourist industry but I do believe that the fishing-lake will be of some interest, too. Enchanting flowers, plants and fishes will bring a special touch to the garden.

For guests who are more interested in sports, fields will be offered for soccer and for other organized sports. I think it will be important to cater for visitors with an athletic mindset.

In such an environment, everyone will find what they are looking for, whether they just want to relax or decrease the effects of chemotherapy or radiation. If there is a place that fits the description for "quality of life", then this is it.

I can testify that in the club the most important purpose is to provide first class customer service. I should not be surprised at all because that is the main principle concerning Kaqun water – helping and caring for people.

The current goal is also to help people. This is an ideal place for patients going through chemotherapy, radiation treatments or recovering from recent surgery – how much they wish for better circumstances, more energy and more freedom in order to combat their disease.

I think this endeavor will be a unique undertaking in the world; it will be a great example how to transform an exhausted patient into a brand new person within ten, seven or even three days!

* * *

Since the bath club has become a part of my daily routine, it means a lot to me to continually observe its operations. I can gladly proclaim that they are becoming very popular in Hungary. The best example for that is the Kaqun Club that exists within the combined facilities of the Szent István and Szent László Rehabilitation Hospitals. After a month of initial start-up, the bath club is running at full capacity.

I was happy to read the statement issued by the administrator of the hospital:

"The special, electrolitically produced high oxygen content water has become very popular among our recovering patients. It is our experience that the bath therapy is beneficial to the patients' well-being and in some cases it accelerates recovery. The oxygen therapy was becoming

popular during its trial runs and the interest in this therapy is still growing. The baths are operating on full capacity."

I am happy because I live really close by and I do not have to commute through the city to get to Kerepes if I do not have the time. I gladly go there for follow-up therapy because – as the statement clearly implies – the Kaqun baths bring a little extra to the patients.

On one instance, during one of my visits, a hospital director mentioned that the Kaqun facility is the shining diamond of the hospital complex. I think that speaks for itself...

* * *

At the basement of the Semmelweis Hospital in Miskolc there is another Kaqun Club. It operates on a totally restored level of the central hospital complex and can be accessed through the main entrance and also from the parking lot which makes it easier to access for disabled patients.

The Kaqun Club has eight bathtubs and the patients are assisted by expert health professionals. At the time I paid a visit there, the director of the hospital mentioned that he saw a great future for the Kaqun therapy since it had wonderful traits to improve on the patients' general well-being. It is the dream of every patient to have better physical condition during recovery.

With its candle lights and flower arrangements, the reception area attracts a lot of visitors. Accompanied with soft music playing, guests cannot help but stop and take in the sight. Not many are able to resist and shortly the patients can enjoy the turquoise blue, warm, oxygen rich water which penetrates and reinvigorates their tired bodies.

I have heard the following phrase several times: "I am coming back because after the bath I feel so light and young!" This is adequate evidence that the bath in Miskolc is fast becoming a popular place to improve on one's well-being.

* * *

Not long ago I was traveling through Austria and as we were driving past a small town a familiar sight caught my eye.

The familiar sign displayed the Kaqun water emblem. I was glad because the bath clubs op-

The Sport Hotel in Rust, Austria houses the Kaqun facility

erated outside Hungary as well and could mean help for people who believed. Among the bath clubs in Europe, the one in Rust is a very important facility. It goes without saying that I just had to go in and pay a visit.

I received a friendly welcome as I was telling them who I was and where I came from.

I was surprised to find out that the club in Rust operates in a very different way. Even though the basic principle is the same, the bath club falls under the supervision of Dr. Bayer who oversees all the affairs of traditional Chinese medicine in Austria. The bath club is located in a Chinese health center where patients specifically go to relax and to participate in rehabilitation, and they are not necessarily suffering from illness but may only have fatigue. They are overwhelmed, depressed or lost their zeal for life and receive rehabilitation for such ailments.

Such programs usually last from Friday to Sunday and patients can participate in physical therapy, get acupuncture done and they may also use the sauna and any of the eight bathtubs; all presented in a Chinese-themed environment. Of course, *chi-kung* and *tai-chi* courses are also offered. I enjoyed talking to the people there who were very excited about the Kaqun water and its remarkable benefits.

* * *

After traveling back home, I went to Kerepes to share my experiences with others and I was very surprised to find out that another Kaqun facility already operates in Holland as well. The owner of that bath club just happened to be visiting Kerepes.

I felt really inspired to go to Holland and find out how the club is being run and what the patients think about the Kaqun water. The Dutch owner explained that product trials took a whole year in Holland. They performed trials with patients suffering from Parkinson's and Alzheimer's diseases and observed what kind of improvements the patients showed. It was such a successful trial run that health insurance companies are planning to incorporate the Kaqun therapy into the treatment programs they provide and they are discussing how they can best support such patients in improving their quality of life.

It was so good to hear all those reports and I felt compelled to go to visit. I became friends with the Dutch bath club owner and when I mentioned traveling to Holland someday, he assured me of his welcome and he told me that he would accept my Hungarian membership card. He also remarked that the conditions of use are the same as in Hungary and asked me to come by and set an appointment.

When I went home I told my wife about my plan to travel to Holland; she said nothing just nodded her head. She knew what the Kaqun water meant to me and she did not try to hold me back. She was just as thankful for the water as I was and she understood my enthusiasm.

I made a firm decision to visit every Kaqun Club. I wanted to hear what others thought about the water...

* * *

A few days later I took off for Holland. The owner welcomed me and spent a long time with me sharing his experiences. He told me that he had suffered from an extreme skin disease. Despite all his efforts no one could help him. He showed me some old photographs of what his face and his skin used to look like. He also elaborated on how many times he had been humiliated and how frustrated he had been. Even his countenance changed as he shifted through his memories: how his self-esteem had totally been destroyed and what kind of superhuman effort it took him to live through each day. Then he reached a point when he did not want to go on anymore.

He got somewhat emotional at that point but then his whole being went under a transformation.

His face lightened up and his memories became all positive when he got to the part where he came to Budapest and visited the Kaqun Club in Kerepes. He heard about the water and actually all he was hoping for was a little relief. He never hoped that he could fully be healed.

According to him, he came to Kerepes four times. Every time he came he took 50-minute baths three times a day and drank nearly a gallon of Kaqun water. By the fourth time he came to visit, his skin disease had completely healed and caused no more pain and problems. As proof he showed me the pictures taken after his recovery.

He told me with a smile that when he had realized that all his health problems were solved by the water, he decided to build a bath club to help others. He added that he welcomes Hungarians because he has positive memories of Hungary.

Since that time, a whole chain of Kaqun Clubs have opened in Holland. When I got home, I relayed the news to everyone; the Kaqun water has gained recognition not just in Hungary but all over Europe.

* * *

Staying Alive!

One day I was taking one of my follow-up bath treatments when I heard a couple talking in Russian behind the separating curtain. Since I do not speak Russian, I only recognized a few words. I was really curious: what do they think of the Kaqun water?

I had finished ten minutes before they did and I found out that they are a married couple who have traveled to Hungary before and they were here to find out more about the water. Their primary purpose was to receive the benefits of the water but the subject was also interesting for them on a professional level. Dr. Oleg Ishchenko is a heart surgeon and his wife, Dr. Irina Ishchenko, is a leading dermatologist from Kiev, Ukraine.

The Ukrainian couple proved to be very friendly and they talked to many of the patients at the club, including me. They wanted to know why I was there. The guests and myself gladly answered their questions. After a few minutes of private conversation among themselves, the couple returned to me and told me that they found my story very fascinating and they wanted to invite me to Kiev to share my experiences with their folk.

I could not believe this was happening to me. I immediately agreed to go because I wanted to see Kiev and even more so after I found out that a bath club had already been established there.

When I went home and told my wife, the poor woman just looked at me. I guess she must have had enough of me being always on the road but she did not protest and accepted being alone for a while.

One morning a courier brought my plane ticket to Kiev. The invitation was for a whole week and it included lodging and meals. As I found out later, they planned other programs for me, too, such as visiting the favorite sights of Kiev.

* * *

With great excitement I set out on my journey. During the flight I recalled the tragic event of Chernobyl from 1986. I was thinking of the effects of it on the Ukrainian people. They must have lived through terrible times; I wondered if I was going to see any traces of that unfortunate nuclear event. I remembered hearing that the nuclear catastrophe caused an increase in the number of cancer cases. Maybe that is the reason why there are so many cancer patients in the Ukraine?

I felt bad for those afflicted and I hoped that the Kaqun water could help them as well. My flight arrived in the evening and Dr. Oleg Ishchenko welcomed me and asked me about my flight.

As we left the airport, I was taking in the sights of Kiev. What a cosmopolitan city – I marveled. I knew that Kiev is one of the oldest cities of Eastern Europe but it was so different from what I expected. Kiev was a modern busy capital.

When we got to my hotel another surprise was waiting: I was taken to a beautiful five-star hotel. My room had two rooms, a bathroom and a kitchen equipped with the latest amenities and a refrigerator stuffed with delicacies. I was invited to take as much as I wanted.

The building that houses the Q Bath of Kiev

Dr. Irina Ishchenko

The next morning, on Monday, I was driven to the Kiev Kaqun Club which is actually named the Q European Oxy System. The club can be found at 22 Kravikaska Street. The Club can be reached by telephone: 0038 044 575 3132, and the toll free number is 8 800 500 9220 which can be used in all of Ukraine. The website is: *http://www.qwater.com.ua*

I was full of expectations when I entered the building; I just wanted to see how the place was set up. The reception was the place where appointments could be set for consultation with Dr. Irina and Oleg Ishchenko.

There is a foyer, a waiting area and eight separate pavilions where the bathtubs are located. The Q European System is a place where compassion and assistance meet the needs of patients. The main purpose is to bring about health and happiness; to increase the patient's belief in success and to improve the quality of their lives.

Dr. Oleg Ishchenko, heart surgeon

I was informed that the Q European Oxy System provides a multitude of services in the area of recreation and health improvement. Their products are: "Q European Oxy System" structured high-oxygen content water which contains 20mg/l oxygen and high-oxygen content water "Q Sport European Oxy System" which contains 30mg/l oxygen. The Q water is extremely beneficial for the health, tastes pleasant and it is recommended to everyone: for the ill and for the healthy as well. If some would like to be proactive about their health and desire vitality and regeneration, the oxygen bath is their solution.

The following food supplements are also recommended by the bath club: D-Lenolate to stimulate the immune system (500 mg capsules in 60 or 180 capsule bottles), and Q Indium-XL which helps the functions of the endocrine system and the immune system (3.0 ml bottles).

I carefully observed everything. I noted how large the foyer was and how well-designed and comfortable the waiting area appeared to be. The employees were very nice and professional. They showed me around the recreational and bath facilities.

I could barely wait to take a bath and I was asked if it felt any different from all the other Kaqun baths I have taken in other countries. I was also taken to the Medicus Enterprise, which is a middle-sized pharmaceutical distribution company.

I was glad to meet other Kaqun Club members and we had a good share of experiences. We told each other our stories, how many baths we had taken and what kind of benefits we had received from them. I told my story as well and my journey from my sufferings until my encounter with the Kaqun water which – I believe – gave me back my health. They seemed glued to my words while they were listening to me intently. I was glad to hear the local patients explain all the wonderful benefits they had received from the water. I felt that my trip was a success because I was able to instill a great amount of strength and belief into others just by sharing my story. The conversation took place in the friendliest atmosphere.

I only had a single thorn in my side. I observed the well-known design and realized that something was different. It said *Q voda* that is Q water. I found that intriguing because in Hungary and in other countries the bath system was known as Kaqun water.

I was curious enough to ask why.

Dr. Oleg Ishchenko just smiled and let me in on a local secret: Kaqun means "diarrhea" in their language. It would be rather hilarious to hear someone say: "Sasha, go buy some bread and eight bottles of diarrhea!" That is why the need for the name change arose and Kaqun water became Q water in the Ukraine. Dr. Ishchenko told me that a multitude of information was available about the Q water on the web and other places.

I enjoyed that day very much and was getting ready for more excitement on the next because I knew I was invited to Kiev's premier Oncology clinic.

The doctors welcomed me with great joy and told me that they were awaiting the presentation of a Hungarian onco-pathologist professor who was there accompanied by his American counterpart and was going to talk about the physiological effects of oxygen.

I was thankful to be invited to the presentation where eighty doctors were present. I found out that this professor receives a great welcome in every other institute around here. I talked to the doctors from the cancer center and heard that studies are being planned concerning the Q water. This product was to be made available for sale within a day in the hospital's pharmacy and a comprehensive case study was in the preparatory stages, using volunteers.

I was told that the case study was based on empirical, that is, practical observation. Chemotherapy and radiation recipients were going to be studied for the beneficial effects of the Q water. If the primary studies showed promising results then clinical studies would follow.

When we were departing from the Institute of Oncology, Dr. Ishchenko received a phone call. He turned to me and asked if I was too tired to accompany him to another health care facility. Of course, I was not tired and gladly accepted the invitation.

We went to another hospital's burn unit. They were treating patients with three different types of burns: chemical burn injuries, scalding cases and fire-burnt patients. If the results managed to persuade doctors about the positive effects of the Q water then the burn patients would be treated in Q baths.

Words cannot express the abundance of experience I received. It was good to see that others were so interested in the Kaqun (Q) water.

* * *

I spent the rest of the week exploring the sights of Kiev and if it wasn't for the occasional golden bulbous church tops, I would have easily mistaken the city for Budapest.

They just looked so similar I felt right at home. As Budapest spreads over the banks of the Danube, lays Kiev on the banks of the Dnieper. The small hills on the right side of the river hide the ancient parts of the city, such as Upper Town, Petchersk, and Pondol. The statue of their Christian pioneer, the Grand Monarch Vladimir, raises the cross much the same way as our Bishop Gellert on the top of the hill named after him.

I have to admit that the "Old Mother" of all Russian cities, Kiev, maintains herself like royalty: she is elegant and European. There is a saying in the Ukraine: "Moscow is big and St. Petersburg is beautiful but Kiev was designed for people."

The most interesting sight for me was the underground city, the Globus, whose existence is only indicated by the tops of buildings located in a flat area. When this shopping center was designed the main concern had been not to interfere with the ancient architecture of the city, so the shopping mall was hid underground. There are 10-mile-long underground tunnels that lead to the shopping facilities. The subterranean tunnels are very large in size and they form a network that covers the whole city. The shopping centers offer a large variety of merchandise from simple inexpensive products to $ 300 socks. I was completely impressed and enjoyed seeing all the famous sights and curiosities.

The sightseeing was concluded with a pleasant dinner in a downtown high rise where I could luxuriate in the night lights of Kiev.

* * *

On the next day I left for home enriched with positive experiences since so many wonderful things had happened to me in Kiev. It was a miracle that I could go at all, let alone spending the whole week in such grandiose circumstances. I was hoping that the Q voda, as the Kaqun water is called there, will help people to get healthy again and give their life back – as it did for me!

(Ever since my visit I have remained in personal contact with Dr. Oleg Ishchenko and his wife. Whenever they come to Hungary I always invite them to my home.)

When I got home I could hardly wait to share my thoughts with the other club members in the course of a club event. I really prepared for that occasion. When we finally got together everyone was giving me their full attention. Many others mentioned that they were also planning to visit Kiev since my experiences inspired them to go. I definitely got some good laughs when I mentioned the reason for the Kaqun water's name change. I talked about the positive opinions that the club members expressed about the water.

What do the skeptics say about the Kaqun water?

Before I left for the club meeting I was browsing the web and despite the numerous positive responses I was disappointed to find some skeptical remarks that had been posted concerning the Kaqun water. Some people expressed their opinions about the water as being a fraud whereas they have never even tried it and never experienced its effects.

(I think honesty demands that an opinion must be founded on something previously experienced. Many will share their sad story of terminal illness when despite all efforts of doctors nothing can be done. The effectiveness of a therapy is best measured by the fact of recovery. There is none more perfect proof than that! I believe that with my illness the participation in traditional cancer treatment would have most likely resulted in my death.)

Such was a condescending remark made by a naturopath who told his/her patient:

"I do not recommend the Kaqun water because it is not produced from pure water."

I was not hiding my outrage in front of my fellow club members. I went to Italy just to personally see the source of the water I have been drinking for many years. I saw the source of the water, the spring breaking through the rock wall six thousand feet up. I had never seen such clear water since it is spring water that receives further purification in the processing plant and it does not contain any preservatives, any coloring agents or flavors. It only contains enriched oxygen added through a special procedure. It is the pureness of the water that sets it apart from other waters!

I would respectfully recommend to that naturopath to take a trip to Italy and witness for him/herself if there is purer water to be found anywhere on this planet...

Another person expressed that he feels cheated because after drinking some bottles of water his chronic headache did not disappear. I already stated that the water is not medicine, not a miracle cure and one needs to realize that not everybody receives the recovery they hope for. Let's think about it: in hospitals where people have the same disease and prescribed the same therapy – does everyone recover? Sometimes people just have to be thankful that they were given a longer lease on life. Maybe the Kaqun water did not heal them but it decreased a patient's pain or elevated someone's spirit...

One of my fellow club members asked to speak. He wanted to support my last few sentences with his tragic story:

"On September 11, 2001 I was in Las Vegas with my wife enjoying the sights and the abundance of entertainment of that city when the tragedy happened. That was a historic day when as a result of the terror attacks the Twin Towers of New York collapsed and buried many innocent people. Everything changed around us and in our lives. We decided to move back to Hungary until things settle down in the US and security once again becomes reality.

We arrived at Ferihegy on November 2nd, 2001 and relished being in Hungary. The border patrol officer, a lady, wished happy birthday to my wife, seeing it was her birthday that day. We never knew how little time she had left...

A few weeks later, without any previous warning, my wife started having acute abdominal pain paired with bloating. Her condition quickly worsened but because of the Christmas holiday, she only entered a hospital on January 2nd. Her abdomen was comparable in size to that of an eight-month-pregnant woman.

A doctor friend of mine escorted my wife, Edit, into the examination room while I waited outside. After numerous tests, he sent her out and asked me to come inside. As I looked him in the eye I knew that there was serious trouble. He told me that my wife had a malignant tumor in her ovary.

That was terrible; the news hit me like lightning from a blue sky. Then I remembered a few strange things that I observed during our stay in Las Vegas: my wife loved the sun but lately she did not tan, instead she avoided the sun. Back then I thought that it was her modesty not wanting to show off being older but now I know that it was a precursor of her illness.

The other symptom that came to my mind was her complaints about being bloated. When I reacted with wanting to take her to a doctor, she blamed her eating habits and refused to see a doctor.

Edit was a strong lady and I knew I could not convince her to get a thorough examination. I did not think that it could be something this bad and I did not push the issue. I did not perceive her being sickly so I did nothing about it. She took care of herself and did not look any different. I regret not being more assertive...

The doctors at the Sports Hospital recommended surgery and the Women's Clinic I agreed to perform the procedure on January 17th. Edit remained at the Sports Hospital from January 2nd to 9th. It had been agreed upon that she could go home until the day of the surgery came but one night she became very ill. She collapsed and lost consciousness. I called my doctor friend at the Sports Hospital who sent an ambulance and they took her in. She was treated and 4 liters of water was drained from her abdominal area.

She was prepared for surgery and the procedure was performed at the Women's Clinic on January 17th. Two teams of surgeons worked on her at the same time. One group was operating from the top and the other from the bottom. The surgery was lengthy and difficult. It seemed like eternity to me.

After the surgery I was told that her condition was so serious that if she had not been operated on at that time, she would have died within forty-eight hours. I left the clinic with a heavy heart and when the phone rang around midnight my heart started skipping beats. I knew that it was the clinic calling.

I was not mistaken. The call came from the intensive care and I was informed that she had got worse and would be taken to another hospital, to the Bronchial Unit of Kútvölgyi Hospital, where she could receive the best care for breathing problems.

I immediately took off to be with her. It was heart-breaking to know that she was not improving but was facing even more difficulties. Her breathing was inadequate and she developed an inflammation in her pancreas. She was in a coma at the time. She had to be put on a respirator for five days. I am still thankful today to the doctor who saved her life by stabilizing her breathing.

She spent twenty days at that hospital and then was transported back to the Women's Clinic I, to the Oncology Department.

I started hoping when I was told that I could take her home. But the situation was that she was allowed to stay at home just to gain strength for chemotherapy and its side effects. When I asked about what to expect as far as chemotherapy was concerned I was informed that it all depended on how she reacted to it.

We were going through a time of hardship. My wife had a Y shaped scar on her abdomen which perforated and leaked. It had to be covered with new dressings all the time. Her condition was worsening instead of improving; she was not gaining any strength which she would have needed. We were facing harder days to come.

It was very painful for both of us to return to the clinic. We were both filled with fear... and hope for the success of the therapy.

At the first stage she received *Taxol* therapy which had to be suspended immediately since it triggered an allergic reaction in Edit's body. Then she was switched to *Ciclo phosphamid/Cisplatin* therapy. She received six series of that. She suffered through hell while the treatments lasted. The headaches, loss of appetite, nausea, weakness, hair loss and other serious symptoms – she had them all.

We heard of the Kaqun therapy and its positive effects during the fall of 2002.

I have to admit being skeptical towards such things. (The reason for that is that I come from a doctor family and I was a paramedic during the 60's. I wanted to become a doctor but after my third attempt at medical school I was told that I was an "outsider" with no chance to be accepted.)

My wife really wanted to try the water – as a side therapy to traditional chemo and I respected her decision. It was not important anymore if I believed in it but giving everything and anything a chance – that was our main principle. I took Edit to the bath club of Dobogókő and she became a member.

During follow-up visits, the doctors did not have any recommendations against trying the Kaqun water as a bath or drinking therapy. The truth is that they admitted to the water's beneficial effects because they saw improvement in Edit's condition.

I also observed that thanks to the water therapy Edit's spirit was lifted. We spent thirty-three years together and I knew her well enough to notice. How beneficial was the Kaqun therapy to her? She endured the negative effects of the chemotherapy much better and she did not feel sick while she was taking the baths and drinking the water...

Unfortunately, her condition worsened again during the summer of 2004. The cancer returned and spread. She died on November 24th. I cannot deny the positive effects of the Kaqun water, even though it could not save Edit's life. She did not recover but it is a fact that the water made her life easier to bear in the last two years. It eased her pain and I cannot deny how much that helped. I am still using the Kaqun therapy, even in Edit's absence, and I remained a club member... "

* * *

The positive influence of the water is beyond doubt, even if such cases as Edit's do occur where there is no recovery. At the same time numerous patients experience significant improvements - even in terminal cases where they were given no chances for survival.

Many club members expressed an outrage similar to mine when they heard about the unfounded negative comments. Péter wanted to tell everyone what has been happening to him since he started coming to the Kaqun Club. It started to seem to me that we were in for an unusual club meeting.

"I first heard about the high oxygen content water back in March 2007 and I have been a club member ever since. I spotted an article about the Kaqun water in a natural health magazine and then my friends helped me search it on the web. Doctors and other medicine-related resources did not mention the existence of the Kaqun water.

When I became a member, my struggle against a viral skin infection (warts) had been dragging on for years. The worst symptoms were affecting the heel of my right foot. I had picked up the infection at a public pool which I was visiting nearly everyday.

I was under treatments done by state health insurance-provided doctors and private doctors as well and their methods were quite similar. My healing process took seven years.

The first symptom was the presence of two warts on my left hand. My dermatologist prescribed Verrum which had to be applied to the warts thickly and completely covering them and a day later they had to be scraped off. This process had to be repeated for three weeks. I was not provided with any further information of the causes or any other recommendations.

Much later, here at the bath club, I found out that I had been given a very strong cell toxin and its purpose and use should have been explained much more carefully. The substance was so strong in fact that it destroyed the surrounding skin areas and the whole section of my skin became a burning inflammation.

At that time I switched doctors and the new therapy was to remove the warts by burning them out. The wart infection returned and I received Verrum therapy again, then the burning process once again.

By that time the infection spread to my feet in another form of the same virus which manifested in the form of small black dots. First it was barely noticeable but as it spread I visited the dermatologist again. I felt a pricking pain as I walked and I saw skin thickening at the affected areas. That symptom made the detection even harder. The treatment was the same again, skin removal and burning out but this time the treated area was much larger and so was the wound. Once again the treatment failed and the infection returned. This time I was recommended to apply **greater celandine** alongside the traditional Verrum therapy.

The long drawn out and fruitless process was frustrating and the ever-worsening skin-thickening made the Verrum treatment and the skin removal nearly impossible for me.

I was not recommended for surgery, I just retuned for check-ups but no other treatments were used besides the use of a wart preventing cream. In the meantime, the health care reform took away my coverage for skin treatments and I had to find a private doctor.

I was receiving regular treatment from August 2006 until February 2007 and this third doctor was trying to help me with a reoccurring infection that had been affecting me for years. No effectual healing method was found and the infection kept getting larger and larger. When the whole area was removed the remaining wound bled profusely but I did not get any comprehensive remedies that would result in complete healing. The scope of infection only revealed itself during the skin removal process.

There were two points of viral concentrations on my feet and reaching their core would have required surgery. I did undergo surgery but the infection reoccurred very soon after and more aggressively. The coming months and years brought three more surgeries in each foot. They were very painful procedures and even the administering of topical pain killers resulted in agonizing pain.

Between the series of surgical interventions I received regular (twice a week) applications of a substance that contained oxygen and the process was called a carbox-ide-solution treatment. The purpose of it was to speed up circulation to get rid of the virus. This remedy was applied with the use of needles directly onto the surrounding areas of the wound. I was given homeopathic recommendations and was told to change my diet. Despite all that, as soon as the wounds had healed, the virus infection returned. The infected area expanded and so freezing also had to be used as a treatment.

After six months of concentrated treatments, the infection suddenly caused a strong inflammation which took up an area of the size of a man's hand. The raw skin was leaking fluids and the whole area was awfully burning and itching at the same time. I was told to scrape off the affected section with the use of a pumice stone. The virus concentration became a deeply cracked, puss-leaking spot. It is difficult to describe this dire condition.

This was the phase where I stopped going to the dermatologist. I want to mention that I understood the good intentions of the doctor and I appreciated his efforts but I started to feel like a guinea pig and felt that should be referred to an oncologist.

I did not have any ideas how to proceed from there and that is when I got the news about the oxygenated water. I did not have any fears or doubts about the water, so trying it out caused no trouble. By that time I was truly frustrated. That is the background of my story.

The Kaqun Lifestyle Club offered the advice of taking daily baths and drinking about a third of gallon of Kaqun water a day. The treatment lasted from March 3rd to June 20th in 2007. The effects of the water resulted in the stoppage of leaking in the next five to six days and then slowly the burning inflammation disappeared. At the same time new skin was growing that became clear and smooth in three to four weeks. The itching slowly faded as well.

I also used an olive based cream and I applied it daily to the edges of the healing skin, to where the infection would not return any more. Five or six weeks later the whole affected area cleared out to the point where the cores of the infection became detectable in the form of black dots.

The bath treatments halted the symptoms and at the end of the second month the stabbing pain had stopped, too. The opportunity for the clearing of the whole skin section has come. That meant that we had to proceed layer by layer, clearing out inactive virus concentrations and could not cause any bleeding because that is how the infection spread.

We were very careful about that and only cleared away about ten percent of the layer at a time. I was still drinking the Kaqun water daily and the soothing baths helped with the regeneration of the skin that had been affected by the removal procedure.

For years I could not stand on the part of my foot correctly where it was infected but as the skin and the disease cleared the pain and itching stopped. By the month of May the layer by layer skin removal and clearing caused no pain at all. I am convinced that the Kaqun water played a pivotal role in this long process of healing.

By the end of June, 2007 I became symptom-free and have been ever since. However, this ordeal had another important effect on my life: I am still drinking the water and every week or every other week I go to take a Kaqun bath.

I am completely healthy and a firm believer of the Kaqun water. That is why I share my knowledge with my friends and colleagues and recommend this therapy to them since it helped me a great deal. One of my co-workers had had a similar infection and after I had sent him to the bath club he achieved the same results but others also came to me for advice.

I am not a doctor and I am a skeptic but still became a devoted fan of the oxygenized water produced through that special process. I supply my aging father with the Kaqun water as well.

The most interesting part of my story is that I had previously been to two naturopaths and later I met with both of them at the Kaqun Club. Even though they were familiar with the water, they never recommended it to me. I also saw one of my dermatologist doctors at the club.

Since that miraculous recovery – that I originally did not believe in – happened to me I tell everyone my story. I was helped and now I want to help others."

* * *

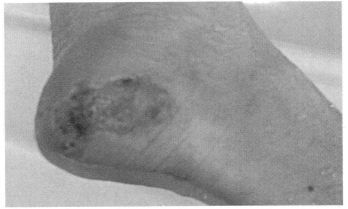

Photo of infected foot

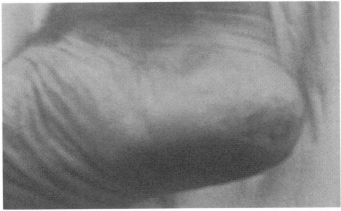

Photo of healed foot

After the end of the story there was a total silence, the club members were staring out to space and then we all started clapping at the same time. We were happy for Péter and him being able to get rid of all his pain.

Péter's story talks for itself, I think. Maybe it is just the right answer to the remark that was posted on the web:

"I wanted to start a new blog after watching the TV program Just Naturally *on the ATV channel. An "expert" was talking about the blessed effects of high oxygen-content water. According to him the Kaqun water reduces the oxygen deficiency of the body, supports regeneration and elevates the body's oxygen level while vitalizing and refreshing the body.*

I do not recommend this trick for anyone. A few glasses of clear water and a bath at home will bring the same results and it is free.

Science says that the human body gains its oxygen from air and not water, and the oxygen does not disperse in the stomach or the intestines, but in the lungs. If this miraculous water contains more oxygen than regular water then it should be very beneficial for creatures who have gills. But it was not recommended to them. Maybe because they cannot pay for it?"

* * *

I believe that all doctors and researcher agree on the fact that we get most of our oxygen through breathing. The structure of the Kaqun water is not entirely understood yet, but one thing we know for sure: regular consumption of

Kaqun water indicates extra oxygen presence in the body and nowadays that can also be measured.

I don't think that even professors know much about the water yet. World-renowned professors in the Ukraine created a comprehensive model of the Kaqun cluster-structure. Several well-known Ukrainian scientists and professors, two American doctors, an Austrian and an Israeli doctor and Professor Emato participated in the study. They produced a special movie about regular water – not Kaqun water – and I think this film is remarkable since we know so little about this very crucial element.

Some time ago I watched a documentary about a simple experiment:

Three identical glass jars were filled with rice and all three jars were filled with water to the point where the water covered the rice. The first bottle was talked to in a very nice voice; it was thanked with a polite voice for its presence. The middle water jar was talked to in angry voice; it was called a stinky rotten vegetable, and the third bottle was left alone, nobody said anything to it.

Three weeks later the first container of water and rice remained clear and fresh along with the rice. The second jug of water and rice became green and it was rotting away full of fungi and bacteria. The third bottle dried out: the water evaporated.

It was relayed to the viewer that this experiment was conducted in all parts of the world but the results were always the same. Skeptics commented that water does not understand the concept of language.

As it turns out, it did not have to! The point was not the type of language that was used but positivity and faith. The focus was on the type of vibration that the sound produced which can change the structure of water!

The same presenter displayed and proved that water reacts to sound and music as well. When he played the music of Beethoven, Bach or Mozart, the water in the process of freezing produced beautiful, well shaped and varied crystal structures but rock music only created distorted and strangely shaped crystals. This further proves that water reacts to vibration which has an effect on its structure. This is also true for people. I never really heard that an audience leaving a classical music concert got into a huge melee. But fights regularly break out after rock concerts. At such times the human body – containing 71% water – is stimulated, its structure changes just the way the water's and behaves differently from a normal situation. That is when I found out that water is capable of carrying positive or negative information.

I wanted to find out how long the music or sound should last near the water before the water's reaction. It takes only seconds.

I think that unbelievers must be laughing by now because many a times they state that whatever is not tangible they do not believe in it and whatever they do see they will doubt. But things and events do exist that we cannot entirely rationalize and their effect can be sensed or experienced!

* * *

Following this presentation, other club members also talked about the skeptic comments to be found on the web. Luckily, however, there are people who have had their own experience considering the beneficial effects of the Kaqun water and stood up for it. One of them is László G. whose blog I will quote and it may serve as an answer to the unbelieving commentator quoted earlier:

"I am László *from Budapest. I read your questions and I thought I should share my experience about the Kaqun water. Since you are not club members I do not expect you to be familiar with the following information.*

The water's structure is transformed through an electrolytic procedure which changes the pH factor as well as the structure of the water. Kaqun water contains water molecules that are different from regular water molecules and thus their chemical and physical parameters are different as well.

The fact that skin breathes was taught in elementary school. The oxygen that is part of regular water is not capable of absorbing into the skin. But the Kaqun water can and we can measure that today in a number of different ways. All you should do is look it up!

Liquids that pass through the digestive system absorb in the large intestine and since the Kaqun is also a liquid it absorbs like any other liquid. The difference is that extra oxygen is left behind for use.

I used to take a lot of medications and for six years no medicine and no prayer helped me. But the Kaqun water convinced me that there is a solution. That is my personal experience and this is no lie!

The Italian address can be found on the label itself. The factory exists and the Kaqun water is manufactured there. OKI, the Hungarian National Institute of Environmental Health has licensed the Kaqun for human consumption. Other information cannot be revealed since copyrights have to be protected. The Kaqun water is licensed in other countries as well.

Truth or mockery?

I have been seriously ill for six years and I underwent every possible cure and treatment that was recommended by modern medicine. Nothing helped me and my ever worsening condition forced me to search for other avenues. However, I did not protest or yell and scream with the backing of consumer protection agencies just because the advertised traditional medications did not help me. We do not even know as much about their effects as we know about mineral water. At least I know what mineral water contains and may or may not choose to drink it.

I am quite sure you have never taken a bath in Kaqun water and you do not even know much about it. But someday you might have to face the disease I had to put up with. That day you will be glad for helpful advice.

This is not a trick. I feel well and I can face my last years with assurance.

I would very much like my letter to be published because spreading the knowledge saves a lot of people from the hope of improvement. I wrote this letter myself and I do not represent any groups or companies.

Respectfully: László G."

* * *

The club members all got worked up about this and one thing I could not call today's meeting was boring. Especially not when Erzsébet asked to be heard. Her story could be a starting point for many of the skeptics and could help many other women who need help in their situations.

"My story starts in the summer of 2007. As a 31-year-old I could call myself a happy wife and mother. I have a two-and-a-half-year-old son and a loving husband. I could call myself lucky not to have faced any serious diseases. The only time I had to go to a hospital was for the delivery of my child and even that happened without any complication.

The six-week check up came and everything was found to be just right. I was given the routine send off: see you in a year for your regular check-up.

A year later I showed up for the examination which resulted in a P 3 reading. Just a little inflammation, remarked the doctor and he gave a prescription. A month later I had to come back for a follow-up exam which indicated a P 2 value and everything seemed to be all right.

The three-month follow up would have fallen on the time of the Christmas holiday so it was delayed until the beginning of January because no laboratories would have been open to provide results.

After the exam in January my doctor told me that he wanted to perform a minor surgery because of the inflammation's presence even if the test came back negative. His comment hit me like lightning. I got really scared because my previous result, the P 2, was totally normal. I was afraid of the procedure and I did not ask for anesthesia and the doctor was against it as well.

He tried to calm me down, explaining the minute nature of the procedure but my thinking was that surgery is surgery. I could not hold my tears back. I remembered my little boy. He was still breast-feeding, we were inseparable. I was very worried what is going to happen to him without me.

We did not appoint an exact date for the surgery but it had to be within two weeks. My days were just dragging on and I could not wait to know what was going to happen. Deep down in my heart I was hoping that my results will be negative; I had never had any problems like that. I even contemplated not having the surgery at all; what if my doctor is simply too concerned? I decided to make my decision after my results come in.

The week went by and the day for the decision arrived. I wanted to take my son to a playhouse for fun activities but then decided to give my doctor a call first to ask him about the results.

There were a few seconds of silence after I made my inquiry then he told me. I heard his voice but only one word occupied my mind: P 4! My whole body was drenched in sweat instantaneously. But that means the presence of cancer cells! I could not pay attention to anything else; that number was thundering in my brain. I was quiet and it took me quite a few seconds to be able to say anything. Crying was squeezing my throat together, my legs got weak and I could barely hold the phone in my hand.

I could barely speak the words: "Does that mean that I have cancer?"

He answered me with a diplomatic response but I felt that I had a serious problem. I knew what a P 4 result meant. The doctor went on to say that the small procedure could not wait anymore, we have to move it up – which also proved my fears to be well founded. We agreed to have the surgery within two days.

My husband waited for me in the car. I cannot remember how I made it to the car. I sat down next to him and told him the bad news. He was shaken up pretty badly but he tried to remain strong. He asked me to go with our son to the playhouse. He probably thought that I would get distracted and calm down a little.

I just nodded in agreement and we went in. What can I say? I do not wish it on anyone to feel the way I did. I still do not know how I had the strength to smile peacefully when inside I was fighting with tears. No one knew what was going on inside of me. I kept thinking that it was my last time there…

I was looking at my son's glowing face as he was playing light-heartedly. I do not want to lose him! I want to see how he starts to walk and begins talking and say: "Mommy!" I want to raise him, me! Desperate thoughts like that were thundering in my mind as well as bitter feelings in my soul.

My family was not told the bad news because the doctor wanted to wait for the results of the tissue samples. They did not know what was going on. If everything is removed that needs to be taken out then why even worry them?

The moment came when I was lying in the operating room. My heart was ready to jump out through my throat. My surroundings, the doctors prepared for the operation were proving my point: surgery is surgery, no matter how small it is.

Unfortunately, the procedure did not go smoothly. The equipment that was supposed to stop the bleeding did not work. Since I was not put under, I had to live through the confusion while lying down on the table unable to do anything. I was an eye and ear witness to the nervous cell phone calls as they were looking for someone who knew how to restart the machine, so it can do its job and stop the bleeding. I was very scared that they would not be able to fix the equipment and I would bleed to death. I imagined hugging my son. I held him close to me like I was afraid that someone will take him away.

Then a louder word called me back to reality. They were still working on the machine. I was watching as they were testing the equipment after they had found another cable. They were finally finishing the surgery that proved to be painful after all. The fifteen-minute procedure took forty-five minutes.

I had nothing else to do but wait for the results. A little more than a week later I received the test results which were adverse and I needed another surgical procedure. I was lucky because I had the best doctors but not even they knew everything about the disease. When I asked what I could do to help myself and do something proactive while waiting for surgery, one of them told me that cancer is an evil disease and there is nothing I could do.

Today I would say that I was living through intolerable weeks but somehow everything was going as it was supposed to. My husband went to work and my son stayed with me at home. We played together, we cooked, we walked, and I changed his diaper... just like before. The only thing that changed was that I could not work at home anymore. My job was such that I could do it at home but I had not noticed before how tired I became after the nightly breast-feedings and after just a few hours of sleep.

I had to wait a month for the next surgery until the scar from the previous procedure healed. I was promised that the "big" surgery will be successful. I was told that I could still have children but I would have one of those risky pregnancies. I believed them and I did as I was told but at the same time it seemed to me that I did not have another choice.

The day I feared finally arrived. I had to go into the hospital the night before. It was a horrible feeling: this was my first night away from my son. I did not leave him by choice but the situation was still very hard to deal with. When no one saw me my tears were flowing and my heart was broken from the pain and the fear that I may never see him again. I knew very well that serious complications could happen. At times likes these people are more likely to think of the negative.

The night finally passed and I was wheeled into the operating room. A surgery like this routinely takes 3-4 hours, while mine took seven hours. When I woke up from the anesthesia, I realized that my legs were terribly aching and I did not feel my left hand. I did not really worry about that since I could barely move at all and most people are just happy to wake up. The brain is not quite clear yet so it is difficult to assess the situation.

I started to suffer more and more because I was hungry but I could not eat. Every piece of me was hurting but I still wanted to go home because I missed my son and my family. I had to stay in for a week. I had to be given shots and this therapy had to continue for the next 42 days, even at home.

I believed that my home environment, my son and my family would do me good and I would get better but instead my strength was disappearing until I became totally weak. I was really discouraged because I went to the hospital under my own strength and barely any symptoms: I was not sick and had no pain but now I cannot even go to the bathroom alone. My husband stayed with me for a week and then my mother and my mother-in-law alternated and came to help me. Even brushing my teeth became a problem. They had to dress me as if I had been a child. My recovery was very slow and I was still unable to move my left hand. I was going through a very difficult time and so was my family.

Then the day finally came when the result of the biopsy arrived and our happiness was overwhelming because I had no cancer cells left in my cervix. I was so happy! But a constant thought would rob me from my joy. I realized that I went through all this for nothing! Had I received surgery that was not even necessary? My son was taken away from me and I had an immeasurable amount of guilt because of it.

Before I totally worked myself into being upset, I calmed myself down. There was no need to cry over spilled milk. I was alive, my son was with me and I could stand up and walk into the garden.

After my check-up examination and stitch removal I received a clean bill of health except for my left hand which was not improving and I had to see a therapist about it. Things started to calm down around me and everybody went on with life. I was told not to worry about the three-month check-up since I was cured.

And that is how I felt. I was finding my old self; I loved playing with my son, I cooked and did all the work I was expected to do. Since the first test went very well and I was told that I could still have beautiful children, I was not worried. I was not really thinking about it and I was not waiting for the result so desperately. I was well and that was all that mattered.

A week later I was expecting the results of the newest biopsy. I remember it was night time and I was visiting somewhere with my son. My husband was calling me on the phone and read me the result: "P 3. Please, call your doctor."

I do not know how I pulled myself together until I got home. Once there, I burst out crying. I had an awful night. Everything was falling apart. My happy and relaxed mind gave way to fear and anxiety. I kept thinking: what was all that suffering for? Is this never going to end? Am I going to live in a constant fear?

The next day I was sitting by the phone with my eyes all red from crying. I was calling my doctor. It took the whole morning because he could not be reached. I had to wait and try again. I had no patience – under the circumstances maybe one can understand the reason for my impatience.

I finally got through him and he told me that I had to go back to the hospital because I needed to have yet another surgery. I had no chance to survive unless a hysterectomy was performed.

I covered my mouth because I did not want to scream into the phone – the doctor's words shocked me! How strange but I have never even thought about such a horrible option. I have never even considered that something like that might happen.

Disappointment and pain overwhelmed me. We so much wanted a little sister to my son. How can I possibly live my life knowing that I am not a real woman anymore? At that moment I felt that I would be empty if I lose my uterus to the disease.

I went to pieces. It was so hard not to cry in front of my little boy but judging from his behavior I think he must have known that there was something wrong. I was so up-set that not even the family's support helped. Their eternal optimism had no effect on me even though I knew that some of them would have given everything – including their own lives – to help me.

My husband went with me to the hospital where I met my doctor. I was still hoping that there would be no need for that drastic surgery. Maybe there is another way, a different therapy to help me. Anything but the surgery! Every little molecule in me was protesting against the removal of my uterus.

I tried to argue against it, used every reason to convince the doctor but I had to accept that I had no other option. If I want to live that is…

After that appointment I talked to anyone and everyone about my situation – something I kept really quiet before. One of our gynecologist friends – to my complete shock – suggested that I should heal myself. After he elaborated on the subject, I signed up for a mind control course which started the following day. That doctor recommended the spiritual response therapy.

Others proposed that I should have magnetic therapy and practice positive thinking. I was told to discover what I really like to do and then search the reason for my illness! That sounded good but how do I start? Not even the doctor knew the explanation for my "evil disease"; what could I do? I was so desperate that I decided to try anything and everything. What did I have to lose? I could only win if one of the alternative therapies worked for me.

I heard about the Kaqun water from a friend and since there was a Kaqun bath near my home where I could take bath therapy and buy the Kaqun water, I started going there.

I have to admit I tried other alternative cures besides the Kaqun. I visited a number of naturopaths, I drank different teas, and I did everything that was recommended because I wanted to have another child.

One of my friends, a general practitioner, asked me to go through the surgery and not to take any risks. She said to think about my little boy and give myself a chance to raise him.

The surgery, all the advice and warnings put me under a lot of pressure and I had terrible mood swings. I came to realize that being surrounded with loving relatives still left me alone with my illness. Nobody knows what will happen, no one knows why I am ill and no one has the correct answer to what I should be doing!

At that point I decided to listen to myself only. I chose to wait with the surgery. I wanted to have another chance to have a better biopsy result the next time. If not then I would go through with surgery…

I do not want to sound like a smart-aleck since I was really unsure of my path. During my decision-making I discovered some other options. I had not tried everything yet but I felt that some methods really did help me improve. Such was the Kaqun water.

While relaxing in the bath and enjoying the smooth touch of the water, I had time to contemplate my life. Today I see many things differently and I know that there is still much to be thought over since no one changes from one day to another. But I am on the right path...

I was drinking the water as part of my therapy and I was taking Kaqun baths. Two months later I went in for another biopsy. After the test taken the doctor told me such positive tidings that I started to believe that he had not remembered me. Then came the proof: the biopsy showed a P 2! The doctor said that my current condition does not warrant a surgery.

Unspeakable happiness and relief came over me. I think the results proved me right. I was smart to wait with the surgery, I was smart to hope and now the Kaqun had become part of my life.

Of course, I am still taking it and I still visit the bath club. I do my best to stay a healthy woman so that I could become a mother again really soon.

It was of great help to me to meet people at the Kaqun Club who were facing or already battled the disease and we could exchange a lot of useful advice and share our ideas.

I learned an awful lot from this experience: one should trust their doctor but if there is a way or method that helps one's condition then the opportunity should be fully explored!"

* * *

At the end of Erzsébet's story I looked around and saw several pairs of eyes, and not only ladies', shining with tears. I was not the only guy to get emotional at times it seemed. I think I can talk for all who were present that day that it was a great feeling to hear another success story. I honestly wish that Erzsébet's disease would never return and she should only remember it as if it had been a bad dream.

The club meeting took longer than usual. We had a good time and I think I had never participated in such a discussion before where so many excited people were present. And it was not over yet.

A young lady volunteered to speak and I had not even noticed that she was with us until then. We were ready to hear her.

"My story started ten years ago. I was thirteen years old and I was becoming aware of the changes taking place in my body. We spent many hours in front of the mirror with my girl friend. I was not happy with my body; I thought I was too fat and that caused me a lot of stress and anxiety. My friend told me that I was only slightly overweight. On top of that worry, my face was covered with ugly pimples. My friend gave me a lot of good advice and a facial cream she herself was also using. I was applying the cream diligently and the pimples started to disappear. My skin was changing to my liking.

One morning, before I took off for school, I took a final look in the mirror and I was shocked at what I saw. I was scared to death to discover that my face was covered with tiny red spots. That afternoon I was supposed to have a date. My very first date! How was I supposed to show up now?

I was so angry I was shaking as I stepped out of the bathroom. I practically ran. I just wanted to pour out my anger on my friend because I thought the cream caused all the red spots.

When I met her in front of the school I let her have it. I told her that I thought that she had been a good friend but I was wrong. It was not bad enough that I was fat; she wanted me to have my face become even uglier than it used to be.

She just looked at me and broke into tears. She had no idea what had happened to me and how I could possibly accuse her of such things? I could not have cared less, I avoided her all day. Right after school I went to the pediatrician and told him why I thought I had such a bad break-out. The doctor looked at me and sent me to a dermatologist. That is where my real suffering started.

The dermatologist gave me a lengthy comprehensive examination. I was told that the cream had nothing to do with my condition – I had a much bigger problem. I had a disease called shingles. This disease is something that usually stressed-out overweight people have and it starts at around the age of thirteen. He told me what the illness was all about. The scalp starts peeling and pieces of skin (dandruff) appear on the hair. The skin starts to get scaly. There is not much hope for a cure but the symptoms are easy to treat.

I got scared to death. Will I have to live with this now? I had tears welling up in my eyes and I could not speak – I was so upset about what the dermatologist told me.

I was given creams, I had to take steroids, I was taking salt baths and I was trying to stick to the prescribed diet. It was 85% vegetables which I did not like but I wanted to get better.

Unfortunately, nothing worked. I did not even feel like going outside. My parents took me out of school and I completed the eighth grade with the help of a private tutor.

The shingles gradually spread over my face and my head and my whole body. Everybody avoided me even though my illness was not contagious. Only that one friend of mine stayed with me and I apologized to her for my accusations on countless occasions.

Of course, my first date was cancelled and I had no chance to meet boys. Years went by and my tears and bitterness never seemed to run out. Do I have to live like this throughout my entire life?

One day my father came home with a big smile on his face. He told me that I did not have to suffer any more – he found a solution to my problem! I thought I was going to faint from excitement. Was there really a way to end my misery? Would I not have to hide from the sun, would I be able to go out into the world, maybe even get a suntan in a bikini?

My father told me that he had heard from someone that the water of the Dead Sea is the only cure. We scraped all of our money together and traveled to the Dead Sea. I felt wonderful because the red spots started to disappear and the accompanying unpleasant symptoms ceased as well.

At last, I could mingle with people, I could wear a low cut dress and I could put on make-up like my friend. We took long walks together and checked out the guys. Before I knew it I had a very handsome boyfriend! I could hardly believe that things had changed for the better and I could still be happy.

My happiness did not last long because the shingles had returned after a long absence and the ordeal started again. I spent the nights crying and my days were filled with fear. My boyfriend left me without saying a word. I was lonely and depressed.

My only friend and my family stood by my side. She came to me one day and told me that her mother talked about a certain type of water called Kaqun that could possibly help me. I had no hope; I had tried so many other things in the past ten years and nothing helped. Why would that water be different? If it was so special then how come no doctor had ever mentioned it?

I went to the club and I talked to a very nice man who happened to be a doctor and he was familiar with my disease. His encouraging words and smile gave me comfort and I started to believe that I can finally escape from the clutches of this dreadful illness.

Before the Kaqun therapy

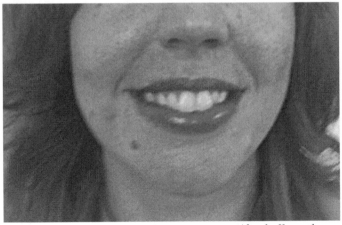

After the Kaqun therapy

I began the bath therapy and started drinking the water. A month later I had to admit that the Kaqun water had an amazing effect: my skin cleared up and all the spots were gone. The shingles have not returned! I hope I am cured. My gratefulness goes to the Kaqun water and to all the doctors and employees who work at the bath club. I am still coming to follow-up baths and I drink the Kaqun water everyday!"

The meeting ended on a positive note. We all knew we had nothing to prove; it all spoke for itself: we were the living proofs! On my way home I was thinking about Erzsébet's case. How many young women die needlessly when they could have been saved the way we had been? How many women had to give up on motherhood because they had a hysterectomy?

I was trying to find a way to help. I decided to be inquisitive much as I was when I was researching oxygen deficiency. I had already heard before that a certain HPV infection was responsible for diseases like that and many people were inflicted and bore the painful consequences but that was not enough information to protect ourselves from it.

I did a thorough research on the subject and I am going to attempt to convey the information I compiled about this insidious virus. If you want to have more information, I recommend searching the web where more detailed information can be acquired. I hope I can bring attention to the HPV virus and many will be helped through this effort.

The Papilloma Virus (HPV)

HPV is an abbreviation for Human Papilloma Virus. What is that?

HPV is a frequently occurring virus affecting men and women alike. It has over a hundred variations. Most of the forms of HPV cause no symptoms, have no consequences and disappear on their own.

About thirty types of HPV are named genital HPV (herpes) because they infect the genitals. Some of the types of this disease may cause cervical cancer or result in unusual cell growth in the cervix that may develop into cancer. Other HPV type diseases result in genital warts or non-malignant cervical anomalies. HPV was also related to some rare forms of diseases, such as vaginal or pubic area cancer or RRP (Recurrent Respiratory Papillomatosis) which illness attacks the upper respiratory regions.

Cervical cancer kills more 650 women a day worldwide. The World Health Organization estimates that 630 million people have HPV. Forty million of HPV patients have pre-cancer indicators on the cervix or have shown cell anomalies on the cervix. Conditions like that may signal the onset of cancer later on.

An infected person may pass on the illness and may not even know that they have the disease because they may not have symptoms or complaints. Sexual activity, even one that does not involve intercourse, may still cause the HPV virus to pass from one person to another.

How does one know whether they have been infected? Since the disease is usually symptom-free, the infected person may not even be aware of the illness. Most HPV infections are discovered through an unusual **Papanicolaou test** results. Pap tests are routine parts of gynecological examinations and they are very helpful in detecting abnormal cell growths before they become pre-cancer anomalies or cervical cancer. Such anomalies could easily result in cancer. They are related to HPV infections and timely diagnosis ensures successful recovery. Periodic exams play a key role in early detection so, please, visit your doctor regularly.

Is HPV curable? There is no proven cure for this dangerous illness but a healthy immune system should be able to destroy the virus. The possible consequences of HPV include the irregular growth patterns of cervical cells; cervical cancer and genital warts are occasionally curable.

Who is susceptible to cervical cancer or pre-cancer conditions? Those women who were infected with certain types of HPV and whose immune systems are unable to kill off the virus. Half of the women suffering from cervical cancer are in the age bracket of 35 – 50 with most of them acquiring the carcinogeneous type of HPV in their teenage years or in their twenties. Most of the women who develop cervical cancer probably have never had a cytological test or a screening.

We must emphasize the importance of regular checkups for all since HPV also affects men. The ever-increasing numbers of foreskin cancer and cancer of the penis prove that the above mentioned infection travels from one person to another.

Showing up for regular examinations is very important because early detection ensures the prevention of most cervical cancers!

Gratitude...

Today I know how much all the knowledge means to me that I gained from the employees of the Kaqun Club and from my fellow patients. I think I can truly say that without all this health preserving information I would be a less blessed person and that would affect your life as well, my dear reader!

Maybe it is no coincidence that I am starting to feel like an "expert". It is hard to believe how much knowledge can be acquired during an illness. On top of that all, I happen to be a very inquisitive person. I like to be informed about what is happening to me and to others because I would like to help as best I can.

* * *

Back then when I was lying on my bed after my latest surgery and it became apparent that my terminal disease had healed and I had no cancer cells in me – I remembered Csilla. She was so adamant that I would recover! She was right! The six months are soon to expire and I would surely show up for our meeting...

Yes, the water helped me and many others who had no hope. It could have helped that young girl who was so excited about her first job interview – if she had known about the water. That is why I decided to share my experience with everybody...

* * *

At the end of my story, I want to thank my wife, my children and my whole family for standing by me during the most difficult times and for their love which strength-ened me and for everything they had done for me.

I want to thank my lakeside neighbor for sending me to a doctor. I have to admit that he was not a harbinger of death as I called him in anger; rather he is my guardian angel!

I owe gratitude to all my doctors and surgeons who operated on me, to all the nurses for their helpfulness but most of all I say thanks to the Kaqun water! They have watched over me, encouraged me and supported me and for the past *six years* they have been guarding my health and my life! Thank you! Thank you! Thank you!

THE BIRTH OF THE BOOK

I did not know who József B. was when he called me and asked me to write his book. Since he was familiar with my books and liked my work, he chose me. I was a little surprised but I did not refuse him because I did not mean to hurt him...

He asked me to give him a chance to meet personally and hear his story, and then I would be free to decide whether to turn him down. He would understand and accept my choice.

I wanted to say that I was too busy and I had no time because I had too much work to do... Excuses were not difficult to find, but as I heard his mechanical voice over the phone – which he later explained – I felt I could not refuse him. We agreed on an appointment in my home.

I admit I was nervous. I had never talked to a person who had a hole in his throat. I had no idea how to act. I was concerned that my patronizing look would be offensive even if it was unintentional. What can I offer him to eat or drink? Can he eat or drink? I was confused.

He called me that he would be arriving in five minutes. I went outside to meet him. I was looking around when he showed up by the gate in a car. Out jumped an agile man and came towards me with a smile on his face.

I was not prepared for that and I was so surprised I could not talk. Then my anxiety disappeared and we shook hands and introduced ourselves.

I liked József from the very first moment. He was in great shape and he appeared to be a completely healthy man. His eyes were sparkling and if it hadn't been for the artificial voice, I would have never thought he had had a terminal illness. His shirt covered the remaining mark of the disease.

We sat down in the living room and had some small talk. Our communication was totally ordinary and I quickly got used to the microphone that helped him talk. The sound was mechanical but it did not bother me.

I was at ease. This man did not need to be pitied. He was energetic, full of vitality, and he had a good sense of humor. I looked at him and said: let's try it. His smile reached down to the bottom of my soul.

I was a little worried when I served cookies and refreshments but he had no trouble taking some of it. József mentioned that he liked sweets. He bakes traditional Christmas desserts for all his relatives because – according to him – he is the best!

I was anxious to ask him a special question. I did indeed ask why it was so important to him that others would get to now his story. Luckily, many people are cured form cancer apart from him, too. I guess that it was not an unusual question.

József smiled and nodded. Then his face turned serious and I could almost see the air vibrating around him while he told me he wanted to publish his story to help others.

First I was surprised at the answer. I did not understand: how does he want to help?

He said he swore after his last surgery – when no cancer cells were found in him – that he would do his best to help others. He wanted to show others how to triumph over sickness! His example could be followed – even if there were many "valleys" and times when he was ready to quit and close to losing his struggle but in the end his will to live overcame. He was hoping to encourage patients who felt they had nothing left and no reason to battle the disease. József wanted others not to give up in a way he had not given up.

After so much suffering and sacrifice he finally found the opportunity that is only given to those who accept it, believe in it and want to live by it. He talked to me about the Kaqun water and its beneficial effects but I did not honestly believe that he was cured by the water. When he told me how the tumor shrank from the bath therapy and how it was found during surgery that the oxygen enclosed the cancer cells into tiny pearls and thus preventing the spreading – well, I started losing my skepticism. Just because I did not experience it, it could still be true! After all there are no harmful substances in the water as it is officially licensed in Hungary. There is nothing in it but spring water and oxygen.

We agreed that we would start the book at the weekend. József would come by and unravel his story and I would write it down…

* * *

As we were getting deeper into the story, so was I brought into this – at times marveling and at other times heart-breaking – tale. There were parts when he had a hard time composing himself and he tried to remain focused.

His memories will probably remain as vivid as they are now. I was watching his eyes and his face, and I was truly touched. He was becoming even more likeable as he did not try to hide his tears. I was affected by the story and I cried with him.

* * *

The pages were filling up and I grew to admire this man who spared no time, effort or energy to do everything in order to help others, sick or healthy. He told me about the importance of prevention! We can do so much to become healthier and to protect ourselves against disease!

József spent a great amount of time gathering more and more information to be able to share it with the reader. He went to Italy to the source of this pure water, just to make sure of its authenticity.

He traveled domestically and abroad to find out about the other Kaqun Clubs, to get to know the people there, to hear their stories and through his experiences we can be part of the many miracles which have had an influence on his life.

He calls our attention to healthy eating habits and what we should consume and what kind of foods we should avoid. Keeping the rules during illness and even after re-covery means a lot when it comes to ideal body functions. He was continually searching for information… to share…

* * *

Staying Alive!

I would have never thought that I would so much enjoy every minute of our conversation. I heard many shocking and interesting stories that were part of the recovery of some of his friends.

I decided to purchase and drink the water and that's what I did. I started drinking it and felt nothing apart from the fact that it proved to be good thirst-quencher... well, honestly, we can say that about other waters, too.

We were at the creation of the last third of the book when my little six-year-old granddaughter started vomiting. From one second to another she became violently ill. She had diarrhea and high fever. Our pediatrician was on vacation and of course it was the weekend. After two days when the vomiting and the fever still continued and her stool started showing blood, I remembered József's water. He said anyone could take it and I decided to give it to her spoon by spoon. I could not believe but her nausea was gone by nightfall and she slept all night. The diarrhea was gone as well and when she woke up the next morning she announced that she was hungry! I kept giving her the water all day and it stayed in her while tap water and tea immediately came out of her. When the pediatrician returned she examined my granddaughter. Her stool was sent to a lab and it turned out that my little one had a very serious salmonella infection which usually requires hospital care.

The doctor was surprised that my granddaughter was doing so well since she had no fever by Monday afternoon and she had an appetite and kept her food and drink down.

Since she received nothing else but the water besides the fever pills, I had to accept that József was right!

I decided to visit a Kaqun Club because I wanted to try what it feels like to take a bath in water that does not lose its temperature in fifty minutes. I think I understand József's enthusiasm for the water. I was so tired when I got into the bathtub. Within seconds I forgot about everything and I felt my need for this water! The water was silky and I loved every minute of my bath.

I was surprised to look into the mirror after the bath: my skin looked smoother, my eyes looked fresher and my body was reenergized. My head felt clearer too even though I had just got done writing two books.

In that moment I decided to become a club member. I wanted to meet the others; I wanted to hear their stories and experiences which can only be done if I am among them.

I realized that I felt really good meeting the club members because they were honest and open. They were capable of giving and receiving love.

I learned a lot from them, primarily from József. He excelled in endurance, in willpower, in caring for one and others, in helpfulness, in good intentions, in faith and in love.

* * *

By the end of the book, I realized something very interesting. All the people who shared about their illness and the people of the stories Joseph conveyed had something in common. They are all men or women from different age brackets who suffered from various diseases but something was the same: every single one of them had *hypoxia* or lack of oxygen. For some it was in the tissues, for some it was near the tissues or near the tumor but all had some type of inflammation in progress.

Today I know from different scientific articles that under the effects of oxygen the immune system strengthens, regains its normal function and the body's self-healing process is restored.

I think what we found out about oxygen deficiency – the way it causes numerous diseases, among them the deadly cancer – is quite thought-provoking. At the same time we also realized – as Otto Wartburg proved – that cancer cells "hate" oxygen!

* * *

I do not regret being József's partner in the creation of this book because I know and feel that it serves a great purpose. It was his will and decision to provide hope and chance for other ill patients to help them in STAYING ALIVE. He did that with his own will, through his recovery and through his faith in the water.

Martha Tailor

Books published by
Martha Tailor so far:

A halál orvosa

Dr. Gyilkos

Téboly

Embólia

Donor

Hipnózis

Vér

Gyilkos tűk

Éhség

Vízió

Zöld halál

Halálos mánia

Gyűlölet

Őrjítő kór

Pokoli kísérlet

Téves diagnózis

Beavatkozás

Megtorlás

Fájdalom

Staying Alive!

Fekély

Rémálom

A megszállott

Kómában fogant

Alagút az agyban (riportkönyv)

Szívbénulás

Operáció

Drogfüggők Esély a gyógyulásra

Leukémia

Ájulás

Cerny Mentő, hogy a kis szív doboghasson

Fertőzés

Kegyetlen terápia

Halálfélelem

Őrült elme

Pokoli láz

Véres bosszú

A halál cinkosa

8.97

LONGWOOD PUBLIC LIBRARY
800 Middle Country Road
Middle Island, NY 11953
(631) 924-6400
longwoodlibrary.org

LIBRARY HOURS

Monday-Friday	9:30 a.m. - 9:00 p.m.
Saturday	9:30 a.m. - 5:00 p.m.
Sunday (Sept-June)	1:00 p.m. - 5:00 p.m.

43817285R00112

Made in the USA
Middletown, DE
20 May 2017